The significance of the Bible in the life, thought and culture of the early Middle Ages can hardly be overstated. Here eleven linked studies, embracing palaeography, art history, history, theology and textual scholarship, examine and interpret the evidence of Bible manuscripts (including gospel books and Psalters) in their cultural context from late antiquity to the thirteenth century. Subjects discussed include the earliest Bible manuscripts, the production of the Gospels in a missionary context, the work of the scriptorium of Tours, the development of the early glossed Psalter, the text of the Old Testament in tenth- and eleventh-century England, the Italian Giant Bibles, the origins of the Paris Bible, the illustration of the early Gothic Psalter and the planning and production of the Hamburg Bible. Together these essays provide a broad-ranging, authoritative treatment of themes which are of central importance for the history and culture of the times.

THE EARLY MEDIEVAL BIBLE

Cambridge Studies in Palaeography and Codicology

This new series has been established to further the study of manuscripts from the Middle Ages to the Renaissance. It will include books devoted to particular types of manuscript, their production and circulation, to individual codices of outstanding importance, and to regions, periods and scripts of especial interest to scholars. Certain volumes will be specially designed to provide students in the field with reliable introductions to central topics, and occasionally a classic contribution originally published in another language will be translated into English. The series will be of interest not only to scholars and students of medieval literature and history, but also to theologians, art historians and others working with manuscript sources.

ALREADY PUBLISHED

Manuscripts and libraries in the age of Charlemagne
by Bernhard Bischoff, translated by Michael Gorman
The early medieval Bible: its production, decoration and use
edited by Richard Gameson

FORTHCOMING TITLES

*Cultural Interplay in the Eighth Century: The Trier Gospels and the making
of a scriptorium at Echternach*
by Nancy Netzer
The 'Miroir Historial' of Jean le Bon
by Claudine Chavannes-Mazel

THE EARLY MEDIEVAL BIBLE

Its production, decoration and use

Edited by

RICHARD GAMESON

Eliot College, University of Kent, Canterbury

CAMBRIDGE
UNIVERSITY PRESS

Published by the Press Syndicate of the University of Cambridge
The Pitt Building, Trumpington Street, Cambridge CB2 1RP
40 West 20th Street, New York, NY 10011–4211, USA
10 Stamford Road, Oakleigh, Melbourne 3166, Australia

First published 1994
Reprinted 1994, 1995

Printed in Great Britain at the University Press, Cambridge

A catalogue record for this book is available from the British Library

Library of Congress cataloguing in publication data

The early medieval Bible: its production, decoration and use /
edited by Richard Gameson. Cambridge Studies in Palaeography and Codicology
p.   cm.
Includes bibliographical references and indexes.
ISBN 0 521 44540 X (hardback)
1. Bible. Latin – History. 2. Bible – Manuscripts, Latin.
3. Illumination of books and manuscripts, Medieval. I. Gameson,
Richard.
BS68.E375 1994
220′.094′0902–dc20 93-16210 CIP

ISBN 0 521 44540 X hardback

The publisher gratefully acknowledges the generous assistance of
the Seminar in the History of the Book to 1500, which granted
a subvention towards the publication of this book.

Contents

vii

Illustrations

Acknowledgements

The authors, editor and publisher make grateful acknowledgement to the following institutions and authorities for photographs and for permission to reproduce them.

Cambridge, University Library, by courtesy of the Syndics (9.4, 9.5, 9.8, 9.12, 9.16, 9.20, 9.23); Cologne, Dombibliothek (7.15, 7.16); Copenhagen, Kongelige Bibliotek (Jacket illustration; 10.1–7); Florence, Biblioteca Medicea Laurenziana (7.18, 7.19, 7.24); Florence, Biblioteca Nazionale Centrale (7.20, 7.21); Frankfurt, Stadt- und- Universitätsbibliothek (5.1); Friuli, San Daniele, Biblioteca Guarneriana (7.11, 7.12, 7.23); Geneva, Bibliothèque Publique et Universitaire (7.8, 7.9, 7.13); Göttweig, Stiftsbibliothek (5.2); Hereford, Cathedral Library, by courtesy of the Dean and Chapter and the Mappa Mundi Trust (2.4); London, British Library (2.1–.3, 9.1); Lucca, Biblioteca Capitolare (7.25); Malibu, J. Paul Getty Museum (5.4, 9.18); Manchester, John Rylands University Library, by courtesy of the Director and the University Librarian (9.2, 9.7, 9.10, 9.13, 9.15, 9.19, 9.22); Mantua, Biblioteca Communale (7.14); Monte Cassino, Archivio della Badia (7.4, 7.7); Oslo, Martin Schøyen (5.5); Oxford, Bodleian Library (5.3, 5.7); Paris, Bibliothèque Nationale (5.8, 7.2, 9.6, 9.9, 9.11, 9.14, 9.17, 9.21, 9.24); Paris, Bibliothèque Ste-Geneviève (9.3); Rome, Biblioteca Angelica (7.1, 7.10); Vatican City, Biblioteca Apostolica Vaticana (7.3, 7.5, 7.6, 7.17, 7.22); Vercelli, Biblioteca Capitolare (5.6).

Contributors

Larry Ayres   *Department of Art History, University of California, Santa Barbara*

Richard Gameson   *Eliot College, University of Kent, Canterbury*

David Ganz   *Department of Classics, University of North Carolina at Chapel Hill*

Margaret Gibson   *St Peter's College, University of Oxford*

Laura Light   *Department of Manuscripts, The Houghton Library, Harvard University*

Patrick McGurk   *Formerly Birkbeck College, University of London*

Rosamond McKitterick   *Newnham College, University of Cambridge*

Richard Marsden   *Girton College, University of Cambridge*

Elizabeth Peterson   *Department of Art, University of Utah*

Erik Petersen   *Department of Manuscripts, The Royal Library, Copenhagen*

Lesley Smith   *Linacre College, University of Oxford*

Preface

That the Bible was central to the life, thought and culture of the early Middle Ages is not in doubt. Bibles or parts of them were the most frequently produced books of the period, and numerous biblical manuscripts still survive. The study of Latin Bible manuscripts is, accordingly, of the greatest significance not only for the palaeographer and textual scholar, but equally for the historian, the art historian and the theologian; and none of these can afford to be ignorant of the others' work in the field.

The chapters in this book elucidate various aspects of latin Bible manuscripts, their production, decoration, interpretation, use and general cultural significance from Antiquity to the thirteenth century. If the main outlines of development during this period have long been appreciated, it is only by subjecting the evidence anew to detailed examination that we can refine our picture, give it three-dimensionality and appreciate its wider implications. Collectively the contributors here demonstrate the wealth and interest of the primary material in this field, and underline how much more can be learned about it by examining and re-examining the manuscripts themselves.

The book originated as a conference held in Oxford in 1990 under the auspices of the Seminar in the History of the Book to 1500. Seven of the chapters were first presented there; the remaining four were written especially for this volume. The Seminar has further supported this publication by a generous grant which enabled it to be illustrated in a fitting manner. Individual acknowledgements will be found in each chapter; here I would like to thank those whose assistance has been invaluable in the making of the book as a whole, namely Linda Brownrigg, Tilly de la Mare, Christine Gameson, Fiona Gameson, Henry Mayr-Harting, Rosamond McKitterick, Margaret Smith and, of course, all the contributors. Finally, I acknowledge with gratitude the support of a British Academy research fellowship, during the tenure of which much of the editorial work was done.

The feast of St Columbanus, 1992

Abbreviations

CCSL Corpus Christianorum Series Latina (Turnhout)
CLA *Codices Latini Antiquiores*, ed. E. A. Lowe, 11 vols. plus *Supplement* (Oxford, 1934–71); 2nd ed. of vol. II (Oxford, 1972)
CSEL Corpus Scriptorum Ecclesiasticorum Latinorum (Vienna)
EETS Early English Text Society (Oxford–London)
MGH Monumenta Germaniae Historica (Hannover–Berlin–Munich)
PL   *Patrologia Latina*, ed. J.-P. Migne, 221 vols. (Paris, 1844–64)

I

The oldest manuscripts of the Latin Bible

PATRICK MCGURK

The police investigation of 19 May 303 into the Cirta (now Constantine) community in Africa reported the seizure of thirty-four biblical manuscripts: one very large, five large, two small, twenty-five of unrecorded size and one made up of four unbound quinions.[1] The figures could suggest that there were a large number of Bible manuscripts in fourth-century Africa. Very many more must have been made when Christianity had survived the persecutions of Diocletian and as it expanded in the following centuries to the barbarian West. Even if Christianity was never to be planted as densely and as intensely in much of the barbarian West as it had been in Africa in the fourth and fifth centuries, there must have been thousands of Latin books of the Bible available in the centuries before 800: indeed they were so numerous that some, no longer wanted or appropriate, came to be discarded and their parchment reused for other texts before that date.[2] Of these probable thousands only 363 have survived and are listed in the palaeographical guide to Latin manuscripts before 800, E. A. Lowe's *Codices Latini Antiquiores* (hereafter CLA), and a large number of these, precious though they may be, are wretched scraps and fragments.[3] The following pages survey the evidence for our oldest Latin biblical manuscripts as it is presented in Lowe's monumental publication. The external characteristics of these books will be considered: their size and appearance; the scripts in which they were written; how their texts were laid out on the page and how these were introduced and concluded; and what changes took place in their external appearance. There will be a brief examination of the decoration and illustrations in early biblical books, and the paper will conclude with a brief survey of their function and use.

---

[1] *Gesta apud Zenophilum*, ed. C. Ziwsa, S. Optati Milevitani libri VII, CSEL 26 (Vienna, 1893), 187–8. This was cited by B. Fischer, 'Bibelausgaben des frühen Mittelalters', *Settimane di studio del Centro Italiano di studi sull'alto Medioevo. X La Bibbia nell'alto Medioevo* (Spoleto, 1963), 519–600; repr. in his *Lateinische Bibelhandschriften im frühen Mittelalter*, Vetus Latina 11 (Freiburg, 1985), 35–100, at 38.

[2] Examples of discarded fifth-century texts include: Paris, Bibliothèque Nationale, lat. 6400G (fols. 113–30), Acts and Apocalypse (Old Latin) with a fragment of the Catholic Epistles (CLA V, 565) reused in the seventh to eighth centuries; Naples, Biblioteca Nazionale, lat. 1 (fols. 1–10, 17–18, 20–1, 23–6, 31–5, 38–40, 44, 49), Kings (Old Latin) (CLA III, 389) reused in eighth-century Bobbio; Vatican City, Biblioteca Apostolica Vaticana, lat. 5763 + Wolfenbüttel, Herzog-August Bibliothek, Weiss 64, Judges and Ruth, (CLA I, 41), also reused in eighth-century Bobbio. Not all reused texts were Old Latin.

[3] Addenda by B. Bischoff and V. Brown in *Mediaeval Studies* 47 (1985), 317–38, cited as CLA Addenda.

For much of the Middle Ages, single-volume Bibles must have been as rare as manuscripts of separate parts of the Bible were common. If surviving evidence is a reliable guide there was only one period of extensive production of large single-volume Bibles, the Carolingian, and this is the subject of David Ganz and Rosamond McKitterick's chapters.[4] Four of these Carolingian Bibles are dated before 800, and are therefore included in CLA (Paris, Bibliothèque Nationale, lat. 9380; Le Puy, Trésor de la Cathédrale, s.n.; Metz, Bibliothèque Municipale, 7; St Gall, Stiftsbibliothek, 75; these are respectively CLA v, 576, vi, 768, 786, vii, 904). Apart from these, only one other single-volume Bible survives intact, and that is the *Codex Amiatinus* (Florence, Biblioteca Medicea Laurenziana, Amiatino 1; CLA iii, 299), which was made at the monastery of Wearmouth–Jarrow sometime before it was taken to the continent in 716.[5] Unless written in a minute hand, Bibles in single volumes would have to be very big. It is for that reason that surviving manuscripts of imposing size, even though they may now provide only part of the Bible text, have been seen as mutilated or truncated remains of such tomes: the fragments from another Wearmouth–Jarrow Bible (London, British Library, Add. 37777 + Add. 45025 + Loan 81, the latter belongs to the National Trust, Kingston Lacy, Dorset; CLA ii, 177, Addenda, 351–2) are a certain example, but the earliest possible candidate is the seventh-century Spanish codex now at León (Cathedral Archives, 15; CLA xi, 1636).[6] Large size is one reason for thinking that two Anglo-Saxon codices, some Gospel fragments in Durham (Durham, Cathedral Library, A. ii. 10 fols. 2–5, 388–9 + C. iii. 13 fols. 192–5 + C. iii. 20; CLA ii, 147) and a manuscript now in the royal collection in the British Library (Royal 1. E. vi; CLA ii, 214), were originally part of a New Testament and a Bible respectively.[7] Texts like the Pentateuch or Octateuch, of course, would make substantial volumes on their own, and it would be a mistake to regard every outsize book as the relic of a single-volume Bible. There would be no difficulty in distributing a text as long as the Bible over two or more volumes which could each be very large.[8] Equally the text could be spread over several smaller volumes as the well-known miniature of Ezra in the *Amiatinus* Bible shows.[9] The six-volume Maurdramnus Bible (Amiens, Bibliothèque Municipale, 6, 7, 9, 11, 12 (fols. 2–192) + Paris, BN, lat. 13174 (fols. 136, 138); CLA vi, 707) is the best-known example from this period –

---

[4] See chs. 3 and 4 below. Large Bibles were produced again in numbers in the eleventh and twelfth centuries, but most were in two or more volumes.

[5] E. A. Lowe, *English Uncial* (Oxford, 1960), 9–13, discusses the identification of the *Codex Amiatinus* with one of the three Bibles known to have been made before 716 at Wearmouth–Jarrow.

[6] The Wearmouth–Jarrow book measures 480 × 335 mm. The León codex measures *c.* 440 × 320 mm and is written in two broad columns of closely packed half-uncial in two columns of 71 to 76 lines.

[7] The Durham fragments measure at least 385 × 250 mm. The size of the leaves is the chief reason for considering them a part of a larger volume like a New Testament. The Royal book measures 470 × 345 mm. Its high quire signatures alone would have suggested that it was part of a Bible. See M. O. Budny, 'London, British Library MS Royal 1. E. vi: the Anatomy of an Anglo-Saxon Bible Fragment' (unpublished Ph.D. thesis, London University, 1985). It is now firmly ascribed to the ninth century.

[8] Two examples of Bibles in two volumes chosen at random are Paris, BN, lat. 11553, the ninth-century second volume of a two-volume Bible from the Paris region, and London, British Library, Royal 1. E. vii and Royal 1. E. viii, an early eleventh-century Anglo-Saxon Bible.

[9] J. J. G. Alexander, *Insular Manuscripts 6th to the 9th Century* (London, 1978), ill. 27.

although as presently constituted these six volumes do not include all the Bible. Other examples in CLA might also be relics of such smaller-scale multi-volume codices.[10] Single volumes of varying sizes devoted to a substantial section of the Bible, such as the Octateuch or the Prophets or the New Testament or the Four Gospels were also produced, just as there might be single volumes of one Gospel (say Matthew or John) or one other text such as Genesis.[11]

A recent survey of early Latin Bible manuscripts by Pierre Petitmengin has divided up the extant material before 600 according to the categories represented by the nine volumes of Cassiodorus's Bible, namely Octateuch, Kings–Job, Histories, Psalms, Solomon, Prophets, Gospels, Epistles and Acts–Apocalypse. Table 1 records the survivors in these same categories at three periods: before 600 (where the figures are based on Petitmengin's), between 600 and 800, and before 800.[12] The number in brackets after each total shows the category's position in the 'league of survivors'.

The high proportion of gospel books among the extant material, over 43 per cent in all periods, is immediately striking; the other popular categories (like the Psalms, Prophets or Epistles) lag far behind. It should, however, be remembered that in the early Middle Ages the greatest effort was spent in the making and keeping of gospel books: they were often the most valued and treasured possessions of a church, monastery or region and this must have helped their survival rate. It is quite possible therefore that this high proportion misleads and that it reflects the favourable conditions for survival rather than the number that was originally made. One other figure might be worth noting, and that is the higher proportion of Psalters from the later period than from the earlier.

---

[10] Possible examples are (i) Milan, Biblioteca Ambrosiana, D. 30 inf. (fly leaves), Ecclesiasticus (CLA III, 330), and D. 84 inf. (back fly leaves) Paralipomena (CLA III, 333), the measurements of the second being *c.* 300 × 230 mm; and (ii) Kremsmünster Stiftsbibliothek, Fragm. I/1 and Mattsee, Stiftsbibliothek, 46 (fly leaf), fragments of two manuscripts of Kings and Prophets, (CLA x, 1445) with identical measurements and numbers of lines (*c.* 380 × 270 mm, written space 305 × 215, two columns of 28 lines).

[11] Examples are (i) Matthew, Würzburg, Universitätsbibliothek, M. p. th. f. 61; CLA IX, 1415, (ii) John, St Gall, Stiftsbibliothek, 60; CLA VII, 902 and (iii) a possible Genesis, Naples, Biblioteca Nazionale, lat. 1 (fols. 11–16, 19, 22, 27–30, 36–7, 41–3, 45–8, 50–2); CLA III, 390.

[12] P. Petitmengin, 'Les plus anciens manuscrits de la Bible latine', *Le monde antique latin et la Bible*, ed. J. Fontaine and C. Pietri (Paris, 1985), 89–123. For convenience CLA is regarded as the corpus and its dates are followed even though some have been revised. Following the revised dates might have reduced the total number of books as some of CLA's borderline eighth to ninth century are now assigned to the ninth. Petitmengin's convention of assigning manuscripts dated in CLA to the turn of a century to the earlier century has been adopted in this table. Thus CLA 'VI–VII' has been assigned to the sixth century. The following Bibles and New Testaments (or Bible and New Testament fragments) have been excluded from the calculations: Bibles: London, British Library, Add. 37777 + Add. 45025 + Loan 81; British Library, Royal 1. E. vi + Oxford, Bodleian Library, Lat. bib. b. 2 (P) + Canterbury, Cathedral Library, Add. 16; these being CLA II, 177, 214, 244 and 262 respectively; Florence, Biblioteca Medicea Laurenziana, Amiatino 1; CLA III, 299; Paris, BN, lat. 9380; CLA v, 576; Amiens, Bibliothèque Municipale, 6, 7, 9, 11, 12 (fols. 2–192) + Paris, BN, lat. 13174 (fols. 136, 138), Le Puy, Trésor de la Cathédrale, s.n., Metz, Bibliothèque Municipale, 7; these being CLA VI, 707, 768 and 786 respectively; St Gall, Stiftsbibliothek, 75; CLA VII, 904; Kremsmünster, Stiftsbibliothek, Fragm. I/1 + Mattsee, Stiftsbibliothek, 46; CLA x, 1445; and León, Cathedral Archives, 15; CLA XI, 1636; New Testaments: Dublin, Trinity College, 52; CLA II, 270; Braunsberg, Lyceum Hosianum, 205 and Fulda, Hessische Landesbibliothek, Bonifatianus 1; these being CLA VIII, 1071 and 1196 respectively. The differences between the above figures for codices before 600 and Petitmengin's are due to the addition of two items from CLA Addenda and the exclusion of the sixth-century New Testament, Fulda, Hessische Landesbibliothek, Bonifatianus 1.

Table 1.

	Before 600	Between 600 and 800	Before 800
Octateuch	10 (3)	25[b] (3)	35 (5)
Kings–Job	9 (4)	17[cd] (6)	36 (2)
Histories	2 (9)	10[cd] (7)	12 (8)
Psalms	5 (6)	31 (2)	36 (2)
Solomon	5 (6)	9[c] (7)	14 (7)
Prophets	8 (5)	21 (5)	29 (6)
Gospels	41[a] (1)	119[e] (1)	160 (1)
Epistles	11[a] (2)	25[f] (3)	36 (2)
Acts–Apocalypse	5[a] (6)	7[bf] (9)	12 (8)

Notes: [a] One item counted thrice (Cambridge, University Library, Nn. ii. 41; CLA ii, 140, Gospels, Acts, Epis.) and three items counted twice (Naples, Biblioteca Nazionale, lat. 2 (fols. 42*, 43–56, 71–5); CLA iii, 395, Acts, Epis.; Ravenna, Archivio Arcivescovile s.n.; CLA iv, 411, Acts, Epis., Apoc.; Paris, BN, lat. 6400G (fols. 113–30); CLA v, 565, Apoc., Acts, Epis.).
 [b] One item counted twice (Brussels, Bibliothèque Royale, II. 1052 (fols. 137–40); CLA x, 1550, Judges, Ruth, Acts).
 [c] One item counted thrice (Stuttgart, Württemburgische Landesbibliothek, HB. ii. 35; CLA ix, 1358, Proverbs, Solomon, Job, Tobias, Esther, Esdras).
 [d] Four items counted twice (Vatican City, Biblioteca Apostolica Vaticana, Pal. lat. 24 (fols. 10–15, 38–53, 72–176); CLA i, 68a, Paral., Tobias–Esther; St Gall, Stiftsbibliothek, 6; CLA vii, 895, Tobias, Judith, Job, Esther; Cassel, Landesbibliothek, Manuskripten-Anhang 19. 1a; CLA viii, 1145, Job, Tobias, Judith, Esther, etc.; Munich, Bayerische Staatsbibliothek, Clm 6239; CLA ix, 1254, Job, Tobias, Judith, Esther).
 [e] One item counted twice (Paris, BN, n.a. lat. 1063; CLA v, 679, Gospels–Epistles).
 [f] Three items counted twice (Rome, Biblioteca Vallicelliana, B. 25ii, CLA iv, 430; Paris, BN, lat. 6400G (fols. 113–30); CLA v, 565; Carlsruhe, Landesbibliothek, Aug. CCXXII (fols. 1–61); CLA viii, 1096, all Acts–Epistles).

The table does not show which books contained both a biblical and a non-biblical text. However Commentaries on the Apocalypse, for example, are found with Apocalypse texts. Rome, Biblioteca Vallicelliana, B. 25ii (CLA iv, 430) includes Bede's commentary along with Acts, the Catholic Epistles and the Apocalypse; and Cassel, Landesbibliothek, Theol. Oct. 5 (CLA viii, 1142) adds to the Apocalypse a copy of Caesarius of Arles' homilies on it. The earliest example of such a combination is the early seventh-century copy of Kings at Verona (Biblioteca Capitolare, II (2); CLA iv, 477) where a copy of Honorius's *Cosmographia* follows immediately after the last book of Kings, but the best-known example is the Book of Armagh where the New Testament is combined with Patrick and Martin of Tours texts (Dublin, Trinity College, 52; CLA ii, 270). There is also an example of a text which was laid out to accommodate a commentary or gloss (Zürich, Staatsarchiv, A. g. 19, no. xii (fols. 24–5 = pp. 61–4; CLA vii, 1008, Ezekiel with commentary and gloss). Here there are three columns per page and text and commentary are visually contrasted. The text in the central column is written in larger script and in fewer lines than the commentary in the outer margins. Though text and commentary are not clearly keyed in to each other as in later medieval glossed or commentary books the format was an advance on that in the

Table 2.

	Before 600	600–800
Uncial	75 (1)	90[a] (6)
Half-uncial	12	9[a] (3)
Rustic capital	3[b]	2 (2)
Majuscule	–	62[a] (4)
Minuscule	–	97 (1)
Other	–	8 (1)

Notes: [a] One of these (Milan, Biblioteca Ambrosiana, G. 82 sup., pp. 209–20, 375–6, 385–6, 449–52, 461–2, 471–4; CLA III, 344b), is counted three times as uncial, half-uncial and Irish majuscule appear in the same manuscript.

[b] One of these three (Vatican City, Biblioteca Apostolica Vaticana, lat. 3806 (fols. 1–2); CLA Supplement, 1766), is made up of the fragmentary canon tables of a gospel book in which the only script was the rustics in the headings and explicits. It is very unlikely that the main script in the Gospels was rustics.

Irish eighth-century Matthew (Würzburg, Universitätsbibliothek, M. p. th. f. 61; CLA IX, 1415) where glosses and commentary accumulate in a haphazard fashion between lines, in margins and on inserted scraps of parchment.

A glance at any handbook on early Bibles, whether Greek, Coptic or Latin, will suggest that most were written in uncials. Table 2 which classifies the scripts in the biblical manuscripts of CLA before and after 600 confirms the truth of that impression. The numbers in brackets indicate manuscripts which have been counted twice since they contain more than one script.[13]

Uncial was dominant before 600, and it remained unchallenged as the favoured script on the continent until the later eighth century and the spread of minuscule scripts: eighth-century manuscripts like the Beneventan or Gundohinus Gospels are clear examples of a continuing, if faltering, practice.[14] Consciously revived among the Anglo-Saxons, its prestige still came to account for a fair proportion of their biblical books – and this in the face of a vigorous and well-established Insular tradition of luxury majuscule codices.[15] The uncial tradition was also consciously recreated in some Carolingian books which testify to a new clarity and design in script and book

---

[13] The same conventions for dating have been adopted here as in the previous table, see note 12 above. 'Bd' uncial books have been counted as uncial. The classes of majuscule and minuscule are taken from CLA, and there has been no attempt to apply other criteria, for instance, the late Julian Brown's different grades of Insular scripts.

[14] London, British Library, Add. 5463 (CLA II, 162) probably 736–60; and Autun, Bibliothèque Municipale, 3 (S.2) (CLA VI, 716) dated 754.

[15] Examples are (i) the Wearmouth–Jarrow books, Durham, Cathedral Library, A. II. 17 (fols. 103–11) (CLA II, 150); and Utrecht, Universiteitsbibliothek, 32 (fols. 94–105) (CLA x, 1587); and (ii) Avranches, Bibliothèque Municipale, 48 (fols. I–II)+66 (fols. I–II)+71 (fols. A–B)+St Petersburg, Saltykov-Scedrin State Public Library, O. v. I. 1 (CLA VI, 730).

making.[16] As is well known, capital scripts, by contrast, came to be associated with pagan texts. The two surviving biblical fragments in rustics, one of the Gospel of John (Aberdeen, University Library, Papyrus 2a; CLA II, 118), and the other from a Greco-Latin version of the Pauline epistle to the Ephesians (Florence, Biblioteca Medicea Laurenziana, P. S. I. 1306; CLA Supplement, 1694) are therefore of great interest.[17] They are both carefully made, and it is impossible to tell whether they represent the chance survival of many more Christian texts in capitals, or whether they are deliberately archaic productions. Rustics or other capital variants were of course used in early and late uncial books for display or for headings or colophons, but they were not again to serve as the main script until the antiquarian productions of the Carolingian period such as the Utrecht Psalter.[18] Capitals appear as a script for accessory texts in the rigorously uncial Anglo-Saxon *Codex Bigotianus* (Paris, BN, lat. 281+298; CLA V, 526), and share a Psalter with uncial in the awkward *Psalterium Duplum* (Vatican City, Biblioteca Apostolica Vaticana, Reg. lat. 11; CLA I, 101) from an as yet unidentified French centre in the later eighth century where a Gallican Psalter text in squarish capitals on the verso faces the Hebrew Psalter text written in uncials. The place of honour in bilingual texts in late antiquity is usually the verso, and if this convention were still being observed in this Psalter it is probable that the script rather than the particular Psalter version was being so honoured.

Half-uncial may have been far less common, but it was used for three famous early Bible manuscripts. The first is the earliest surviving copy of the Vulgate Gospels, the St Gall codex of the early fifth century (St Gall, Stiftsbibliothek, 1395 (pp. 7–327)+ St Gall, Stadtbibliothek s.n.+St Paul in Carinthia, Stiftsbibliothek, 25. 4. 21a+ Zürich, Staatsarchiv, A. G. 19, no. II (fols. 2–5)+Zürich, Zentralbibliothek, C. 43 (offset)+C. 79b (fols. 4–7)+Z. XIV. 5; CLA VII, 984). This has marginalia which have been related to notes added to an earlier exemplar probably by Jerome and by an unknown second scholar.[19] Its modern editor regarded it as a book 'presumably intended for personal rather than public use: but for a person of high office of some importance'.[20] The second is the sixth-century Italian Gospel book now at Split (Chapter Library, s.n.; CLA XI, 1669). This is written in a careful half-uncial (making it perhaps the most formally written of the early half-uncial biblical books). It was used liturgically in the early eighth century, and has marginalia from the tenth to eleventh

[16] An example of Carolingian uncial before 800 is Abbeville, Bibliothèque Municipale, 4 (1); CLA VI, 704. See the discussion by R. McKitterick, 'Carolingian Uncial: A Context for the Lothar Psalter', *British Library Journal* 16 (1990), 1–15.

[17] Good reproductions and useful discussion of both in R. Seider, *Paläographie der lateinischen Papyri. II. 2* (Stuttgart, 1981), 115–18, pl. 43a–b.

[18] See W. Koehler and F. Mütherich, *Die Karolingischen Miniaturen* IV: *Die Hofschule Kaiser Lothars–Einzelhandschriften aus Lotharingien* (Berlin, 1971) pls. 62–79 for reproductions of the two Carolingian Aratea, London, British Library, Harley 647 and Leiden, Universiteitsbibliothek, Voss. lat. Q. 79. A full colour facsimile of the second manuscript was published as *Aratea: ein Leitstern des abendlandischen Weltbildes*, by Faksimile Verlag Luzern (Lucerne, 1987). The commentary volume has papers by B. Bischoff, B. Eastwood, T. Klein, F. Mütherich and P. F. J. Obbema. A recent survey of the history of rustics is J. Autenrieth, '*Litterae Virgilianae*': *vom Fortleben einer römischen Schrift* (Munich, 1988).

[19] B. Bischoff, 'Zur Rekonstruktion des Sangallensis (Σ) und der Vorlage seiner Marginalien', *Biblica* 22 (1941) 147–58, repr. in his *Mittelalterliche Studien*, 3 vols. (Stuttgart, 1966–81), I, 101–11.

[20] C. H. Turner, *The Oldest Manuscript of the Vulgate Gospels* (Oxford, 1931), xxvi.

centuries concerning the ecclesiastical histories of Spalato and Nona. The third is the earliest surviving Latin single-volume Bible, the León palimpsest (Cathedral Archives, 15; CLA XI, 1636), which is written in a crowded half-uncial. Interestingly all three books are written in two columns. In contrast half-uncial usually appears in books in long lines; this applies both in the more utilitarian scholarly manuscripts, such as those carefully uncovered by Caroline Hammond Bammel, and in other texts, both biblical and non-biblical, early and late, such as the fifth- to sixth-century Verona Pentateuch fragments (Biblioteca Capitolare, IV (4) fols. 1–2); CLA IV, 479), the Irish seventh-century so-called Ussher Gospels (Dublin, Trinity College, 55; CLA II, 271) and the seventh- to eighth-century Anglo-Saxon Douce Primasius (Oxford, Bodleian Library, Douce 140; CLA II, 237).[21]

There is less variety of range and quality of script before 600 than in the later period. There is nothing before 600, and indeed before 700, for example, to compare with the cursively written and relatively utilitarian early eighth-century copies of Kings in Verona (Verona, Biblioteca Capitolare, III (3); CLA IV, 478) and of the New Testament in Paris (BN, n.a. lat. 1063; CLA V, 679) or with the minutely written, apparently personal Irish pocket gospel books of the eighth and early ninth centuries (e.g. Dublin, Trinity College, 59 and 60 (the books of Dimma and Mulling); CLA II, 275 and 276). It is very likely that personal small copies of biblical books in half-uncial (or in the unfortunately termed quarter-uncial hand) or just possibly even in cursive hands, were made before 700 but they have not survived.[22] As has already been noted, the creation of new scripts in the seventh and eighth centuries, whether majuscule in the British Isles, or lower grade scripts both there and on the continent, challenged the dominance of uncial. These new scripts affected the appearance and layout of many codices and these changes will be touched on later. It should be noted that the simple listing of scripts gives no impression of the great variety in size and scale of letters and the disposition of the writing on a page. These scripts varied from the minute hands in the Irish books to the monumental uncial of over 5 mm high in the fifth-century palimpsest Prophets book in the Vatican (Biblioteca Apostolica Vaticana, lat. 3281; CLA I, 14). The Irish books were personal and easily portable copies, the Vatican copy of the Prophets was meant for display and for reading in public.

A recent sale catalogue of Sotheby's included a minute leaf from a Greek Gospel of Mark of possible fifth-century date: it measured 67×67 mm and represented a type of small codex familiar from the finds of early Greek papyri, a fair number of which were listed by E. G. Turner in his pioneering *The Typology of the Early Codex*.[23] Famous among these dwarfs is the Greek Gospel of Mani, dating from the fourth to fifth

---

[21] On such half-uncial literary manuscripts see C. P. Hammond Bammel, 'Products of Fifth-century Scriptoria Preserving Conventions used by Rufinus of Aquileia', *Journal of Theological Studies* 35 (1984), 347–93, at 379–93.

[22] For a discussion of some quarter-uncial see *ibid.*, at 379–93. One wonders in what script the Gospels carried by St Maximus (according to Gregory of Tours) were written: 'habens ad collum, cum evangeliorum libro, ministerium quotidianum, id est patenulam parvam cum calice', Gregory of Tours, *De Gloria Confessorum*, ch. 22, MGH, *Scriptores rerum Merovingicarum* (Hannover, 1885), I. ii. 311.

[23] *Sotheby's, Western Manuscripts and Miniatures*, 18 June 1991 (London, 1991), item 68. E. G. Turner, *The Typology of the Early Codex* (Philadelphia, 1972).

centuries and measuring 38×45 mm.[24] It has been suggested that some of these books may have served as amulets. The smallest Latin Bible manuscript, indeed early Latin codex, is the uncial Gospel of St John in Paris (BN, lat. 10439; CLA v, 600) dating from the turn of the fifth and sixth centuries, which measures 71×51 mm, with eleven lines per page confined to a written space of 45×34 mm. It may have been worn as an amulet before it was deposited inside the eleventh-century reliquary of the Virgin's shirt at Chartres where it was found in 1712. Other small books such as the Irish pocket Gospels or the Wearmouth–Jarrow Stonyhurst Gospels (to which a talismanic function has also been posited) are about twice as large as the Chartres St John. The smallest of the Irish books, the Cadmug Gospels now at Fulda (Hessische Landesbibliothek, Bonifatianus 3; CLA vii, 1198) measures 127×100 mm and is only slightly smaller than Stonyhurst, the dimensions of which are 135×93 mm (English Province of the Society of Jesus, on loan to London, British Library, Loan MS 74; CLA ii, 260).

Other notable formats include tall and narrow volumes in Egypt, their dimensions sometimes recalling those of consular diptychs and some of these could have been designed for tall and narrow ivory covers. The narrowest Latin volume is the Fulda New Testament codex of Victor of Capua, which includes a Latin version of the Diatessaron, and which dates at the latest from 536–7 (Hessische Landesbibliothek, Bonifatianus 1; CLA viii, 1196). It is just over twice as tall as it is wide (288×140 mm), and is proportionately just slightly narrower than its nearest rival, the late eighth- to early ninth-century Gospel fragments from Besançon (Bibliothèque Municipale, 184 fols. 58–74; CLA vi, 731), which measures 340×175 mm.[25] At the other end of the scale of course were the single-volume Bibles. The *Codex Amiatinus* (Florence, Biblioteca Medicea Laurenziana, Amiatino 1; CLA iii, 299) measures 505×340 mm and has 1,030 folios. The oldest surviving Tours Bible, St Gall, Stiftsbibliothek, 75 (CLA vii, 904) represents an early stage in Bible production at that celebrated centre and is even larger in format measuring 540×395 mm, but its text has been compressed into 418 folios.

Some impression of the range of sizes of our biblical manuscripts can be obtained by arranging them in different groups according to size.[26] (See table 3.) There is a perceptible increase in the average size over these four centuries. This might be usefully complemented by table 4 which shows three arithmetic means: (i) of the total

---

[24] Cologne, P. colon., inv. 4780. E. G. Turner, *Greek Manuscripts of the Ancient World*, 2nd edn, rev. by P. J. Parsons (London, 1987), item 83.

[25] CLA vi, 731 says that 'the narrow length suggested that the Gospel book was meant to have an ivory cover'. The book contains Jerome's letter to Pope Damasus which opens with the words *Nouum opus* and a Gospel capitulary.

[26] The groups are those used by C. Bozzola and E. Ornato, *Pour une histoire du livre manuscrit au moyen Âge. Trois essais de codicologie quantitative*, 2nd edn (Paris, 1983), 218. The conventions used for dating are those adopted in earlier tables, see note 12 above. The fifth-century tally includes books dated 'IV–V' by CLA. Some items from CLA have been excluded because it has not been possible to reconstruct their original size. Measurements in CLA are not sharp or detailed enough to apply the interesting experiments in C. Bozzola *et al.*, 'Noir et blanc. Premiers résultats d'une enquête sur la mise en page dans le livre médiéval', *Il libro e il testo*, ed. C. Questa and R. Raffaelli (Urbino, 1984), 195–221, or in D. Muzerelle, 'Normes et recettes de mise en page dans le codex pré-Carolingien', *Les débuts du codex*, ed. A. Blanchard (Turnhout, 1989) 125–56.

Table 3.   Categories

	A	B	C	D
Fifth century	0%	36.66%	60%	3.3%
Sixth century	0%	37.5%	59.37%	3.125%
Seventh century	6.52%	47.52%	41.3%	4.34%
Eighth century	5.05%	60.11%	27.52%	7.34%

A where the sum of height and width of a page is over 670 mm B between 491 and 670 mm C between 321 and 490 mm D 320 mm or less

Table 4.

	Total page size	Size of written space (i) two columns	(ii) long lines
Fifth century	463.23 mm	343.52 mm	331.17 mm
Sixth century	465.12 mm	392.43 mm	342.13 mm
Seventh century	510.89 mm	442 mm	332.64 mm
Eighth century	509.13 mm	434.55 mm	343.06 mm

size of page, (ii) of the total size of written space for books written in two columns (with no deduction made for the inter-columnar marginal space) and (iii) of the written space for books written in long lines.

These figures can only give the crudest of guides to size and averages not least because it is difficult to know how representative is the surviving evidence. The samples are very small and therefore easily subject to many distortions. The figures both for total size of page and of written space in two columns for the seventh century, for instance, were affected by one or two large volumes such as the León palimpsest Bible or the Durham Gospel fragments. Conversely the apparently anomalous stability in size of written space of manuscripts written in long lines between the fifth and eighth centuries could be affected by the many small books in this category which survive from the eighth and the turn of the eighth and ninth centuries.

The figures do show that books were bigger in the eighth century than in the fifth, the switch from a class C to a class B majority being particularly noticeable. What they do not convey is the differences between individual biblical books. Appropriately for a verse text, Psalters tended to be written in long lines, and they also tended to be smaller than other books, particularly Gospels. In the eighth century, for instance, the average mean total page size of Psalters was 454 mm as against the 509 mm of Bible manuscripts as a whole, or the 508 mm of all gospel books. Curiously enough, eighth-century gospel books originating in England tend to be larger than contemporary volumes produced elsewhere, their average being 568 mm as against 474 mm – or against 495 mm if the small Irish pocket books are excluded. The sizes of the written space confirm this contrast, the Anglo-Saxon average for two columns being 457 mm against 408 mm, and for long lines 419 against 373 mm. Large dimensions are also a feature of some non-biblical Anglo-Saxon manuscripts. The exceptional size of the Durham Cassiodorus manuscript (Durham, Cathedral Library, B. ii. 30; CLA ii, 152, measuring 429 × 295 mm) has always been noted, and more recently CLA Supplement, 1746 drew attention to the similarity in the dimensions of written space and in the number of lines between the Cassiodorus and two other probably Northumbrian manuscripts, a fragment of the second Pauline epistle to the Corinthians (Paris, BN, lat. 9377 (fol. 3); CLA Supplement, 1746) and a Pliny in Leiden (Universiteitsbibliotheek, Voss. lat. F. 4; CLA x, 1578). If no Anglo-Saxon Gospels reach these proportions, they are nevertheless often substantial. They are, however, matched by the sizes of certain elaborate Continental copies like the *Codex Beneventanus* (London, British Library, Add. 5463; CLA ii, 162; 355 × 255 mm) or the sumptuous products of the first court school of Charlemagne such as the Harley Gospels (London, British Library, Harley 2788; CLA ii, 198; 367 × 255 mm) or the Gospels at Abbeville (Bibliothèque Municipale, 4 (1); CLA vi, 704; 355 × 247 mm). It may therefore be that the greater size of Anglo-Saxon Gospels reflects nothing more than the chance survival of a greater number of more sumptuous books originating in this island than from elsewhere. It need not suggest, for instance the use of larger skins. The limitations of the evidence make it impossible to draw firm conclusions on such matters.

The ratio of books written in two columns (or more) to those in long lines does not alter much during the period, only increasing slightly in the eighth century. However this increase would be much greater if two groups of books were excluded from the calculations: those with Irish connections and those from Rhaetian or Allemannic scriptoria. Most Irish books were written in long lines and their numbers affected the ratio in the eighth century. Many Bible manuscripts from Swiss scriptoria were small and small books tend naturally to be written in long lines. As an example the Bible manuscripts in the hand of the well-known St Gall scribe, Winithar, might be mentioned. His Bible books range in size from 245 × 155–9 mm (St Gall, Stiftsbibliothek, 2 (pp. 301–568), Acts and Apocalypse; CLA vii, 894) to 285 × 200 mm (St Gall, Stiftsbibliothek, 70, Pauline Epistles; CLA vii, 903). The case of the Maudramnus multi-volume Bible seems to confirm the association of long lines with a small format. The largest and possibly the first volume of the set, the Pentateuch (Amiens, Bibliothèque Municipale, 6) is of a good size (380 × 260 mm) and is written in two columns whereas the others, which are all smaller (within the range 300–15 × 200 mm), are in long lines (all of them are in CLA vi, 707). Two or even three columns are used in small books as the pocket Gospels of Dimma or Mulling (Dublin, Trinity College, 59 and 60; CLA ii, 275 and 276) show, but these are written in extremely small hands. It would have been difficult to write a stately capital or majuscule script over two columns on a small page, and, in any case, such a layout would have produced an unwieldy and bulky book for all but the shortest text.

If two columns were not suitable for large formal scripts in small books, it is striking how narrow the columns can be in some large two-column formal books, the proportion being between 1:4 and 1:5.[27] This is a persistent, though occasional, feature in our manuscripts from the late fourth-century Vercelli Gospels (Biblioteca Capitolare, s.n.; CLA iv, 467, written space 170 × 105 mm, single columns measuring 170 × 40 mm) to the eighth-century Irish Milan Gospel of Matthew fragments (Biblioteca Ambrosiana, D. 10 sup. (front fly leaves); CLA iii, 327; calculated written space *c.* 220 × 140 mm, single columns measuring *c.* 220 × 52 mm) and the late eighth-century Douai Gospels from the area of St Amand (Douai, Bibliothèque Municipale 12; CLA vi, 758; written space 240 × *c.* 135 mm, single column 240 × 45 mm). In the earliest manuscripts such narrow columns seem to be an established variant. In later books like the Douai Gospels and its sister early ninth-century Livinus Gospels at Ghent (Ghent, Archives of the Cathedral of St Bavo, s.n.), it is one of many deliberately chosen archaic features.[28]

The characteristics of the oldest manuscripts which were enumerated by Lowe many years ago in two classic articles were common to biblical and non-biblical codices alike.[29] This is equally true of the features mentioned above – the constraints imposed by a small layout and the choice between long lines and two or more columns. The greater opulence of a large number of biblical manuscripts did, however, set them apart from other classes of text. There are extant splendid late Antique manuscripts of Virgil, and the Carolingian reproductions of pagan illustrated texts such as the Aratea or the comedies of Terence provide vivid evidence of others now lost. In the period before 800, however, and perhaps after 550 or so, it is likely that the only new sumptuous books were biblical and that most of these were Gospels. The Bible texts written in gold and silver on purple parchment which have survived from the fifth and sixth centuries are splendid examples of the de luxe products strongly denounced by Jerome.[30] The Old Latin Brescia Gospels (Brescia, Biblioteca Queriniana, s.n.; CLA iii, 281) is one distinguished representative of this category, and its sister manuscript the Gothic *Codex Argenteus* now at Uppsala (Kungliga Universitets Biblioteket) may have belonged to Theoderic the Ostrogoth.[31] The sixth-century purple Old Latin Psalter, now at Paris (BN, lat. 11947; CLA v, 616), is written in silver and gold in very well-spaced-out letters between two ruled lines 6 mm

---

[27] These proportions may be compared with 1:3 for the sixth-century 'St Augustine's' gospels (Cambridge, Corpus Christi College, 286; CLA ii, 126) or 1:2.9 for the eighth-century *Codex Beneventanus* (London, British Library, Add. 5463: CLA ii, 162).

[28] P. McGurk, 'The Ghent Livinus Gospels and the scriptorium of St Amand', *Sacris Erudiri* 14 (1963), 164–205, at 175–8.

[29] E. A. Lowe, 'Some facts about our oldest Latin manuscripts', *Classical Quarterly* xix (1925), 197–205 and 'More facts about our oldest Latin manuscripts', *Classical Quarterly* xxii (1928), 43–62; both repr. in his *Palaeographical Papers*, 2 vols. (Oxford, 1972), i, 187–202 and 251–74.

[30] 'Inficitur membrana colore purpureo, aurum liquiescit in litteras, gemmis codices vestiuntur, et nudus ante fores earum Christus emoritur', Jerome, *Epist.* 22. 32 (CSEL 54, 193).

[31] For a facsimile see *Codex Argenteus Upsaliensis* (Upsala, 1927). On the *Codex Argenteus* see J.-O. Tjäder, 'Der Codex argenteus in Uppsala und der Buchmeister Viliaric in Ravenna', *Studia Gothica* (Stockholm, 1972), 144–64. On Gothic manuscripts see P. Scardigli, *Lingua e storia dei Goti* (Florence, 1964), 218–28 (the 1973 German edition was not available).

apart on beautifully prepared parchment. A counterpart just within this period is the purple Abbeville Gospels (Bibliothèque Municipale, 4 (1); CLA vi, 704) which was a product of the first court school of Charlemagne and was written in gold uncials again between two ruled lines. Another product of the same school, which, though written in gold, is not on purple leaves, the already-mentioned Harley Gospels (London, British Library; CLA ii, 198) has decorated frames for each column on every page.

Although written neither in gold nor in silver and not on purple leaves, elaborate uncial Gospels like the Anglo-Saxon fragments from Avranches (Bibliothèque Municipale, 48 (fols. I–II) + 66 (fols. I–II) + 71 (fols. A–B) + St Petersburg, Saltykov-Scedrin State Public Library, O. v. I. 1; CLA vi, 730) or the Mondsee folios now divided between Nuremberg and New York (Nuremberg, Germanisches Nationalmuseum, 27932 + Nuremberg, Stadtbibliothek, Fragm. 1 + New York, Pierpont Morgan Library, M 564; CLA ix, 1347) arrange their text spaciously on the page guided by double ruled lines. The changes in the appearance of books which took place in the seventh and eighth centuries (partly in association with new scripts) brought concepts of luxury different from those of the late Antique uncial tradition. The Book of Kells (Dublin, Trinity College, 58; CLA ii, 274), written in stately majuscules between two ruled lines and with a wealth of exuberant illuminations on every page, is a striking witness to these new concepts, concepts which seem to have developed quickest and furthest in the British Isles. The plain symmetrical uncial page gave way to one where ornament was dominant. The innumerable decorated initials at the opening of verses, and sometimes of pauses, along with the frequent runovers sequestered by decorative flourishes broke up the pages of text even where an uncial type layout may have lain behind the work of the Insular scribe and artist.[32] The massive initial pages with overall rich patterning (where the sense of the text was less important than the announcement of an opening) combined with the intricate convolutions of the full-decorated carpet pages to proclaim the beginnings of texts in ways utterly different from those in their uncial elders and betters. The script in all these luxury books was written between two ruled lines. This simple device made capital or majuscule script more regular and even, and was used in many de luxe manuscripts.[33]

The frequent use of runovers and their demarcation by flourishes or guiding creatures gave the pages of Insular books a distinctive appearance.[34] A much more striking difference was the separation of words. The ancient practice of *scriptio continua*

---

[32] It is difficult, for instance, to assess how much the rigorous symmetry of the Lindisfarne Gospels (London, British Library, Cotton Nero D. iv; CLA ii, 287) owes to the Anglo-Saxon scribe-artist himself and how much to an uncial exemplar.

[33] It does, however, appear in two much more modest books, the Greco-Latin Pauline epistle in rustics of the fourth to fifth centuries (Florence, Biblioteca Medicea Laurenziana, P. S. i. 1306; CLA Supplement, 1694) and a seventh-century Mark fragment (Hannover, Kestner-Museum, CUL. i. 44 (365), CLA Supplement, 1699) which is written in small unpretentious uncials.

[34] An account of runovers in the early Middle Ages might be useful. They are found much more in Insular books and are decoratively more obvious. The pages of the Book of Kells show many striking examples, see the colour facsimile published by Faksimile Verlag Luzern, *The Book of Kells*, ed. Peter Fox, 2 vols. (Lucerne, 1990).

was replaced by word separation, and this was one of the most important contributions made by Irish scribes to what Malcolm Parkes has called the 'grammar of legibility'.[35] Sections were also more completely separated by initials and careful, modulated punctuation broke text up into intelligible and constituent parts. These features as much as the already-mentioned divergent treatment of the page helped to change the appearance of the book, biblical and non-biblical alike.[36]

Through these innovations Insular scribes made texts as a whole more legible, but in the case of biblical books there were already various conventions for laying out and punctuating text which the Irish adopted and which were not radically changed during the centuries with which we are concerned here. Biblical books were divided in differing ways. In the Psalter each Psalm would be clearly separate, but most other books would be divided into chapters or sections, the Gospels, particularly Vulgate texts, being also further divided into the very numerous Eusebian sections.

Additionally there could be further divisions into verses and into sense pauses within verses. There were three methods of showing these further divisions, some more thorough than others. The first method was particularly suitable for poetical books. In it each verse is given a new line: an early example is the Greco-Latin sixth- to seventh-century Psalter at Verona (Biblioteca Capitolare, I (1); CLA IV, 472), but the practice is found throughout the period, particularly in the Psalms.

The other two methods contrasted visually with each other. In the first of these the text is laid out in a block, and presents a monolithic appearance on the page. In the second the text is laid out *per cola et commata*, and each division and pause, every *colon* (clause) and *comma* (phrase), starts on a new line: in this way the page is broken into sense lines.[37] Both methods were used throughout our period. In the former there would be scarcely perceptible breaks for verses and pauses; and chapters, and also sometimes – in the case of the Gospels – Eusebian sections would be the chief chinks in the almost solid rectangle (or square) of script. However, within this apparently solid block of script there would be discreet punctuation either by marks or by the slightest of gaps between phrases or verses. Bonifatius Fischer's edition of the Naples palimpsest of I–IV Kings reproduces these varying gaps and marks very faithfully, and shows that the text was punctuated almost as carefully, if not as obviously and as comprehensively, as one arranged *per cola et commata*.[38] Later practitioners of this

[35] M. B. Parkes, 'Insular scribes and the grammar of legibility', *Grafia e interpunzione del latino nel medioevo*, ed. A. Maierù (Rome, 1987), 15–29; repr. in his *Scribes, Scripts and Readers* (London, 1991), 1–18.

[36] *Ibid.*

[37] 'Nemo cum Prophetas versibus viderit esse descriptos, merito eos aestimet apud Hebraeos ligari et aliquid simile habere de Psalmis vel operibus Salomonis; sed quod in Demosthene et Tullio solet fieri, ut per cola scribantur et commata, qui utique prosa et non versibus conscripserunt, nos quoque utilitati legentium providentes interpretationem novam novo scribendi genere distinximus', Jerome, *Prologus in Isaia propheta, Biblia Sacra iuxta vulgatam versionem*, 2 vols. ed. R. Weber (Stuttgart, 1969–75), II, 1096.

[38] B. Fischer, 'Palimpsestus Vindobonensis', *Beiträge zur Geschichte der lateinischen Bibeltexte* (Freiburg, 1986), 308–438, at 324–5, 333–81. D. C. Parker, *Codex Bezae: An Early Christian Manuscript and its Text* (Cambridge, 1992), 30–4, also discusses fruitfully the differing punctuation 'phenomena' in the bilingual Bezae. He notes eight such 'phenomena': lines projecting into the margin with initial letters; the indentation of citations; double, medial and high points; a small space; a large space with a medial point in it; and a large space sometimes followed by an initial letter.

method sometimes gave up some of the sensitive punctuation: the MacRegol Gospels (Oxford, Bodleian Library, Auct. D. II. 19; CLA II, 231), for instance, has hardly any breaks in its solid pages apart from those marking chapters or the occasional Eusebian section while Carolingian books punctuate carefully by signs but not by gaps between words. The second method *per cola et commata* has become associated with Jerome, but this method of dividing the text according to sense lines is ancient and was known to Demosthenes and Cicero. It is interesting that the already-mentioned earliest Vulgate Gospels, the St Gall Gospel fragments, is, in spite of its possible antecedents by Jerome's circle, by no means consistently laid out *per cola et commata*, and the sixth-century Milan Gospels (Biblioteca Ambrosiana, C. 39 inf.; CLA III, 313) is almost as inconsistent. The method is wasteful of space, and the *Codex Amiatinus* is perhaps the only extant single-volume Bible to lay out much of its text in this way. The single-volume Tours Bibles, by contrast, compress their text into far fewer pages than the *Codex Amiatinus* by the simple expedient of laying out the page (and column) in a block while carefully punctuating each *colon* and *comma*. Like any elaborate system of punctuation it is difficult to reproduce exactly and faithfully. The Lorsch Gospels (Bucharest, Central Library, s.n. + Vatican City, Biblioteca Apostolica Vaticana, Pal. lat. 50) of Charlemagne's court school, and slightly beyond the upper limit of CLA, is a luxury codex and ornate frames enclose each column of text on a page.[39] However, in the absence of bounding lines within these frames, the scribes found it much more difficult to dispose their careful uncials *per cola et commata* than their colleagues had been able to do in the slightly earlier Harley Gospels. It is perhaps worth noting that most Irish books were arranged in blocks (a factor sometimes contributing to their archaic appearance) though a few are disposed *per cola et commata* (e.g. Milan, Biblioteca Ambrosiana, D. 10 sup. (front fly leaves)). In others where the text is laid out in a solid block (e.g. parts of the Book of Mulling, Dublin, Trinity College, 60; CLA II, 276) the punctuation occasionally reproduces a text originally laid out according to the method recommended by Jerome.[40]

Single bounding lines enclosed the writing space in most Irish books, even in one as elaborate and obviously paragraphed as the Book of Kells. Text arranged in a block does not need double bounding lines since initial letters are either entirely contained within the text block or, if they project beyond it, may do so only a little way. Conversely text arranged *per cola et commata* is best guided by double bounding lines.[41] The beautiful uncial in the sixth-century Harleian Gospels (London, British Library, Harley 1775; CLA II, 197) is arranged *per cola et commata*. It has double bounding lines set quite widely apart. Every new verse or sense pause has two or sometimes three initials within these bounding lines which are never crossed by the rest of the text. The

---

[39] See the facsimile, W. Braunfels, *The Lorsch Gospels* (New York, 1967).

[40] The Irish pocket gospel book in the British Library (Add. 40618; CLA II, 179) curiously relegates initials to the margin even when a new sentence begins in the middle of a line. An analogous practice is that found in some Greek books (e.g. British Library, Royal 1. D. v–viii, the *Codex Alexandrinus*) of projecting a letter into the margin at the beginning of a line when the new section had begun in the middle of the previous line.

[41] R. Raffaelli, 'La pagina e il testo. Sulle funzione della doppia rigatura verticali nei CLA', *Il libro e il testo*, ed. C. Questa and R. Raffaeli (Urbino, 1984), 3–21.

final line of a verse is further distinguished by a slight indent. Citations in turn are indented further and sometimes marked by a *diple* in the margin. By these means the text was more clearly articulated on the page.

In addition to their segregation between double bounding lines, by the eighth century initial letters were further distinguished by being decorated and by being larger than the letters of normal script. The background to the Irish scribal practice of opening a section with a larger letter which was integrated with the text by the gradual diminuendo of the following letters down to text size (as in, for example the Psalter called 'Cathach of St Columba', Dublin, Royal Irish Academy, s.n.; CLA ii, 266) has been sought in late Antique texts written in the form of 'literary cursive'. Julian Brown pointed to one early manuscript written in such a script and containing grammatical treatises of Probus and Charisius (Naples, Biblioteca Nazionale, lat. 2, (fols. 76–111, 140–56, 159; CLA iii, 397a) which begins paragraphs 'with an enlarged letter followed by a gradual diminuendo of letters coming down to standard text size'.[42] As important as the emergence of the decorated initial with diminuendo was the switch of emphasis from the colophon recording the end of a text to the initial or initials graphically announcing its opening. An Old Latin gospel book like the probably African *Codex Bobiensis* of the turn of the fourth and fifth centuries (Turin, Biblioteca Nazionale, G. vii. 15; CLA iv, 465) announces the change from Mark to Matthew by devoting a whole page of well-spaced-out large uncials interlined with dashes and strokes to the words: *euangelium cata Marcum explicit. Incipit cata Mattheum feliciter.* By contrast a plain tall initial *L* alone announces the restrained opening of Matthew: *Liber generationis.*[43] In the later Vulgate Cividale Gospels which are ascribed to the beginning of the sixth century (Cividale, Museo Archeologico, s.n. + Prague, Knihovna Metropolitní Kapitoly, Cim. 1 + Venice, San Marco, s.n; CLA iii, 285) the visual accent is more evenly distributed between explicit and incipit: the transition between Luke and John is managed by an explicit in capitals in one column and a longer decorated initial *I* (*In principio*) at the top of the second.[44] In the Gundohinus Gospels of 754, greater emphasis is being given to the incipit. The Gospels and accessory texts open with a much larger decorated letter, some lines of coloured and filled out capitals and a column of script larger than that in the text whereas the explicit consists of a few lines of elongated rustic capitals.[45] Similarly in the Lindisfarne Gospels of *c.* 700, the explicit is far less important than the opening of the Gospel which is announced by a fully-decorated page dominated by an extremely large initial of great height and lines of large integrated and angular capitals.[46] The emphasis on the colophon has been seen as an inheritance from the roll where the end was the

[42] T. J. Brown, 'The Oldest Irish Manuscripts and their Late Antique Background', *Ireland and Europe. The Early Church*, ed. P. Ní Chatháin and M. Richter (Stuttgart, 1984), 311–27, at 317–18.

[43] For a facsimile see C. Cipolla, *Il codice evangelico k della Bibl. Universitaria di Torino* (Turin, 1913).

[44] C. Nordenfalk, *Die Spätantiken Zierbuchstaben* (Stockholm, 1970), pl. 41.

[45] Autun, Bibliothèque Municipale, 3 (S.2); L. Nees, *The Gundohinus Gospels* (Cambridge, Mass., 1987), pls. 20, 24 and 29.

[46] For the Lindisfarne Gospels, see the plates in either E. G. Millar, *The Lindisfarne Gospels* (London, 1923), or J. Backhouse, *The Lindisfarne Gospels* (London, 1981) or the facsimile T. Kendrick *et al.*, *Evangeliorum quattuor Codex Lindisfarnensis*, 2 vols. (Olten and Lausanne, 1956–60).

appropriate place for an announcement. If this were the case, the tradition persisted for many centuries long after the roll had been abandoned for most texts. The switch to an emphatic opening was partly the result of the development of the decorated initial, which Nordenfalk has traced to its late antique beginnings in a masterly survey.[47] The focus on the opening initial in turn pulled towards it the capital letters which had hitherto only been found in the colophon. As with the change from an uncial to a majuscule book, old practices survived alongside the new, and the focus was sometimes only fitfully shifted: an explicit could still be emphasised in the eighth century.

Three early extant Latin manuscripts bear witness to the existence of cycles of biblical illustration: the Quedlinburg Itala, the Cambridge so-called 'Gospels of St Augustine' and the Ashburnham Pentateuch. The earliest of the three is the fifth-century Quedlinburg Itala, a manuscript of Samuel and Kings (Berlin, Deutsche Staatsbibliothek, theol. lat. fol. 485 + Quedlinburg, Stiftskirche, Treasury, s.n.; CLA VIII, 1069). Only four illustrated pages survive, each with several scenes, but consideration of the original size of the manuscript suggests that it once contained some two hundred or more illustrations.[48] The sixth-century 'Gospels of St Augustine' (Cambridge, Corpus Christi College, 286; CLA II, 126) probably had, when complete, eight pages of miniatures, two to each Gospel, of which only those for Luke survive. One page contains twelve scenes from the Passion in square compartments within a rectangular frame, while the second had a representation of St Luke below an arch with his symbol in the lunette, and twelve scenes from Luke's Gospel set in compartments between two pairs of columns on either side of the evangelist. Originally therefore the manuscript could have had forty-two scenes from the life of Christ on the large rectangular miniatures, and a further forty-two scenes on the portrait pages devoted to episodes in the relevant Gospel.[49] The seventh-century Ashburnham Pentateuch (Paris, B.N., n.a. lat. 2334; CLA V, 693a) has nineteen partially- or fully-illustrated pages devoted to Genesis and Exodus. These generally contain several scenes within a single frame unified by a common background of landscape or architecture.[50] The manuscript is incomplete and it must have lost an uncertain number of illustrations.

The large cycles of illustrations for Genesis, Exodus, Kings and the Gospels which were current at an early date, as revealed by these manuscripts, have left hardly any other traces in the codices of CLA. The one extant complete single-volume Bible, the often mentioned *Codex Amiatinus*, has only three illustrations: on preliminary leaves before the Old Testament are a diagram of the Tabernacle with its vessels of ritual, and a picture of Ezra the scribe writing in front of a cupboard containing the Bible in nine

[47] Nordenfalk, *Spätantiken Zierbuchstaben.*

[48] The most recent study is I. Levin, *The Quedlinburg Itala. The Oldest Illustrated Biblical Manuscript* (Leiden, 1985). The calculation of the original number of individual scenes is based on the assumption that the codex had sixty illustrated pages, see K. Weitzmann, *Late Antique and Early Christian Book Illumination* (New York, 1977), 15.

[49] F. Wormald, *The Miniatures in the Gospels of St Augustine* (Cambridge, 1954); repr. in his *Collected Writings I: Studies in Medieval Art from the Sixth to the Twelfth Centuries* (London, 1984), 13–35.

[50] For a facsimile see O. v. Gebhardt, *The Miniatures in the Ashburnham Pentateuch* (London, 1883).

volumes; while a full-page miniature of Christ in majesty with the four evangelists and their symbols precedes the New Testament.[51] The paucity of illustrations in this Wearmouth–Jarrow Bible is one of the reasons which suggest that extensive cycles were unlikely in complete Bibles. The complete Bible made a very big book, a much bigger book than had been illustrated in Antiquity, and much cumulative experience would have been needed before it could be richly decorated. There were many codices of individual biblical texts, and these attracted illustrations. Among these besides the aforementioned Itala and Pentateuch, the only extant codices with illustrations in this period were gospel books and Psalters. The Eusebian canon tables were often placed under arcades and acted as a unifying decorated introduction to a gospel book and were occasionally embellished with symbols of the evangelists or busts of the apostles.[52] A picture of the appropriate evangelist with or without his symbol, or, sometimes in Insular books, the symbol on its own would precede each Gospel. The Psalter could have illustrations at specified points in the book, corresponding to the established divisions. The eighth-century copy of Cassiodorus' Commentary on the Psalms now in Durham originally had three full-page miniatures corresponding to the tripartite division of the Psalter.[53] The Anglo-Saxon Vespasian Psalter once probably opened with the now misplaced picture of David and his musicians; it has historiated initials at Psalms 26 and 52, and probably had another one at the opening of Psalm 1 (not to mention a carpet page between the Psalms and canticles).[54] In discussing only extant illustrated codices of pre-ninth-century date, only a small part of the evidence is being considered, but even to list the possible early illustrative cycles as revealed in later copies would overload this survey.

The contents and additions of some of these books can tell us how they were used. Many served in the liturgy: this is true not merely of Gospels but also of copies of the Pauline Epistles, of Psalters and of some other books. Two formally written sixth-century uncial Gospels may be taken as examples. Copious notes in different scripts in the margins of the Ancona Gospels (Chapter Archives, s.n.; CLA III, 278) suggest that it was used liturgically for some time, particularly in the seventh and eighth centuries, though some marginalia were added as late as the tenth. The uncial Milan Gospels (Biblioteca Ambrosiana, C. 39 inf.; CLA III, 313) has liturgical marginalia in seventh-century cursive indicating North Italian use. In neither case of course do the additions reveal when the books ceased to be of service; nor, when they were superseded, whether they were elevated to a higher, or relegated to a lower, status. A few liturgical notes and corrections in the Greco-Latin *Codex Claromontanus* of the Pauline Epistles (Paris, BN, gr. 107 + 107a + 107b; CLA v, 521), in the Greco-Latin *Codex Bezae* of Acts (Cambridge, University Library, Nn. II. 41; CLA II, 140), in the fifth-century Old Latin Darmstadt Prophets (Landes und Hochschulbibliothek, 895 + 3140 + Donaueschingen, Hofbibliothek, 191 (flyleaf) + Fulda, Hessische Landesbibliothek,

---

[51] See Alexander, *Insular Manuscripts*, 32–5, ills. 23–7, fig. 27.
[52] C. Nordenfalk, *Die Spätantiken Kanontafeln*, 2 vols. (Göteborg, 1938).
[53] R. A. B. Mynors, *Durham Cathedral Manuscripts to the End of the Twelfth Century* (Oxford, 1939), 21.
[54] Alexander, *Insular Manuscripts*, 55–6, ills. 143–6, fig. 7. Facsimile and study by D. H. Wright, *The Vespasian Psalter*, Early English Manuscripts in Facsimile XIV (Copenhagen, 1967).

Aa 1a + St Paul in Carinthia, Stiftsbibliothek, s.n. + Stuttgart, Württemburgische Landesbibliothek, HB II. 20, II. 54, VII. 1, VII. 12, VII. 25, VII. 28, VII. 29, VII. 30, VII. 39, VII. 45, VII. 54, XI. 30, XIV. 14, XIV. 15 (all fly leaves and offsets); CLA VIII, 1174) and in the eighth-century Vatican Pauline Epistles (Biblioteca Apostolica Vaticana, Reg. lat. 9; CLA I, 100) show that these too had been used in this way. The capitularies added to eighth-century Gospels (e.g. Biblioteca Apostolica Vaticana, lat. 5465 (fols. 1–170); CLA I, 24a; lat. 7016; CLA I, 51) or Pauline Epistles (Biblioteca Apostolica Vaticana, Reg. lat. 9; CLA I, 100) show that they were meant for the liturgy, though in the case of the more luxurious books of Charlemagne's court school which were similarly equipped (Abbeville, Bibliothèque Municipale, 4 (1); CLA VI, 704), it might be doubted whether much regular use of this nature was ever invisaged. (Marks added in the Gospels for the Passion indicating either changes of tone or of speakers, must be treated with caution as evidence for use of the books in question during Holy Week. These could have been copied mechanically from an exemplar. Only the evidence of marginal reading marks made by pen or dry point would confirm use during the reading of the Passion, but these unfortunately have not often been recorded.) Nevertheless despite its limitations, the evidence does indicate that a fair number of the biblical books in CLA served in the liturgy.

It was thought worth extending the active life of some codices. Thus the Ashburnham Pentateuch had replacement leaves (Paris, BN, n.a. lat. 2334; CLA, V, 693a and 693b) added at a later date, the Matthew of the fifth-century *Codex Claromontanus* Vatican City, Biblioteca Apostolica Vaticana, lat. 7223 (fols. 1–66; CLA I, 53) was completed by the Gospels of Mark, Luke and John in the seventh-century part of lat. 7223. (fols. 67–283; CLA I, 54). Other books were thought worth copying. Thus the gospel book Perugia, Biblioteca Capitolare, 2 (CLA IV, 408) of the eighth to ninth century copied the sixth-century Perugia, 1 (CLA IV, 407), presumably at Perugia, and today provides a guide to the latter's defective text.

Many of our manuscripts were designed or were destined to be studied and commented upon: the most striking example of this is the Irish eighth-century Würzburg Matthew (Universitätsbibliothek, M. p. th. f. 61; CLA IX, 1415) which has innumerable marginal glosses and yet others on a large number of inserted leaves or scraps. Another working copy is the eighth-century Trinity Cambridge Pauline Epistles (Trinity College, B. 10. 5 + London, British Library, Cotton Vitellius C. VIII; CLA II, 133) which has many interlinear glosses and marginalia by contemporary and later Anglo-Saxon hands. Many of these, ascribed to the hand responsible for the main text, are derived from Pelagius' Commentary on the Epistles. The Old English or High German glosses added to a very large number of books – some as prestigious as the Lindisfarne (CLA II, 187) and MacRegol Gospels (Oxford, Bodleian Library, Auct. D. II. 19; CLA II, 231), both with tenth-century interlinear glosses, or the Vespasian Psalter (London, British Library, Cotton Vespasian A. I; CLA II, 193) with interlinear glosses added in the ninth century – clearly answered a need though in the case of the most precious books they surely would not often have been used for teaching purposes. (One wonders what sort of book was used by a teacher like Theodore of Tarsus at Canterbury when commenting on the text of the Pentateuch and the Gospels.) Bilingual books, Greco-Latin, or Gothic-Latin, were obvious aids to study in areas where two languages were current, and their history has recently been elucidated by D. C. Parker.[55] Texts are arranged sense line by sense line, and it is not surprising that Parker found that this tradition had broken down when the Carolingians resumed the practice of bilingual texts.[56] Unlike the *Codex Bezae* which arranges its Latin and Greek texts on facing pages in sense lines, the Bodleian Graeco-Latin *Codex Laudianus* Acts (Laud. gr. 35; CLA II, 251) arranges its bilingual text side by side on the same page with one or two words per line rather like early school glossaries of the classics.[57] The earliest Greco-Latin Psalter (Verona, Biblioteca Capitolare, I (1); CLA IV, 472) dates from *c*. 600, and has been used as an aid for studying Greek.[58]

Most of our books were corrected at one time or another. The two Italian gospel books traditionally associated with St Augustine of Canterbury (Cambridge, Corpus Christi College, 286; CLA II, 126 and Oxford, Bodleian Library, Auct. D. II. 14; CLA II, 230) were clearly handled in Anglo-Saxon England. An eighth-century English hand added captions in uncial to some of the illustrations in the first, while the second bears eighth- to ninth-century corrections and additions in an Anglo-Saxon hand. The sixth-century Italian Harleian Gospels (London, British Library, Harley 1775; CLA II, 197) was corrected at two different periods, first by a contemporary writer, and again in the ninth century, the second phase including some attention to the Eusebian canon table numbers and many lection notes.[59] Beyond this it shows few signs of wear and tear apart from the flaking of ink on flesh sides. One book, the sixth-century Cividale Gospels (Museo Archeologico, s.n. + Prague, Knihovna Metropolitní Kapitoly, Cim. 1 + Venice, San Marco, s.n.; CLA III, 285) was prestigious enough to serve as a distinguished visitors' book at Aquileia from the ninth century onwards. Others were regarded as safe homes for entering documents or charters (e.g. the Lichfield Gospels, Cathedral Library, 1; CLA II, 159; or the Book of Kells, Dublin, Trinity College, 58; CLA II, 274). Very many came to be associated with local saints. The association is chronologically improbable in the cases of the seventh-century St Chad with the eighth-century Lichfield Gospels and of the seventh-century St Columbanus with the fourth- to fifth-century *Codex Bobiensis* (Turin, Biblioteca Nazionale, G. VII. 15; CLA IV, 465); but it is plausible or, at least, acceptable palaeographically, in the cases of St Germain (496–576) with the beautiful sixth-century purple Old Latin Psalter (Paris, BN, lat. 11947; CLA V, 616), of St Eusebius (+371) with the fourth- to fifth-century Vercelli Gospels, (Biblioteca Capitolare, s.n.; CLA IV, 467) and of St Marcellinus,

---

[55] Parker, *Codex Bezae*, 50–69.   [56] *Ibid.*, 63–6.   [57] *Ibid.*, 69.

[58] G. Turrini, *Millenium scriptorii Veronensis dal IVo al XVo secolo* (Verona, 1967), pl. 8 shows a double page.

[59] The early corrections here and in the *Codex Fuldensis* of Victor of Capua (Fulda, Hessische Landesbibliothek, Bonifatianus 1; CLA VIII, 1196) observe Greek syllabification, a reflection of their Italian sixth-century context. It has not been remarked that the Tironian notes added in the ninth century to the Harleian Gospels mark the beginning (with the sign for 'hic' or by the use of an appropriate Eusebian section) and end (with the sign for 'usque') of numerous lections.

bishop of Ancona from 550, with the sixth-century Ancona Gospels (CLA III, 278). Some books were embellished with jewelled covers: thus the Lindisfarne Gospels (CLA II, 187) in the eighth century, if its tenth-century colophon can be believed, and the Carolingian Arsenal Gospels (Paris, Bibliothèque de l'Arsenal, 599; CLA V, 517) by the twelfth century, if the note of that date on fol. av is reliable. Others may have been put in a precious metal box, as the Vercelli Gospels was by Duke Berengaria in 885; while yet others, especially in Ireland, came to be regarded as relics and enshrined.[60]

Reference has already been made to C. H. Turner's view that the earliest manuscript of the Vulgate Gospels, the fifth-century St Gall Gospels (CLA VII, 984) was a copy for personal and not public use.[61] The view receives support from CLA's reference to its 'pleasingly irregular' half-uncial (in contrast to the regular and formal uncial of many contemporary books), and from the scholarly and non-liturgical character of the marginalia. Now sadly depleted, it must have been a good size personal copy, having dimensions of c. 230 × 180 mm. Smaller in format (177 × 120 mm), but bulkier and more luxurious than the St Gall codex, is another possible personal copy, the sixth-century Italian Harley Gospels (CLA II, 197). Written in formal uncials well laid out on the page, and prefaced by the earliest complete Latin architectural canon tables (arcades in fact of great elegance), with its beginning and end mutilated, it runs to 468 folios. Again there are no signs of liturgical use (before the ninth century) and it could have made a hefty personal book for someone of rank.[62] An early eighth-century New Testament in Paris (BN, n.a. lat. 1063; CLA V, 679) is extremely cursively written, abounding in ligatures and some features of Merovingian charter script. Slightly smaller than the St Gall Gospels (220 × 145 mm), it does not look like a book which could have been read easily in public, and has no liturgical notes. It is tantalising to speculate whether it was used by a layman or cleric, but little is known of its history until a nineteenth-century report of its being one of the chief treasures of the Beauvais Chapter. Another possible personal copy is a Verona fragment of Kings in eighth-century cursive half-uncial (Biblioteca Capitolare, III (3); CLA IV, 478), but too little has survived of the manuscript for any evaluation of its function to be much more than a guess.

The pocket gospel books were clearly personal copies.[63] Most are Irish, and, written in small and often cursive hands, they might be seen as the private gospel books mentioned in the lives of Irish saints.[64] One of them has been regarded as an amulet; this is the textually selective Stowe St John (Dublin, Royal Irish Academy, D. II. 3 (fols. 1–11); CLA II, 267), which was placed in a *cumdach* in 1045–52 with the Stowe Missal (Dublin, Royal Irish Academy, D. II. 3 (fols. 12–67; CLA II, 268), the

[60] Examples are the book shrine of the Gospels of St Molaise and that usually known as the shrine of the Stowe Missal (see below).

[61] Turner, *The Oldest Manuscript*.

[62] A. Petrucci, 'L'onciale Romana. Origini, sviluppo e diffusione di una stilazzazione grafica altomedievali (sec. VI–IX)', *Studi Medievali* series 3, 12 (1971), 75–135, at 109.

[63] P. McGurk, 'The Irish pocket Gospel book', *Sacris Erudiri* 8 (1956), 249–70.

[64] *Ibid.*, 249–50.

manuscript with which it is now bound. Two other small copies of John, the Wearmouth–Jarrow Stonyhurst Gospels (London, British Library, Loan 74; CLA II, 260) and the Chartres codex (CLA V, 600), the smallest of all early extant Latin manuscripts, have also been considered possible amulets.[65] The Stonyhurst John was found in the coffin of St Cuthbert at the saint's translation in 1104. It has some lection crosses but shows little sign of use. As has already been stated, the sixth-century Chartres St John was found in the reliquary of the shirt of the Virgin at Chartres in 1712, and the report of that date spoke of its having been a relic of St Lebuinus, bishop of Chartres (+ *c*. 556). It has crosses marking liturgical pericopes and could have been used for the liturgy. One of these three books may have begun life as an amulet and could be the heir to the early tradition of miniature books like the already mentioned Mani Gospel.[66] The occasion for the making of the Stonyhurst John could well have been the translation of St Cuthbert in 698, a date which is palaeographically acceptable. If so, it would be Wearmouth–Jarrow's offering for an occasion which may also have stimulated the production of the Lindisfarne Gospels, and it might be regarded as offering the tomb the magical protection with which the fourth Gospel was specifically endowed. The other two books, however, may have started out as personal copies, the Stowe St John with its passages for private reading, and the Chartres codex as a convenient book for personal reading and occasional liturgical use. Their use (whether real or imagined) by holy men may have made them relics and such a change may have also happened with the other pocket books.

If these books became relics, this was not their original function. It has been suggested that the two most famous Insular books, the Lindisfarne Gospels and the Book of Kells, may have been made for particular local sacred occasions, the first for the translation of St Cuthbert in 698, the second for the shrine of St Columba.[67] Whatever the truth of either hypothesis, many of the great Insular gospel books should rightly be placed in the context of monastic communities and local shrines, and some of them can be seen as offerings to a local patron saint.[68] However, whilst this might be true of books like the Lichfield or MacRegol Gospels, which lack the customary aids to liturgical use, it must be remembered that the sumptuously illuminated Barberini Gospels (Vatican City, Biblioteca Apostolica Vaticana, Barb. lat. 570; CLA I, 163) was clearly used as a lectionary. Barberini has marginal section references, whether Eusebian or chapter, which make it easy to handle even without lection notes.

The *Codex Beneventanus* (London, British Library, Add. 5463; CLA II, 162) was written by a monk Lupus for Ato, who has been plausibly identified with an abbot of

---

[65] T. J. Brown, *The Stonyhurst Gospel of St John* (London, 1969), 28–44. Much of what follows on the three small books (Stowe, Stonyhurst and Chartres) is based on these pages of Brown, though the conclusion drawn differs a little from his.

[66] Turner, *Greek Manuscripts*, item 83.

[67] For Lindisfarne see Alexander, *Insular Manuscripts*, 35–40. The dating of Lindisfarne to 698 and the association of the translation of St Cuthbert was first made by T. J. Brown in Kendrick *et al.*, *Codex Lindisfarnensis*, II. On Kells, see P. Meyvaert, 'The Book of Kells and Iona', *Art Bulletin* 71 (1989), 6–19, at 12–13.

[68] G. Henderson, *From Durrow to Kells: The Insular Gospel-Books 650–800* (London, 1987) places these books firmly in their context.

San Vincenzo al Volturno (736–60). The multi-volume Maurdramnus Bible, the colophon to Amiens, Bibliothèque Municipale, 11 (CLA vi, 707) records, was made at the command of the abbot of that name '*propter Dei amorem et propter compendium legentium*', that is 'for the love of God and for the convenience of lectors reading in church'.[69] The St Gall manuscript of Ezekiel, the minor Prophets and Daniel, (St Gall, Stiftsbibliothek, 44 (pp. 1–184); CLA vii, 899) was written for St Gall at the command of John II, bishop of Constance (760–81), who was also abbot of St Gall and Reichenau. The layout and script of all three books would have made them easy to read in church. The Bible manuscripts written by Winithar of St Gall (e.g. St Gall, Stiftsbibliothek, 2 (pp. 3–294); CLA vii, 893a; St Gall, Stiftsbibliothek, 2 (pp. 301–568); CLA vii, 894; and St Gall, Stifstbibliothek, 70; CLA vii, 903) would also have been very suitable for this function, their lesser discipline and awkwardness of layout reflecting differing scribal standards, not a different purpose. There are a large number of gospel books and fragments now in Durham Cathedral Library, all large, all elaborate products. They could all well have been made for use in church and monastery. The smaller scale books like the Hereford (Cathedral Library, P. i. 2; CLA ii, 157) and Royal Gospels (London, British Library, Royal 1. B. vii; CLA ii, 213) were probably made for, or at, less exalted institutions or lesser scriptoria.[70]

The *Codex Amiatinus* was made by the monks of Wearmouth–Jarrow and taken as a gift to the Pope by Abbot Ceolfrith in 716. It is one of the few documented gifts of biblical books of this period, and should be seen as a gift from the most romanised of Anglo-Saxon establishments in exchange for what it had received from Rome. Two books of the court school of Charlemagne were made to order, and are examples of a new lay patronage. The Dagulf Psalter (Vienna, Österreichische Nationalbibliothek, lat. 1861; CLA x, 1504) was written at the order of Charlemagne as a present for Pope Hadrian (+795) while the Ada Gospels (Trier, Stadtbibliothek, 22; CLA ix, 1366) were commissioned by the lady of that name, who may have been the illegitimate daughter of Pippin (+after 823). A third product of this same school, the purple Gospels at Abbeville (Bibliothèque Municipale, 4 (1); CLA vi, 704) may have been the evangelary which Angilbert, abbot of St Riquier (790–814), said was given by Charlemagne to that house. These three codices show lay direction and patronage of a kind not recorded since Constantine ordered the mass production of Bibles to equip the new churches he intended to build in Constantinople.[71] The fifth-century Gothic Gospels written in gold and silver on purple pages, the *Codex Argenteus Upsaliensis*, which was probably made for Theodoric the Ostrogoth, is the only other early extant example of such patronage. However, the conditions behind the making of the purple Gothic codex for Theodoric were quite different from those behind the Carolingian commissions or behind the preparing of Insular or Merovingian books in the seventh

---

[69] See W. M. Lindsay, 'The old script of Corbie: its abbreviation symbols', *Revue des Bibliothèques* xxii (1912), 407. I owe this reference and the rendering of the colophon to D. Ganz, *Corbie in the Carolingian Renaissance* (Sigmaringen, 1990), 44, note 33.

[70] See Richard Gameson, ch. 2, below.   [71] Eusebius, *Vita Constantini*, iv, 36.

and eighth centuries. Books in the fifth century were still being written for, and in, households as well as in communities, and a commercial book trade still existed.[72]

Pierre Petitmengin has pointed out that most purple codices of the fifth and sixth centuries have Old Latin texts.[73] Appropriately enough it is as though Jerome's invective against de luxe manuscripts had had an effect on the presentation of Vulgate manuscripts in particular. If a royal connection can be seen in the case of the Gothic codex, the evidence for the other purple books suggests an association with cathedrals from an early date: the purple Trent and Verona codices were very probably preserved in their town cathedrals, and could well have been made for them, commissioned by eclesiastics or presented by wealthy lay people. The gospel book had a crucial validating role at councils and assemblies, which luxury purple books would have carried out most impressively. The verses of the Carolingian scribe Godescalc are very evocative in this context: 'Golden letters on purple pages promise the heavenly kingdom and the joys of heaven by the shedding of rosy blood'.[74] Jerome might condemn the extravangance of the luxury codex, but the opulence, the purple and gold and silver were for Christ.

---

[72] Two workshops are attested. That of Gaudiosus 'librarius ad vinculas S Petri civitate Romana' is found in the ninth-century Angers, Bibliothèque Municipale, 24 (20), fol. 125v. Gaudiosus seems to have flourished *c.* 500. See D. De Bruyne, 'Gaudiosus, un vieux libraire', *Revue Bénédictine* xxx (1913), 343–5.

    Viliaric antiquarius, the scribe of the sixth-century Florence, Biblioteca Medicea Laurenziana, Plut. 65. 1 (CLA III, 298), presumably also had a workshop: 'confectus codex in statione magistri Uiliaric antiquarii'. On him see Tjäder, 'Codex argenteus' at 150–6.

[73] Petitmengin, 'Les plus anciens manuscrits', 99.

[74] D. Ganz, 'Preconditions for Caroline Minuscule', *Viator* 18 (1971), 23–44, at 30. I am extremely grateful to the editor, Richard Gameson, for a helpful and rigorous reading of this paper which much improved its clarity. I am responsible for faults and errors which remain.

2

The Royal 1. B. vii Gospels and English book production in the seventh and eighth centuries

RICHARD GAMESON

London, British Library, MS Royal 1. B. vii is a gospel book of probable eighth-century date (see ills. 2.1–3).[1] Its preparation, script and decoration all testify to an origin in an Insular milieu, and its textual affiliations with manuscripts from Lindisfarne and Wearmouth–Jarrow accord with E. A. Lowe's ascription of it to England, 'probably Northumbria' on palaeographical grounds.[2] Small additions in Caroline minuscule[3] hint either that the book was on the Continent during the ninth century or that it was used in England in circles which included Continental personnel at this time. Whatever the truth of this matter, the volume was definitely in England during the tenth century, for in 925 or thereabouts the manumission of one Eadhelm by King Athelstan was recorded in a blank space on fol. 15v.[4] It has been suggested that the manuscript might actually have belonged to Athelstan at the

---

[1] Reproductions may be found as follows.
Fol. 4v: our ill. 2.3 (detail).
Fol. 9r: G. L. Micheli, *L'enluminure du haut Moyen Age et les influences irlandaises* (Brussels, 1939), fig. 215.
Fol. 10v: J. J. G. Alexander, *Insular Manuscripts 6th to the 9th Century*, A Survey of Manuscripts Illuminated in the British Isles 1 (London, 1978), ill. 72.
Fol. 13r: T. Kendrick, T. J. Brown, R. L. S. Bruce-Mitford *et al.*, *Codex Lindisfarnensis*, 2 vols. (Olten and Lausanne, 1956–60), II, pl. 33(f).
Fol. 14v: our ill. 2.2
Fols 14v + 15r: L. Webster and J. Backhouse, eds., *The Making of England: Anglo-Saxon Art and Culture AD 600–900* (British Museum exh. cat., 1991), no. 84, p. 120.
Fol. 15r: Alexander, *Insular Manuscripts*, ill. 71.
Fol. 15v: M. Lapidge and H. Gneuss, eds., *Learning and Literature in Anglo-Saxon England, Studies Presented to Peter Clemoes* (Cambridge, 1985), pl. XI (full page); Alexander, *Insular Manuscripts*, ill. 70 (detail).
Fol. 38r: F. G. Kenyon, *Facsimiles of Biblical Manuscripts in the British Museum* (London, 1900), pl. XII.
Fol. 55r: our ill. 2.1.
Fol. 84r: G. F. Warner and J. P. Gilson, *Catalogue of Western Manuscripts in the Old Royal and King's Collections*, 4 vols. (London, 1921), IV, pl. 6 (full page); Alexander, *Insular Manuscripts*, ill. 73 (detail).
Fol. 130v: CLA II, 213.
[2] CLA II, 213.
[3] Fols. 55r (*diens*), 75r (*ferebant* – correcting *dicebant*). Both are written in a lighter brown ink than that which was used for the main text. The sample is too small to admit confident interpretation; however they are clearly the work of different hands, and the second hand may well also have been responsible for the punctuation which was added in the same light brown ink between fols. 73r–77r.
[4] Printed in *Select Historical Documents of the Ninth and Tenth Centuries*, ed. F. E. Harmer (Cambridge, 1914), no. XIX. For the script see N. R. Ker, *Catalogue of Manuscripts Containing Anglo-Saxon* (Oxford, 1957), no. 246.

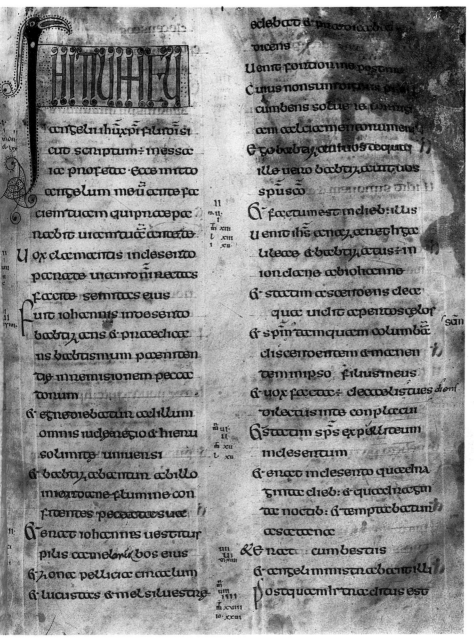

2.1   *London, British Library, MS Royal 1. B. vii, fol. 55r. Page size: 280 × 220 mm*

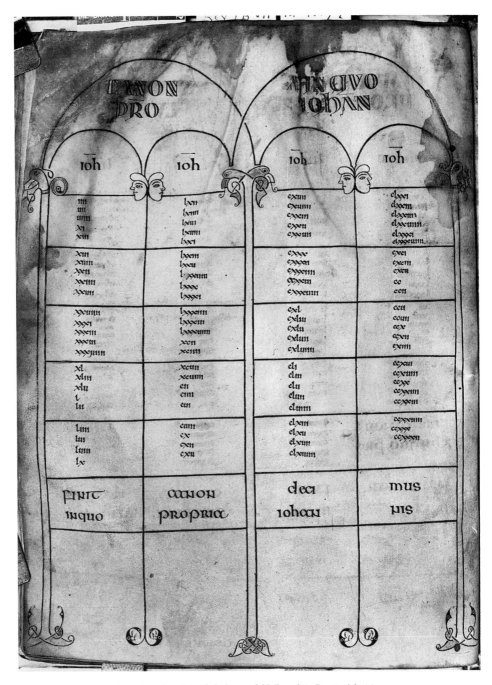

2.2   *London, British Library, MS Royal 1. B. vii, fol. 14v.*

scme potenus exsup scribi
mb: quasinfronce notta
inuenies quiautequot del-
is q: inquines similia dixe
runt ueniens etiam conelu
qua euangelia preundenu
mentum quem contanei——is
uidebis copostos p̄ singu
los numeros cooq:eos insi
is pnopnusq:locis similia
dixisse neppenies
in argumentum ima
attheus iniudea si
cut inordine pri
mus ponum euar
gelium iniudea pr
mus scribsit cuius uocacac
codm expuplicanis acab:
fit duonum ingeneracion
xpi principia p̄ sumens un
us cuius pruma cncumcis

2.3   *London, British Library, MS Royal 1. B. vii, fol. 4v (detail)*

time.[5] In fact, this provides the only certain knowledge we have about the history of
the volume during the entire medieval period since, apart from the laconic testimony
of a few very minor textual additions made in the late eleventh or early twelfth
century,[6] of a line of neumes that is possibly contemporary,[7] and of some dry-point
sketches of probable twelfth-century date,[8] its subsequent fortunes until its accession
into the royal library are equally obscure.[9] As the early history of many Insular
manuscripts is comparably enigmatic – the date, the location, even what side of the
Irish Sea or the North Sea they were written being uncertain – we lack an adequate
frame of reference for placing ill-documented volumes like Royal 1. B. vii. No
speculations concerning its origin will be offered here; the purpose of the present
study is rather to define with new precision its relative position within the corpus of
early Insular gospel books, and to explore such general insights as it may offer into the
world of book production in early Christian Anglo-Saxon England.

In comparison with the various other, more famous manuscripts that tend to
shape modern perception of the appearance of an Insular gospel book, Royal 1. B. vii
is an unpretentious volume. It consists of 155 folios, measuring in their present
trimmed state[10] *c*. 280 × 220 mm, with a written area of *c*. 220–30 × 158–70 mm, the
width of the individual columns being *c*. 68 mm. Thus, although bigger than the Book
of Durrow,[11] and approximately the same size as the St Gall Gospels[12] and the
(severely cropped) Cambridge–London Gospels,[13] it is significantly smaller than the
Lindisfarne, Durham, Echternach, Lichfield, St Petersburg (formerly Leningrad)
and Barberini Gospels, the Book of Kells, the Stockholm Codex Aureus, the
Codex Bigotianus and the fragmentary gospel book from Wearmouth–Jarrow that
is now in Utrecht.[14] The volume is divided into twenty quires, all but four of

---

[5] See S. Keynes, 'King Athelstan's Books', *Learning and Literature*, ed. Lapidge and Gneuss, 143–201, at 185–9.
[6] Fols. 73r, *MARCUM* (rustic capitals) and *IHS*; 75r (upper margin), *falsu[m] tes[timonium]*; 76v, *u* and
      lamatabtani (Mark *15*, 34: above the corrected phrase *Heloi heloi lema sabacthani*); and possibly also 86r,
      LUC.
[7] Fol. 77r (above *Et aduoluit lapidem ad ostium monumenti*: Mark 15.46).
[8] Fols. 4r (standing figure – between columns at the bottom of the page) and 112r (inner margin: hands, one
      projecting from a sleeve).
[9] It appears in the Royal catalogue of 1666 (fol. 3). The rather crude ink chapter numbers in the upper margin
      were possibly added around this time. H. Wanley, *Librorum Veterum Septentrionalium Catalogus* (vol. II of
      G. Hickes, *Linguarum Veterum Septentrionalium Thesaurus* (Oxford, 1705)), 181, believed that it had formerly
      belonged to Christ Church, Canterbury. M. R. James, *The Ancient Libraries of Canterbury and Dover*
      (Cambridge, 1903), 532, assigned it to St Augustine's, Canterbury. Neither gives his reasons.
[10] The extent of the trimming is most readily apparent in the canon tables, the capitals and bases of which have
      been cropped at the outer edge.
[11] Dublin, Trinity College, MS 57 (Alexander, *Insular Manuscripts*, cat. 6; CLA II, 273): 245 × 145 mm.
[12] St Gall, Stiftsbibliothek, MS 51 (Alexander, *Insular Manuscripts*, cat. 44; CLA VII, 901): 295 × 215–20 mm.
[13] Cambridge, Corpus Christi College, MS 197B + London, British Library, MS Cotton Otho C. v (Alexander,
      Insular Manuscripts, cat. 12; CLA II, 125): 285 × 212 mm.
[14] Respectively: London, British Library, MS Cotton Nero D. IV (Alexander, *Insular Manuscripts*, cat. 9; CLA II,
      187): 340 × 240 mm
         Durham, Cathedral Library, MS A. II. 17 + Cambridge, Magdalene College, Pepysian MS 2981(19)
      (Alexander, *Insular Manuscripts*, cat. 10; CLA II, 149): 344 × 265 mm
         Paris, Bibliothèque Nationale, MS lat. 9389 (Alexander, *Insular Manuscripts*, cat. 11; CLA V, 159): 335 ×
      225 mm

which[15] are or were regular quaternions. Most of the quires are signed in the centre of the lower margin on the final verso; in addition nearly half are marked with a cross in the top left-hand corner of the first recto.[16] The first and last pages of the book as a whole are noticeably more discoloured and stained than the rest, attesting to greater wear and tear. Of moderate thickness,[17] the parchment of Royal is stiff and greasy. The codex is quite plump and although this is partly due to the cockling of the leaves and to the way the quires have been 'thrown out' on individual guards in modern times, it is also a reflection of the quality of the membrane. The parchment is arranged in the Insular manner of hair side facing flesh within the quire, with a hair side outermost. Although there are no pricks in the inner margins, the disposition of direct and transmitted dry-point ruling makes it clear that the bifolia were folded, not open, when they were ruled[18] – again in accordance with Insular practices. Double or occasionally triple[19] vertical bounding lines were ruled in dry-point to define each column of text; single horizontal ones were provided to guide the script itself. Typically, the horizontals start neatly at the innermost of the two verticals, but overrun irregularly the outer ones. Owing to slips made on the first attempt, a couple of the vertical lines had to be re-ruled.[20] The number of lines per page varies between 27 and 30; the bottom line is occasionally left blank.[21]

Although decoratively very simple, the canon tables are clearly laid out, and they were prepared separately from the body of the book with their own ruling pattern to facilitate this. The numbers are carefully aligned and their subdivision into groups is

---

Lichfield, Cathedral Library, MS 1 (Alexander, *Insular Manuscripts*, cat. 21; CLA ii, 159): 308 × 235 mm

St Petersburg, Saltykov–Scedrin State Public Library, MS F. v. 1. 8 (Alexander, *Insular Manuscripts*, cat. 39; CLA xi, 1605): 349 × 242 mm

Vatican City, Biblioteca Apostolica Vaticana, MS Barberini lat. 570 (Alexander, *Insular Manuscripts*, cat. 36; CLA i, 63): 340 × 250 mm

Dublin, Trinity College, MS 58 (Alexander, *Insular Manuscripts*, cat. 52; CLA ii, 274): 330 × 250 mm

Stockholm, Kungliga Biblioteket MS A. 135 (Alexander, *Insular Manuscripts*, cat. 30; CLA xi, 1642): 395 × 314 mm

Paris, Bibliothèque Nationale, MS lat. 281, 298 (Alexander, *Insular Manuscripts*, cat. 34; CLA v, 526): 345–50 × 262–75 mm

Utrecht, Universiteitsbibliotheek, MS 32, fols. 94–105 (Alexander, *Insular Manuscripts*, cat. 8; CLA x, 1587): 330 × 255 mm

[15] The exceptions are: Qq. ii (discussed in the text below); x (8, with leaf 6 cancelled); xv (10); and xix (4). The other two quires that are now irregular were originally quaternions: Q. xvii (which lacks leaf 2); and Q. xviii (which has gained a ninth leaf – leaf 9 (fol. 151) properly belongs to Q. xix (it has the direct ruling whose transmitted impression appears on fol. 152r) but is currently mistakenly bound as the final leaf of the previous quire). N.b. the system of quire numbering which is followed here, as throughout this article, is based on counting all the quires. It is thus generally one in advance of the contemporary numbering system which ignores the second quire (that containing the canon tables). See further n. 16 below.

[16] The signatures occur as follows: fol. 8v, **I**; 30v, **III**; 38v, **IIII**; 46v, **V**; 70v, **VIII**; 77v, **VIIII**; 85v, **X**; 93v, **XI**; 101v, **XII**; 109v, **XIII**; 119v, **XIIII**; 127v, **XV**; 134v, **XVI**; and 142v, **XVII**. The crosses are found as follows: 23r (Q. iv); 31r (Q. v); 47r (Q. vii); 71r (Q. x); 78r (Q. xi); 128r (Q. xvii); 135r (Q. xviii); and 152r (Q. xix).

[17] Sample measurements were all within the range 0.23–0.28 mm.

[18] The same is true of the Vespasian Psalter (London, British Library, MS Cotton Vespasian A. i): see D. H. Wright, *The Vespasian Psalter*, Early English Manuscripts in Facsimile xiv (Copenhagen, 1967), 18–19, where it is reasonably deduced that the ruling was accomplished with the help of a set square.

[19] Triple rulings defining one of the four vertical boundaries are found in Qq. iii, vii and xiii. It is difficult to perceive a positive motive for the phenomenon: it seems most likely that the margin which was originally ruled was judged unsuitable and one of the two lines was consequently redrawn.

[20] Clearly discernible, for example, on fols. 81r and 94r.   [21] E.g. on fol. 40.

emphasised by firmly drawn horizontal lines, making them very easy to follow. The text of the tables was corrected at an early date, probably soon after they had been written.

The main text of the book is written in black-brown ink, *per cola et commata* (in sense units), two columns to the page, in Insular half-uncials, by, it would seem, a single scribe whose hand Lowe justly described as 'rather cramped'. The minims are, on average, about 2 mm tall. They are thus approximately two-thirds the height of those in the Lindisfarne Gospels and the Book of Durrow, half the height of those in the Durham, Lincoln College[22] and Worcester[23] Gospels, and just over a third that of those in the Book of Kells and the Lichfield Gospels. Although he used a formal book-hand, the scribe's writing is notable for its irregularities and unevenness in comparison with that of the volumes I have just mentioned. The triangular serifs vary in weight and angle; round letter-forms differ in shape, and tend to be square rather than circular; **b**s and **l**s have a sharp 'break' in their backs; while the headstrokes of **g**s and **t**s tend to be set slightly higher than the general headline of the minims as a whole. The shape of a given letter can vary appreciably, and the lateral space it occupies alters accordingly. (Separate from such 'accidental' irregularity, the scribe's treatment of the letter **N** involved considerable deliberate variation, for he regularly elongated its diagonal stroke – up to a maximum of 30 mm – in order to help justify the line in question.) Moreover, the constituent parts of letters like **d**, **e**, **p** and **r** are less carefully joined to each other than in more controlled work: the scribe seems to have been writing with the maximum haste that was compatible with maintaining the formal book hand. Word division is relatively fluid – or at least not particularly pronounced – but given that there are rarely more than five words per column line, and often only two, this seldom causes any ambiguity. Abbreviations are used sparingly, and the only practice worthy of note is the regular use of two wavy lines to indicate suspension or contraction.

The 'rubric' and column titles in the canon tables were written by the same scribe in an enlarged, more evenly spaced version of the same script.[24] The headings, by contrast, were supplied in Insular capitals that are quite distinct in form – they are characterised by their squat proportions, by the use of wedge- or bulb-shaped terminals, and by the juxtaposition of thick limbs defined by double strokes and filled with colour with thin limbs and serifs defined by a single stroke – nevertheless there is no reason to think that they are not also the work of the same hand. There are numerous runovers in the text and these are written at the end of the line above or below, as appropriate,[25] isolated by a diagonal stroke. The various subdivisions of the text are clearly indicated. The first line of each chapter is written in orangey-red ink

[22] Oxford, Lincoln College, MS 92, fols. 165–6 (CLA II, 258).
[23] Worcester Cathedral Library, Add. MS 3 (CLA II, 264).
[24] Except at the end of Canon IX (fol. 13v) where the requisite text was supplied in uncials by another hand. For a useful review of the Insular system of scripts as a whole see T. J. Brown, 'The Irish Element in the Insular System of Scripts to circa A.D. 850', in *Die Iren und Europa im frühen Mittelalter*, ed. H. Löwe, 2 vols. (Stuttgart, 1982), I, 101–19.
[25] The same procedure was sometimes followed in the case of the first lines of chapters (written in minium): e.g. fols. 63v, 92v, 93r, 93v, 135r and 147r.

(minium) in Insular half-uncials,[26] and headed by an enlarged (one-line-high) orange, calligraphic initial or monogram[27] set in the ruled border – all by the one scribe. Eusebian sections are mostly introduced by an enlarged (three-quarters of a line high) orange initial, the appropriate correspondences being noted in the margins, again probably the work of the same hand. The ordinary verse initials are smaller in scale, but are periodically embellished by orange dots.[28] Attention is drawn to quotations within the text by the provision of two or three points and a comma (. . ,) in the margin to the left of the lines in question, a form of citation mark which is common in early Anglo-Saxon manuscripts.[29] Interestingly, there are possibly as many as nine different correcting hands of eighth- or early ninth-century date,[30] demonstrating that a number of people were interested in the book at this time, and perhaps even providing some insight into the size of the scriptorium in which it was produced. Evidence of a more casual attitude towards the book at a comparable date is provided by the crude dry-point sketch of a vine scroll which was added in the lower margin of fol. 51v.[31]

In its contents, their arrangement and the original Italo-Northumbrian type of text itself, Royal is closely related to the Lindisfarne Gospels, with which it shares also its table of lections – *capitula lectionum* and 'quasi-capitulary', complete with the famous Neapolitan feasts.[32] Consequently, it has reasonably been suggested that both manuscripts derive from the same textual exemplar.[33] Interestingly, in addition to the correction of minor mistakes and the supplying of omissions in the margin, parts of the text were actually erased and rewritten *in rasura* shortly after it was completed, to bring it into line with the so-called mixed Italian textual recension. (It is difficult to decide whether or not this was for the most part done by the original scribe; it is certainly the work of a similar hand.) This is the version that was followed in the Durham Gospels, another manuscript of probable Lindisfarne origin and of late

---

[26] Except fol. 77r where minuscule was used.

[27] Most commonly *ET*, but also *IN* (*In illo*) and *SI* (*Simile*).

[28] Each of the beatitudes is headed by an enlarged initial, while the first contains within its bowl a cross of red dots.

[29] See P. McGurk, 'Citation Marks in Early Latin Manuscripts', *Scriptorium* 15 (1961), 3–13, at 7.

[30] My provisional apportionment of this work to different hands is as follows:
  i) 21r
  ii) 28r
  iii) 37r and 50v
  iv) 32r, 33r, 44r, 48v, 49r, 49v, 50v, 56r, 64v, 70r, 74r, 77v, 85v, 94r, 103v, 128r and 145v (lower)
  v) 42r, 43r and 137v
  vi) 51r
  vii) 55r and 107r
  viii) 57v and 104r (lower)
  ix) 63r

[31] Now cropped, the motif may be compared with sculptured forms on shafts at Hexham (2 and 3) and Stamfordham, Northumberland (R. Cramp, *Corpus of Anglo-Saxon Stone Sculpture I, County Durham and Northumberland*, 2 vols. (Oxford, 1984), II, pls. 173 (915, 917), 175 (926) and 219 (1245)).

[32] *Codex Lindisfarnensis* II, 34–46.

[33] See Warner and Gilson, *Catalogue* I, 10–11; *Codex Lindisfarnensis* II, 33–7 and 43–6 (where it is suggested that the exemplar was probably a sixth-century Neapolitan gospel book written in uncials, but lacking canon tables, or a Wearmouth–Jarrow copy of such a book); and C. D. Verey, T. J. Brown and E. Coatsworth, *The Durham Gospels*, Early English Manuscripts in Facsimile XX (Copenhagen, 1980), 69, n. 26.

seventh- or early eighth-century date.[34] Unfortunately, the paucity of our knowledge concerning the distribution and the chronology of adoption of different recensions – not to mention concerning contemporary perception of them – makes it very difficult to assess the particular implications of this painstaking editorial revision. However a parallel circumstance is found in the Echternach Gospels, where marginal corrections assimilate the original Italo-Northumbrian text to a different family (in this case the 'Irish' one),[35] and the general points that the distinction between versions was clearly recognised in some centres at this time and that local interest in one of them as opposed to another could be sufficient to lead to emendation are worthy of note in themselves. Moreover, the fact that the text of the *Codex Amiatinus*, one of the three giant pandects produced at Wearmouth–Jarrow during the abbacy of Ceolfrith (688–716), was compiled from a wide range of disparate traditions both alerts us to the variety of types of texts that were available in England at this time, and reminds us that far more elaborate editorial activity had been practised at another Northumbrian centre at an early date.[36] At thirty-six places in Royal's text the start of a liturgical reading is marked in the margin, sometimes by a rubric written in a compressed Anglo-Saxon minuscule, at other times by a cross. (Again it is difficult to judge whether this is the work of the original hand; on balance it is probably not.) Another imponderable link with the Durham Gospels is provided by the fact that these rubrics seem to descend from a set akin to those found in that book.[37]

Royal's canon tables, and in particular Canon I, have different affinities, indicating that the book cannot have been copied entirely from the same exemplars as the Lindisfarne Gospels, and further highlighting the complexity of the inter-relationship between the extant Anglo-Saxon gospel manuscripts. In terms of the arrangement of the numbers in Canon I, Royal is affiliated to the Lindisfarne and St Petersburg (formerly Leningrad) Gospels; and, as Patrick McGurk has shown, the type of source that lies behind the pattern found in these three books is represented by the canon

---

[34] See *Novum Testamentum Domini Nostri Iesu Christi Latine secundum editionem S. Hieronymi ad codicum manuscriptorum fidem*, ed. J. Wordsworth and H. J. White, 3 vols. (Oxford, 1889–1954), I: *Quattuor Evangelia; Verey et al., Durham Gospels*; and C. Verey, 'The Gospel Texts at Lindisfarne at the Time of St Cuthbert', *St Cuthbert, His Cult and His Community to AD 1200*, ed. G. Bonner, D. Rollason and C. Stancliffe (Woodbridge, 1989), 143–50, at 147–8. The relative chronology of the Durham and Lindisfarne Gospels is still debated: compare most recently, *ibid.*, 146, n. 20; and R. Bruce-Mitford, 'The Durham-Echternach Calligrapher', *St Cuthbert*, 175–88, esp. 179.

[35] See *Codex Lindisfarnensis* II, 32.

[36] Florence, Biblioteca Medicea Laurenziana, MS Amiatino 1 (Alexander, *Insular Manuscripts*, cat. 7; CLA III, 299). For a summary of its heterogeneous text see R. Loewe, 'The Medieval History of the Latin Vulgate', *The Cambridge History of the Bible II: The West from the Fathers to the Reformation*, ed. G. W. H. Lampe (Cambridge, 1969), 102–54, at 113–18.

[37] The lection notes occur in Royal at the following points: 22r (Matt. 8.5); 23r (Matt. 9.10); 86r (Luke 1.57); 86v (Luke 2.1); 87v (Luke 2.21); 88r (Luke 2.42); 88v (Luke 3.1); 91r (Luke 4.16); 100v (Luke 8.40); 104r (Luke 10.16); 112v (Luke 15.15); 113r (Luke 16.1); 116r (Luke 18.9); 126r (Luke 24.13); 131r (John 1.29); 133v (John 4.5); 143r (John 10.22); 145v (John 12.20). See further Verey *et al.*, *Durham Gospels*, 26ff. Other gospel books written or owned in Anglo-Saxon England which have liturgical notes are listed in H. Gneuss, 'Liturgical Books in Anglo-Saxon England and their Old English terminology', *Learning and Literature*, ed. Lapidge and Gneuss, 91–141, section D.

tables in the Burchard Gospels.[38] This is a sixth-century Italian uncial codex, but its canon tables are a later addition by a Wearmouth–Jarrow hand. Now, variants in the texts distance Lindisfarne and St Petersburg on the one hand from Royal and Burchard on the other. Thus while an exemplar or a close relative of the Burchard tables would seem to have been the model for Royal, a different exemplar (but one with a similar pattern for Canon I) lies behind Lindisfarne and St Petersburg.

The decoration of Royal 1. B. vii, which is all by one hand, most probably that of the original scribe, is limited in scope and unambitious in execution. The twelve pages of canon tables are accommodated on a quire of their own (fols. 9–14) – the only quire that consists of three bifolia in a book that is largely composed of regular quaternions; also the only one that is ignored in the numbering of the quire signatures. Owing to the practicalities of an economic layout, this had to stand between the prefatory material to Matthew (*Argumentum, capitula lectionum*, list of feasts) at the end of quire I, and the Gospel text itself which starts at the beginning of quire III.[39] Looking at the canon tables themselves, we find that all four pages of the outer bifolium of the quire (i.e. fols. 9r, 9v, 14r, and 14v) have identical decorative designs, while throughout the remaining folios (10–13) the scheme on the recto of each leaf is repeated on the verso, perhaps having been traced through the leaf. These expedients, by which the scribe greatly simplified his task, inevitably mean that the designs which actually face each other on each opening do not match.[40] The forms that were thus expeditiously executed are themselves very simple. Whereas in other Insular gospel books the columns and arches of the canon tables are rendered in double lines, either shaded to simulate three-dimensional columns[41] or filled with various two-dimensional decorative patterns,[42] in Royal the arcades are rendered for the most part by single black lines. Embellishment is restricted to linear human heads, beast heads, rudimentary interlace, spirals and attenuated bird forms which were supplied at the top and bottom of each column as capitals and bases.

There are no evangelist portraits in the book. The beginnings of the four gospel texts are introduced merely by crude eight-line-high initials consisting of a plain ink body with rudimentary terminal decoration of maladroit interlace and bird heads, the

---

[38] Würzburg, Universitätsbibliothek, M. p. th. f. 68 (CLA IX, 1423ab). The relationship between the tables in these manuscripts and the conclusions which may be drawn from it are discussed in Patrick McGurk, 'The Disposition of Numbers in Latin Eusebian Canon Tables', in *Philologia Sacra: Studien zu Bibel und Kirchenvätern für Hermann J. Frede und Walter Thiele zu ihrem Siebzigsten Geburtstag*, ed. R. Gryson, 2 vols., Aus der Geschichte der Lateinischen Bibel 24–5 (Freiburg, 1993), 242–58. I wish to record my gratitude to Patrick McGurk both for kindly supplying me with a copy of this important paper in advance of publication, and also for his helpful comments on an earlier draft of the present study.

[39] This was probably a space-saving side-effect of the dual wish a) to fit the canon tables exactly onto a single quire; and b) to begin Matthew's Gospel on the first recto of a new quire.

[40] Interestingly, the same expedient was used in the most opulent surviving Anglo-Saxon manuscript, namely the Stockholm Codex Aureus, with the same consequences.

[41] E.g. Trier, Domschatz, MS 61 (Alexander, *Insular Manuscripts*, cat. 26, ill. 108); formerly Harburg über Donauwörth, Schloss Harburg, Fürstlich Öttingen-Wallersteinische Bibliothek, MS I. 2. 40. 2 now Augsburg, Universitätsbibliothek (*ibid.*, cat. 24, ills. 121–2); and the Stockholm Codex Aureus (*ibid.*, ill. 147).

[42] E.g. the Lindisfarne, St Petersburg and Barberini Gospels (*ibid.*, ills. 32, 188–91 and 173). N.b. after fol. 1r, the canon tables in Barberini were left unfinished: on fols. 1v–4r the architectural frame was drawn but remained devoid of filling, while on fols. 4v–6v not even the outline of the arches was supplied.

majority of the shape being outlined by red dots. In the case of Mark and Luke the initial is followed by a row of two-line-high *litterae notabiliores*, filling the width of the column; in Matthew and John, by contrast, only one, lesser capital was supplied. The incarnation initial in Matthew is conceived according to the former, slightly more elaborate mode. Here the wish to fill the width of the column led the scribe to include four *litterae notabiliores* after the decorated chi: most unusually therefore, the *au* of *autem* is afforded the same status as the rho and the iota of the sacred name. Also noteworthy in this case is the fact that two of the four *litterae notabiliores* are so stylised that they no longer represent the correct letter shapes: the rho looks like an *n*, the *a* like an *H*. Whilst the latter is still appreciable as a rectilinear, open-topped *A*, the former is more dramatically distant from the requisite letter shape. In point of fact its form was probably derived from that of the combined rho–iota digraphs that are common in this context in de luxe manuscripts,[43] the iota having then been erroneously repeated here. This prominent slip, if such it be, is analogous to the glaring misspelling (*eret* for *erat*) written in display script on the first page of John's Gospel in the Cambridge–London Gospels.[44] In addition to the initials that have been mentioned, simpler decorated letters conceived in the same mode head the preface to each gospel,[45] the capitula to Matthew and Mark,[46] and the three general prefatory texts, *Novum opus*, *Plures fuisse* and *Eusebius Carpiano*.[47]

Only three pigments are used in the book – yellow (orpiment), green (verdigris) and orangey-red (minium), the latter often now dulled owing to oxydisation. They are very sparingly applied to the decoration, occuring merely in the capitals and bases of the canon tables, at the terminals of the gospel initials and the chi–rho, and in or around some of the *litterae notabiliores*. Furthermore, of the initials, it is only in the **L** of Matthew's Gospel and the chi–rho, the first major initials in the book, that all three colours are found; in the case of Mark, Luke and John red and yellow alone were used. On the other hand, minium was, it will be recalled, extensively deployed throughout the text itself: in addition to the initial at the beginning of most of the Eusebian sections, the entire first line of each *capitulum* is written in red. This is a feature which is paralleled in several Wearmouth–Jarrow books, and its ultimate source was probably Italian manuscripts.[48]

Since as a whole Insular manuscript art is characterised by individual virtuosity within a widely shared general repertoire of forms and designs, the business of identifying meaningful parallels between the ornamentation of different books is highly proble-

---

[43] E.g. in the Lindisfarne, Echternach, Lichfield and Barberini Gospels (*ibid.*, ills. 44, 51, 6 and 170). For interesting comments on Anglo-Saxon perception of the chi–rho monogram in general see G. H. R. Hersley and E. R. Waterhouse, 'The Greek Nomen Sacrum Xpi- in some Latin and Old English Manuscripts', *Scriptorium* 38 (1984), 211–29, esp. 220–9.
[44] Alexander, *Insular Manuscripts*, ill. 49.   [45] Fols. 4v, 52r, 78v and 128r.
[46] Fols. 5r and 52v. Those to Luke and John are plain red.
[47] Respectively fols. 1r, 2v and 3v.
[48] Compare the Wearmouth–Jarrow Gospel Book fragment in Utrecht, the *Codex Amiatinus* and the Stonyhurst Gospel of St John (Stonyhurst College s.n., now British Library, loan MS 74: CLA II, 260). See further *Codex Lindisfarnensis* II, 44 and 94.

matic. Moreover, in the case of Royal 1. B. vii, the decoration in question is clearly set apart from the mainstream of the genre as we are familiar with it, owing to its restraint and maladroitness. Nevertheless the affiliations of the various basic design-types that the scribe-artist of this manuscript attempted are worth reviewing.

Arranged on twelve pages, the canon tables belong to Nordenfalk's 'shorter Latin series'.[49] Given the number of Insular gospel books that have lost their canon tables, the range of possible 'local' analogies for those in Royal is somewhat prescribed; however the twelve-page system is found in the Stockholm Codex Aureus, the Barberini Gospels and the St Petersburg Gospels,[50] and this last volume also provides a counterpart for their position between the first gospel and its prefatory material. The parsimonious, single-line realisation of the arcades in Royal, which was motivated by considerations of economy and ease, is without parallel as has been mentioned. Nevertheless, considering the actual forms that are thus economically rendered, we find that the basic double 'n and m' arch outline is most closely and consistently matched in the St Petersburg Gospels, and interestingly it is this same manuscript which offers the best analogies for the use of curling beasts and single-strand interlace for the column bases.[51] As for the use of human heads as capitals, this is a feature which is paralleled only in the Barberini Gospels.[52] The implications for Royal of these loose affiliations with the Barberini and, particularly, the St Petersburg Gospels are difficult to assess, not least because these two manuscripts are themselves somewhat enigmatic: generally dated to the later eighth century, both are of unknown origin and early provenance and neither has yet received the attention it deserves.[53] For the St Petersburg Gospels, on the other hand, these connections are perhaps more significant, since taken along with the fact that the book shares lection notes with Lindisfarne and Royal[54] and a canon table exemplar with Lindisfarne, they point to Northumbria as the most likely place of origin.

Analogies for the decoration of Royal's initials are more numerous. The conception

---

[49] C. Nordenfalk, *Die Spätantiken Kanontafeln*, 2 vols. (Göteborg, 1938); also *Codex Lindisfarnensis* II, 33–4.

[50] The numbers of pages over which the canon tables are distributed in relevant manuscripts of Anglo-Saxon origin are as follows – Barberini: 12; St Petersburg: 12; Stockholm Codex Aureus: originally 12 (only 8 surviving = fols. 5r–8v); Lindisfarne: 16; Echternach: 23; *Codex Amiatinus*: 7; British Library, MS Royal 1. E. vi (Bible fragment): 5. Twelve pages of canon tables are also found in the Maesyck, Harburg, Trier and Cutbercht Gospels, manuscripts written and decorated in Insular style on the Continent (Alexander, *Insular Manuscripts*, cats. 23, 24, 26 and 37).

[51] See *ibid.*, ills. 190–1.   [52] Fols. 2v and 3r.

[53] Carl Nordenfalk (*Karl der Grosse* (Council of Europe exh. cat., Aachen, 1965), no. 398) attributed the St Petersburg Gospels to southern England and dated it *c*. 800; Lowe (CLA XI, 1605) ascribed it to Northumbria because of textual similarities with the Lindisfarne Gospels and the *Codex Amiatinus*, whilst noting Kentish features in the script; T. J. Brown favoured Northumbria (*Codex Lindisfarnensis* II, 33). For a review of the (lack of) evidence and the opinions concerning the Barberini Gospels see Alexander, *Insular Manuscripts*, 61–2. F. Henry, *Irish Art during the Viking Invasions* (London, 1967), 60–1, proposed a Northumbrian origin; while T. D. Kendrick, *Anglo-Saxon Art to A.D. 900* (London, 1938), 144–7, favoured southern England (Mercia) 'with some hesitation', an attribution repeated without discussion in D. Wilson, *Anglo-Saxon Art* (London, 1984), 91. Most recently M. P. Brown in 'The Lindisfarne Scriptorium from the late seventh to the early ninth century', *St Cuthbert*, ed. Bonner *et al.*, 151–63, at 155 and in Webster and Backhouse, eds., *The Making of England*, cat. 160, has admitted both Mercia and Northumbria (?York) as possibilities.

[54] See D. Wright, 'Addenda' in P. McGurk, *Latin Gospel Books from A.D. 400 to A.D. 800* (Brussels, 1961).

of the major initials, plain ink bodies with terminal embellishment, may be paralleled in a number of de luxe manuscripts – but, significantly, it is the design of their secondary not their primary initials that it echoes. The **F** of *Fuit in diebus* and several of the *litterae notabiliores* after the chi–rho in the Echternach Gospels,[55] various of the ordinary Psalm initials in the Vespasian Psalter[56] and the *litterae notabiliores* that follow the initial to Psalm 40 in the Lothian Psalter,[57] to mention several cases, are masterly examples of the type of secondary letter design that the scribe-artist of Royal 1. B. vii followed with less panache for his five principal initials. The closest general parallel in terms of scale, conception and usage for these initials in Royal 1. B. vii is provided by Leiden, Universiteitsbibliotheek, Voss. Lat. F. 4, a manuscript attributed to Northumbria on the grounds of its script and dated to the first half of the eighth century.[58] The fact that this fragmentary book, although of generous dimensions, is not a liturgical volume but a copy of Pliny, *Historia naturalis*, makes the same point. The start of the volume as a whole is lost and the surviving initials – which are, incidentally, more skilfully executed than those in Royal – head the capitulae and the beginnings of individual books, further underlining the fact that the decoration of our gospel book was not only second-rate in execution but also second-grade in conception.

The affinities of the *litterae notabiliores* that follow the initials in Royal are, as we would expect, with the secondary and tertiary display lettering of de luxe manuscripts. Because of the simpler form of these capitals as a class, the discrepancy between the standard of the interpretations in Royal and those in other books is less pronounced than was the case with the decoration we have just examined. Such capitals owe their general dynamic to the juxtaposition of forms based on stylised Insular half-uncial book-script, with others probably derived from Insular, Runic and Roman epigraphic forms, spiced with the occasional Greek character.[59] As the uncial-based forms are rounded, whilst those of epigraphic origin are angular, the result is generally a dialogue between curvilinear and rectilinear forms. Although collectively distinctive, such lettering is characterised by its flexibility and formal diversity: individual virtuosity within broad parameters, not conformity to set forms, is its hallmark. Each practitioner interpreted the forms in his own ways. A variety of shapes may be used for a single letter in one manuscript and each one of them can establish rapprochements with the lettering in different books. Consequently, whilst finding parallels for individual letters is easy, identifying significant sub-groups within the family as a whole is a difficult and delicate task. Most of the individual letter forms used in Royal

[55] Alexander, *Insular Manuscripts*, ills. 53 and 51.   [56] See Wright, *Vespasian Psalter*.

[57] New York, Pierpont Morgan Library, M 776, fol. 40r (Alexander, *Insular Manuscripts*, cat. 31, ill. 150; for a reproduction of the whole page see D. Miner, *Illuminated Books of the Middle Ages and Renaissance* (Baltimore, 1949), pl. I).

[58] Alexander, *Insular Manuscripts*, cat. 18, ills. 66 and 68–9; CLA x, 1578.

[59] See *Codex Lindisfarnensis* II, 75–7; N. Gray, *A History of Lettering* (Oxford, 1986), 56–64, 242–7; R. D. Eaton, 'Anglo-Saxon Secrets: Run and the Runes of the Lindisfarne Gospels', *Amsterdamer Beitrage zur alteren Germanistik*, ed. A. Quak and P. Vermeyden (Amsterdam, 1986), 11–27; and R. I. Page, 'Roman and Runic on St Cuthbert's Coffin', *St Cuthbert*, ed. Bonner *et al.*, 257–65, at 258.

are indeed paralleled in a variety of manuscripts. The exceptions are the unusual **A** and rho that were discussed earlier and which are without parallel, and the grid-like **O** which reappears only in Cologne, Dombibliothek, 213, a strikingly handsome *Collectio canonum*, assigned to Northumbria and probably of early eighth-century date.[60] In contrast to the alternation of curvilinear and rectilinear forms that is found in most manuscripts, the *litterae notabiliores* in Royal as a whole are striking for their consistent pronounced, elongated rectilinearity, and this too is a feature that is most closely matched in the more elegant display lettering of Cologne 213.

Although there is no consensus in such general affinities as may be found for Royal's limited repertoire of ornamentation which suggests that this volume should be grouped with a particular surviving manuscript or manuscripts, the decoration is entirely compatible with the attribution of the book to Northumbria which is suggested by the script and lent further credence both by the original text and by the corrections. What these comparisons have principally achieved, however, is to elucidate more precisely the nature of the decoration and its limitations. The key point is that whilst the singularity of style and idiosyncrasy of detail were the result of maladroit execution, the restraint was a carefully planned economy based on beginning the hierarchy of calligraphic ornament that was used to decorate and articulate the text one grade lower than was the case in a de luxe book. Although the decoration is very limited in scope and crude in execution, the programme as a whole follows the system that we find in the more elaborately conceived Insular gospel books: the text is divided in much the same way, and the relative importance of the various subdivisions within the volume as a whole is clearly indicated; it is just that the decorative accent at a given point has been downgraded.

It is quite understandable, then, that Royal 1. B. vii should have become the Cinderella of Insular manuscript art, its decoration reasonably characterised in the standard catalogue of the illuminated manuscripts from this period as suggestive of a Continental copy of Insular work,[61] and omitted altogether from a recent monograph devoted to Insular gospel books.[62] Yet the volume remains worthy of our attention – and not, it will be argued here, despite the modest standard of its general execution and script, and the low quality of its artwork, but rather precisely because of this.

Additional to the consequences of its unimposing appearance, Royal 1. B. vii has suffered eclipse, one suspects, because of the accidents of fortune that resulted in its preservation in the same library as the Lindisfarne Gospels, arguably the finest example of the genre of book to which it belongs. Allied in textual tradition, likely to have emanated from the same geographical area, and further comparable in that they are both in the main probably the work of single scribe-artists, these two gospel books

---

[60] Alexander, *Insular Manuscripts*, cat. 13, ill. 60; CLA viii, 1163; see also, G. Henderson, *From Durrow to Kells: The Insular Gospel-Books 650–800* (London, 1987), 88–90; and *The Making of England*, eds. Webster and Backhouse, cat. 126.

[61] Alexander, *Insular Manuscripts*, 48. [62] Henderson, *Durrow to Kells*.

are nevertheless poles apart in almost every detail of their realisation. The carefully selected and prepared parchment of the Lindisfarne Gospels, with minimal discrepancy of colour-tone and texture between hair and flesh sides, meticulously ruled with a faint direct impression on both sides of each page,[63] presents a strong contrast to the lower quality of that in Royal, the hair side of which is often easily distinguishable from the flesh side, and which was ruled several – sometimes as many as five – leaves at a time. Whilst double horizontal dry-point lines were supplied for each line of text in Lindisfarne to ensure maximum regularity of script, single rulings sufficed to guide that in Royal, as was noted above. Lindisfarne, a large volume with more folios but fewer lines to the page, is altogether more spaciously laid out and written; and while its text script is the canonical example of Phase II Insular half-uncial,[64] that of Royal is a less regular, more compressed version of the same letter-forms. In comparison with the wealth, variation and finesse of the decoration of the former, that of the latter appears impoverished in extent and inept in execution; and its three colours, sparingly applied, pale into insignificance (figuratively and literally) beside the generous range of pigments which enliven the pages of Lindisfarne.[65] The point need hardly be pressed: the basic fact that there is a world of difference between the Lindisfarne and the Royal 1. B. vii Gospels is self-evident and this simple truth is the key to our interpretation of the latter book.

Before turning to the general conclusions which may be drawn from this fact, it is worth digressing for a moment to remind ourselves that few, perhaps none, of the other surviving Insular gospel books can match the comprehensively superlative quality of the Lindisfarne Gospels. The Durham Gospels, for example, may originally have had more decoration, equally well executed, but its preparation was less meticulous – single not double horizontal lines were supplied to guide the script and they were ruled several pages at a time – and its palette was more restricted. Moreover the scribe downgrades from Insular half-uncial to minuscule at the ends of lines and in runovers in order to save space. Conversely, although the Lichfield Gospels (which could probably also boast a more extensive programme of full-page illumination in its original state, had a generous palette and used paint more subtly)[66] seems to have been prepared with equal care, parts of its major decoration are less perfectly executed and the figural drawing, particularly that of St Mark and the four symbols page, is considerably less skilful.[67] The Cambridge–London Gospels is a smaller volume than these, with a less ambitious decorative programme. Although the designs of its two

---

[63] For this and what follows see *Codex Lindisfarnensis* ii, 61ff.

[64] For detailed discussion of its characteristics see *ibid.*, 64–74 and 89–106; also T. J. Brown, 'Northumbria and the Book of Kells', *Anglo-Saxon England* 1 (1972), 219–46. For convenient summaries see CLA ii, xv–xvi and M. P. Brown, *A Guide to Western Historical Scripts from Antiquity to 1600* (London, 1990), no. 16.

[65] *Codex Lindisfarnensis* ii, 263–72.

[66] Unlike Lindisfarne, colours are here mixed and superimposed: see *ibid.*, 275–6.

[67] The scholar who has studied the manuscript in the most detail, W. Stein, 'The Lichfield Gospels' (unpublished Ph.D. thesis, University of California, Berkeley), seems to have been struck by its provincial qualities in comparison with the other de luxe volumes. (I have not seen Dr Stein's work; this conclusion is reported by Henderson, *Durrow to Kells*, 126–9.) See further Bruce-Mitford, 'Durham-Echternach Calligrapher', 187–8.

surviving evangelist symbols are certainly elegant, the proportions of the one remaining major initial are less successful: its 'strokes' are too long and thin. This book, too, was sometimes ruled several pages at a time and, as the 'tram lines' that furrow the symbol page of St John's eagle demonstrate, in striking contrast to Lindisfarne, insufficient care was taken to prevent the ruling from impinging unattractively on the full-page decoration.[68] Furthermore, its system of decorated canon tables broke down after Canon VIII, Canons IX and X being left devoid of arches.[69] As for the Echternach Gospels, the verve of its calligraphy and artwork notwithstanding, there is little doubt that it was altogether more economically conceived and hastily executed.[70] There are no carpet pages as such, rather carpet and evangelist symbol seem to be conflated on one page in each case,[71] and three of these pages remained unfinished;[72] the principal initials only occupy part of the first column of the following verso; the palette is limited to yellow, orange, pink and purple;[73] the main body of the text is written not in Insular half-uncial but in set minuscule; and the initials to the Ammonian sections are not decorated but are simply rendered in black, outlined with orange dots.

The extent to which these gospel books differ in terms of their preparation, make-up and decoration is interesting in itself; however these are, of course, merely distinctions of finesse: the fact that all the books that have just been mentioned are volumes *de luxe* is not in doubt. When, on the other hand, we turn to the less familiar territory of a gospel (presumably gospel book) fragment at Leipzig,[74] to another gospel book which survives simply as a single leaf (fol. 75) in British Library, Cotton Tiberius B. v,[75] and, in particular, to the Hereford Gospels,[76] we find ourselves notably closer to the conception of Royal 1. B. vii, and we return to the main thrust of our enquiry. Of possible Northumbrian origin, the dimensions of the Leipzig fragment are nearly identical to those of Royal. It contains Matthew 1.2–6.4. Up to chapter 1, verse 20, the text is written on single ruled lines in a stately Phase II Insular half-uncial, but thereafter a compressed Anglo-Saxon minuscule with majuscule

---

[68] This can be seen most clearly in colour reproductions: P. Verzone, *From Theodoric to Charlemagne*, Art of the World XXVII (London, 1967), 169; P. Hunter-Blair, *Northumbria in the Days of Bede* (London, 1976), frontispiece; and Webster and Backhouse, eds., *The Making of England*, 118.

[69] See Henderson, *Durrow to Kells*, 71. Compare the Barberini Gospels.

[70] *Codex Lindisfarnensis* II, 96–7.

[71] The Book of Durrow, in which the symbols appear isolated within a frame that is a simple rectangle in shape (having an internal filling of ornament) might represent a possible complementary prototype for this approach. In Echternach (and Cambridge–London) the frames are, with the exception of the first (fol. 18v), undecorated but their actual form has become more complex and they interact directly with the symbol. Unlike Echternach, Durrow of course has separate carpet pages. For further discussion of the Echternach symbol page designs from a different perspective see W. Dynes, 'Imago Leonis', *Gesta* 20 (1981), 35–41.

[72] See Bruce-Mitford, 'Durham-Echternach Calligrapher', 179.

[73] See *Codex Lindisfarnensis* II, 97, n. 4; and F. Avril and P. D. Stirnemann, *Manuscrits Enluminés d'Origine Insulaire VIIe–XXe Siècle* (Paris, 1987), no. 1, pp. 2–3.

[74] Leipzig, Universitätsbibliothek, MS Rep. I. 58a + Rep. II. 35a (Alexander, *Insular Manuscripts*, cat. 15, ill. 67; CLA VIII, 1229 and *Supplement*, 1229).

[75] CLA II, 190. Lowe reasonably suggests that it was bound into this volume by Robert Cotton.

[76] Hereford, Cathedral Library, MS. P. I. 2 (Alexander, *Insular Manuscripts*, cat. 38, ills. 197–9; CLA II, 157). Of recent commentators, P. Sims-Williams, *Religion and Literature in Western England 600–800* (Cambridge, 1990), 181, seems to favour an origin for the book in Wales; Webster and Backhouse, eds., *The Making of England*, cat. 91, suggest West Midlands or Wales.

elements was used. Only one of the six folios which survive has decoration and that contains the chi–rho. This is a restrained four-line-high monogram, more expertly executed but otherwise comparable both in scale and design to the chi–rho in Royal. It seems reasonable to presume that the four other major initials in the book would have been similar in scope. Nothing is known for certain about the early history of the manuscript.

The Tiberius leaf is also from Matthew's Gospel: it was the final page. All that remains of the original work now, unfortunately, is twelve lines of one column containing verses 15–19 of chapter 28. Owing to erasure on the one hand and fire damage on the other, it is difficult to be certain about the original dimensions of the page; however, the text was certainly written in two columns of at least 28 lines, each column being *c*. 75 mm wide, the space between the lines being *c*. 9 mm. That the original codex was a relatively modest book is clear from both the parchment and the script. The membrane is greasy and the hair folicles are easily visible; the hand, which Lowe fairly described as 'not very expert' is an irregular Insular half-uncial which is rectilinear in general proportions (the minims are *c*. 3 mm high). Like Royal the book was used to receive documents in the late Anglo-Saxon period: the surviving page includes two manumissions and a notice of a guild assembly at Exeter, all in Old English.[77] External features point to Northumbria as a likely place of origin, while the Old English notices demonstrate that the book subsequently came to Exeter – again like Royal it would seem to have migrated from the north to the south of the country.

The Hereford Gospels, which could date from as late as the beginning of the ninth century and which is of early Herefordshire provenance but uncertain, possibly western English or Welsh origin, is a smaller volume (see ill. 2.4). The text, which is arranged, not in columns, but in single long lines, is written in a hasty, angular, hybrid Insular minuscule, displaying Celtic symptoms. As in Royal, it seems to be the work of a single scribe, who was probably also the decorator. Again like Royal there is no ornament within the body of the text: subsections are indicated simply by plain ink capitals. The only decoration in the book is the initial page at the beginning of each gospel (that to Luke is lost, as, incidentally, is the page with the chi–rho which was presumably also embellished). Emulating the major initial pages of de luxe books, yet greatly reduced in scale and complexity, the three surviving incipits reveal grandiose aspirations tempered by limited resources and talent. In each case the page in question is bounded by a plain frame with a straightforward, single-strand interlace twist at the corners. The initial monogram runs the length of the page, extending beyond the frame, and it is followed by three lines of display capitals, the first (and largest) of which is emphasised by a frame of its own, an outgrowth of the main frame. The interlace, fretwork, spirals and animal head or leg terminals that embellish the initials are rudimentary both in conception and execution; the palette is restricted to two colours, a distinctive orange and yellow; and one or more lines of ordinary hybrid

[77] Ker, *Catalogue*, no. 194.

2.4   Hereford, Cathedral Library, MS P. 1. 2, fol. 102r. Page size: 225 × 170 mm

minuscule text appear within the frame at the bottom of the page.[78] Furthermore, it should be pointed out that the most interesting and novel aspect of the initial designs themselves – the grid of diamonds that links the two uprights of the *Ini(tium)* monogram and the lattice of circles that joins those of *Inp(rincipio)* – also in fact represents an economy. In the Echternach Gospels, it will be recalled, carpet and evangelist symbol were apparently conflated on one folio, being followed by the major initial on the verso; in Hereford there are no portraits and what we see here is a conflation (a visually more blatant one incidentally) of carpet and principal initial. While the decoration of the initial pages in the Hereford Gospels is considerably more elaborate than that in Royal, the book as a whole is a more modest construction; in general it provides a most interesting analogy for Royal 1. B. vii.

The superlative quality of the Lindisfarne Gospels is a striking tribute to the training, talent and patience of its scribe and decorator, Eadfrith, but equally it is a reflection of its projected function and context. That this splendid volume, written 'for God, for St Cuthbert and for all the saints whose relics are on holy island', quite probably for the occasion of Cuthbert's translation in 698, by the bishop (or future bishop) of Lindisfarne,[79] bound and covered by a monk who was eventually to be his successor to the see, embossed by an anchorite, subsequently taken by the community on their travels along with the relics of St Cuthbert and the cross of Æthelwold (the aforementioned binder of the gospels), the details of its manufacture becoming part of their folk-lore,[80] that this volume was intended as the principal ceremonial gospel book of the Lindisfarne community need not be doubted. Projected purpose, quality of materials and choice of scribe and artist were directly related: the most important task merited the best materials and the finest craftsman. The costly, carefully selected materials from which the book was made underline that it was a project of great importance to the Lindisfarne community; correspondingly, we may presume that the task of writing and decorating it devolved upon Eadfrith because, quite simply, he was recognised as the most talented scribe-artist available.[81] We are less knowledge-

[78] As one line appears in Matthew, two in Mark and four in John, it is tempting to see this as a deliberate progression; the unfortunate loss of the beginning of Luke prevents confirmation or rejection of the hypothesis.

[79] For text and translation of, and commentary on, the colophon which provides these details see *Codex Lindisfarnensis* II, 5–16. For biographical details of Eadfrith see *ibid.*, II, 17–20.

[80] Being written down at the end of the book itself in the tenth century by Aldred, the priest, the glossator of the manuscript. It is interesting that the information was committed to writing only after the migration from Lindisfarne to Chester-le-Street – and a significant time afterwards at that. The physical disjunction was probably an important factor in providing the community with an incentive to preserve such traditions the more carefully. One might further speculate that the demise of the last of the 'original' Lindisfarne community was ultimately perhaps both a catalyst for the making of the record and a precondition of the dramatic decision to gloss the treasured book throughout in Old English. The information was subsequently reiterated in the early twelfth century by Simeon of Durham in his *Historia Dunelmensis Ecclesiae*, Bk III, 12 (*Symeonis monachi Opera omnia*, ed. T. Arnold, 2 vols. (London, 1882–5), I, 68); see further *Codex Lindisfarnensis* II, 5. On the circumstances and rationale of Simeon's work as a whole see A. J. Piper, 'The First Generations of Durham Monks and the Cult of St Cuthbert', *St Cuthbert*, ed. Bonner *et al.*, 437–46.

[81] For more pointed reflections on the possible house politics surrounding Eadfrith's association with the book see M. P. Brown, 'Lindisfarne scriptorium', 154–5.

able about the original setting of the other volumes that have been discussed,[82] but the fact that the most luxurious were designed for a particularly important purpose – to adorn an altar or to become the personal possession of a bishop – is self-evident. Other volumes that have not so far been mentioned but which were certainly destined for an exalted context had an equally splendid format. For example, the (now lost) gospel book which the controversial but colourful and dynamic Bishop Wilfrid commissioned and which was subsequently kept in the church of Ripon as a memorial to him, actually being mentioned in the epitaph that was inscribed on his tomb, was written in gold on purple parchment and either covered in gold or kept in a gold shrine – the acme of opulence;[83] while the three pandects whose preparation Ceolfrith, abbot of Wearmouth–Jarrow, supervised at the end of the seventh century, one to reside in each of the chapels of the twin community he ruled, the third to accompany him on his final pilgrimage to Rome as a gift to the Pope, were of monumental size and were written throughout in stately uncials.[84] The point need not be laboured. All that it is crucial to stress in this context is the simple but easily forgotten fact that these volumes, the volumes which, understandably, have been the subject of the most extensive study by modern scholars, present only the achievements of the greatest Insular scribes and artists working on the most important projects. This of course is precisely what the moderate sized, modestly conceived books – Hereford, Leipzig, Tiberius and, of course, Royal 1. B. vii – are not, and therein lies their significance.

Surviving evidence, documentary and archaeological, attests to the existence of some ninety churches in England in the seventh century[85] and suggests that by the mid-ninth century the number of ecclesiastical foundations was over two

[82] The Echternach Gospels, which still belonged to Echternach at the end of the Middle Ages and exerted a formative influence on the design of some of its eighth-century manuscripts, was clearly one of the early possessions of that house, which was established by Willibrord in 698. It was possibly prepared as a foundation gift from Lindisfarne (*Codex Lindisfarnensis* II, 103–4), alternatively perhaps being provided by some arm of the monastic *familia* of Egbert, Willibrord's mentor (Henderson, *Durrow to Kells*, 91–7). See further D. O'Croinin, 'Rath Melsigi, Willibrord and the earliest Echternach Manuscripts', *Peritia* 3 (1984), 17–49 and his 'Is the Augsburg Gospel Codex a Northumbrian Manuscript?' *St Cuthbert*, ed. Bonner *et al.*, 189–201; and N. Netzer, 'Willibrord's scriptorium at Echternach and its relationship to Ireland and Lindisfarne' *ibid.*, 203–12. For the interesting suggestion that the Cambridge–London Gospels may have been prepared in Northumbria as a gift for St Augustine's, Canterbury, see Henderson, *Durrow to Kells*, 91–2.

[83] *The Life of Bishop Wilfrid by Eddius Stephanus*, ed. B. Colgrave (Cambridge, 1927), ch. XVII, 36; with *Bede, Historia Ecclesiastica* v, 19 (*Bede's Ecclesiastical History of the English Nation*, ed. B. Colgrave and R. A. B. Mynors (Oxford, 1969), 528). Otherwise Wilfrid is not recorded to have been interested in books and, apart from his own biography, there is no evidence that he fostered literary activities. See further P. Hunter-Blair, *The World of Bede* (London, 1970), 163–4.

[84] Bede, *Historia abbatum*, ch. 15 (*Venerabilis Baedae Opera Historica*, ed. C. Plummer, 2 vols. (Oxford, 1896), I, 402). See further CLA II, 177; E. A. Lowe, *English Uncial* (Oxford, 1960), 18–19, pls. VIII–IX; R. L. S. Bruce-Mitford, 'The Art of the Codex Amiatinus', Jarrow Lecture 1967 (Jarrow, 1968); also n. 36 above. For reflections on the practical realisation of the project see R. G. Gameson, 'The Cost of the Codex Amiatinus', *Notes and Queries* 237/1 (1992), 2–9. For the identification of one of the copies which remained in England with a much-admired Bible reputedly given to the church of Worcester by Offa and there in the eleventh century see most recently Sims-Williams, *Religion and Literature*, 182.

[85] R. Morris, *The Church in British Archaeology* (London, 1983), 35–8.

hundred.[86] These may well be minimum figures rather than close approximations to the actual totals. The size, composition and activities of most of these places are shadowy at best, but clearly each one of these 'minsters' would have needed at least one gospel book; the larger foundations most probably owned multiple copies. Indeed multiple copies of the Bible as a whole would seem to be a precondition of the ideal articulated in the seventh clause of the Canons of Clovesho (747) amongst other places, where it is decreed that bishops, abbots and abbesses should endeavour to ensure that their entire communities read Scripture as much as possible.[87] Of course we know that some of the volumes in question and certainly all of the earliest were imported by the Roman and Irish missionaries, or subsequently obtained from Continental allies – indeed at least two Italian gospel books which belong to this class are still extant[88] – but against these one may set the additional copies made in England during the eighth century that were exported to supply the Anglo-Saxon missionaries in Germany;[89] not to mention those that were removed from circulation by being interred with the dead,[90] any which may have been essentially the private property of individual ecclesiastics, and those that were needed to replace older copies which had become damaged or

[86] For a convenient cartographical synthesis of such written and archaeological evidence as survives for the existence of early foundations see J. Campbell, ed., *The Anglo-Saxons* (Oxford, 1982), fig. 72. See also the comments of J. Campbell, 'The First Century of Christianity in England', *Ampleforth Journal* 76 (1971), 12–29, at 14–16 (reprinted in his *Essays in Anglo-Saxon History* (London, 1986), 49–67, at 51–3).

[87] *Councils and Ecclesiastical Documents relating to Great Britain and Ireland*, ed. A. W. Haddan and W. Stubbs, 3 vols. (Oxford, 1871), III, 364–5. Compare Aldhelm's letter to Sigegyth (*Aldhelmi Opera*, ed. R. Ehwald, MGH, *Auctores Antiquissimi* 15 (Berlin, 1919), 497), and, from another point of view, Boniface ep. x (*Die Briefe des heiligen Bonifatius und Lullus*, ed. M. Tangl, *Monumenta Germaniae Historica Epistolae Selectae* I (Berlin, 1916), 10).

[88] Namely Cambridge, Corpus Christi College, MS 286 (CLA II, 126; McGurk, *Latin Gospel Books*, 25; see further F. Wormald, *The Miniatures in the Gospels of St Augustine* (Cambridge, 1954)); and Oxford, Bodleian Library, MS Auct. D. II. 14 (CLA II, 230; Lowe, *English Uncial*, 17, pl. IV; McGurk, *Latin Gospel Books*, 40), which is also traditionally known as the 'Gospels of St Augustine'. A possible third candidate is the Italian sixth-century Burchard Gospels (see n. 38 above) restored in English uncial, though whether in England or on the Continent is arguable (cf. Lowe, *English Uncial*, 17, and D. H. Wright, 'Some Notes on English Uncial', *Traditio* 17 (1961), 441–56). Other extant manuscripts of Continental (mainly Italian) origin dating from before c. 800 which were demonstrably, or likely to have been, in England at an early date are CLA II, 127, 153, 164, 251; VII, 1139; IX, 1430a and *Supplement*, 1740. See further Bede, *Historia ecclesiastica*, ed. Colgrave and Mynors, I, 29; and Hunter-Blair, *World of Bede*, ch. 20. For documentary evidence for the dispatch of books from Gaul c. 700 see *Vita Bertilae Abbatissae Calensis*, ed. W. Levison, MGH, *Scriptores rerum Merovingicarum* 6 (Hannover and Leipzig, 1913), 95–109, ch. 6.

[89] The reality of this traffic in books in general is underlined by correspondence: e.g. Boniface's letters to Nothelm, Eadburh (twice) and Hwætberht (respectively, *English Historical Documents I, c. 500–1042*, ed. D. Whitelock, 2nd edn (London, 1979), 810, 811, 812 and 824–5); Lul's letter to Dealwine, and Cuthbert's to Lul (respectively, *ibid.*, 815–6 and 831–2). A comparable philosophy is seen in Alcuin's wish, expressed to Charlemagne, that students be dispatched from Tours to York to acquire copies of texts he knew to be available there (S. Allott, *Alcuin of York* (York, 1974), 12). The fundamental account of W. Levison, *England and the Continent in the Eighth Century* (Oxford, 1947), esp. ch. VI, should now be read in the light of R. McKitterick, 'Anglo-Saxon Missionaries in Germany: Reflections on the Manuscript Evidence', *Transactions of the Cambridge Bibliographical Society* 9/4 (1989), 291–329. Notwithstanding the renewed debate concerning the particular circumstances in which it was produced (see n. 82 above), the Echternach Gospels, like Cologne 213, is clearly tangible evidence for the export of Insular books, scribes and scribal practices to Germany at this time.

[90] As was the Stonyhurst Gospel of St John (found in the tomb of St Cuthbert when it was opened in 1104): see C. F. Battiscombe, ed., *The Relics of St Cuthbert* (Oxford, 1956), 356–62 and 362–74; and T. J. Brown, *The Stonyhurst Gospel of St John* (London, 1969).

worn out.[91] To suggest that at least three hundred gospel books must have been produced in England in the two centuries following the arrival of St Augustine is speculation, but it is a speculation that seems far more likely to err on the side of underestimation than the reverse. And of course gospel books were not the only volumes that had to be acquired or produced at this time and on this scale. The study of the Bible as it was zealously recommended from the late seventh century onwards ideally required a complement of grammatical texts and patristic commentaries.[92] The various centres which seem to have offered advanced education, such as Canterbury, Malmesbury, Nursling, Breedon, Barking, Wimborne, Bath, Thanet, Lindisfarne, Wearmouth–Jarrow and York, were presumably satisfactorily equipped in this respect,[93] and by the late eighth century some of them may have ranged well beyond it:[94] mention was made above of the eighth-century copy of Pliny's *Historia naturalis* which is now in Leiden and is ascribed to Northumbria.[95] Now, although only the relatively restricted number of houses that were concerned to build up such a library would probably have required the copying of a wide range of different texts, and whilst pandects or even complete multi-volume sets of biblical books are likely to have been rarities outside the larger foundations,[96] nevertheless an uncertain but surely not inconsiderable number of centres will probably have wanted more than just a rudimentary book collection,[97] and each of the aforementioned two hundred or more 'minsters' would certainly also have needed a psalter and a couple of service books (namely a sacramentary and a gradual) at the very least.[98] Moreover it is worth

[91] Durham, Cathedral Library, MS A. ii. 16 + Cambridge, Magdalene College, Pepysian MS 2981 (18) (Alexander, *Insular Manuscripts*, cat. 16; CLA ii, 148a–c), in which most of the surviving part of the three synoptic gospels are written in uncial (the remainder being written in Insular half-uncial) assigned to the eighth century, but John is written in Anglo-Saxon half-uncial of later eighth-century date and belongs to a different textual family, provides an interesting example of a gospel book that was repaired or completed probably a generation or so after the original campaign of work. The hazards to which manuscripts could be exposed in a missionary context are dramatically suggested by the fate of St Boniface's books at the time of his martyrdom at Dokkum in 754. The looting heathens carried off the chests in which his books were kept; then, when they found manuscripts, not treasure to be their contents, they scattered them across the fields and marshes (*Vita Bonifatii auctore Willibaldo*, ed. W. Levison (*Scriptores Rerum Germanicarum in usum scholarum* (Hannover, 1905), 1–57; trans. C. H. Talbot, *The Anglo-Saxon Missionaries in Germany* (London, 1954), at 56–8). Codex Bonifatianus 2 in the Hessische Landesbibliothek, Fulda (CLA viii, 1197), a copy of Isidore's *Synonyma* written in Luxeuil minuscule, is supposedly the manuscript with which Boniface defended himself against his assailants, the episode being reflected in the fact that it is almost cut through.

[92] H. M. R. E. Mayr-Harting, *The Coming of Christianity in Anglo-Saxon England* (London, 1972), ch. 12; and Sims-Williams, *Religion and Literature*, ch. 7.

[93] See H. Gneuss, 'Anglo-Saxon Libraries from the Conversion to the Benedictine Reform', *Settimane di studio del centro italiano di studi sull'alto medioevo* 32 (1986), 643–88, esp. 651–61.

[94] Suggestive in this respect, although its precise status is debatable, is the list of books owned by Æthelbert, archbishop of York, and bequeathed to Alcuin *c.* 778, which includes a wide range of authors. See *Alcuin, The Bishops, Kings, and Saints of York*, ed. P. Godman (Oxford, 1982), 120–6, with lxv–lxvi; M. Lapidge, 'Surviving Booklists from Anglo-Saxon England', *Learning and Literature*, ed. Lapidge and Gneuss, 33–89, at 45–9; and Gneuss, 'Anglo-Saxon Libraries', 655–7.

[95] See n. 58 above.

[96] For surviving Anglo-Saxon Bibles and fragments see the discussion by Richard Marsden, ch. 6 below.

[97] The problem of these 'secondary status' libraries is considered by Gneuss, 'Anglo-Saxon Libraries', 669–72.

[98] Three de luxe psalters of Anglo-Saxon origin and a fragment of a fourth are extant: Berlin, Deutsche Staatsbibliothek, MS Hamilton 553; London, British Library, MS Cotton Vespasian A. i; New York, Pierpont Morgan Library, M 776; and Basle, Universitätsbibliothek, N. i. 2, fol. 1 (respectively: CLA viii, 1048; ii, 193; xi, 1661; and vii, 850; Alexander, *Insular Manuscripts*, cats. 14, 29 and 31). On early service

remembering that in the late ninth century King Alfred considered several non-liturgical texts, notably Gregory the Great's *Regula pastoralis* and *Dialogi*, Augustine's *Soliloquia*, Boethius' *De consolatione philosophiae* and Orosius' *Historiae adversus paganos*, to be books which *all* men ought to know;[99] and circumstantial evidence suggests that the first of these at least had been widely regarded as a desideratum in previous centuries.[100]

The mechanics, the organisation and the geographical distribution of the scribal activity that was necessary to supply this demand is largely obscure and likely to remain so. Lack of evidence renders it impossible, for example, to gauge the extent to which such books were written locally in small cells, perhaps by single scribes working in relative isolation, as opposed to in the scriptoria of larger foundations, being subsequently distributed. (The case of the Irish master-scribe Ultan who is known to have been attached to a cell of Lindisfarne probably in the first half of the eighth century suggests that the former practice was not unknown at least;[101] while the recent discovery of styli at Flixborough, South Humberside, has demonstrated that writing was practised at a centre which would not otherwise be associated with literary culture.[102]) It is uncertain how many important scriptoria were active in England at this time – there are only three or four for whose scribal practices we have identified concrete evidence,[103] while several undoubtedly significant writing centres, including Whitby and Malmesbury, are entirely unrepresented in the corpus of

---

books in England see Mayr-Harting, *Coming of Christianity*, ch. 11, with appendix II; and G. G. Willis, 'Early English liturgy from Augustine to Alcuin' in his *Further Essays in Early Roman Liturgy*, Alcuin Club Collections 50 (London, 1968), 189–242. For a convenient classification and listing of extant manuscripts see Gneuss, 'Liturgical Books'.

[99] *King Alfred's West-Saxon Version of Gregory's Pastoral Care*, ed. H. Sweet, 2 vols., EETS os 45 and 50 (Oxford and London, 1871), I, 6–8. For a convenient summary of the programme of translations see *Alfred the Great*, trans. S. Keynes and M. Lapidge (Harmondsworth, 1983), 28–35.

[100] The principal evidence is: 1) the existence of several early fragments of the text (see CLA II, 188, 229 and 264); 2) the likelihood that it had been intimately associated with Christianity in England from the arrival of St Augustine (see Alfred's metrical preface to his translation: *The Anglo-Saxon Poetic Records*, ed. G. P. Krapp and E. V. K. Dobbie, 6 vols. (London and New York, 1931–42), VI: *The Anglo-Saxon Minor Poems*, 110); 3) the fact that it was the one book alongside scripture that Bede especially urged Archbishop Egbert of York to read and ingest (see n. 113 below); and 4) its presence and primary status in Alfred's literary programme.

[101] *Æthelwulf, De Abbatibus*, ed. A. Campbell (Oxford, 1967), ch. VIII (pp. 18–22). For recent speculations concerning the attribution of extant work to Ultan's hand see D. O'Croinin, 'Pride and Prejudice', *Peritia* 1 (1982), 352–62, at 362 (favouring the Durham Gospels at Rath Melsigi); Henderson, *Durrow to Kells*, 122–9 (suggesting the Lichfield Gospels); and Bruce-Mitford, 'Durham-Echternach Calligrapher', 187–8 (preferring the Durham Gospels).

[102] Webster and Backhouse, eds., *The Making of Britain*, cat. 69 (a, v and 2).

[103] The three scriptoria of whose activities we have some picture, although not free from controversy, are: 1) Lindisfarne (see principally *Codex Lidisfarnensis*; Verey *et al.*, *Durham Gospels*; M. P. Brown, 'Lindisfarne scriptorium'; also the literature cited in n. 82 above); 2) Wearmouth–Jarrow (see O. Arngart, *The Leningrad Bede*, Early English Manuscripts in Facsimile II (Copenhagen, 1952); Lowe, *English Uncial*; Wright, 'Notes'; and M. B. Parkes, 'The Scriptorium of Wearmouth–Jarrow', Jarrow Lecture 1982 (Jarrow, 1983)); and 3) Canterbury (see Wright, 'Notes', 448–50; Wright, *Vespasian Psalter*; C. Nordenfalk, *Celtic and Anglo-Saxon Painting* (London, 1977), 94–107; and Alexander, *Insular Manuscripts*, cats. 29, 30 and 32). The fourth scriptorium, where the ground is slightly less secure, is Minster-in-Thanet. For the attribution of Oxford, Bodleian Library, MS Seldon Supra 30 to this centre see CLA II, 257, and N. P. Brooks, *The Early History of the Church of Canterbury* (Leicester, 1984), 201. In addition circumstantial evidence makes Minster an attractive candidate for the place of origin of the Stockholm Codex Aureus – and certainly more compelling than Canterbury. Finally it is possible that some headway may yet be made with a fifth scriptorium: note should be

surviving attributable manuscripts. Moreover, it is even obscure what an 'important scriptorium' meant in terms of manpower.[104] But whilst we cannot hope to know upon how many writing centres, of what size, the onus of meeting the demand for gospel books devolved, we can be reasonably certain that it was not enough. It is in this context that the fact that, although we do not know in absolute terms how long it took to make a given Insular gospel book, there is no doubt that it took considerably less time to prepare a volume like Royal 1. B. vii than one like the Lindisfarne Gospels assumes great significance.

That heavy demand for books could cause serious problems even for the largest writing centres is demonstrated by the case of Wearmouth–Jarrow. By the early eighth century the community of this twin foundation totalled more than six hundred members (though whether they were all monks is uncertain) and it had an impressive history of literary activities.[105] Yet in the second half of the century the international demand for copies of the works of its outstanding and prolific house author, Bede, seems to have caused something of a crisis in the scriptorium, leading, so it is suggested, to significant changes in scribal practice.[106] Uncial, the stately, expansive, time-consuming script in which earlier products of the house were written, seems to have given way for general purposes to a version of Insular minuscule, a speedier, more compact, lower-grade book-hand. Now elsewhere in England at this time and earlier a similar downgrading to Insular minuscule was evidently countenanced as an expedient to hasten production of the sacred gospel text itself: the Echternach Gospels, it will be recalled, commences with one page in a stately majuscule but thereafter is largely written in a formal minuscule; similarly the Leipzig fragment begins in half-uncial but continues in a compressed minuscule; while the Hereford Gospels is entirely written in a regular but unimposing hybrid minuscule.[107] It was equally acceptable, if circumstances demanded it, to entrust this work to scribes of the

made of the thoughtful suggestion that the Durham Cassiodorus, Durham, Cathedral Library, MS B. ii. 30 (CLA ii, 152) is a York book (see D. Bullough, 'Alcuin and the Kingdom of Heaven', *Carolingian Essays. Andrew W. Mellon Lectures in Early Christian Studies*, ed. U.-R. Blumenthal (Washington DC, 1983), 1–69, at 18–22).

For the importance of Whitby see P. Hunter-Blair, 'Whitby as a centre of learning in the seventh century', *Learning and Literature*, ed. Lapidge and Gneuss, 3–32; for York see Hunter–Blair, 'From Bede to Alcuin', *Famulus Christi*, ed. G. Bonner (London, 1976), 239–260; and *Alcuin*, ed. Godman, esp. lx–lxxv.

104   Estimates of numbers can only be made in relation to the three aforementioned scriptoria and must rest on the triply uncertain basis of a) distinguishing hands in b) such manuscripts as have survived and are attributable and c) are presumed to be broadly contemporary. The minimum figure afforded by this sketchy foundation for Lindisfarne and Wearmouth–Jarrow *c.* 700 is nine and eight respectively.

105   For the size of the community see *Vita Ceolfridi Abbatis Auctore Anonymo*, ed. C. Plummer (*Venerabilis Baedae Opera Historica*, i, 388–404), ch. 43. For modern accounts of its literary activities see, *inter alia*, Hunter-Blair, *World of Bede*, esp. chs. 15–18 and 21; M. L. W. Laistner, 'The Library of the Venerable Bede', *Bede His Life, Times and Writings*, ed. A. H. Thompson (Oxford, 1935), 230–66; Lowe, *English Uncial*; and Bonner, ed., *Famulus Christi*, esp. chs. 2, 3, 9 and 14.

106   Parkes, 'Scriptorium of Wearmouth–Jarrow'. It is not impossible that some books were written in minuscule at an earlier date but have not survived.

107   For Echternach see *Codex Lindisfarnensis* ii, 96–7; for Leipzig and Hereford see nn. 74 and 76 above. Incidentally, in addition to being employed for the last line of many pages in the Durham Gospels, minuscule was regularly used throughout smaller gospel books produced in Ireland from the eighth century onwards: e.g. British Library, Add. MS 40618; Dublin, Trinity College, MSS 52, 59, 60 (parts I and II); and Fulda, Hessische Landesbibliothek, MS Bonifatianus 3 (CLA ii, 179, 270, 275–77; and viii, 1198).

second rank, to prosecute the task with rapidity and to confine decoration of the text to the minimum. And clearly circumstances did require it. Volumes like Royal and Hereford, perhaps the second-grade product of a major scriptorium and the master-piece of a provincial scribe respectively, throw invaluable light on this otherwise occult world of mass gospel-book production, the need to organise which must have been an important preoccupation of the young, expanding missionary church in Anglo-Saxon England.

Considered in its own right, Royal 1. B. vii is an entirely satisfactory copy of the four gospels: the text is easily legible and it is competently written throughout in an imposing book-hand; subdivisions are clearly indicated – a plain initial and red ink are no less efficient than a decorated initial in achieving this – and appropriate marginal and prefatory apparatus facilitates usage. It appears substandard only if volumes like the Lindisfarne Gospels are regarded as the norm, which of course they were not. On the contrary, it is Royal itself, along with Leipzig, Tiberius and Hereford, that offers a better gauge of the general appearance of the great majority of early Anglo-Saxon gospel books, the type of volumes that had to be produced in some quantity year after year, which were widely distributed, and which saw active service day in, day out. Lindisfarne is a ceremonial copy, Royal is a working one. The point is underlined at the outset by the fact that Royal's simply ornamented canon tables have significantly fewer errors than the much more handsomely decorated ones in Lindisfarne; it is subsequently reinforced by the fact that it is far more convenient actually to read from a volume in which the first page of the gospels contains a substantial portion of text, written in a standard book-hand, than from one in which only a single sentence may be seen before the page has to be turned, and that sentence is written in display capitals which sacrifice clarity of letter-form in order to convey visually the numinous import of the sacred words. That a relatively high percentage of the de luxe volumes should have been preserved, whilst a very low proportion of their originally far commoner, ordinary counterparts have survived is hardly to be wondered at; on the contrary it is precisely what we should expect: as well as the extra care with which they were no doubt kept, they would as a matter of course have been subject to considerably less wear and tear.[108] It is arguably no coincidence that two of our four lower-grade codices, that is fifty percent of the sample, survive merely as fragments, one indeed as but a single damaged page. The de luxe books, by contrast, were designed to be treasured rather than used – as is, of course, still the case. However this adds very considerably to the historical value of their few extant humbler counterparts. As rare examples of the type of gospel books that were probably familiar to, and actually used by, a wide range of clergy in the early Anglo-Saxon church, Royal 1. B. vii, the Leip-zig fragment, the Tiberius leaf and the Hereford Gospels are of great significance.

---

[108] Boisil, prior of Melrose, owned a seven-quire copy of the Gospel of St John, which was possibly unbound: St Cuthbert read one quire to him each day during the week before he died (*Vita sancti Cuthberti auctore Beda*, VIII: *Two Lives of St Cuthbert*, ed. B. Colgrave (Cambridge, 1940), 180–4). This provides a striking example of a book which was well-suited to daily use and which was unlikely to last very long.

They remind us of the imbalance of our sample and to some extent they enable us to correct it.

The lone representatives of a once very important class of book, these volumes provide crucial insight into the norms of seventh- and eighth-century liturgical book production, norms which are easily overlooked. This in its turn offers a valid but little-exploited standpoint from which both to view their de luxe counterparts and to consider some of the social functions of these codices as a whole. Much modern analysis of the book production of the period focuses exclusively on the great decorated gospel books and is diachronistic in orientation, that is it tends to examine the de luxe volumes principally as a class unto themselves, in order of age, comparing and contrasting each with its predecessor(s) and/or successor(s) as appropriate. The importance of Royal, Leipzig, Tiberius and Hereford is that they provide us with a wider cross-section of material and enable us to take an alternative, synchronistic approach to the de luxe codices – viewing them in a lateral perspective by comparing them with broadly contemporary lower-grade versions of the same text. The resultant dialogue poses as many questions as it answers, but three general points may briefly be raised in conclusion here.

In the first place, the comparison between the de luxe volumes and their more modest counterparts serves to confirm (if confirmation were needed) that most of the Insular gospel books with which the modern student is principally familiar were indeed masterpieces, surely exceptional in their own day: we are fortunate enough to possess a selection of seventh- and eighth-century books which is unrepresentative in including a high percentage of the finest quality work.

Secondly, the contrast between high- and low-grade gospel books can be seen to reflect a fundamental dichotomy in the Anglo-Saxon church itself. In the later seventh century, the problems and uncertainties that characterise the history of English Christianity in the middle of the century having passed,[109] certain sectors of the church began to enjoy conspicuous prosperity.[110] From this point onwards one is struck by the disparity between the impressive economic stability and prosperity, the well-ordered life and the evident spiritual fervour of certain centres, notably the great foundations such as Lindisfarne, Wearmouth–Jarrow and Canterbury, on the one hand; on the other by the more exiguous basis on which the institutionalised church was established throughout the land as a whole. Notwithstanding the local chapels that are known to have been founded on lands belonging to great monasteries, and such rural churches as were built at the instigation of lay thegns on their properties,[111] the problems involved in establishing an effective network of local Christian centres, evangelising the countryside as a whole and sustaining its conversion were formidable: the church lacked sufficient resources in terms of bases, trained personnel

---

[109] See Hunter-Blair, 'Whitby as a centre of learning', 14–17.
[110] See Campbell, 'First Century of Christianity in England'.
[111] See Bede, *Historia ecclesiastica* v, 4–5, and 12; *Vita Cuthberti*, ch. 34; *Aldhelm, The Poetic Works*, trans. M. Lapidge and J. Rosier (Woodbridge, 1985), 8; and more generally J. Blair, 'Minster Churches in the Landscape', *Anglo-Saxon Settlements*, ed. D. Hooke (Oxford, 1988), 35–58.

and equipment (of which books were of course a fundamental part) adequately to consolidate the initial missionary ventures and gains 'in the field'.[112] This was one of the aspects of the Northumbrian church in 734 which Bede identified as a cause for concern,[113] and, whilst his celebrated letter to Egbert, archbishop of York, undoubtedly reflects a cloistered viewpoint and is polemical in intent, his fear that the existing provisions for continuous, widespread pastoral care were inadequate was surely sound. The splendour of manuscripts like the Lindisfarne Gospels clearly relies on, and reflects, the internal world of the prosperous ecclesiastical centres, their outstanding cultural and spiritual achievements and their extensive material resources (not to mention the foundations, despised by Bede, which were flourishing under the aegis, if not within the *familia*, of entrepreneurial thegnly dynasts). The same centres were probably responsible for producing many of the lower grade volumes like Royal 1. B. vii which had to be made in much greater numbers; but these books, by contrast, can be seen as material witnesses to the problems involved in establishing and supporting Christianity at a local level throughout the length and breadth of England in the seventh and eighth centuries.

Yet the difference between de luxe and lower grade gospel books was not merely a passive reflection of the dichotomy within the Christian establishment which we have just summarised: it was surely also part of the system of ranking that existed in the church, a system that was consciously fostered and actively maintained; and this is the third and final point. The church in England, as elsewhere, was, and had been from its inception, a hierarchical organisation. Individuals and institutions necessarily varied, and, no less crucial, had to be seen to vary, in rank, status and importance. The point is underlined by the very first clause in the earliest Anglo-Saxon written law code, that of Æthelberht of Kent (602–3?), where the differing status of individual ecclesiastics is reflected in the amount of compensation that was due if their property were stolen (Church property commanded twelve-fold compensation, a bishop's eleven-fold, a priest's nine-fold, a deacon's six-fold and a clerk's three-fold).[114] Needless to say corresponding stratification is enunciated by specifically ecclesiastical ordinances such as the *Dialogue of Egbert*[115] – where we are told that the testimony of priests, deacons and monks is valued according to the importance of their position (*secundum gradus promotionis*), that of the first being worth twice that of the second, which is in turn double that of the third – and is embedded within wider ranging documents such as

---

[112] See in general, M. Deanesley, *The Pre-Conquest Church in England* (London, 1961), ch. IX; and Mayr-Harting, *Coming of Christianity*, ch. 14. The important collection of essays, *Pastoral Care before the Parish*, ed. J. Blair and R. Sharpe (Leicester, 1992), appeared after this study had been written. A. Thacker, 'Monks, preaching and pastoral care in early Anglo-Saxon England', 137–70, is the most relevant in this context.

[113] Letter to Egbert, Archbishop of York: *Councils and Ecclesiastical Documents*, ed. Haddan and Stubbs, III, 314–26; trans. *English Historical Documents*, ed. Whitelock, 799–810. For important comments on its context and interpretation see P. Wormald, 'Bede, Beowulf and the Conversion of the Anglo-Saxon Aristocracy', *Bede and Anglo-Saxon England*, ed. R. T. Farrell, British Archaeological Reports 46 (Oxford, 1978), 32–95, esp. 51–8; A. Thacker, 'Bede's Ideal of Reform', *Ideal and Reality in Frankish and Anglo-Saxon Society*, ed. P. Wormald (Oxford, 1983), 130–153, esp. 133–4 and 149–53; and Sims-Williams, *Religion and Literature*, 126–34.

[114] *The Laws of the Earliest English Kings*, ed. F. L. Attenborough (Cambridge, 1922), 4.

[115] Section I: *Councils and Ecclesiastical Documents*, ed. Haddan and Stubbs, III, 404.

the *Penitential of Egbert*,[116] where heavier penalties are required for a given misdemeanor from the more important orders. That such a hierarchy could occasionally lead to abuse, and that the career structure it defined could sometimes be a distraction, with individual self-interest impeding rather than fostering the growth of the church as a whole, is not in doubt. The difficulties which Archbishop Theodore faced when trying to subdivide the over-large existing dioceses into more efficient and manageable administrative units are a case in point.[117] But equally the efficient ordering and organisation of the church undoubtedly relied upon, and presupposed, a clearly perceived pecking-order, and since the system had the unshakeable recommendation of tradition and universality, it is no surprise to find that it was carefully maintained. As primary indicators of status in a society which was well-attuned to assessing them as such, the material possessions of the church, particularly moveable ones,[118] are likely to have been subject to a considerable degree of manipulation, implicit and explicit, designed to help define the status quo – and also to support attempted departures from it. At a basic level, what was the proper accoutrement of a bishop, a deceased holy man or a prestigious monastic community was patently not appropriate for a local cleric, an ordinary monk or a small church, and items were clearly conceived and acquired or supplied accordingly. Howsoever his character and career may be judged, the architectural grandeur of Wilfrid's principal churches and the splendour of his gold-on-purple gospel book were entirely concordant with the magnificence that was a bishop's due, and are celebrated as such by his biographer.[119] Similarly, notwithstanding Bede's reticence on the subject of monastic wealth, it is readily apparent that Wearmouth–Jarrow cut an imposing figure in terms of its possessions and decorations which was wholly concordant with the size of the community, its land-holding and its cultural importance, not to mention the thegnly status of its founder-abbot (although this, of course, was something that it had in common with lesser houses). As the most important and widely distributed tool of the Christian religion, it is inconceivable that gospel books, whatever their intrinsic spiritual importance, were exempt from this system; on the contrary they are likely to have been commissioned and designed, or prepared and dispatched, in full accordance with it. It is hardly coincidence that what is arguably the finest extant Insular gospel book is firmly associated with the cult of the redoubtable St Cuthbert as it was energetically fostered at one of the wealthiest and most important monasteries of the day.[120]

No less than the promulgators of the synodal decrees which defined the relationship

---

[116] *Ibid.*, 416–31.

[117] See Brooks, *Church of Canterbury*, 71–6; and M. Roper, 'Wilfrid's Landholdings in Northumbria', *Saint Wilfrid at Hexham*, ed. D. Kirby (Newcastle-upon-Tyne, 1974), 61–79.

[118] R. Hodges, *The Anglo-Saxon Achievement* (London, 1989), 108, draws attention to the contrast between the relatively small scale of Anglo-Saxon churches on the one hand, and the extent of their moveable wealth on the other.

[119] Eddius Stephanus, *Vita Wilfridi*, ed. Colgrave, chs. xvii, xxii (pp. 34–6 and 44–6); and E. Gilbert, 'Saint Wilfrid's Church at Hexham', *Saint Wilfrid*, ed. Kirby, 81–113.

[120] On the energy with which Cuthbert's cult was promoted at Lindisfarne see D. Rollason, *Saints and Relics in Anglo-Saxon England* (Oxford, 1989), 105–10.

between the various orders of the church while trying to regulate their behaviour, the scribes and artists of the scriptoria which supplied gospel books to an ecclesiastical hinterland were actively involved in assessing the clerical hierarchy and designating positions within it. Royal 1. B. vii could have been supplied with simple evangelist portraits, separate carpet pages and more decorated initials for relatively little additional expenditure of time and labour if such had been regarded as appropriate; evidently it was not. It is greatly to be regretted that we do not know the original setting for which this particular book was prepared; however the likelihood is strong that Royal 1. B. vii and other now lost volumes of a lesser grandeur were designed economically, not merely owing to restrictions of time and pressure of demand, but also because this was what the nature of their prospective contexts was adjudged to require.

The comparison between the Lindisfarne Gospels and Royal 1. B. vii usefully reminds us that, as is commonly the case throughout the history of manuscript production, so too in early Anglo-Saxon England, the books whose decoration was the most carefully planned and which enhanced the meaning of the text most fully and innovatively, the books which actually determined the thrust of calligraphic practices and manuscript art, were the least well known to, and used by, contemporary society in general. Moreover we may reasonably conclude that this was not only a passive reflection of the diverse and problematic nature of the early church in England as a whole, but also a positive device that was inevitably deployed alongside many others, ranging from penitential penalty to dress, to maintain and develop the hierarchy of the young, growing Christian establishment and to define the individual church or cleric's place within it.

3

Mass production of early medieval manuscripts: the Carolingian Bibles from Tours

DAVID GANZ

The copying of complete texts of the Bible, contained in only one or two volumes, which characterised the scriptoria of St Martin's and Marmoutiers at Tours during the course of the ninth century, constituted a new development in medieval book production. While multi-volume and single-volume Bibles had been copied before, and the scriptorium at Wearmouth–Jarrow had made three copies of the Bible, whose layouts and similarities await study, the multiple reproduction of the biblical text during a sixty-year period cannot be paralleled. Only the attempt by the abbey of Micy to provide several copies of the Bible recension prepared by Theodulf of Orléans deserves mention here. Theodulf's text was continuously revised during his lifetime, and was conceived as an accessible reference work, and so he chose a very small, three column 61-line format, with quires of five leaves. The copying involved elaborate scribal preparation, and the Bibles were produced within a short space of time. Six copies survive and two others have left traces,[1] and there is clear evidence that Theodulf's text was used to improve biblical texts throughout the Carolingian empire.[2]

Carolingian book production was decisively affected by the steady supply of Bibles and gospel books which were copied at Tours. Forty-six Bibles and eighteen gospel books have survived from the period before 853; only three Bibles and seven gospel books may be dated later in the ninth century, an indication of the severe effects of Viking attacks on Tours in the reign of Charles the Bald, notably the burning of St Martin's Abbey in 853, 872 and again in 903.[3] So the Tours scriptoria were perhaps copying two full Bibles per year, for more than half a century. Nor was book production at Tours restricted to these Bibles: the abbey of St Martin was also copying the works of classical, patristic and Carolingian authors. Works of Cicero,

---

[1] E. Dahlhaus-Berg, *Nova antiquitas et antiqua novitas. Typologische Exegese und isidorianisches Geschichtsbild bei Theodulf von Orléans* (Cologne, 1975), 39–61. The manuscripts are: Stuttgart, Württemburgische Landesbibliothek, HB II. 16; London, British Library, Add. 24142; Le Puy, Trésor de la Cathedral (CLA VI, 768); Paris, Bibliothèque Nationale, lat. 9380 (CLA V, 576); Paris, Bibliothèque Nationale, lat. 11937; and Copenhagen, Kongelige Bibliotek, N. K. S. 1. I have examined the manuscripts in London and Paris.

[2] See further the essay by Rosamond McKitterick, ch. 4 below.

[3] B. Fischer, *Die Bibel von Moutier-Grandval* (Bern, 1971), 49, repr. in his *Lateinische Bibelhandschriften im frühen Mittelalter*, (Freiburg, 1985) – hereafter cited as Fischer, 'Die Bibel'; E. K. Rand, *The Earliest Books of Tours* (Cambridge, Mass., 1934).

Servius, Hegesippus, Augustine, Orosius, Priscian, Isidore, the Paris Council of 829, Amalarius, Paul the Deacon, were all copied between 820 and 860.[4] What has not been sufficiently acknowledged is that many of these volumes were also produced for libraries outside Tours. The earliest volumes to survive from the Tours scriptorium, produced from *c.* 730, were copied in order to supply the needs of a community of libraries. That sort of scriptorium was far more common than we have tended to realise, especially if we have focused on twelfth-century scriptoria. Like the scriptorium of Luxeuil, which affirmed its monastic values through the extensive copying of works of spirituality both for individual patrons and for religious foundations linked to that prominent house, the scribes of Tours shared their resources by copying on commission. Their mass-produced gospel books, their Bibles and the anthology of texts which commemorate and celebrate the life and miracles of St Martin, set Tours at the centre of a network of ecclesiastical spirituality. This was in marked contrast to most Carolingian scriptoria, which copied chiefly for their own libraries, occasionally duplicating a rare text or the work of a house author.

Only one of the Tours Bibles, the Moutier Grandval Bible in London, has been studied in sufficient detail to clarify how it was copied.[5] Art historians have surveyed the illustrations which enhance three Tours Bibles, and the canon tables and decoration of others.[6] Some of the most important contributions to an understanding of how the Bibles of Tours were made come from the publication of surviving fragments of these Bibles, in Obermachtal,[7] Braunschweig and Wolfenbüttel, Munich, Munich and Augsburg,[8] Trier, Berlin, Cornell, Bloomington and Malibu.[9] This paper draws on my examination of fragments in Chapel Hill, London, Munich, Trier, Wolfenbüttel and Yale; and of complete and incomplete Bibles in London, Munich and Paris. It offers a number of observations and suggestions, vitiated by the incomplete and overhasty examination of the Bibles, the neglect of the evidence of gospel books and the impossibility, except in Paris, of setting Tours Bibles side by side.

Several complete Carolingian texts of the Bible predate the Bibles produced at Tours: the most celebrated, and the earliest is Metz, Bibliothèque Municipale, 7, copied before 791, which perished in 1944.[10] Fulda, Aa 10–11 was copied at

---

[4] E. K. Rand, *A Survey of the Manuscripts of Tours. Studies in the Scripts of Tours* 1 (Cambridge, Mass., 1929).

[5] London, British Library, Add. MS 10546: J. Duft *et al.*, *Die Bibel von Moutier-Grandval, British Museum Add. MS 10546* (Bern, 1971).

[6] W. Koehler, *Die karolingischen Miniaturen I: Die Schule von Tours*, 2 vols. (Berlin, 1930–3); C. Nordenfalk, 'Methodische Fortschritte und materieller Landerwerb in der Kunstforschung', *Acta Archaeologica* 3 (1932), 276–88; and 'Beitrage zur Geschichte der turonischen Buchmalerei', *Acta Archaeologica* 7 (1936), 281–304; and H. L. Kessler, *The Illustrated Bibles from Tours*, Studies in Manuscript Illumination 7 (Princeton, 1977).

[7] A. Dold, 'Neuentdeckte Blatter einer unbekannten Bibelhandschrift von Tours', *Zentralblatt für Bibliothekswesen* 48 (1931), 169–77.

[8] H. Spilling, 'Fragmente einer Alcuin-Bibel aus Konstanz', *Bibliotheksforum Bayern* 9 (1981), 211–21.

[9] F. Mütherich, 'Die touronische Bibel von St. Maximin in Trier', in *Kunsthistorische Forschungen O. Pächt zu seinem 70 Geburtstag*, ed. A. Fosenauer and G. Weber (Salzberg, 1973), 44–54.

[10] CLA vi, 786.

Reichenau for Constance;[11] Würzburg acquired a multi-volume Bible under Bishop Hunbert (832–42);[12] fragments survive from a multi-volume Freising Bible.[13] St Riquier had a large two-volume Bible which is now Paris, Bibliothèque Nationale, lat. 45+93. St Germain also had an excellent vulgate text.[14] Salzburg had a multi-volume Bible.[15] Clearly Alcuin's revised text, widely copied at Tours, was not exclusive, and at Metz and Reichenau a single- or two-volume format had already been adopted for the Bible before 800.

The evidence of the surviving complete Tours Bibles in Monza, Cologne, London and Paris suggests that a complete Bible consisted of some 450 leaves, measuring *c*. 480 × 375 mm, with 50–2 lines per page. To copy a Tours Bible required some 210–25 sheep, whose shaped skins measured around 525 × 760 mm. The dimensions of Carolingian sheep and their price await study, but it has been suggested that sheep this size required available pasture throughout the winter. The format of the Bible was a marked improvement on the 1,030 leaves of the *Codex Amiatinus* and the estimated 920 leaves of Ceolfrith's smaller pandect,[16] or the 72-line format of the two-column eighth-century Spanish half-uncial Bible, León, Cathedral, MS 15. Though the size of the sheet was much larger, the number of leaves required to copy a Tours pandect was less than that required to copy the multi-volume Bibles of Corbie, St Gall or Würzburg. But the saving in parchment depended on the excellence and the uniformity of the scribes who copied the *c*. 85,000 lines of Alcuin's text.

The clearest account of the purpose of the Tours pandects is that given in the several prefatory poems which Alcuin composed as presentation inscriptions to accompany copies of the Bible made during his lifetime.

> Ad decus ecclesiae propria simul inque salutem.   (Carmen 67)

As an ornament of the church and for his own salvation.

> Hic est fons vitae, hic sunt praecepta salutis,
> Hunc dictante Deo scripsere in secula sancti, . . .
> Esset in ecclesia ut praesto legentibus ille.
> In quo quisque legat Domini dulcissima verba,
> Sit memor auctoris, illum qui scribere iussit, . . .
> Tuque valeto legens, tibi maxima cura legenti
> Sit precor, ut recto resones caelestia sensu
> Verba Dei, Christi merces tibi magna manebit.   (Carmen 66)[17]

This is the fount of life these are the precepts of salvation, the saints wrote this for centuries at God's dictation. It should be in the church for the readers, and whosoever reads the sweetest words of the Lord, let him remember the author who ordered it to be written. Farewell to you

---

[11] B. Fischer, 'Bibeltext und Bibelreform unter Karl dem Grossen', in *Karl der Grosse. Lebenswerk und Nachleben II: Das geistige Leben*, ed. B. Bischoff (Düsseldorf, 1965), 156–216, at 202.

[12] *Ibid.*, 200.   [13] *Ibid.*, 208.   [14] *Ibid.*, 183–4.

[15] Fischer, 'Die Bibel', 59.60. The Salzburg Bible survives as the fragment CLA x, 1445.

[16] Fischer, 'Die Bibel', 59.   [17] MGH, *Poetae aevi Karolini* i, 285.

who are reading I pray you take care of the reading, so that you resound the heavenly words of God with the right meaning and the great reward of Christ will remain for you.

> Hos lege tu, lector felix, feliciter omnes
> Ad laudem Christi propriumque in secla saluti.
>   (Carmen 68 in the Tours Bibles now in Zürich and Bamberg.)[18]

Two Carolingian Bibles which were not copied at Tours preserve the longest of Alcuin's poems.[19] The contents of the Bible are listed in detail, and their harmonies clarified:

> Continet iste uno sancto sub corpore codex
>   Hic simul hos totos, munera magna Dei;
> Quisque legat huius sacrato in corpore libri
>   Lector in ecclesia verba superna Dei
> Distinguens sensus, titulos, cola, commata voce
>   Dicat ut accentus ore sonare sciat.[20]

This codex contains in one holy body all these things at the same time, the great gifts of God. Whosoever as a reader in church reads in the sacred body of this book the high words of God distinguishing the meanings, titles, cola and commata with his voice, let him say with his mouth as he knows the accent sounds.

The volumes were clearly produced for the church, and for the reader reading in the church, and the novelty of having the complete Bible in one volume is mentioned. The poems affirm that the reader's task is to convey the clarity of the text and of its subdivisions. Tours Bibles are community books.

The poems reveal that Alcuin prepared a copy of the Bible for Charlemagne which was completed early in 800, a second Bible which was presented to Charlemagne for his palace chapel at Aachen at Christmas 801, two copies for Tours, a further Bible for Bishop Gerfrid of Laon and a Bible commissioned by an *ancilla Dei* named Ava. So from 800 Alcuin was able to ensure that the text which he had assembled could be copied every year, perhaps at the rate of two Bibles in one year. That required a steady supply of high-grade parchment (holes and flaws are almost unknown in the pages of Tours Bibles) and a group of scribes who were expert calligraphers. Eleven years before, Charlemagne had commanded that Bibles and liturgical texts be copied by skilled and senior scribes.[21] The three gospel books and six Bibles which Fischer dates before Alcuin's death in 807, together with the six lost Bibles mentioned by Alcuin himself, show that by *c.* 800 Tours scribes met these standards. No earlier Tours manuscript now extant contains a copy of a biblical text. Yet if the St Gall Bible, or the earliest Paris Bible fragment, Bibliothèque Nationale, lat. 8847, are set beside the Theodulf Bibles or the gospel books of the court school, their standard of book production is markedly inferior.

18 *Ibid.*, 287; see Koehler, *Die karolingischen Miniaturen* I, 209.
19 Vienna, Österreichische Nationalbibliothek, lat. 1190; Fischer, 'Die Bibel', 57.
20 MGH, *Poetae aevi Karolini* I, 288–92.   21 Admonitio Generalis: MGH, *Capitularia* I, 60.

It would be wrong to assume that the contents of a Tours Bible were fixed during Alcuin's lifetime. As Fischer has shown, it was possible to alter the order of the books, the prefatory material and the chapters.[22] For instance, in the Tours Bibles in Berlin and St Gall, the Apocalypse precedes the Pauline Epistles, unlike other Bibles which end with the Apocalypse. After Fridugisus, Alcuin's successor as abbot of St Martin's, the Pauline Epistles include the apocryphal letter to the Laodiceans. There seems to be no clear explanation of why some Bibles have a list of chapters for the book of Ruth while others have none. Zürich starts the series of prefaces and summaries for the Gospels, found also in Bern, Munich, Grandval, Rorigo, Bamberg, Vivian and Cologne. The layout of the canon tables also developed so that they occupied four pages, as Nordenfalk and Fischer have shown.

A further illustration is found in Bern, Moutier Grandval, Bibliothèque Nationale, lat. 250, Munich, Rorigo, Vivian and Cologne, where the Pauline Epistles are preceded by a table, the Concordia Epistularum, akin to the canon tables in its arcade format, which is not included in Zürich, Bamberg, Berlin or Bibliothèque Nationale, lat. 47. Chronology does not explain why certain volumes have this table, but its systematic references to the Pauline Epistles may establish different functions for the copies which include it as opposed to those which do not.

Fischer has shown that the chronology of Tours Bibles cannot be established on textual grounds. But it is clear that Abbot Adalhard (834–43) supervised a revision of the Gospel text, bringing it closer to the text of the gospel books of the Palace School. This revision is dated to circa 840. The text of the Palace School was also adopted at Metz, Rheims, Salzburg and St Amand. The Tours text was used to revise Bible texts in the Carolingian empire, at Aniane, at Micy under Theodulf, at St Germain, at Chelles, at the Reichenau and at St Gall.

Few attempts have been made to establish the number of scribes who collaborated in the production of Tours Bibles. Rand suggested that eight scribes worked on the Rorigo Bible, Bibliothèque Nationale, lat. 3; at least four main scribes in Bamberg; six hands in Vivian, Bibliothèque Nationale, lat. 1; about a dozen hands in British Library, Harley 2805 (237 leaves); about a dozen hands in the surviving portion of Bibliothèque Nationale, lat. 68 (159 leaves). He identified some sixteen hands in Bibliothèque Nationale, lat. 11514 (207 leaves); and at least half a dozen hands in Zürich; but Rand and Homburger distinguish only two hands in Bern 3–4, one hand in the surviving portion of Bibliothèque Nationale, lat. 47 (176 leaves) (I suspect that there may be a second hand at the end of the Gospel of Matthew.) Bruckner distinguishes twenty-four scribes in Moutier Grandval.[23] So a Bible might need between two and twenty-four scribes. Rand also linked Bibliothèque Nationale, lat. 11514, Harley 2805 and Bibliothèque Nationale, lat. 68, and suggested that 11514 and 68 have a common scribe.

Only in the Monza Bible is there a scribal signature. This reads, 'Hos tandem dignos exaravit dextera libros exiguus Christo devotus famulus almo Amalricus atque hic sua

---

[22] This paragraph summarises Fischer, 'Die Bibel', 65–77.
[23] J. Duft *et al.*, *Die Bibel von Moutier-Grandval*, 114–16.

otio frangit' which might perhaps be rendered, 'The poor devout servant of Christ Amalric wrote (ploughed) these worthy books with his right hand and here he stopped for a rest'. Another scribe in the same Bible wrote a prayer at the end of the book of Malachi. In addition Bischoff noted the signature of one Hildebertus beside the quire signature on a bifolium in Munich (Bayerische Staatsbibliothek, Clm 29158) containing portions of Isaiah and Jeremiah.[24] Neither of these scribes is known in other manuscripts, though Amalricus may be the *magister* and correspondent of Lupus of Ferrières. The most celebrated listing of Tours scribes is found in the scribal signatures in the Tours copy of the third decade of Livy, and those reflect the division of labour in the copying of the volume. This may also explain the signature of Hildebertus. Otherwise the scribes of Tours Bibles were silent.

But there is considerable evidence of the attention given to the accurate copying of the scriptural text. **REQ** *requisitum est*, and the equivalent in Tironian notes are found at the ends of quires throughout Harley 2805, Bibliothèque Nationale, lat. 68, and lat. 3 and the Moutier Grandval Bible. *Requisitum est* was translated by Rand as 'collated with the original'. It is significant that this collation of the text was done quire by quire presumably before the volume was bound. The notes recorded the activity of a corrector. But while this practice seems to have been standard at Tours from the mid-eighth century, it was rare in other Carolingian scriptoria. Tours systematically strove to ensure the accuracy of its Bible texts. In Harley 2805 there are traces of contemporary correction in the Psalter on fol. 220v.

The separate sections of the text are distinguished by simple initials followed by a line in uncial or sometimes in half-uncial. The explicit is always copied in rustic capitals. Incipits occupy several lines, in square capitals, and are followed by uncial for the first line of the book. All openings are decorated with an initial. Red is used for the capitals of the text, for the incipit or explicit and for initials. Care is taken to begin each book at the start of a page, often a new folio and, when possible, a new quire. Initials are used for the prologue to the Pentateuch and for Genesis, for the Psalms and the Gospels. St Gall and Monza extend the titles of books over two columns, but Bibles of the second period confine these titles to one column. They begin each chapter within a book on a new line, which St Gall and Monza did not do consistently. In Zürich and Munich the separate Gospels have initials as do the Pauline epistles. Munich and Bern also distinguish Acts, Kings and Proverbs. Prologues are copied entirely in half-uncial. Within a book each chapter begins on a new line, with an initial in the margin. This required the ruling of a separate narrow column beside the column of text. This change in ruling format will be discussed below. Both the contents and the divisions of a Tours Bible develop over time. Developments in script and layout make it almost impossible to distinguish hands, save for certain features of display script in Bibles copied after the 830s.[25]

[24] B. Bischoff, 'Die turonische Bibel der Munchener Staatsbibliothek', in his *Mittelalterliche Studien* 1 (Stuttgart, 1966), 34–40.

[25] I am grateful to James Hayes and Stan Knight, calligraphers who have spent many years studying the script of Tours, for helpful discussions of this script. Stan Knight has published some of his observations, with superb photographs in 'Scripts of the Grandval Bible', *The Scribe* 44 (1988), 13–14; 45 (1989), 6–10; 48 (1990) 3–6.

The chief purpose of this elaborated hierarchy of scripts, which distinguish the books of Tours from the products of other Carolingian scriptoria, is to enhance the legibility of the text, just as Alcuin's poem had urged the reader of his Bible to distinguish 'the meanings, titles, cola and commata with his voice, let him say with his mouth as he knows the accent sounds'. The Bible is copied for public reading in church and the lector must be able to convey the internal divisions of the text he reads. During the second stage in the development of Tours Bibles, the small Caroline minuscule used to copy the chapter lists at the beginning of each book of the Bible was also used for the text of the Gospels and the Psalter. The probable explanation for the use of this very small script is that Gospels and Psalter would not be read from a Bible, but from a gospel book or a Psalter. It is found in Zürich, Harley, Moutier Grandval, Munich, Trier and Bibliothèque Nationale, lat. 47.

The contents and the divisions of a Tours Bible developed over time. By the 830s the scribes of Tours had refined the layout of their Bibles, and perfected their script so that it is almost impossible to distinguish hands without using features of display script as the defining criterion. Ligatures are rarer in the minuscule script. The earliest scribes had frequently joined **r** to a following vowel, as in Bibliothèque Nationale, lat. 11514 and Harley 2805. **NT** ligatures, and **re** and open **a** are found in Harley, for example on fols. 29r, 35r and 41v, and in Munich on fol. 214. Open **a** is also found in Bibliothèque Nationale, lat. 68, copied under Fridugisus.

The ruling of Tours Bibles was first explored by Pater Dold, who recognised that the layout of the page changed from the early Bibles, ruled in two columns with a central margin, to the later Bibles with outer and inner marginal columns beside the columns of text.[26] There is a remarkable consistency in the measurements of these columns. Bibliothèque Nationale, lat. 68 and Harley 2805 both have rulings of 122, 24, 122. The new scheme, found in Moutier Grandval, Rorigo, Bern and Munich, is 6, 125, 6, 18, 6, 125, 6. Later the text column was narrowed from 125 to 115 mm, as in Trier, Wolfenbüttel, and Bibliothèque Nationale, lat. 47 and 250. In lat. 250 there is a change in the ruling pattern after fol. 49, at the start of Acts. The Gospels are written in a unique scheme in which the central column is flanked by two pairs of columns each 7 mm wide. The ruled lines for the text are normally 7 or 8 mm apart.

The actual process of copying is clarified by a set of marginal notes. In quire XLI of the Moutier Grandval Bible the separate leaves are labelled in the lower margin 'in primo folio', 'in secundo folio', 'in iii folio', 'in vi folio', 'in vii folio'. Rand believed that these were directions to ensure that the text of Ezra fitted into this quire.

This corresponds to the evidence of the script, where compressed passages of text show how the scribes collaborating in the copying of Tours Bibles tried hard to fit the blocks of text which were assigned to them into a predetermined format, a fixed number of columns. The Gospels, when they were copied in the tiny capitular minuscule, frequently required compression so as to ensure that each Gospel fitted the requisite space. Clear examples are found in Clm 12741 at the start of the Gospel of

---

[26] Dold, 'Bibelhandschrift von Tours', 170–3.

Mark and during the Gospel of John on fols. 334 and 337r; in Bibliothèque Nationale, lat. 47 at the end of Matthew; and at the end of the Gospel of John on fols. 48r–v of lat. 250 and on fol. 81v at the end of the quire. The Psalter was also copied in tiny Tours minuscule and might require compression, as is found in both Harley 2805 and the Moutier Grandval Bible. In Harley on fol. 224 there is compression to fit the preface to the Psalms into one column, and on fol. 234 during the Psalms. Compression is found in the texts of the Psalter on fols. 239r–240v and 242 of Moutier Grandval. Harley 2805 may have been copied more hastily than some Tours Bibles, if compression is a reliable guide: it occurs on fol. 92v at the end of Ruth, fol. 98v, fol. 129v col. 2, and 130v at the end of Malachi and fol. 221v to complete the book of Job. In the Moutier Grandval Bible the Pauline epistles are often compressed to ensure that a new epistle begins a new page. There is also compression at the end of quire 12 before the work of a new scribe in quire 13.

The text was copied in quires, as is confirmed by the patterns which recur in the division of the text. Both Bamberg and Zürich end the Book of Ruth at the end of quire 12, while in Monza, Berlin, Bibliothèque Nationale, lat. 250, Rorigo, Vivian and Cologne, Matthew occupies nine or ten leaves, Mark five or six, Luke ten and John seven. (Unfortunately the foliation varies too much for these correspondences to mean that a particular Gospel will be found on the same pages in different manuscripts.) This degree of standardisation ensured that before the copying of a Tours Bible began it would have been possible to estimate how much parchment would be needed, and it made it much easier to divide the task of copying among a number of scribes. The illustrations of Moutier Grandval and Vivian are all on singletons inserted into the text.

But the apparent uniformity of Tours Bibles has been overemphasised, and Fischer took the format as a criterion for rejecting attribution of some volumes to Tours. Bibliothèque Nationale, lat. 9397, copied at Marmoutiers, has portions of Sapientia, Ecclesiasticus, Matthew and Mark in two columns of 25 lines. Troyes 29 has portions of the Old Testament in two columns of 46 lines. A fragment of Job in the Beinecke Library at Yale, clearly copied in the perfected style of Tours, also has a 25-line format. Such volumes cannot have contained complete Bible texts, but they suggest that the scriptorium was still able to experiment. However the standard format of 50 to 52 lines proved the most suitable, and was used widely.

Angelomus of Luxeuil, in his commentary on Genesis composed for the emperor Lothar, Charlemagne's grandson, refers to the Aachen copy of the Bible which Alcuin had corrected for Charles, and took pains to emend, and which he himself had inspected.[27] Tours Bibles were seen as royal Bibles, and as normative Bibles. We have seen that the text was influential throughout the Carolingian empire. The links between the Bible and the ruler persisted throughout the ninth century. Bibles and Tours gospel books were presented to emperors and their relations. Both Charles the Bald and Lothar, his brother, seem to have had their own copies which were later

---

[27] PL cxv, 180D.

presented to religious houses. Metz received the Vivian Bible, which had been presented to Charles the Bald, perhaps at his coronation in 869. Lothar presented a Tours Bible with inscriptions and illustrations to the abbey of Prüm in 852. The Rorigo Bible, Bibliothèque Nationale, lat. 3 was presented to the abbey of Glanfeuil, on the Loire, by Count Rorigo, the son-in-law of Charlemagne and the father of Charles the Bald's archchancellor Louis, abbot of St Denis and St Riquier. Rorigo was also related to the abbot of Glanfeuil. Moutier Grandval may have received its Bible from Luitfrid, the son of Hugh of Tours and brother-in-law of the emperor Lothar. Bibliothèque Nationale, lat. 250, from St Denis may have been presented to that abbey by Hilduin, archchaplain and abbot of St Germain, St Denis and St Martin of Tours. Regensburg may have obtained its Bible during the abbacy of Bautrich, the archchancellor of Louis the German. So in several cases we can link Tours Bibles to prominent court personalities.[28] It is hard to believe that they were not produced for specific foundations, or at times for individual clergymen. This was how Alcuin had envisaged his Bibles.

No other Carolingian scriptorium was engaged in such persistent copying of so long a text, such persistent copying of a single text and such extensive supplying of its products to individuals and communities throughout the empire. Such mass production transformed the nature of the Carolingian scriptorium, and also transformed the study of the Bible in the Carolingian world. But to understand the scribal side of that transformation we should recall a quotation from Edward Johnston, a salutary reminder of how far we are removed from what we attempt to study.

While I am working at the board in front of you I am thinking of doing my duty; it is expected of me (like Nelson), I have to put it across. While I am working at home by myself I am thinking of doing my best. But the old scribes were so superb because if they thought at all it was neither of their Duty nor of their Best, but they wrote because it was so much a part of them. If they were thinking of anything it was of the Psalm or Gospel, or whatever they were writing.[29]

LIST OF TOURS BIBLES AND FRAGMENTS (IN CHRONOLOGICAL ORDER)

Paris, Bibliothèque Nationale, lat. 8847: ff. 177; 455 × 330 mm; from 39 to 51 lines
St Gall, Stiftsbibliothek, 75: ff. 420; 545 × 401; 51 (50) lines
Monza, Biblioteca Capitolare, G. 1: ff. 400; 515 × 375; 51 lines

---

[28] Fischer, 'Die Bibel', 95–8.
[29] The weight of the volumes concerned means that I am very glad to thank the library staff, especially in London and Paris, who carried Tours Bibles to my desk. They were never portable. I should also like to thank Professor Michael Cothren for his kindness in measuring Tours Bibles in Paris for me, and Professor Padraig O'Neill for discussions of the Tours Psalter text. The librarians of the Episcopal Library in Trier, the Beinecke Library in Yale and the Lower Saxon State Archives in Wolfenbüttel have been generous with information and photographs of fragments in their collections, as have Christopher de Hamel at Sotheby's and Richard Linenthal at Quaritch. Dr Mildred Budny has allowed me to read a forthcoming paper on the inserted leaves in the Vivian Bible

Paris, Bibliothèque Nationale, lat. 11514: ff. 207; 483 × 350; 50 (51) lines
Paris, Bibliothèque Nationale, lat. 68: ff. 159; 512 × 390; 50 lines
London, British Library, Harley 2805: ff. 237; 525 × 365; 51 lines
Basle, Universitätsbibliothek, A. N. I. 3: ff. 174; 518 × 380; 51 lines
Bern, Burgerbibliothek, 3–4: ff. 209 + 158; 460 × 355; 51 (52) lines
Zürich, Zentralbibliothek, Car. C. 1: ff. 421; 490 × 362; 50 (49) lines
Paris, Bibliothèque Nationale, lat. 250: ff. 105; 494 × 362; 50 lines
Munich, Bayerische Staatsbibliothek, Clm 12741: ff. 353; 512 × 378; 51 lines
Berlin, Deutsche Staatsbibliothek, Hamilton 82: ff. 435; 490 × 362; 52 lines
Paris, Bibliothèque Nationale, lat. 3: ff. 409; 500 × 372; 51 (52) lines
London, British Library, Add. 10546: ff. 449; 495 × 375; 51 lines
Bamberg, Staatsbibliothek, Bibl. 1: ff. 423; 477 × 362; 50 and 51 lines
Paris, Bibliothèque Nationale, lat. 1: ff. 423; 500 × 380; 51 lines
Cologne, Dombibliothek, 1: ff. 382; 500 × 355; 51 lines
Paris, Bibliothèque Nationale, lat. 47: ff. 176; 380 × 112; 49 lines

Fragments

Chür, Bischofliches Archiv, Prophets
Munich, Bayerische Staatsbibliothek, Clm 29158, Isaiah and Jeremiah
Stuttgart, Hauptstaatsarchiv, Bu IX b nr 626, John
Karlsruhe, Generallandesarchiv, 65/2800 and 67/523, Exodus
Chapel Hill, Wilson Library, MS 526, Psalms (? from Harley 2805)
Obermachtal and Beuron, Paralipomenon and Macchabees
London, British Library, Sloane 1044, fol. 5, Deuteronomy
Munster, Staatsarchiv, VII 2 (4), Acts
Wolfenbüttel, Niedersächsisches Staatsarchiv, 1 2, Joshua, Psalms, Prophets
Basle, Universitätsbibliothek, N. I. 6, fol. 2, Luke
Aarau, Staatsarchiv 3739, Paralipomenon
Paris, Bibliothèque Nationale, n.a. lat. 2633 fol. 12, Leviticus
Trier, Bistumsarchiv, 95 1/2, Psalms

4

Carolingian Bible production: the Tours anomaly

ROSAMOND MCKITTERICK

No one doubts that the contribution of Tours to Bible production in the ninth century was considerable. The process of the famous enterprise for producing a corrected Bible text at Tours inaugurated in the time of the English abbot Alcuin, is also clear. Yet as Bonifatius Fischer has stressed, the Alcuin Bible was part of a general effort to produce a correct text of the Bible rather than the official text produced on Charlemagne's command.[1] It was not an edition but essentially a corrected and tidied up text, with a particular sequence settled on (though not consistently observed) for the books of the Old and New Testaments, together with chapter divisions, the choice of the Gallican rather than the Roman Psalter, the Vulgate translations and selections made by Jerome for all the books. There were also successive if gradual revisions under Fridugisus and Adalhard. The Alcuin Bible was put together from a number of different books of the Bible, containing different, primarily Frankish, variants of their respective texts, which were in use locally in the Tours region rather than copied from some kind of Ur-text for the whole Bible. There is no hint that Alcuin made a special effort to seek out texts nor that he drew on all those available to him such as Paris, Bibliothèque Nationale, n.a. lat. 2334 (the Ashburnham Pentateuch).[2] The diverse sources are apparent also in the schemes of illustration which are the 'products of several projects undertaken at different times to illustrate the full Bible as a single unit'.[3]

The presentation of the text, moreover, was distinctive in its layout, with large one-volume pandects in a standard format of two columns of 50–52 lines each on large pages, with a written space averaging about 360×260 mm and with generous margins. The script is a distinctive and uniform formal minuscule, of a Tours type which I should wish to define as 'export quality script', with equally distinctive capitals and uncials used in the headings and half-uncial for prefaces and prologues.[4]

---

[1] B. Fischer, 'Bibeltext und Bibelreform unter Karl dem Grossen', in *Karl der Grosse. Lebenswerk und Nachleben II: Das geistige Leben*, ed. B. Bischoff (Düsseldorf, 1965), 156–216. See also his 'Bibelausgaben des frühen Mittelalters', *La Bibbia nell'alto Medioevo*, Settimane di Studio del Centro Italiano di Studi sull'alto medioevo x (Spoleto, 1963), 519–600 and *Die Alkuin-Bibel*, Vetus Latina 1 (Freiburg, 1957).

[2] CLA v, 693a and b, and Fischer, 'Bibeltext und Bibelreform', 174.

[3] H. L. Kessler, *The Illustrated Bibles from Tours*, Studies in Manuscript Illumination 7 (Princeton, 1977).

[4] I discuss the idea of 'export quality' script in 'Carolingian Book Production: Some Problems', *The Library*, 6th series, 12 (1990), 1–33.

The possible influence of the Tours Bible, therefore, could be exerted in three different spheres: firstly in the actual text; secondly in the order of the books, the definition of the scriptural canon and the chapter divisions and headings; and thirdly in the physical format and layout.

A scriptorium's work in copying a particular text thereby propagates that version of the text. Palaeography and text are interdependent and cannot be considered in isolation from each other. Let us first, therefore, examine the question of Alcuin's text. Inflated claims have been made for the extent of its influence and for the degree to which Tours dominated the market in Carolingian Bibles. Raphael Loewe, for example, in his authoritative survey of the development of the medieval Vulgate in the *Cambridge History of the Bible*, while emphasising that 'the textual influence of Alcuin's Bible was less widespread than its external features and it is to these and not to any *official* sponsorship that is due the prominence which Alcuin's text came to enjoy throughout the [Carolingian] Empire', went on to assert that the 'Vulgate was henceforth to be, effectively, Alcuin's text'. Loewe acknowledged what he described as the 'conservatism of monastic scriptoria [which is] demonstrated by the continued production of pre-Alcuinian and mixed Alcuinian texts', but he nevertheless suggested that the 'sedulous introduction of Alcuinian corrections indicates that the strictly Alcuinian text was, by the late ninth century, coming to be regarded as a norm'.[5] This is cautiously worded, it is true, but the fact remains that Loewe cites only one specific manuscript, British Library, Harley 2797, written at Ste Geneviève in Paris, to support this conclusion. There are, of course, others, as Fischer has made clear.[6] We know, for example, that Chelles adopted the Alcuin Bible almost immediately, hardly surprising in view of the relationship between Alcuin and Abbess Gisela.[7] Extensive, though not exclusive, use, moreover, was made of the Alcuinian Bible at St Gall in the time of Abbot Hartmut, a use perhaps encouraged by the connection between St Gall and Tours represented by the fact that Abbot Grimald, Hartmut's predecessor, had studied at Tours under Alcuin. St Gall, Stiftsbibliothek 75, the earliest Tours pandect extant, certainly appears to have reached St Gall by the mid-ninth century, and many subsequent biblical texts produced in the St Gall scriptorium show evidence of its inspiration.[8] Other centres such as Rheims, Corbie, Amiens, Salzburg, Mondsee and Fleury, and the north Frankish centre which produced the Bible of *c.* 822, Paris, Bibliothèque Nationale, lat. 11504–5, clearly made sporadic use of the Alcuinian text but usually alongside others.[9] The last named volumes, for example, followed the Alcuin Bible in the arrangement of books, prologues, summaries and text introductions, but the text of Proverbs was a mixture of Alcuin and Theodulf, while much of the remainder of the book is *Vulgata* with Old Latin versions of Tobit and Judith

[5] R. Loewe, 'The Medieval History of the Latin Vulgate', *The Cambridge History of the Bible II: The West from the Fathers to the Reformation*, ed. G. W. H. Lampe (Cambridge, 1969), 102–54.
[6] Fischer, 'Bibeltext und Bibelreform'.
[7] *Ibid.*, 184, evidenced in Châlons-sur-Marne, Archives de la Marne, 3 J 1 (I, 10) and Oxford, Bodleian Library, Douce 176 (CLA II, 238).
[8] Fischer, 'Bibeltext und Bibelreform', 206.   [9] *Ibid.*, 174–5.

(which agree with the so-called Bible of St Riquier), and of James and I Peter. A Spanish text type is followed for the Octateuch.[10] Vienna, Österreichische National-bibliothek, lat. 1190, possibly written for Abbot Rado of Saint Vaast (808–15), betrays some Alcuin influence in its text, but the order of the books is neither Alcuinian nor Theodulfian.[11] The court school of Charlemagne, on the other hand, drew on an entirely different, non-Alcuinian, set of texts.[12] The fact that the scholastic Paris Bible text of the thirteenth century was 'basically' the text of Alcuin does not necessarily prove that Alcuin's text was widespread, nor that it was the outcome of a universal acceptance of Alcuin's text before the twelfth century. It is rather a consequence of its selection from those available within the region in which the Paris Bible later became current; possibly, too, because it represented the text of Jerome and therefore patristic authority. Due to the problems of mass production, the Paris Bible itself was subject to much variation, and only in the canonical order of the books and revised chapter divisions did it achieve uniformity and enjoy widespread influence – largely as a consequence of the reputation of the Paris schools and the work of the exegetes themselves.[13]

The wealth of Carolingian Bible production seems to indicate, in fact, that what Loewe describes as 'sedulous introduction of Alcuinian corrections' is a massive overstatement of the case, at odds with Fischer's view of the limited influence exerted by Alcuin's text and unjustified in terms of the extant evidence. This is particularly important in relation to our assessment of the recognised rival edition produced at the same time as Alcuin, namely, that of Theodulf of Orléans.[14] Loewe's assertion concerning Theodulf's edition of the Bible, for example, must be challenged. Loewe claimed that it suffered from the competition of the contemporary, more precisely planned and successfully disseminated Alcuinian version, despite the survival of the Theodulfian edition in twelfth- and thirteenth-century Paris Bibles. It simply does not follow that *as a result* (my emphasis) of Theodulf's Bible succumbing to the superiority of Alcuin's Bible (in itself a questionable notion) manuscripts containing Theodulf's Bible are not numerous and its influence was not great. This is an entirely circular argument, and it takes insufficient account in any case of the impressive degree of organisation, didactic intent and achievement, not to mention the sheer profession-alism and elegance, of the substantial group of Theodulfian Bibles produced under his supervision.

---

[10] *Ibid.*, 189.　　[11] *Ibid.*, 184–5.

[12] These are clearly analysed in W. Koehler, *Die karolingische Miniaturen II: Die Hofschule Karls des Grossen* (Berlin, 1958) and III: *Die Gruppe des Wiener Krönungsevangeliars. Metzer Handschriften* (Berlin, 1960).

[13] Loewe, 'The Medieval History', 147, and cf. Laura Light on the Paris Bibles, ch. 8 below.

[14] Fully discussed by E. Dahlhaus-Berg, *Nova antiquitas et antiqua novitas. Typologische Exegese und isidorianisches Geschichtsbild bei Theodulf von Orléans* (Cologne, 1975), esp. 39–76. Theodulf's biblical citations have also been analysed by Ann Freeman in the course of establishing Theodulf's authorship of the *Libri Carolini*: 'Theodulf of Orléans and the *Libri Carolini*', *Speculum* 32 (1957), 663–705; 'Further Studies in the *Libri Carolini*. I. Palaeographical problems in Vaticanus Latinus 7207. II. Patristic Exegesis, Mozarabic Antiphons, and the Vetus Latina', *Speculum* 40 (1965), 203–89; 'III. The Marginal Notes in Vaticanus Latinus 7207', *Speculum* 46 (1971), 597–612. See also P. Meyvaert, 'The Authorship of the *Libri Carolini*: Observations Prompted by a recent book', *Révue Bénédictine* 89 (1979), 29–57.

It is perhaps unfair to pick on Loewe. I do so, however, to highlight the tenuousness of the current orthodoxy on Carolingian Bible production which his article summarises. It must be admitted, too, that demonstrating the extent to which an assumption of the Alcuinian text's influence is unwarranted is fraught with difficulties, due primarily to the dearth of detailed work on Bible texts in use in the Carolingian world. Time after time in Fischer's list of Bibles produced in the early Carolingian period he adds the note that the text of a particular Bible manuscript has not been investigated.[15] In Hartmut Hoffmann's magisterial survey of tenth-century manuscripts there is a considerable number of biblical texts, notably Gospels, and one full Bible, Berlin, Deutsche Staatsbibliothek theol. lat. fol. 336, and these texts also need further research.[16] It is not only the exact nature of extant Bible texts, whether pandects, separate books or groups of books such as the Psalter, Apocalypse, Pentateuch, Prophets, Gospels or Pauline and Catholic Epistles that are often unknown. We also do not know precisely which texts were employed for the abundance of gospel and epistle lectionaries, in sacramentaries and other liturgical books, nor by individual Carolingian scholars in their exegesis of scripture.[17] We have to bear in mind, too, that these scholars were dependent on earlier patristic authors who themselves may not necessarily have used the Hieronymian redaction of the Bible exclusively, if at all. Where we do have information, in the case of no less a scholar than Alcuin himself, we find that he did not use his own pandect text of St John in his commentary on this Gospel, for there is evidence of different readings in his citations.[18] Theodulf of Orléans, on the other hand, is the Carolingian scholar whose version of and citations from the Bible have been the most rigorously studied, particularly in his work on images in the *Libri Carolini*.[19] What we need is knowledge about Carolingian scholars comparable to that which we now possess about Theodulf.

Obviously a proper understanding of the Bible in the ninth century will only be possible once such identification has been done. Noting the place of a particular manuscript within the text tradition to which it belongs is, indeed, one of the criteria for describing a manuscript all too seldom observed. It is an urgent desideratum for all those responsible for cataloguing Carolingian manuscripts, whether for sale, for libraries or in their own scholarly work, to endeavour to identify to which recension

---

[15] Fischer, 'Bibeltext und Bibelreform' and see also his collected studies, *Beiträge zur Geschichte der lateinischen Bibeltexte* (Freiburg, 1986), especially 'Das Neue Testament in lateinischen Sprache', 156–274.

[16] H. Hoffmann, *Buchkunst und Königtum im ottonischen und frühsalischen Reich*, Schriften der MGH, Band 30, 1 (Stuttgart, 1986). The Berlin Bible, of Werden provenance, is equipped with didactic additions drawn from patristic and Carolingian commentaries and merits further examination for what it may reveal of Ottonian Bible study.

[17] M. L. W. Laistner, *The Intellectual Heritage of the Early Middle Ages* (New York, 1972) has useful studies of commentaries on the Old Testament and St Matthew in the early Middle Ages which identify their use of patristic authors but do not speculate on the precise text of the Bible used. For an excellent survey of Carolingian Bible study see J. J. Contreni, 'Carolingian Biblical Studies', *Carolingian Essays. Andrew W. Mellon Lectures in Early Christian Studies*, ed. U.-R. Blumenthal (Washington DC, 1983), 71–98.

[18] Noted by P. Corssen, *Die Trierer Ada-Handschrift* (Leipzig, 1889), 59 and reiterated by Fischer, 'Bibeltext und Bibelreform', 174.

[19] See n. 14 above.

each particular Bible text belongs as a matter of course, bearing in mind the necessity to distinguish between spelling differences and mistakes, and actual variants.[20]

Given these imprecisions, let me rehearse in outline what is known about Bibles other than that of Alcuin in the Carolingian period. In the first place, Tours was not the first, nor the only, centre to embark on the production of a corrected, let alone an edited, text of the Bible in the early Carolingian period. In fact, Alcuin's rather minimal effort, with spelling and grammar regularised, was only one among many others, often, as in the case of that of Theodulf of Orléans, far more scholarly and intelligent. Indeed, the work of Bonifatius Fischer and his predecessors has amply demonstrated the enormous variety of Bible texts and combinations of particular variants of particular books.[21] Almost everywhere where there were any pretensions to intellectual life, there appears to have been an effort to produce a Bible text, drawing on every available text to do so, which included both local and imported exemplars.

Not only is there the familiar rival to Alcuin's Bible, that is the version of Theodulf of Orléans produced under his supervision and possibly in the scriptorium of St Mesmin de Micy; there is also the less familiar one (as far as its text, as distinct from its innovative letter forms, is concerned) produced by Maurdramnus of Corbie in several volumes now in Amiens (Bibliothèque Municipale, MSS 6, 7, 9, 11 and 12, and Paris, Bibliothèque Nationale, lat. 13174 fols. 136 and 138) and apparently based on local biblical texts to hand.[22] Fischer even went so far as to suggest that the Maurdramnus minuscule (the earliest datable pure Caroline minuscule) used for this Bible was actually evolved deliberately as a new Bible script, though the implications of this suggestion for the development of Caroline minuscule have not yet, so far as I know, been fully explored.[23] Corbie continued to produce this text or texts close to it, not least the so-called Corbie Bible (Paris, Bibliothèque Nationale, lat. 11532–3) of the mid-ninth century, though in this there is influence from both the Alcuinian and Theodulfian redactions.[24] That the Marudramnus text itself exerted some influence is suggested by the splendid tenth-century Pentateuch which was at St Peter's (or St Lucain), Beauvais by the twelfth century. Formerly in the Phillipps library (2860), it was sold at Sotheby's on 21st November, 1972, and is now in a private collection in Switzerland. The text shows a remarkable affinity with that of the Maurdramnus Bible and suggests that as far as Corbie and its region was concerned, the Alcuinian version was of minor importance.

The famous Metz pandect, Bibliothèque Municipale, 7, destroyed in 1944, which preserved the Old Latin rather than the Jerome translation of Tobit, manifests various other signs of independence. It is worth noting that the text, apart from Tobit, is

---

[20] As Koehler does in such exemplary fashion in *Die karolingischen Miniaturen* (Berlin, 1935–), especially in vols. II and III devoted to the court school manuscripts of Charlemagne.

[21] Fischer, 'Bibeltext und Bibelreform' and, notably, S. Berger, *Histoire de la Vulgate pendant les premiers siècles du moyen âge* (Paris, 1893).

[22] CLA VI, 707.

[23] Fischer, 'Bibeltext und Bibelreform', 186, and cf. Stanley Morison, 'Notes on the development of Latin script', in *Selected Essays on the History of Letter-Forms in Manuscript and Print*, ed. D. McKitterick, 2 vols. (Cambridge, 1981) I, 250–3.

[24] Berger, *Histoire*, 104–8.

connected with that of the Ada group of manuscripts, as is that of the Lorsch Bibles, of which we now have a magnificent fragment (Book 2:13–4:19), Oslo, Schøyen Collection 617, in addition to the evidence that is already well known.[25]

Fischer has described, for the early Carolingian period at least, the different Bible recensions made in Brittany, Fleury, Paris, Chelles, northern France, Corbie, St Riquier, St Vaast, St Bertin, Cambrai, St Amand, Laon, Rheims, Metz, eastern France, Trier, the court at Aachen, the Rhine-Maas region, the Anglo-Saxon missionary centres such as Echternach, Werden, Fulda, Würzburg and Mainz, and East Frankish and Alemannian monasteries such as Lorsch, Schuttern, Murbach, St Gall, Reichenau and Chur, as well as in the different centres in Bavaria such as Augsburg, Regensburg, Freising, Benediktbeuern, Tegernsee, Salzburg, Mondsee and Kremsmünster, not to mention those of northern Italy such as Biasca, Monza, Milan, Bobbio, Verona and Ravenna and of central Italy and Monte Cassino.[26] Such diversity clearly demonstrates the many responses to the need for an accurate and a reliable Bible text in the Carolingian world, and how Tours was simply one of very many in this.

One can point in detail to such attempts at producing a Bible text as Paris, Bibliothèque Nationale, lat. 11553, probably written at St Germain-des-Prés in the early-ninth century, which was possibly a copy of a north Italian pandect though some Old Latin readings are added.[27] Even in the Paris region itself, uniformity was not achieved, for a different Bible text was produced at St Denis, represented, for example, by Vatican City, Biblioteca Apostolica Vaticana, Reg. lat. 7 of the mid-ninth century.[28] Some centres appear to favour the Theodulf Bible as much as the Alcuinian. Alternatively, at the very least, as in the case of Paris, Bibliothèque Nationale, lat. 2 from St Amand, the manuscripts display knowledge and use of the Theodulf Bible.[29] Others are simply composites of the various Frankish, Italian and Spanish recensions available in Gaul before the Carolingian period and based on similar texts to those used by Alcuin and Theodulf. Examples are the Stuttgart Psalter produced at St Germain-des-Prés in the 820s,[30] the Poitiers Gospels, Poitiers, Bibliothèque Municipale, 17, of the late-eighth century put together from a

---

[25] Metz pandect, CLA VI, 786 and see Fischer, 'Bibeltext und Bibelreform', 191–2. For the Schøyen fragment see *Bookhands of the Middle Ages: Part V, Medieval Manuscript Leaves*, Bernard Quaritch Catalogue 1147 (London, 1991), 7–8, with plate.

[26] Fischer, 'Bibeltext und Bibelreform' with full details of the manuscripts and references.

[27] Fischer, 'Bibelausgaben', 576–86.

[28] Fischer, 'Bibeltext und Bibelreform', 183–4.

[29] As the manuscript was a gift to Charles the Bald from Abbot Gauzlin of St Amand, who was also bishop of Paris, the text of this Bible is of more than incidental interest and might be associated with a continuing interest in the promotion of a particular Bible text on the part of the Frankish kings. On the context see R. McKitterick, 'Charles the Bald (823–877) and His Library: The Patronage of Learning', *English Historical Review* 95 (1980), 29–47 and 'Royal Patronage of Culture in the Frankish Kingdoms under the Carolingians: Motives and Consequences', *Committenti e produzione artistico-letteraria nel'alto medioevo occidentale, Settimane di Studio del centro Italiano di Studi sull'alto Medioevo* 39 (Spoleto, 1992), 93–129.

[30] Stuttgart, Württembergische Landesbibliothek, Bibl. fol. 23 and see the full account of the text in *Der Stuttgarter Bilderpsalter. Bibl. Fol. 23 der Württembergischen Landesbibliothek*, ed. B. Bischoff *et al.*, 2 vols. (Stuttgart, 1965–8).

number of different versions,[31] the Trier Apocalypse,[32] and the two-volume 'St Riquier Bible', Paris, Bibliothèque Nationale, lat. 45 and 93, whose Old Testament follows a Spanish type even though the New Testament follows Alcuin.[33]

It would seem from this impressive catalogue that, in accordance with the *Admonitio Generalis*' identification of the need for correct texts of the catholic books used for the Christian religion in 789,[34] many centres in the Carolingian world were working to produce a correct Bible text within the means at their disposal. As we have seen, a few in due course made some use of the Alcuin Bible text, others of the Theodulfian, still others of both, but some, perhaps most, in so far as can be determined from the work so far done, were more or less independent from the Alcuinian version.

It is, moreover, not only the early Carolingian period that was one of *biblica mixta*; it is clear from surviving manuscripts that despite the production of the Alcuinian text, many centres remained attached to their own local or regional texts; the diversity of Bible texts consulted, cited and produced appears to have continued throughout the Carolingian period. Look, for example, at the continued production of the Old Latin versions of the New Testament, for the most part mixed with other texts. Of the eighty-seven different manuscripts which represent witnesses to the Old Latin version in one form or another listed by Metzger, those from the Carolingian regions dating from the end of the eighth century or later number no less than fourteen.[35] They are:

St Gall, Stiftsbibliothek, 48, s. ix (St Gall) (Gospels)

St Petersburg, Saltykov-Scedrin State Public Library, O. v. I. 3, s. viii (Corbie) Matthew predominantly Vulgate[36]

Paris, Bibliothèque Nationale, lat. 13169, s. x (?St Germain), Gospels

Vatican City, Biblioteca Apostolica Vaticana, Pal. lat. 177, s. viii/ix from Lorsch, Jerome *In Mattheum* with OL sections of Matthew[37]

Vendôme, Bibliothèque Municipale, 2, s. x, citations from Gospels in Eusebian canon tables.

---

[31] CLA vi, 821, probably written in Amiens for Bishop Jesse (799–836) and indicative therefore of his interest in provision of a text of the Bible.

[32] Trier, Stadtbibliothek, 31, see *Die Trierer Apokalypse*, ed. R. Laufner and P. K. Klein, 2 vols. (Graz, 1975).

[33] Fischer, 'Bibeltext und Bibelreform', 188–9. This Bible was not produced in St Riquier, however, but in Paris 820/840, perhaps in St Denis. Fischer, furthermore, has indicated the possibility, raised by the list of relics, that production may have been in a convent of nuns, of which Argenteuil is a likely possibility. Although he then dismisses this on the grounds that a group of women are hardly to be credited with the editing work of the text manifest in these codices, there may be supporting parallel evidence of female scholarship to make the indications not as absurd as Fischer assumed. See, for example, R. McKitterick, 'Frauen und Schriftlichkeit im Frühmittelalter', in *Weibliche Lebensgestaltung im frühen Mittelalter*, ed. H.-W. Goetz (Cologne, 1991), 65–118. The text of Düsseldorf, Universitätsbibliothek, A 14, the Epistles of Paul, is related to Paris, Bibliothèque Nationale, lat. 45 and 93, and there may therefore be a connection between the different convents underlying this, and thus an active and productive interest in the text of the Bible on the part of some nuns and canonesses in associated centres that has in any case, already been remarked at Chelles by B. Bischoff, 'Die Kölner Nonnenhandschriften und das Skriptorium von Chelles', *Mittelalterliche Studien* 1 (Stuttgart, 1966), 16–33, esp. 27.

[34] MGH, *Capitularia* i, No. 22, c. 72, pp. 59–60.

[35] B. Metzger, *The Early Versions of the New Testament. Their Origin, Transmission and Limitations* (Oxford, 1977), esp. 293–319.

[36] CLA xi, 1624.   [37] CLA i, 79.

Poitiers, Bibliothèque Municipale, 17, s. viii ex, from Amiens, citations from
  Gospels in Eusebian canon tables[38]
St Petersburg, Saltykov-Scedrin State Public Library, F. v. 20, Graeco-Latin
  Pauline Epistles
Cambridge, Trinity College Library, B. 17. 1, s. ix, St Gall, Graeco-Latin Pauline
  Epistles
Dresden, Landesbibliothek, A. 145b, s. ix, Pauline Epistles, twin of Trinity B. 17. 1
Paris, Bibliothèque Nationale, lat. 653, *c.* 800, from N. Italy, fragment of Hebrews[39]
Oxford, Bodleian Library, Laud lat. 108, s. viii/ix, Pauline Epistles
Munich, Bayerische Staatsbibliothek, Clm 29055a, s. ix, Schaftlarn, fragment of
  Hebrews
Monza, Biblioteca Capitolare, 1–2/9, s. ix/x, portions of Pauline Epistles
St Petersburg, Saltykov-Scedrin State Public Library, Q. v. I. 39, s. ix, Corbie,
  Epistle of James

Some of the remaining manuscripts, for the most part dating between the fourth and
the eighth centuries, appear to have been owned by, or present in, active Carolingian
centres. Cases in point are St Gall, Stiftsbibliothek, 1394, a seventh-century copy of St
John's Gospel, and Paris, Bibliothèque Nationale, lat. 6400G, fols. 113–30 (Acts,
Catholic Epistles and Revelation) possibly written in Italy in the fifth century but later
at Fleury (in palimpsest).[40] Presumably, therefore, such volumes were in a position to
continue to exert an influence on a Bible text in use in that particular monastery. Old
phrases and particular renderings of sections of the biblical text could thus have
remained a familiar and habitual element in the regular readings and worship of a
community.

So far I have outlined the present state of knowledge about texts of the Bible
available and in use in the Carolingian world, indicated its deficiencies and suggested
that it is incorrect to accept the current assumptions concerning the triumph and
influence of Alcuin's Bible. But how are we to account for this extraordinary
assumption, of which I have to say I have been as guilty as everyone else up till now,
of superiority and success on the part of Alcuin's recension?[41] It can only be due to
the sheer impressiveness and quantity of Tours Bible production. Consequently, in so
far as is possible given the deficient state of present knowledge, not least my own, I
wish to spend the rest of this paper exploring the general nature of Tours Bible
production and its implications in the context of Carolingian Bible production as a
whole.

First, we need to determine whether there are any special features of the production
and distribution of Tours Bibles which may throw light on the actual, as distinct from
the supposed, 'market' for this particular text. On the face of it, Tours Bible
production is certainly impressive. Tours produced a remarkable number of
one-volume Bibles or pandects – apparently the favoured format for the Alcuin

---

[38] CLA vi, 821.   [39] CLA v, 527.   [40] CLA vii, 978a and CLA v, 564a.
[41] R. McKitterick, 'Carolingian Book Production', 30–1.

Bible text – in the course of three or four decades in the first half of the ninth century.[42]

Two pandects can probably be dated to Alcuin's own time, St Gall Stiftsbibliothek, 75, and Monza, Biblioteca Capitolare, G. 1, as well as three gospel books and a Psalter.[43] These are, however, very modest and far from organised or uniform in appearance. It is in the abbacy of Fridugisus (807–34) that the distinctive format for the Tours Bibles was developed. The relevant volumes include:

Basle, Universitätsbibliothek, A. N. I. 3 (Bible fragment)

Bern, Burgerbibliothek, 3–4 (Bible)

London, British Library, Add. 11848 (Gospels)

London, British Library, Harley 2805 (Bible)

New York, Pierpont Morgan Library, Morgan 191 (Gospels)

Oslo, Martin Schøyen collection, 624 (Bible fragment – Ezekiel)

Paris, Bibliothèque Nationale, lat. 25 (New Testament)

Paris, Bibliothèque Nationale, lat. 68 (Bible)

Paris, Bibliothèque Nationale, lat. 11514 (Bible fragment)

Stuttgart, Württembergische Landesbibliothek, HB. II. 40 (Gospels)

Zürich, Zentralbibliothek, C. 1 (Bible)

Unfortunately, the immediate destination of these Bibles is uncertain. It may be the case that St Gall, Stiftsbibliothek, 75, for example, was actually copied for St Gall, but we are only certain of its being there from the mid-ninth century onwards, that is, half a century after its completion. The provenance of the Zürich Bible can only be established from the end of the thirteenth century when it was in the library of the Dominicans in Zürich.[44] Only from the sheer quantity of Tours Bibles of uniform format, from their later provenance and as I have suggested elsewhere, from the quality of script, 'export script', employed for their production, can we surmise that these Bibles were produced for export rather than for home use.[45]

We are in a slightly stronger position with the magnificent Bibles and splendid gospel books surviving from the time of the lay abbots Adalhard (834–43) and Vivian (844–51). Paris, Bibliothèque Nationale, lat. 3, the Rorigo Bible, appears to have been a gift from Count Rorigo to Glanfeuil and was presumably commissioned for this purpose,[46] London, British Library, Add. 10546, the Moutier Grandval Bible, may

---

[42] For full details on these manuscripts see L. Delisle, 'Mémoire sur l'école calligraphique de Tours au IXe siècle', *Mémoires de l'Institut national de France. Académie des Inscriptions et Belles-lettres* 32 (1886) 29–56; E. K. Rand, *A Survey of the Manuscripts of Tours. Studies in the Script of Tours* 1 (Cambridge Mass., 1929); W. Koehler, *Die karolingischen Miniaturen I: Die Schule von Tours*, 2 vols. (Berlin, 1930–3) and Kessler, *The Illustrated Bibles from Tours*.

[43] Paris, Bibliothèque Nationale, lat. 260 and 17227, and London, British Library, Harley 2760 (Gospels) and Harley 2793 (Psalter).

[44] M. Germann, 'Die Karolingische Bibel aus Tours. Ein Monument der Minuskelschrift um 825/30', *Zentralbibliothek Zürich. Schatzkammer der Überlieferung*, ed. A. Cattani and B. Weber (Zürich, 1989), 11–13, and Anhang 141–4.

[45] R. McKitterick, 'Carolingian Book Production', 30–1.

[46] Berger, *Histoire*, 214.

have been copied for that monastery,[47] the Gospels in Nancy, Nancy Trésor de la Cathédrale (Arnaldus Gospels), were arguably commissioned for the cathedral,[48] Bamberg, Staatsbibliothek, Bibl. 1, the Bamberg Bible, was the gift of Henry II to Bamberg and may therefore have been in royal or lay ownership before that.[49] Paris, Bibliothèque Nationale, lat. 1, the First Bible of Charles the Bald, was actually presented to the king by Count Vivian in about 846,[50] and certain Gospel Books, such as the Prüm Gospels (Berlin, Deutsche Staatsbibliothek, theol. lat. fol. 733) and the Lothar Gospels (Paris, Bibliothèque Nationale, lat. 266) seem also to have been destined for royal patrons.[51] We can only guess at the original destinations for some of the other volumes, such as the gospel books, Paris, Bibliothèque Nationale, lat. 274, Wolfenbüttel, Herzog-August Bibliothek, 2186, Basle, Universitätsbibliothek, B. II. 11, St Petersburg, Saltykov-Scedrin State Public Library, Q. v. I. 21, Laon, Bibliothèque Municipale, 63 or Paris, Bibliothèque Nationale, lat. 9385.

The extant Bibles with an Alcuinian text which were not produced at Tours may provide witnesses to the dissemination of this text from places other than Tours. The volumes in question are Rome, Biblioteca Vallicelliana, B. 6, possibly from Rheims;[52] the Bible of San Paolo fuori le Mura, Rome (the Third Bible of Charles the Bald) also possibly produced at Rheims and presented to Charles the Bald *c*. 870;[53] Cologne, Dombibliothek, 1, presented to Cologne by Archbishop Hermann (890–925);[54] Vienna, Österreichische Nationalbibliothek, lat. 1190; and Angers, Bibliothèque Municipale, 1–2.[55] Some of these, too, seem to have been destined, at least in the case of the San Paolo Bible, for wealthy patrons, whether clerical or lay. The Angers Bible, however, looks more modest and ordinary than the others, which may indicate that it had a practical, everyday liturgical function rather than being a book reserved on the altar as a sacred, seldom-used, holy symbol.[56]

Although unfortunately we do not know where all these manuscripts were produced, the fact that only a very few centres actually produced a pure, as distinct from a mixed, Alcuinian text, is nevertheless clear. This reinforces our impression that the direct influence exerted by Tours was quite limited. One might compare, too, the case of the Theodulf Bibles. Although in terms of quantity, Tours far surpassed Micy in the production of Bibles, the essentially limited copying of the pure text outside the

---

[47] *Ibid.*, 209–11.   [48] *Ibid.*, 248–9.

[49] On its earlier provenance P. E. Schramm and F. Mütherich, *Denkmale der deutschen Könige und Kaiser I: Ein Beitrag zur Herrschergeschichte von Karl dem Grossen bis Friedrich II*, 2nd edn (Munich, 1981), no. 128, p. 162, and pl. 128.

[50] See R. McKitterick, 'Charles the Bald and His Library'.

[51] See, for example, D. Bullough, '*Imagines regum* and Their Significance in the Early Medieval West', in *Studies in Memory of David Talbot Rice*, ed. G. Robertson and G. Henderson (Edinburgh, 1975), 223–77, at 223.

[52] Fischer, 'Bibeltext und Bibelreform', 181.

[53] See J. Ghaede, 'The Bible of San Paolo fuori le Mura in Rome: Its Date and Relation to Charles the Bald', *Gesta* 5 (1966), 9–21 and E. Kantorowicz, 'The Carolingian King in the Bible of San Paolo fuori le Mura', *Late Classical and Medieval Studies in Honor of Albert Matthias Friend Jnr* (Princeton, 1955), 287–300.

[54] Berger, *Histoire*, 212–13.

[55] Fischer, 'Bibeltext und Bibelreform', 174.

[56] Compare my comments on the dissemination of texts in 'Royal Patronage of Culture'.

home centre is very similar.[57] Yet, as David Ganz has stressed, Tours' export of Bibles to other centres indicates the serving of particular interests outside Tours.[58]

Tours Bibles certainly witness to the dissemination of the text, but their provenance and original destination suggest rather more than this. Given the fact that the Tours Bibles extant are those written for export, and the chance nature of their survival, it is reasonable to suppose that these survivors represent but a portion of what Tours once produced. They witness to a Bible produced in prodigious quantities but for a specific and limited market. I suggest that it is possible to make a distinction between the lavish and expensive gospel books and Bible texts that Tours copied for export, produced in such a way as to mark them immediately as Tours products on the one hand, and the texts produced on the basis of appreciation of the Alcuinian text, using it as one of the local or available base texts from which to construct a Bible on the other. Tours exported grand Biblical codices, and its scriptorium was organised in such a way as to enable one part of its activities to be devoted to the provision of a particular text on a remarkably lavish scale. It is important to appreciate the significance of the original commission for many of these books, such as the Bibles for Charles the Bald, the Gospels for Lothar and the various volumes prepared as munificent gifts for cathedrals or wealthy monasteries. Tours Bibles in some respects therefore represent the Fabergé eggs of Carolingian book production.

Nevertheless, Tours endeavoured to disseminate a Tours text as well as a Tours book. It is simply because the books were for such a small and wealthy élite that the text had in fact such limited impact. When one compares Tours Bibles with the biblical texts produced elsewhere, not least such products as Angers, Bibliothèque Municipale, 1 and 2, the Tours Bibles stand out as exceptional in their grandeur of format and lavishness of production. Two comparable non-Tours pandects, on the other hand, as far as size and magnificence are concerned, were also made for a wealthy patron, namely, King Charles the Bald, at Rheims and at St Amand respectively (San Paolo fuori le Mura and Paris, Bibliothèque Nationale, lat. 2).[59]

To suggest that the business of supplying a restricted and wealthy market limited the actual dissemination of the Alcuinian Bible text is not to deny that Tours may well have wished the Alcuinian Bible to become the normal text in use in the Carolingian world. Nevertheless, allowing ourselves to be dazzled by the magnificence of the *format* in which Alcuinian texts survive has misled us into an overestimation of the extent of the *text*'s influence. The received view has rested on too imprecise and impressionistic a knowledge of the Alcuinian version of the Vulgate and its dissemination; it was based on an inadequate understanding of the influence and standing of Tours' place in relation to Carolingian book production as a whole; it extrapolated, without any justification whatsoever, from the finest and in consequence probably the least typical examples of Carolingian Bible production to generalise about the production of biblical manuscripts at all levels and in all regions; it assumed

---

[57] Dahlhaus-Berg, *Nova antiquitas*, 39–76.   [58] See ch. 3 above.
[59] For the circumstances see R. McKitterick, 'Charles the Bald and His Library'.

that a normal and uniform text was required by the Carolingians, and it has made us seek to recognise such a normal text in the Bible from Tours.

Should we in fact be thinking of a uniform text as a concept accepted by the Carolingians? On the contrary, are we not bound to acknowledge the strength of local use and familiarity as far as the Bible text is concerned? Although in many respects uniformity of text over the entire Carolingian empire was attempted in the case of sacramentaries or mass books, of homiliaries, of the Gospels and epistle lectionaries, of canon law and, in the reign of Louis the Pious, of the Rule of Benedict, in practice we know how much diversity of text and usage remained. The emphasis was on *correctio* and *emendatio* rather than on complete *unitas*, which simply was not and probably could not have been achieved.

There are, notwithstanding these great limitations, other ways in which the Alcuin Bibles of Tours could exert an influence, if only by way of establishing precedents and workable models. One way to explore this would be to investigate the evidence for the adoption of the Alcuinian organisation and sequence of books and to see how this became accepted in due course as the definitive arrangement of the scriptural canon. Unfortunately, insufficient precise information about Carolingian Bibles and parts of Bibles is as yet available for conclusions to be drawn on this matter.

Another possible area in which Tour Bibles could have exerted an influence was in that of format. Is the distinctive format of the Tours Bibles found elsewhere? It is essential to bear in mind that resolving the problems of presenting a lengthy text in a one-volume format may be very similar in different centres, yet such resolution may nevertheless be independent. Thus one would need to look for precise adoption of the Tours 50–52 line two-column arrangement to be certain that Tours' example was being followed. On format I shall be brief, for David Ganz has already provided an admirable exposition of the principal features of a Tours Bible.[60]

Both the Zürich and the Moutier Grandval Bibles can be taken as the standard or classic format for the Tours Bible. Their massive one-volume format, with 50–52 lines, was adopted for the non-Touronian copies of pure Alcuinian texts. Elsewhere, however, as in the case of the Theodulf Bibles, a very different size and format was adopted. Theodulf arranged the text in three (later two) columns of tiny writing in a page of modest size, apparently far more suited to private study. Parallels have been drawn between Theodulf's design and the Cava Bible produced in Spain in the mid-ninth century, with the suggestion that the three-column small-format Bible was an earlier Spanish idea. The influence, however, may have run the other way – directly from Theodulf to some centre in northern Spain.[61] Alternatively, as in the case of the Metz Bible, which may have antedated Tours production, a large format was adopted with fewer lines of writing on the page.[62] The designers of other Bibles

---

[60] See ch. 3 above.

[61] La Cava dei Tirreni, Biblioteca della Badia, ms. memb. I, illustrated in J. Williams, *Early Spanish Manuscript Illumination* (London, 1977), pls. 1 and 2, pp. 40–3.

[62] Metz, Bibliothèque Municipale, 7, CLA VI, 786, destroyed in 1944 though full-size photographs of the entire manuscript exist in the abbey of S. Girolamo in Rome.

chose to have more lines, and even as many as 60, as in the case of the Second Bible of Charles the Bald from St Amand.[63] The St Amand Bible is in fact a crucially important book to consider. With its extensive use of prologues, running titles and hierarchy of scripts to set out the text as clearly as possible, it establishes beyond doubt that Tours had no monopoly of intelligence when it came to the presentation of scripture. Whether St Amand's example was emulated among Franco-Saxon centres or further afield remains to be established. Other disciplined and well-organised scriptoria could evidently achieve a similar mastery of the problems presented by the sheer magnitude of the task of copying the whole Bible, or indeed smaller units of biblical books, and making them visually accessible to the reader.

The consequence of the generous proportions of Tours' design is of course an enormous, heavy and cumbersome volume, even though the layout and script is wonderfully clear. The large format might preclude any notion of private study, though we cannot assume from our own difficulties in studying these Bibles that private study was not envisaged. Every effort has been made in the Tours Bibles to ensure ease of reference. The principal impression, in fact, is of the overwhelmingly didactic nature of the lay-out, with the summaries of the purport of each book set out at the beginning with enlarged letters, the list of the books in the Bible in the sequence determined by Alcuin, the deployment of different scripts to make certain portions of the text – *capitula*, prologues and headings – stand out, the running titles, so that one always knows exactly where one is within the text and the clear divisions of the text itself, enhanced by the use of initials and the hierarchy of scripts.[64] Various key passages in the text are made to stand out, such as the Ten Commandments and the Beatitudes. The Commandments in the Moutier Grandval Bible, for example, are each given red capital letters. In the Moutier Grandval Bible, furthermore, the presentation of the text is immaculate, with even columns, measured and elegant script, line ends practically justified and each letter separated. Words are not quite so clearly separated from each other, and in places the text reads as *scriptura continua*. Presumably to the practised *lector* this would present no difficulties, for the text would, after all, be familiar. One should, however, be wary of anachronistic assumptions concerning layout and punctuation in relation to reading out loud.[65] We simply do not know enough about the process of reading aloud to discard such indications as the manuscript itself may afford us of a scribe's intention as far as oral communication of his writing was concerned. Given that the text is didactic in its presentation and was easy to follow as far as its general structure was concerned, it might be more plausible to suggest that the didactic function was a public rather than a private one, with the prologues playing as important a role as the text of scripture itself. It was a Bible for communication, in a context we cannot at present reconstruct. Analogy with the two Ceolfrith Bibles housed in the chapels of Wearmouth and Jarrow may be helpful here.

---

[63] Paris, Bibliothèque Nationale, lat. 2.

[64] This has already been remarked upon by Contreni, 'Carolingian Biblical Studies'.

[65] On reading and singing for example see L. Treitler, 'Reading and Singing: On the Genesis of Occidental Music-writing', *Early Music History* 4 (1984), 135–208.

They acted as definitive reference copies, so that anyone could find the passage he wanted, but they were surely also used for public reading.[66]

The Tours attention to presenting a text that was easy to follow may well have been influential and this is something that should be tested in relation to other Carolingian Bibles. The idea of a pandect, on the other hand, had little currency. It is striking how many biblical texts from the Carolingian period continue to be copied in separate books or groups of books.[67] The necessary scribal and technical adaptation which enabled the Paris Bibles to be produced in small format, on thin skins with tiny writing, had not yet been made.[68]

By way of summary, what I wish to stress is the wholly didactic presentation of the biblical text. Whether for private scholarship as in the case of the Theodulf Bibles or for public instruction as may be the case with the Tours Bibles, we have to see the scribal and technical innovations in the presentation of scripture within the context of an educational enterprise, for instruction, elucidation and edification.[69] The text itself, clearly presented by means of format and selected scripts, was augmented by the choice of accompanying prologues and explanatory treatises, such as Jerome on Hebrew names.[70] That the tenth-century Bible from Werden, now in Berlin, should incorporate headings from the commentaries of Jerome, Hrabanus Maurus, Alcuin and Bede, with their explanatory and didactic prologues, is entirely consistent with this essentially educational tradition in Carolingian Bible production.[71]

The central importance of the Bible to the Carolingians, the extent to which it provided models of kingship, government, warfare, historical writing and interpretation, public praise and private devotion, its central place in the intellectual preoccupations of the Frankish scholars, the dominance of the Psalter in the private and public prayer of the Frankish people and the inspiration it offered to the artists and poets of the Carolingian world are all fully acknowledged. What we have to add, moreover, is the extraordinary determination with which monasteries, churches and individuals with private chapels set out to equip themselves with the texts they needed.[72] I hope to have made clear in this paper the following three conclusions. The Bible text produced for any one person or centre was not necessarily the same as that

---

[66] *Vita Coelfridi Abbatis Auctore Anonyme*, ed. C. Plummer, *Venerabilis Baedae Opera Historica*, 2 vols. (Oxford, 1896) I, 395, ch. 20. I am grateful to Richard Gameson for pointing this out to me.

[67] Quite apart from many examples in extant manuscripts, the library catalogues make clear how many of the biblical books were still shelved separately or in thematic groups in Carolingian libraries. For references to these see my *The Carolingians and the Written Word* (Cambridge, 1989), 165–210.

[68] See the comments, however, of C. de Hamel, *Glossed Books of the Bible and the Origins of the Paris Booktrade* (Woodbridge, 1984), especially 14–37, and the excellent section on the Bible in *Mise en page et mise en texte du livre manuscrit*, ed. H.-J. Martin and J. Vezin (Paris, 1990), 57–111.

[69] Here I echo Contreni, 'Carolingian Biblical Studies'.

[70] Useful observations on these supporting texts are to be found in *The Cambridge History of the Bible II*, ed. Lampe.

[71] Berlin, Deutsche Staatsbibliothek, theol. lat. fol. 336 and see H. Hoffmann, *Buchkunst und Königtum*, 143–4.

[72] Note the specific instance of such provision in Anglo-Saxon England discussed by Richard Gameson in ch. 2 above. On the general context for this provision see my *The Frankish Church and the Carolingian Reforms, 789–895*, Royal Historical Society Studies in History 2 (London, 1977).

of their neighbours. As in so many other spheres of Carolingian life, we have diversity within unity and one text, the Bible, with many different recensions and methods of presenting it. It is an eclecticism familiar within the Carolingian world, and as Richard Marsden has made clear, in Anglo-Saxon England as well.[73] Finally, no one text of the Bible, whether Alcuinian, Theodulfian, Corbeian, Hofschule or any other, was dominant.[74]

[73] See ch. 6 below.
[74] I am very grateful to Richard Gameson for his comments on and careful reading of the text of this paper.

5

Carolingian Glossed Psalters

MARGARET GIBSON

Volumus ut Unroch habeat Psalterium nostrum duplum . . . Berengarius alium Psalterium
uolumus ut habeat cum auro scriptum . . . Adalardus tercium Psalterium uolumus ut habeat,
quod ad nostrum opus habuimus . . . Rodulphus uolumus ut Psalterium cum sua expositione
habeat, quem Gisla ad opus suum habuit.

Eberhard, count of Friuli, *a* 867[1]

I. THE GENRE

The Carolingian patron commissioning a luxury Psalter had a wide range of options.
He could have parallel versions in two, three or even four columns.[2] Eberhard's own
Graeco-Latin 'Psalterium duplex' still survives, having passed to the Vatican Library
via Paul Petau (*ob.* 1614), and Queen Christina of Sweden.[3] He could have a *codex
purpureus* with the text written in gold: when the page is held against the sunlight the
letters seem to float in a purple haze.[4] He could have gold on plain parchment – still
luxurious, but more legible.[5] He could commission fine initials and, in some

[1] P. E. Schramm and F. Mütherich, *Denkmale der deutschen Könige und Kaiser I: Ein Beitrag zur Herrschergeschichte von Karl dem Grossen bis Friedrich II*, 2nd edn (Munich, 1981), 93–5, at 94. Although his title is from the north Italian march, Eberhard's family lands were in north-west Francia, in the region of Tournai.

[2] The prototype of such parallel versions was Origen's *Hexapla* edition of the Old Testament, which medieval scholars knew only through Jerome's description: *Commentarium in Titum* 3.9 (PL XXVI, 595 AB). Triple and quadruple Psalters in French libraries are conveniently accessible in V. Leroquais, *Les psautiers manuscrits latins des bibliothèques publiques de France*, 3 vols. (Mâcon, 1940–1), II, 475, with references. Outside France see, for example, the great quadruple Psalter (Gallicanum, Romanum, Hebraicum, transliterated Greek) that was written in 909 for Abbot Salomo III of St Gall: Bamberg, Staatsbibliothek, Bibl. 44 (A. 1. 140). For the Rhineland see Cologne, Dombibliothek, 8 and Essen, Münsterschatz, s.n., twin quadruple Psalters of the eleventh century: see R. Kahsnitz, *Der Werdener Psalter in Berlin: MS. theol. lat. fol. 358* (Düsseldorf, 1979), 101–4 and R. Drögereit, 'Griechisch-Byzantinische aus Essen', *Byzantinische Zeitschrift* 46 (1953), 110–15, at 114.

[3] Biblioteca Apostolica Vaticana, Reg. lat. 11, later eighth century: see A. Wilmart, *Codices Reginenses*, 2 vols. (Vatican City, 1937–45), I, 26–30 and CLA II, no. 101.

[4] Fine examples are the Angilberga Psalter, written anno 827, presumably for Louis the Pious (Piacenza, Biblioteca Communale Passerini-Landi, 2) and Oxford, Bodleian Library, Douce 59 (mid-ninth century: Rheims). See respectively Schramm and Mütherich, *Könige und Kaiser*, I, 129, no. 40 and O. Pächt and J. J. G. Alexander, *Illuminated Manuscripts in the Bodleian Library*, 3 vols. (Oxford, 1966–73), I, no. 416.

[5] See the Milanese Psalter of the later ninth century which is now Vatican City, Biblioteca Apostolica Vaticana, lat. 83: A. von Euw, *Liber Viventium Fabariensis: das karolingische Memorialbuch von Pfäfers in seiner liturgie- und kunstgeschichtlichen Bedeutung*, Studia Fabariensia 1 (Bern/Stuttgart, 1989), 126, with references.

circumstances, full-page miniatures or intercalated narrative drawing.[6] Here we are concerned with Count Eberhard's fourth option, a Psalter with its own marginal gloss ('cum sua expositione'). Set adjacent to the text in a smaller script, the annotation is a planned element in the *mise-en-page*. A gloss of this kind is sharply distinct from the marginal and interlinear notes in a school text. There the comments are brief reminders of facts or arguments to be explicated by the master in class; the original corpus of notes may be expanded and corrected over the years. In a Glossed Psalter, by contrast, the annotation is complete from the moment of production; and it is deployed in the margins of the page only, never between the lines. It is a learned embellishment to a volume which is distinguished by variety of ornament and elegance of script at least as much as by the quality of its text.

Perhaps two dozen Carolingian Glossed Psalters survive today, some in excellent condition, others merely fragments.[7] They are paradoxical volumes, technically innovative but exegetically conservative. The strict *mise-en-page* inhibits additions, clarifications, readers' comments; there is no scope for second thoughts or new material. At the same time they cast a long shadow into the twelfth century, where they are the prototype for the *Glossa Ordinaria* to the Bible as a whole.[8] Whether as a single book (e.g. Genesis) or several related books (e.g. the Pentateuch) the *Glossa Ordinaria* is organised on essentially the same principles of ruling and deployment as are the Carolingian Glossed Psalters.

II. THE MANUSCRIPTS

The prerequisites for an elegant and intelligible glossed page are that the script of text and apparatus be clearly differentiated, and that the page be ruled to accommodate a marginal gloss.[9] That both techniques were well understood in Fulda *c.* 800 may be seen in Frankfurt, Stadt- und Universitätsbibliothek, MS Barth. 32 (ill. 5.1).[10] The text is articulated through a hierarchy of four Insular scripts, used respectively for the major initials, the *tituli* preceding each psalm, the Psalter-text and the marginal gloss. The text is in Insular half-uncial, the gloss in a minuscule that is sometimes Insular and sometimes early Carolingian. The same uncertainty prevails in the collects, which are

---

[6] Two outstanding examples of Psalters with intercalated narrative drawing are Utrecht, Universiteitsbibliotheek, 32 (the Utrecht Psalter), from Rheims; and Stuttgart, Württembergische Landesbibliothek, Bibl. fol. 23 (the Stuttgart Psalter), from St Germain-des-Prés. Both seem to have been made in the 820s.

[7] I hope to review the group as a whole in a monograph.

[8] The classic study is B. Smalley, *The Study of the Bible in the Middle Ages*, 3rd edn, rev. (Oxford, 1983), 46–52, with references. See also C. F. R. de Hamel, *Glossed Books of the Bible and the Origins of the Paris Booktrade* (Woodbridge, 1984), with good plates; M. T. Gibson, 'The Twelfth-century Glossed Bible', in *Papers presented to the Tenth International Conference on Patristic Studies held in Oxford in 1987*, ed. E. A. Livingstone, Studia Patristica XIX–XXIII (Leuven, 1989), XXIII, 232–44; and my 'The Place of the *Glossa Ordinaria* in Medieval Exegesis', in *Ad Litteram: Authoritative Texts and their Medieval Readers*, ed M. Jordan and K. Emery Jr (Notre Dame, Ind. and London, 1992), 5–27.

[9] See the lucid and wide-ranging discussion by G. Powitz, 'Textus cum commento', *Codices Manuscripti* 5 (1979), 80–9.

[10] G. Powitz and H. Buck, *Die Handschriften des Bartholomaeusstifts und des Karmeliterklosters in Frankfurt am Main*, Kataloge der Stadt- und Universitätsbibliothek Frankfurt am Main 3. ii (Frankfurt am Main, 1974), 66–70.

in Carolingian minuscule (fols. 4–16), then in Insular, then Carolingian once more (fol. 122v). The gloss to each psalm is preceded by a note summarising its content and meaning; these notes are in a rather crabbed Insular minuscule.[11] The page is ruled initially for 25 lines of text, then for 28; there are correspondingly 49 and 55 lines of marginal annotation. The gloss is ruled at half-spacing against the text. Although the text-ruling does not cross the narrow columns to the left and right, text and gloss are on the same grid. Each gloss begins with a lemma, linking it to the relevant passage in the text; there is no further mechanism for identifying and placing individual glosses. Within the context of surviving Fulda manuscripts, which are rather few and widely scattered, Barth. 32 may be dated to the first quarter of the ninth century.[12] In particular the introductory notes to each psalm would present difficulties to readers not thoroughly at home with Insular script – and such readers were becoming rare by the 830s. Furthermore the Psalter-text itself is the Romanum, which from the 790s onwards was being replaced by the Gallicanum throughout Carolingian Europe.[13]

The Frankfurt Psalter is a splendid folio volume, ruled and written by a practised hand. Although today it is unique, in its own time we can scarcely believe that it was even experimental. Its confident execution implies a well-established genre, in which the art of integrating text and apparatus was completely understood in Fulda c. 800.

What may be seen as the classic type of Carolingian Glossed Psalter was made in St Gall in the mid-ninth century. Three such manuscripts survive: Göttweig, Stifts-bibliothek, 30;[14] its now fragmentary twin Munich, Bayerische Staatsbibliothek, Clm 29315/3 + Regensburg, Bischöfliche Zentralbibliothek, fragmenta s.n.;[15] and St Gall, Stiftsbibliothek, 27.[16] A further close relation is Vercelli, Biblioteca Capitolare, 149,[17] written in Salzburg but indebted to the St Gall tradition for both text and layout. The likely point of exchange is the court of Louis the German at Regensburg, where Abbot Grimalt of St Gall was for some years chancellor.[18] All four manuscripts are

---

[11] B. Fischer, 'Bedae de titulis psalmorum liber', in *Festschrift Bernhard Bischoff zu seinem 65 Geburtstag*, ed. J. Autenrieth and F. Brunhölzl (Stuttgart, 1971), 90–110 and pl. 2. See further section iii below.

[12] Powitz and Buck, *Die Handschriften*. For the Fulda library as a whole see now S. Krämer, *Handschriftenerbe des deutschen Mittelalters* 3 vols., Mittelalterliche Bibliothekskataloge Deutschlands und der Schweiz, Ergänzungs-band I (Munich, 1989–90), I, 280–4, with references.

[13] See B. Fischer, 'Bibeltext und Bibelreform unter Karl dem Grossen', in *Karl der Grosse. Lebenswerk und Nachleben II: Das geistige Leben*, ed. B. Bischoff (Düsseldorf, 1965), 156–216; repr. in his *Lateinische Bibelhandschriften im frühen Mittelalter*, Vetus Latina 11 (Freiburg, 1985), 101–202, at 164–6.

[14] B. Bischoff, *Südostdeutschen Schreibschulen und Bibliotheken in der Karolingerzeit*, 2 vols. (Wiesbaden, 1974–80), II, 44–5, with bibliography; useful plates in K. Holter, 'Zum Ornament eines karolingischen Psalters in Göttweig', *Österreichische Zeitschrift für Kunst und Denkmalpflege* 17 (1963), 174–9. For an overview of St Gall manuscripts see A. Bruckner, *Scriptoria Medii Aevi Helvetica*, 14 vols. (Geneva, 1935–78), II–III, *Schreibschulen der Diözese Konstanz: St Gallen I–II*.

[15] B. Bischoff, 'Bücher am Hofe Ludwigs des Deutschen und die Privatbibliothek des Kanzlers Grimalt', in his *Mittelalterliche Studien*, 3 vols. (Stuttgart, 1966–81), III, 187–212, at 194. The Munich fragment is illustrated in Schramm and Mütherich, *Könige und Kaiser* no. 11, 467.

[16] Bruckner, *Scriptoria Medii Aevi Helvetica* III, 59 and pl. III (= Ps. 2).

[17] Bischoff, *Schreibschulen* II, 189–90.

[18] Grimalt was abbot of St Gall 841–72 and intermittently chancellor to Louis the German 833–70: J. Fleckenstein, *Die Hofkapelle der deutschen Könige*, 2 vols., MGH, Schriften 16 (Stuttgart, 1959–66), I, 168–76, with references; see further *Helvetia Sacra* III. i. 2, ed. E. Gilomen-Schenkel (Bern, 1986), 1275–7.

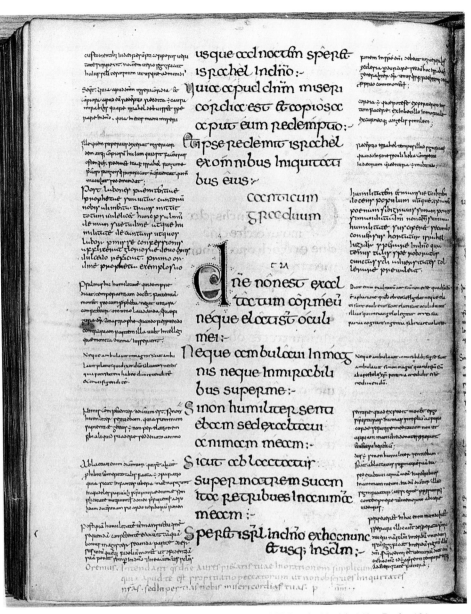

5.1   *Frankfurt, Stadt- und Universitätsbibliothek, MS Barth. 32, fol. 163v: Psalm 131*

ruled in the 'Fulda' manner of a common grid, with the gloss at half-spacing (see ill. 5.2). In Göttweig 30 and the Munich-Regensburg fragments the scribe has achieved a more elegant *mise-en-page* by setting every second gloss in the right-hand margin. Thus the reader's eye is led step by step downwards to the appropriate line of text. These

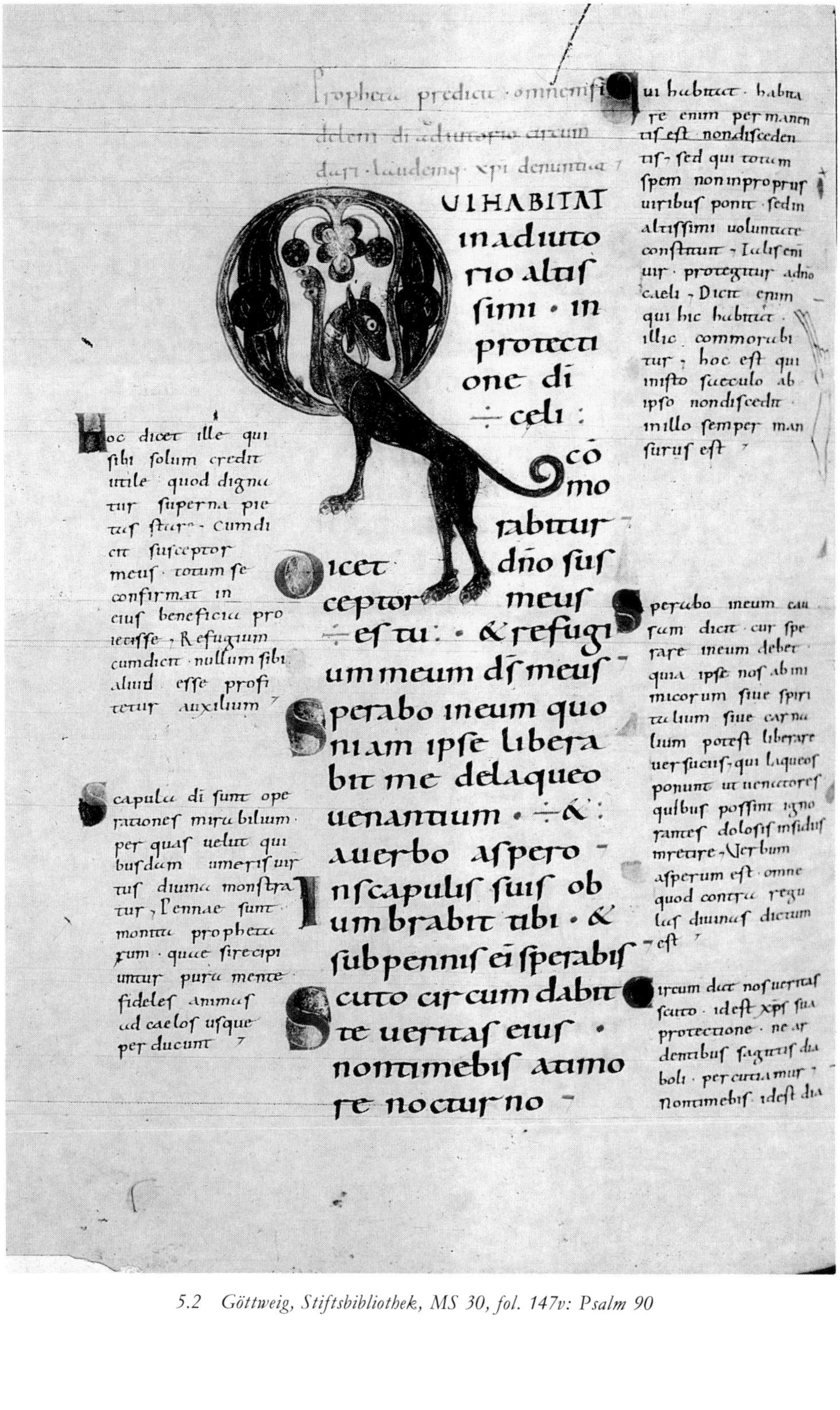

5.2 *Göttweig, Stiftsbibliothek, MS 30, fol. 147v: Psalm 90*

manuscripts have common parameters: in size, in lines per page, in the accommodation of the gloss and in the embellishment of the initials to Psalms 1, 51 and 101.[19] Where they go beyond the Fulda precedent is in their text. Not only does the Gallicanum displace the Romanum for the Psalter proper, but it carries with it – in addition to the *tituli* and collects[20] – (i) a series of prefaces to the Psalter, (ii) an annotated liturgical supplement, (iii) an extended litany and (iv) a major collection of prayers.

(i) The prefaces to the Psalter

The ten prefaces in Göttweig 30 and St Gall 27 are broadly patristic in content – Augustine, Jerome, Cassiodorus, Isidore. There is a comparable series in the Salzburg manuscript, and here too the tradition continues into the eleventh century and beyond.[21] The choice and order of these prefaces were never completely stabilised.

(ii) The liturgical supplement

Six Canticles from the Old Testament are followed by eight more recent Canticles and Creeds. They may be introduced by the 'additional' Psalm 151, 'Pusillus eram'. The sequence adopted in ninth-century Fulda and St Gall remains the norm in all the other manuscripts discussed below.[22] It is:

OLD TESTAMENT

   I   Confitebor tibi domine: Isaiah 12.1–6
  II   Ego dixi: Isaiah 38.10–20
 III   Exultauit cor meum: I Kings 2.1–10
 IV   Cantemus domino: Exodus 15.1–19
  V   Domine audiui: Habakkuk 3.2–19
 VI   Audite coeli: Deuteronomy 32.1–43

---

[19] The measurements are: Göttweig 30, page 352 × 268 mm, text + gloss 290 × 220 mm, text 29 lines; St Gall 27, page 320 × 240 mm, text + gloss 194 × 167/175 mm, text 20 lines; Vercelli 149, page 281 × 238 mm, text + gloss 215 × 195 mm, text 28 lines.

[20] The *tituli* in the Frankfurt Psalter are normally the opening verses of the relevant Psalms; the St Gall tradition is the much more elaborate Series VI: P. Salmon, *Les 'Tituli Psalmorum' des manuscrits latins*, Collectanea Biblica Latina 12, Études liturgiques 32 (Paris, 1959), 149–86. For the collects in the Frankfurt Psalter see L. Brou, *The Psalter Collects from the V–VIth Century Sources*, Henry Bradshaw Society 83 (London, 1949), 174–227. This so-called 'Romana' series is the text normally found in Glossed Psalters right across Europe: see Brou's list of manuscripts (p. 174).

[21] In principle see F. Stegmüller, *Repertorium Biblicum Medii Aevi*, 11 vols. (Madrid, 1940–80), I, nos. 358–452, with references.

[22] See Leroquais, *Les psautiers manuscrits* I, lv; H. Schneider, *Die altlateinischen biblischen Cantica*, Texte und Arbeiten ... Beuron I. 29–30 (Beuron/Hohenzollern, 1938), 50–8, *et passim*; and, still very useful, J. Mearns, *The Canticles of the Christian Church Eastern and Western in Early and Medieval Times* (Cambridge, 1914), 62–7.

INTER-TESTAMENTAL AND LATER

VII	Benedicite: Daniel 3.57–88
VIII	Te deum
IX	Benedictus: Luke 1.69
X	Magnificat: Luke 1.48
XI	Nunc dimittis: Luke 2.29
XII	Gloria
XIII	Pater noster: Luke 11.3
XIV	Apostles' Creed
XV	Athanasian Creed ('Quicunque uult')

With the exception of Psalm 151, which is never annotated, all these texts can carry a gloss; the 'Quicunque uult', for instance, is often explicated in detail.

(iii) The litany

The Glossed Psalters from St Gall and their German successors contain an extended litany, at the beginning or the end of the manuscript.[23] In two of the St Gall books it is an opportunity for quite elaborate 'canon table' decoration.[24]

(iv) The collection of prayers

The two principal St Gall manuscripts include a major collection of prayers at the beginning (Göttweig 30) or at the end (St Gall 27);[25] the Salzburg manuscript has a comparable collection at the end.[26]

The vigour of the German tradition may be seen in the southern Bavarian monastery of Tegernsee in the mid-eleventh century. Four luxury Psalters, so closely related as certainly to reflect the same exemplar, were made there *c.* 1060.[27] In Oxford, Bodleian, MS Laud lat. 96 (ill. 5.3) – which may here stand for them all – the *mise-en-page* has been simplified to two equal columns: 23 lines of text in the inner column and 45 lines of gloss at half-spacing in the outer. The Laudian manuscript and its three fellows solve the technical problem of relating apparatus to text both elegantly and (in codicological terms) at low risk. Here at last is a formula which will keep text and apparatus in step throughout the manuscript. In these books the luxury Glossed

---

[23] The Tegernsee litany is printed from Munich, Clm 18121 by M. Coens, 'Anciennes litanies des saints', *Analecta Bollandiana* 54 (1936), 5–37, at 30–6.

[24] Göttweig 30, fols. 1v–4, and Munich, Clm 29315/3, the latter reproduced by Schramm and Mütherich, *Könige und Kaiser*.

[25] For the genre see A. Wilmart, *Precum Libelli Quattuor Aevi Karolini* I (Rome, 1940); Wilmart's projected discussion (II) was never published. The Glossed Psalters contain much that appears to be new.

[26] I am grateful to Monsignor Giuseppe Ferraris, the Chapter Librarian of Vercelli, for his welcome, and the access that he permitted to Vercelli 149 and 62.

[27] Munich, Bayerische Staatsbibliothek, Clm 18121; Oxford, Bodleian Library, Laud lat. 96 and Rawl. G. 163; Vatican City, Biblioteca Apostolica Vaticana, Ross. lat. 184.

5.3   *Oxford, Bodleian Library, MS Laud. lat. 96, fol. 9v: Psalm 4*

Psalter has achieved its definitive form.[28] In other respects the Tegernsee manuscripts follow Carolingian precedent. The *tituli* and collects agree with those in the manuscripts from St Gall. The prefaces are similar, the liturgical supplement is identical and the litany, too, has much in common with the St Gall text. The major development is in the collection of prayers, which has been altered and amplified; it

---

28 A German example of the more traditional three-column solution is Fulda, Hessische Landesbibliothek, MS Aa 42 (s. xi; Weingarten).

ends with an otherwise unrecorded abridgement of the Psalter, 'written by St Jerome at the dictation of an angel'.[29] The major initials to Psalms 1, 51 and 101 are each allocated a full page, which they do not quite fill; with their painted purple background they are inferior versions of initials in a *codex purpureus*.[30]

South of the Alps the picture is more complex. In the first place German manuscripts were sent to Italy. The Salzburg manuscript now in Vercelli may have reached Piedmont within a generation of its production; it was certainly there by the twelfth century. Manuscripts might be copied in Italy from German exemplars. Northern antecedents, as in the characteristic initials of Trier and Echternach, are very noticeable in the fragment that is now Malibu, J. Paul Getty Museum, MS 83 MK 92 (ill. 5.4).[31] But there are also indigenous Italian manuscripts, which still await detailed study. A book that has only just returned to scholarly attention is the so-called 'Psalter of St Romuald', the first half of which (Psalms 1–99.3) is still in the sacristy of San Salvatore, Camaldoli (diocese of Arezzo).[32] Mabillon saw the complete manuscript in March 1686, and noted that the gloss extended as far as the Canticles.[33] By 1750 the latter half of the manuscript had been removed and apparently lost. Pages were removed, writes Magnoald Ziegelbaur, as curios or as relics to other Camaldolese houses.[34] In the late 1950s one further page reached the Rosenthal collection, whence it has just passed to Mr Martin Schøyen, by whose generous permission it is reproduced here (ill. 5.5).[35] This fragment is currently the only accessible part of the Romuald Psalter; nevertheless it permits us to surmise what the manuscript as a whole is like. Text and commentary were written by the same ninth-century scribe: a central column of text (61 mm) with the gloss in only slightly narrower columns (*c*. 58 mm) to left and right. The idiosyncratic capitals of the text contrast with the unremarkable minuscule of the commentary. Each gloss begins in the left-hand column and ends in the right-hand column, approximately half the gloss being on each side. The opening lemma is at the level of the text to which it refers. Thus whoever designed the page

---

[29] Laud lat. 96, fols. 225ra–59va: *inc. prol.* Porro propter hoc breuiatum est hoc psalterium . . . *expl.* cantat assidue; title, IN CHRISTI NOMINE INCIPIT PSALTERIVM A SANCTO HIERONIMO VT DICITVR ANGELO SE DOCENTE COMPOSITVM. *inc.* Verba mea . . . *expl.* ego seruus tuus sum.

[30] That the design of the initial pages was borrowed from another model, and imperfectly adapted to Laud lat. 96 may be seen from the wide useless margin (lower 72/85 mm; outer 60/66 mm) on all sides; from the ruling, which is the normal text and gloss ruling of the rest of the volume; and from the omission of the gloss to Psalm 1.1, which ought to have been accommodated on the first of the initial pages (fol. 7).

[31] Formerly MS Ludwig VIII. 1: see A. von Euw and J. M. Plotzek, *Die Handschriften der Sammlung Ludwig*, 4 vols. (Cologne, 1979–85), I, 308–10, with colour plate of recto (Te deum). I am very grateful to the Getty Museum for its generosity in providing photographs of this manuscript.

[32] The manuscript is ninth century (ill. 5.5). Its association with St Romuald (*c*. 952–1027) derives from Peter Damian's account of Romuald's vision of God the Father directing him to expound the Psalter: *Vita Romualdi*, ed. G. Tabacco, Fonti per la Storia d'Italia 94 (Rome, 1957), cap. 50, 92–3. Mabillon records the inscription: Istud Psalterium scripsit et glosauit manu sua propria sanctissimus ac beatissimus Romualdus, sicut praeceperat sibi Deus, quando fuit raptus in paradisum, celebrans Missam in eremo Sytriae, ut scribit beatus Petrus Damianus Presbyter Cardinalis in legenda sua: *Museum Italicum*, 2 vols. (Paris, 1687), I, 181; cf. M. Ziegelbaur, *Centifolium Camaldulense* (Venice, 1750), 71–2.

[33] J. Mabillon, *Annales Ordinis Sancti Benedicti: saec. IV* (Paris, 1707), 275.

[34] Ziegelbaur, *Centifolium Camaldulense*, cap. lxxxiv, 71.

[35] Psalms 99.3–100.3, identified and analysed in a letter to Bernard Rosenthal from Bernhard Bischoff, 1959; *Bookhands of the Middle Ages: Part V, Medieval Manuscript Leaves*, Bernard Quaritch Catalogue 1147 (1991), no. 5; now Schøyen Collection, Oslo, MS 620.

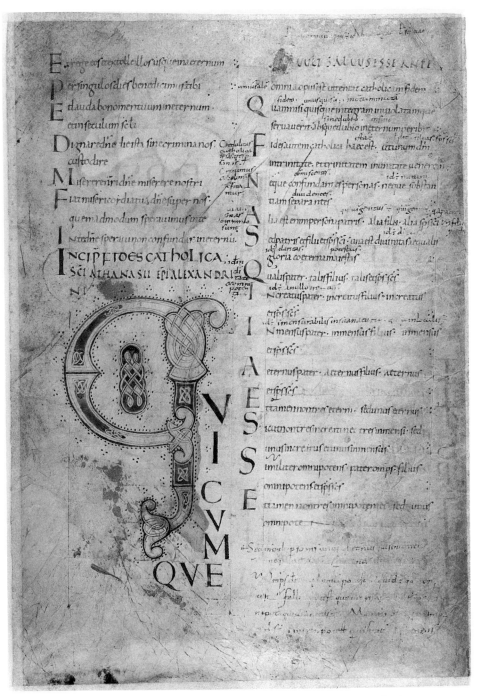

5.4   *Malibu, J. Paul Getty Museum, MS 83. MK. 92v: Athanasian Creed*

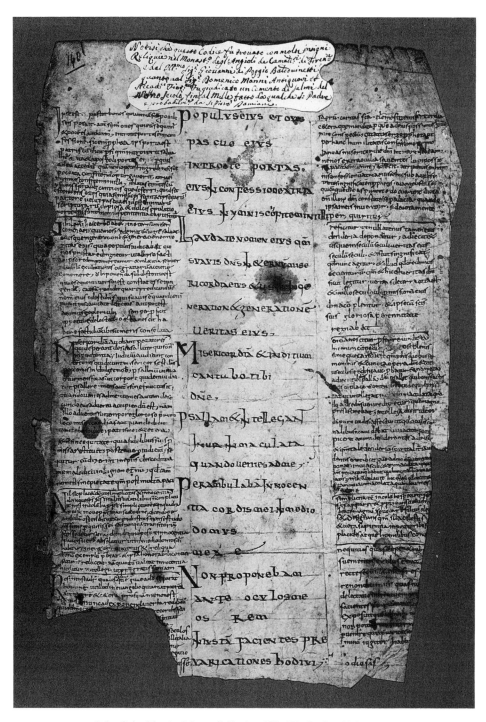

5.5   *Oslo, Martin Schøyen Collection, MS 620: Psalms 99.3–100.3*

had to plan the maximum length of each gloss, and the point of division. Beyond that, the layout is unsophisticated. The ruling relates to the text only, and in the absence of *tituli* and collects no provision need be made for introductory initials or contrasting scripts.

A characteristic feature of Italian Glossed Psalters is their intercalated narrative drawings. These are disposed freely on the page, beside or within the text. A fine early example is Vercelli, Biblioteca Capitolare, 62, in which the Psalmist is shown time and again addressing Christ (ill. 5.6).[36] This is a volume of the mid- to later ninth century, which may well be local to Vercelli itself. Certainly the formulae for the drawings reappear in Piedmont in the Warmund Psalter of *c.* 1000, a manuscript that is still in the Chapter Library of Ivrea.[37] The gloss to Vercelli 62 is set at half-spacing against the text and identified by alphabetical reference-signs.[38] Another ninth-century Psalter, attributable to Milan, survives only in two binding fragments; these indicate that it too may have had a systematic gloss and intercalated drawings.[39] The tradition is sustained in a book that is a few decades beyond our limit of *c.* 1050. Rome, Biblioteca Vallicelliana, MS E. 24 has extensive discussion of the *titulus* and brief notes to the rest of each Psalm. Every so often a scene from the life of Christ is set within the Psalter text: for instance the Last Supper (Psalm 41, *Sicut ceruus*: fol. 73v), the Crucifixion (Psalm 89, *Domine refugium*: fol. 133) and the Descent into Hell (Psalm 106, *Confitemini domino*: fol. 152v). Scholarly opinion locates this Psalter in Umbria, or perhaps in Rome itself.[40]

The most puzzling region is west of the Rhine. The two great illustrated Psalters that survive from Rheims and Paris in the 820s – respectively the *Utrecht Psalter* and the *Stuttgart Psalter* – were not designed to carry annotation.[41] The principal Glossed Psalter to survive from ninth-century France is Laon, Bibliothèque Municipale, MS 14, a book in which Psalms 114–50 and the Canticles are a twelfth-century replacement; Psalms 1–23 are also missing from the beginning. The Carolingian rump, Psalms 24–113, is ruled at half-spacing throughout for a systematic gloss, but only Psalms 24–67 have the annotation entered in the space provided.[42] The script

---

[36] Vercelli 62: see Bischoff, *Schreibschulen* II, 59; the drawings on fols. 60 and 124 are reproduced in A. M. Brizio, *Catalogo delle cose d'arte e di antichità d'Italia VIII: Vercelli*, Ministero della Educazione Nazionale: Direzione Generale delle Antichità e Belle Arti (Rome, 1935), 102–3.

[37] Ivrea, Biblioteca Capitolare, 30 (LXXXV): see L. Magnani, *Le miniature del sacramentario d'Ivrea e di altri codici warmondiani* (Vatican, 1934), pl. xlviia.

[38] The measurements are: page 360 × 295 mm; text 238 × 140 mm; inner gloss panel 45 mm; outer gloss panel 50 mm; boundary columns 9 mm; 26 lines of text per page, 51 lines of gloss. See further section iii below.

[39] Dillingen-an-der-Donau, Studienbibliothek, Fragm. 25 + Schøyen Collection, 74: see R. McKitterick, 'Carolingian Book Production: Some Problems', *The Library*, 6th series, 12 (1990), 1–33, at 23–4 and fig. 6 (Schøyen fragment); Gibson, 'Place of the *Glossa Ordinaria*', pl. 3 (Dillingen fragment).

[40] Good description, with bibliography, by L. Avitabile in 'Censimento dei codici dei secoli X–XII: Roma, Biblioteca Vallicelliana', *Studi Medievali* 3rd series, xi. 2 (1970), 1013–74, at 1062–3. See in particular E. B. Garrison, *Studies in the History of Medieval Italian Painting*, 4 vols. (Florence, 1953–62), II, 86–90, and figs. 82–9.

[41] The gloss to *Stuttgart*, Psalms 1–16 is a tenth-century addition made in South Germany: see B. Bischoff, 'Die Handschrift: paläographische Untersuchung', in *Der Stuttgarter Bilderpsalter. Bibl. fol. 23 der Württembergischen Landesbibliothek*, ed. B. Bischoff *et al.*, 2 vols. (Stuttgart, 1965–8), II, 15–30, at 19.

[42] Page 289 × 257 mm; text 244 × 63 mm; inner gloss panel 63 mm; outer gloss panel 56 mm; 27 lines of text per page, 53 lines of gloss; simple red major initials.

5.6   *Vercelli, Biblioteca Capitolare, MS 62, fol. 65r: Psalm 50*

indicates a Parisian house, perhaps St Denis.[43] An incomplete, and less extensive, gloss is found at the end of the century in Troyes, Bibliothèque Municipale, MS 615, provenance unknown.[44] Fifty years later a Glossed Psalter from Fleury, now Orléans,

[43] J. J. Contreni, *The Cathedral School of Laon from 850 to 930: Its Manuscripts and Masters*, Münchener Beiträge zur Mediävistik und Renaissance-Forschung 29 (Munich, 1978), 46, n. 30. For the specifically 'St Denis' provenance I am indebted to Professor Bischoff, who dates the manuscript to the second third of the ninth century.

[44] A fragment (fols. 1–137: Psalms 21–143), now bound in with a Romance text: see Leroquais, *Les psautiers manuscrits* II, 234–5. The formal gloss ceases at Psalm 68 (fol. 52).

Bibliothèque Municipale, MS 48, has extensive and systematic annotation, for which the only provision made in the *mise-en-page* is the narrow central column of text and the wide margins. The gloss is neither ruled, nor contained within a ruled panel, nor correlated with the lines of text.[45] These three manuscripts are competently executed, without being in any real sense luxury productions.

The Glossed Psalter as a luxury manuscript is established in France at the very end of the tenth century, continuing into the 1050s and 60s. The initial impulse may well have been Byzantine, not as the source of text or illumination, but as the model for the *mise-en-page*. Greek Psalters of the ninth and tenth centuries, if glossed, are framed by a 'catena' of apparatus in the upper, lower and outer margins of a double opening (ill. 5.7).[46] This is exactly the format of the superb St Bertin Psalter of *c.* 999 (Boulogne, Bibliothèque Municipale, MS 20),[47] and the ambitious, but poorly executed, St Denis Psalter of a generation later (Paris, Bibliothèque Nationale, MS lat. 103: ill. 5.8).[48] In both these manuscripts the apparatus frames a double opening of text: the visual analogy with older and indeed contemporary Greek Psalters with a 'catena' gloss is very striking. This 'Byzantine' formula may be contrasted with the two-column solution reached in Tegernsee *c.* 1060 (ill. 5.3). At the same time, the St Bertin Psalter is markedly innovative in its illumination, having prefatory miniatures, historiated initials showing scenes from the life of Christ and marginal drawings.[49] St Denis, by contrast, had third-rate artists, who had access to very much older models.[50]

Later French Psalters returned to the *via regia* of a central text with apparatus in the inner and outer margins. Metz, Bibliothèque Municipale, MS 14 (now destroyed) was one such, datable to the first third of the eleventh century.[51] A fine volume from St Germain-des-Prés, Paris, Bibliothèque Nationale, MS lat. 11550, datable to *c.* 1030, was designed originally with the gloss in the inner margins only, and the Bedan

---

[45] *Les Manuscrits de Fleury* (Orléans exh. cat., 1980), no. 6, with pl. of p. 222. I have to thank the Institut de Recherche et d'Histoire des Textes, Paris, for the opportunity to see the Troyes and Orléans manuscripts in microfilm.

[46] A fine example is Oxford, Bodleian Library, MS Auct. D. III. 17, written in Constantinople in the later tenth century. See ill. 5.7 (fols. 52v–53r: Ps. 23); details in I. Hutter, *Corpus der byzantinischen Miniaturenhandschriften* I, *Oxford, Bodleian Library*, Denkmäler der Buchkunst 2 (Stuttgart, 1977), 13, no. 7.

[47] Leroquais, *Les psautiers manuscrits* II, 94–101 and III, pls. XV–XXI. I am most grateful to Susan Lowrie for the loan of a microfilm of this manuscript and for her generous and hospitable assistance in studying it. The St Bertin Psalter has recently been mentioned as an example of *mise-en-page* by G. Lobrichon, 'Le Psautier d'Otbert', in *Mise en page et mise en texte du livre manuscrit*, ed. H.-J. Martin and J. Vezin (Paris, 1990), 174–8. I take the opportunity to register friendly but radical dissent from Professor Lobrichon's argument and its conclusions.

[48] Leroquais, *Les psautiers manuscrits* II, 30–2.

[49] Plates in Leroquais, *Les psautiers manuscrits* III, pls. XV–XX and full discussion by R. Kahsnitz, 'Der christologische Zyklus im Odbert-Psalter', *Zeitschrift für Kunstgeschichte* 51 (1988), 33–125, with references.

[50] The Psalter is divided by four Evangelist portraits taken ultimately from Carolingian models. The intercalated picture of Nathan rebuking David (II Sam. 12) has details reminiscent of late Antique official portraits: Psalm 101 (fol. 87v). The initial to Psalm 50, *Miserere mei* (fol. 44v), showing a naked man wrestling with two peacocks, is a remote echo of a much more sophisticated design.

[51] Leroquais, *Les psautiers manuscrits* I, 251–4 and III, pl. XXII.

5.7 *Oxford, Bodleian Library, MS Auct. D. III. 17, fols. 52v–53r: Psalm 22*

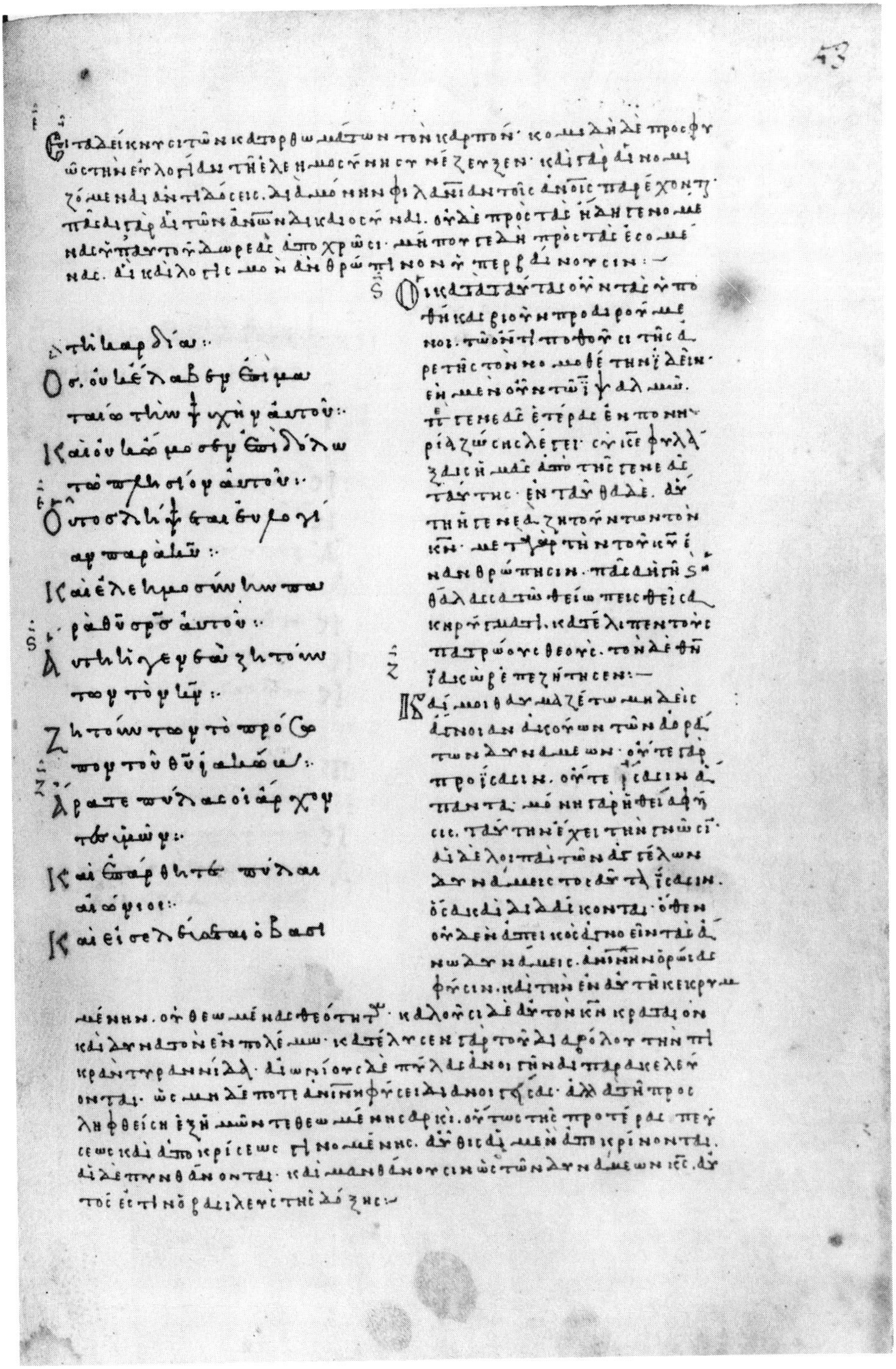

5.8   *Paris, Bibliothèque Nationale, MS lat. 103, fols. 12v–13r: Psalms 11–13.1*

Usequequo dne obliuisceris me infinem ·

Usquequo auertis faciem tuam ame ·

quandiu ponam consilia in anima mea ·

Dolorem incorde meo per diem

Usquequo exaltabitur inimicus mr sup me ·

respice & exaudime dne ds mr

inlumina oculos meos ne umquam obdormiam in mortem ·

nequando dicat inimicus mr preualui aduersus eum ·

Qui tribulant me exultabunt si motus fuero ·

ego aut in misedia tua speraui ·

Exultabit cor meum insalutari tuo · cantabo dno qui

bona tribuit mihi · & psallam nomini dni altissimi ·

Ne auertas faciem tuam anobis omptr dr ne inimici nri

exaltate aduersus nos · sed ita cor nrm salutaris tui

exultationem infunde · ut facias nos somnium secunde

mortis euadere infinem

DIXIT INSIPIENS IN CORDE SVO · NON EST DS ·

Corrupti sunt & abhominabiles facti sunt instudiis

suis · non est qui faciat bonum · non est usq adunum

Dns de caelo prospexit sup filios hominum

ut uideat si est intelligens aut requirens dm

Omnes declinauerunt simul inutiles facti sunt ·

non est qui faciat bonum non est usq ad unum

Explanationes on the outer.[52] Within a few years a further gloss was added to the outer margins of Psalms 1–47 (fols. 8v–71v). This additional material corresponds to the gloss in the St Denis Psalter – a book which is also close to lat. 11550 in its glossed hymnal. The Psalter of St Germain-des-Prés has its apparatus set at half-spacing to the text. It opens with full-page drawings of the Crucifixion with symbols of the Evangelists (fol. 6) and David and his musicians (fol. 7v).[53] Finally a mid-eleventh century luxury Psalter of great interest, but not strictly a Glossed Psalter from its inception, is the Psalter of Angers Cathedral, Amiens, Bibliothèque Municipale, MS fonds l'Escalopier 2.[54] This was the principal Psalter in Angers cathedral when Berengar of Tours was an archdeacon there; and it is of course attractive to speculate that he had a hand in the construction of its apparatus. But as an example of *mise-en-page* l'Escalopier 2 should be set aside.

Systematic annotation was a recognised option in a luxury Psalter *c.* 800–*c.* 1050. Visually it took different forms in Germany, Italy and France, but textually there are common traditions, to which we now turn.

III. THE EXEGESIS

Exegesis of the Latin Psalter begins with Hilary of Poitiers (d. 367) and continues through Augustine (d. 430) to Cassiodorus (d. *c.* 580). But although Hilary's name was known, and the text occasionally available, the two studies that were genuinely accessible throughout the earlier Middle Ages were the *Enarrationes in Psalmos* of Augustine and the *Expositio Psalmorum* of Cassiodorus.[55] The great anomaly is Jerome. His revision and translations of the Psalter render him the expositor *par excellence*,[56] yet he left no authentic commentary; the *Breviarium* of Jerome is a work of the mid-seventh century.

During the seventh century this patristic inheritance was reworked in the earliest of the medieval commentaries: the *Glosa ex traditione seniorum* (first half of the seventh century), drawing principally on Augustine;[57] the *Breviarium* of Pseudo-Jerome (mid-seventh century), using the *Glosa* and Cassiodorus;[58] above all the series of introductions to individual Psalms which is attributed to Bede (*c.* 700 +). This 'liber de titulis

---

[52] *Ibid.*, II, 105–10 and III, pls. XXX–XXXI. *Pace* Leroquais, this is a single manuscript, which must be dated after 1029 (St Martial established in the calendar) and should perhaps be dated after 1031, in that the illuminator, Ingelard, was employed by Abbot Adelard (1031–63): see C. Samaran and R. Marichal, *Catalogue des Manuscrits en Ecriture Latine portant des indications de date, de lieu ou de copiste, III Bibliothèque Nationale fonds latin (Nos. 8001 à 18613)*, ed. M. T. d'Alverny (Paris, 1974), 241.

[53] For the David imagery see H. Steger, *David Rex et Propheta*, Erlanger Beiträge zur Sprach- und Kunstwissenschaft VI (Nürnberg, 1961), *passim*; this MS described at 199–201 (no. 30).

[54] Leroquais, *Les psautiers manuscrits* I, 16–19, with pls. XXIII–XXVIII.

[55] Augustine, *Enarrationes in Psalmos*, ed. E. Dekkers and J. Fraipont, CCSL 38–40 (Turnhout, 1956); Cassiodorus, *Expositio Psalmorum*, ed. M. Adriaen, 2 vols., CCSL 97–8 (Turnhout, 1958).

[56] Details lucidly set out by Leroquais, *Les psautiers manuscrits* I, xxvii–xl.

[57] H. Boese, *Die alte 'Glosa psalmorum ex traditione seniorum': Untersuchungen, Materialen, Texte*, Vetus Latina 9 (Freiburg, 1982).

[58] PL XXVI, 821–1270: for the date see 'Glosa psalmorum', p. 80.

psalmorum' (as Fischer called it),[59] or 'Titulatio' (in the language of the St Germain-des-Prés Psalter),[60] consists of excerpts from Cassiodorus, abridged, slightly reordered and deployed as a continuous commentary with lemmata. It circulated well into the eleventh century, both in its original form and as an element in a Glossed Psalter. Finally the commentary in the Mondsee Psalter (pre-778), for which Cassiodorus is again the prime source, is another witness to the systematic study of the Psalter in pre-Carolingian Europe.[61]

All these early commentaries are 'continuous': that is, they consist of lemmata of text, each followed by its exposition. The more elegant and difficult alternative was the planned text with apparatus: the Glossed Psalter as such. Here the preferred source is Cassiodorus, sometimes in the Bedan *Titulatio*, often quarried directly from the original text. The picture can be drawn in broad outline, although much remains to be explored.

(A) Germany

The apparatus to the Frankfurt Psalter has three elements: the Bedan *Titulatio*, direct quotation and adaptation of Cassiodorus, and some new material. Fischer's suggestion that the apparatus to Psalms 1–4 is 'Irish' and the rest (Psalms 5–150) 'Cassiodoran' I find hard to understand.[62] But it may well be that an older continuous commentary or commentaries, substantially Cassiodoran in character, contributed to the apparatus. The major tradition, however, was established in St Gall and maintained in Tegernsee. With or without the Bedan *Titulatio*,[63] it consists of Cassiodorus' exposition freely altered and adapted, with extensive new material. It appears to be independent of the apparatus that had already been developed in Fulda. Now the annotation extends beyond Psalm 150 through the Canticles and the Lord's Prayer to the concluding Athanasian Creed, the *Quicunque uult*. The attribution of the Tegernsee version to Bruno, bishop of Würzburg (*ob*. 1045) may indicate the patron who commissioned a volume, rather than the 'author' of an already traditional gloss.[64]

(B) Italy

Here it is rash to venture even a hypothesis, so many libraries remain unexplored. In Vercelli the text already seen as a continuous commentary in Mondsee appears as a

[59] See Fischer, 'Bedae de titulis psalmorum liber'.

[60] Paris, Bibliothèque Nationale, lat. 11550, fol. 221v.

[61] F. Unterkircher, *Die Glossen des Psalters von Mondsee*, Spicilegium Friburgense 20 (Freiburg, 1974). Not only is the commentary textually indebted to Cassiodorus; the Mondsee manuscript opens with full-page icons of Christ and David which are manifestly in the same tradition as the two icons of David in Durham, Cathedral Library, MS B. ii. 30, an abridged Cassiodorus of s. viii 2/4. See J. J. G. Alexander, *Insular Manuscripts 6th to the 9th Century*, A Survey of Manuscripts Illuminated in the British Isles 1 (London, 1978), no. 17 and pls. 74–5.

[62] Fischer, 'Bedae de titulis psalmorum liber'; noted by Powitz and Buck, *Die Handschriften*, 69.

[63] St Gall 27 has the *Titulatio* throughout, as does Vercelli 149 (Salzburg); for the latter see M. Vattasso, 'Del *Libellus de psalmis* di Einhardo felicemente ritrovato', *Bessarione* 31 (1915), 92–104. Göttweig 30, the Regensburg–Munich fragments and the four Tegernsee manuscripts do not have the *Titulatio*.

[64] See further M. T. Gibson, 'The Psalter-commentary attributed to Bruno, bishop of Würzburg', *Studi Medievali*, forthcoming.

marginal gloss in Vercelli 62.[65] As usual, the basic source is Cassiodorus. The Schøyen fragment may testify to an Augustinian tradition, but we need more evidence. Finally the *Breviarium* of Pseudo-Jerome makes an unexpected appearance in Camaldoli as the only element so far identified in the Romuald Psalter.[66]

(C) France

In broad terms the French version may be seen first in the ninth century: in Laon, Bibliothèque Municipale, MS 14 (?St Denis), in Orléans, Bibliothèque Municipale, MS 48 (Fleury)[67] and in Troyes, Bibliothèque Municipale, MS 615 (provenance unknown). The St Bertin Psalter is surprisingly close to Laon 14; the 'excerptor' of the gloss, who is named in a prefatory poem,[68] must have been working from a very similar manuscript. The primary gloss in the St Germain-des-Prés Psalter is an abridged version of the same;[69] the gloss in the Angers Psalter (l'Escalopier 2) should probably be classed as 'scholastic' and considered elsewhere. As to the lost Metz manuscript, the single extant photograph indicates that the gloss may have been in the same tradition as the primary gloss in the Psalter of St Germain-des-Prés.

IV. THE CONTEXT

Whether they are seen as seventh- to eighth-century commentaries visually redeployed on the page, or in the longer perspective of the Latin Fathers, the Glossed Psalters are a tight little genre within the context of early medieval book production. Their prototypes, their analogues and their influence, cannot be examined here in detail. But we can identify the main lines of enquiry.

Valid prototypes do not survive. Irish scholars of the seventh and eighth centuries commented on parts of the Bible, and on grammatical and other secular texts. Occasionally such commentary survives in the form of marginal and interlinear annotation. But it is never deployed as a formal marginal gloss: the page is ruled for text alone, and the gloss is accommodated casually, here and there, as space permits. The gloss may be quite substantial; but it is not visually integrated with its text. Indeed one tantalising fragment now in Zurich illustrates a quite different *mise-en-page*, whereby text and commentary are set up in a tricolumnar format with the text as the second column.[70]

---

[65] Note 36 above, and see Unterkircher, *Die Glossen des Psalters von Mondsee*, 13–15, *et passim*.

[66] I am indebted to Rosamond McKitterick for this identification.

[67] Contrary to Leroquais' assumption (*Les psautiers manuscrits* I, 289), the commentary in Orléans 48 is not that of Smaragdus: see F. Rädle, *Studien zu Smaragd von Saint-Mihiel*, Medium Aevum Philologische Studien 29 (Munich, 1974), 99–100.

[68] Me compsit Heriueus, et ODBERTVS decorauit, / *Excerpsit Dodolinus*, et hos Deus aptet Olimpo: Leroquais, *Les psautiers manuscrits* I, 94–5.

[69] That is the gloss in the inner margins only.

[70] Zürich, Staatsarchiv, A. G. 19, no. XII: see CLA VII, 1008.

The *mise-en-page* of the Glossed Psalter was rarely applied to other books of the Bible. A fine manuscript of the Pauline Epistles, that was written for Bishop Arn of Salzburg *c.* 800, has its commentary intercalated after every phrase or verse.[71] This is a formula already seen in all the early manuscripts of the *Glosa ex traditone seniorum* and in the Mondsee Psalter; the annotation is indeed planned, but not as a gloss. Another manuscript of the Pauline Epistles, now in the Chapter Library of Ivrea, does have an extensive and contemporary marginal gloss, but again the ruling relates to the text only.[72] By the 860s however the scriptorium of Weissenburg (Alsace) was producing manuscripts of most parts of the Bible which broadly conform to the principles of the Glossed Psalter: the annotation is delimited by a panel on each side of the text.[73] More than a century later two perfect examples of a formally-glossed Bible text were written at Reichenau for Otto III.[74] But throughout the whole period *c.* 800–*c.* 1050 such manuscripts are few and far between. Although the technique of the integrated glossed page was sufficiently known, it was not widely adopted.

Hazardous though it is to assert a negative, I would argue that the integrated glossed page is never found in the texts that were routinely explicated in a Carolingian school. Donatus and Priscian, Virgil, Boethius and Martianus Capella: all were widely available and closely read. The evidence is in the marginal and interlinear annotation, which can show successive masters returning to tackle the same crux.[75] They may be drawing on a common stock of material, the text of their exegesis may be relatively stable; but visually it is random. Only in the late tenth century, in the circle of Dunstan at Canterbury, are there a few texts which cross the divide: Boethius, Juvenal and Prudentius.[76]

Schoolmasters were always reluctant to accept the constrictions of a *mise-en-page* that was too elegant to be emended. The integrated glossed page remained a rarity until the twelfth century, when it first became common to proceed to higher studies in Bible, in law and in medicine. In all these fields the definitive work of reference was a text and commentary laid out as an integrated glossed page.[77] The *Glossed Bible* consisted of a series of eight or ten volumes, with a marginal and interlinear gloss formally deployed throughout. This *mise-en-page* differs from that of the Carolingian Glossed Psalters in

---

[71] Budapest, National Library, Széchényi 1: Bischoff, *Schreibschulen* II, 114–15; text edited by H. J. Frede, *Ein neuer Paulustext und Kommentar*, Vetus Latina 7–8 (Freiburg, 1973–4).

[72] Ivrea, Biblioteca Capitolare, 28 (LXXIX): Bischoff, *Schreibschulen* II, 104–5.

[73] See W. Kleiber, *Otfrid von Weissenburg* (Munich, 1971), 136–7, *et passim*; Gibson, 'The Place of the *Glossa Ordinaria*'.

[74] Bamberg, Staatsbibliothek, MSS Bibl. 22 (Song of Songs and Daniel) and Bibl. 76 (Isaiah); see F. Mütherich, 'The Library of Otto III', in *The Role of the Book in Medieval Culture*, ed. P. F. Ganz, Bibliologia 3, 2 vols. (Turnhout, 1986), II, 11–25, at 13; Gibson, 'The Place of the *Glossa Ordinaria*'.

[75] A good example is Oxford, Bodleian Library, MS Auct. T. I. 26 (SC 20622), a handsome Carolingian volume of Priscian: plate in M. T. Gibson, 'Milestones in the Study of Priscian', *Viator* 23 (1992), 19–33.

[76] For Boethius and Juvenal see Oxford, Bodleian Library, MS Auct. F. I. 15 (SC 2455) and Geneva, Bibliotheca Bodmeriana, MS 175 (Boethius only), both English. For Prudentius see Oxford, Bodleian Library, MS Auct. F. III. 6, in which some pages have half-space ruling for the gloss.

[77] Smalley, *Study of the Bible*, 52–6 (civil and canon law: note by H. Kantorowicz). The *mise-en-page* of standard medical texts still requires further study.

two respects: the presence of an interlinear gloss as well as a marginal, and the continuation of every second line unbroken across the page. The former is a significant variation, which derives from the use of the Psalter and the Pauline Epistles as textbooks in the schools of northern France and the Rhineland.[78] The latter – which has attracted more scholarly attention – is the only feature that consistently distinguishes the ruling of the old Carolingian Psalters from that of the new *Glossed Bible*. It should not obscure our perception of the luxury Glossed Psalter as the prototype of the *Glossed Bible*, not in its substance but in the well-tried principles of its *mise-en-page*.

[78] M. T. Gibson, 'The Twelfth-century Glossed Bible'.

6

The Old Testament in late Anglo-Saxon England: preliminary observations on the textual evidence

RICHARD MARSDEN

The high profile enjoyed by the Gospels and the Psalms in the devotional life of the Benedictine monasteries, and in the surviving manuscript evidence for that life, tends to obscure the essential role played also by the non-psalmodic books of the Vulgate Old Testament.[1] 'Quae enim pagina', runs the question in the last chapter of the Rule of Benedict, 'aut qui sermo diuinae auctoritatis ueteris ac noui testamenti non est rectissima norma uitae humanae?'[2] Little scholarly attention has been paid either to the form in which the Old Testament books circulated or to the texts which they transmitted during the monastic revival of the second half of the tenth century in England.[3] The surviving primary material is, admittedly, sparse. It amounts to one Bible (which lacks the first half of Genesis in the original form) and single leaves from two others, to which we may add Old Testament books or extracts copied into a handful of other, non-biblical manuscripts.[4] Yet even these few witnesses are a valuable potential source of knowledge, not only about manuscript production during the late Anglo-Saxon period but also about the history of the Vulgate, in particular the relationship between its Continental and Insular texts. In what follows, I survey the available material, including the neglected London, British Library, Royal 1. E vii–viii, and outline the results of a preliminary analysis of it.

---

[1] For useful surveys of gospel books and Psalters, with some bibliography, see H. Gneuss, 'Liturgical Books in Anglo-Saxon England and their Old English Terminology', in *Learning and Literature in Anglo-Saxon England, Studies Presented to Peter Clemoes*, ed. M. Lapidge and H. Gneuss (Cambridge, 1985), 91–141, at 106–9 and 114–16, respectively. However, the detailed history of the Anglo-Saxon Psalter and gospel book texts, along with an account of other New Testament books, remains to be written.

[2] *Benedicti Regula*, ed. R. Hanslik, CSEL 75 (Vienna, 1960), 164. 'For what page, what phrase in that divine authority, the Old and the New Testament, does not represent a most proper standard of human life?'

[3] H. H. Glunz's *History of the Vulgate in England from Alcuin to Roger Bacon* (Cambridge, 1933), despite the broad scope of its title, is an account only of gospel book transmission. It is marred by unsupported statements.

[4] By contrast, twenty Latin gospel books survive which were probably written in England between the mid-tenth and mid-eleventh centuries, thirteen of them between about 980 and 1020; P. McGurk, 'Text', in *The York Gospels*, ed. N. T. Barker (London, 1986) 43–63, at 43–4.

SOME PROLEGOMENA

Two of our three surviving Latin Bible manuscripts from the late Anglo-Saxon period
are mere fly-leaf fragments. Columbia, Missouri, University of Missouri Library,
Fragmenta Manuscripta 4, preserves portions of the minor prophets, Micah, Nahum
and Habakkuk. It was written in England during the second half of the tenth century
but its specific origin is unknown.[5] London, British Library, Add. 34652, contains
the end of the text of Song of Songs and the beginning of a capitula list for Wisdom
and has been dated on palaeographical grounds to the first quarter of the eleventh
century, but its specific origin in England is again unknown.[6] By contrast, and by
great good luck, our third biblical witness offers an almost complete text of the Old
Testament, although unfortunately some twenty of the original leaves, including those
containing all of Genesis as far as 20.35, have been replaced at later periods. This is the
two-volume Bible, London, British Library, Royal 1. E. vii–viii, which has received
little attention but whose importance can hardly be overstated.[7] The manuscript
probably dates from the end of the tenth century and has customarily been attributed,
purely on circumstantial evidence, to the scriptorium of Christ Church, Canterbury.
This is unlikely, though the manuscript was indeed at Christ Church immediately after
the Conquest, as we shall see.

Direct evidence for the Old Testament in the earlier Anglo-Saxon centuries is
hardly less sparse than that for the later years. I know of only eight witnesses for the
whole period up until the beginning of the monastic reforms of the mid-tenth century.
These are listed chronologically, along with the later witnesses, in an appendix to this
paper.[8] Only the last of the eight, a fly-leaf fragment containing portions of Numbers

---

[5] No. 811 in H. Gneuss, 'A Preliminary List of Manuscripts written or owned in England up to 1100', *Anglo-Saxon England* 9 (1981), 1–60 (hereafter 'Gneuss'), where it is listed as University of Missouri–Columbia Library, Rare–L/PA3381/.A1/.F7, fol. 4. It consists of a single leaf, trimmed to 172 × 128mm, badly damaged in places. I have established (from photographs kindly supplied by Linda Voigts of the University of Missouri) that it contains the text of Micah 7.15–20 and Nahum 1.1–6 (recto) and Habakkuk 2.5–17 (verso).

[6] Gneuss, no. 289; *Catalogue of Additions to the Manuscripts in the British Museum in the Years 1894–1899. Part 1. Descriptions* (London, 1901), 28, item 5 (where the manuscript is assigned to the late twelfth century).

[7] Gneuss, no. 449; G. F. Warner and J . P. Gilson, *Catalogue of Western Manuscripts in the Old Royal and King's Collections*, 4 vols. (London, 1921), I, 20–1; N. R. Ker, *Medieval Libraries of Great Britain: A List of Surviving Books*, 2nd edn (London, 1964), 36. Further bibliographical information is given below.

[8] A ninth manuscript, a bifolium containing parts of Judges, written in a cursive minuscule of the early ninth century and now in the private collection of T. Takamiya, Tokyo (formerly Doheny A-S 1), was assigned tentatively in a recent study to a southern English scriptorium; M. P. Brown, 'A New Fragment of a Ninth-Century English Bible', *Anglo-Saxon England* 18 (1989), 33–43. Bruce Barker-Benfield has shown, however, that the Tokyo leaf belongs with thirty-two leaves surviving in Düsseldorf, Landes- und Stadtbibliothek A.19 (on permanent loan to the Heinrich-Heine-Universitätsbibliothek, Düsseldorf). These are the remains of a Heptateuch, probably written by an Insular scribe in the monastery of Werden on the Ruhr. See B. C. Barker-Benfield, 'The Werden Heptateuch', *Anglo-Saxon England* 20 (1991), 43–64, and CLA Supplement, 1685. It is probable that British Library, Royal 1. E. vi, with Canterbury, Cathedral Library, Add. 16 and Oxford, Bodleian Library, Lat. bib. b. 2 (P), copied in the first half of the ninth century, probably at St Augustine's, Canterbury, is the remains of another complete Bible, but only the gospels and a fragment of Acts survive. See CLA II, 214 and 244; Gneuss, no. 448; Warner and Gilson, *Catalogue*, I, 20; P. McGurk, 'An Anglo-Saxon Bible Fragment of the Late Eighth Century', *Journal of the Warburg and Courtauld Institutes* 25 (1962), 18–34; M. O. Budny, 'London, British Library MS Royal 1. E. vi: the Anatomy of an Anglo-Saxon Bible Fragment' (unpublished Ph.D. thesis, London University, 1985).

and Deuteronomy and dating from the first part of the ninth century, was written in southern England.[9] All the others are Northumbrian both in provenance and, with one exception, in origin. The exception is the earliest manuscript, a sixth-century fragment of Maccabees written in Italy, whence most of the exemplars for the Northumbrian Bibles probably came.[10] Five more of the eight earlier witnesses are fragmentary also, but one is a volume of five wisdom books from the eighth century, surviving almost complete in London, British Library, Egerton 1046.[11] The most celebrated of the early Anglo-Saxon witnesses is the *Codex Amiatinus*, Florence, Biblioteca Medicea Laurenziana, Amiatino 1.[12] Written at Wearmouth–Jarrow some time before 716, and probably the last of three such pandects ordered by Abbot Ceolfrith, it was sent almost at once to Italy.[13] As well as being the earliest complete Vulgate to have survived anywhere, *Amiatinus* is our only complete pre-Conquest English Bible.[14]

Can any general deductions be made from these manuscripts about the form of Old Testament biblical manuscripts and the manner in which they circulated in Anglo-Saxon England? Michelle Brown has drawn attention to the relationship between page size and Bible form in the earlier Anglo-Saxon witnesses.[15] Those manuscripts associated with complete Bibles, viz. *Amiatinus* and the surviving leaves from one of its sister pandects,[16] have a large format, with a text area of about *c.* 360 × 260 mm on pages of *c.* 505 × 340 mm. Part-Bibles, with only a selection of Old Testament books and therefore demanding far less space, have smaller pages. The Egerton wisdom codex has a text area of 260 × 200 mm on pages of 310 × 225 mm. If these criteria are applied to our two late biblical fragments, it must be concluded that both of them, the Columbia leaf (whose text area I estimate to have been approximately 350 × 240 mm)

---

[9] Oxford, Bodleian Library, Lat. bib. c. 8 (P), with Salisbury, Cathedral Library, 117, fols. 163–4, and Tokyo, T. Takamiya, private collection (formerly Cheltenham, Phillipps Collection 36183); CLA II, 259; Gneuss, no. 646.

[10] Durham, Cathedral Library, B. IV. 6, fol. 169; CLA II, 153; Gneuss, no. 245. On the Italian connection, see B. Fischer, *Lateinische Bibelhandschriften im frühen Mittelalter*, Vetus Latina 11 (Freiburg, 1985), 68–9 and R. Marsden, 'Theodore's Bible: the Pentateuch', in *Archbishop Theodore, 690–1990: Commemorative Studies on his Career and Influence*, ed. M. Lapidge (forthcoming).

[11] CLA II, 194a and 194b; Gneuss, no. 410. The manuscript consists of two complementary parts, in cursive minuscule and hybrid minuscule.

[12] CLA III, 299; Gneuss, no. 825. See esp. S. Berger, *Histoire de la Vulgate pendant les premiers siècles du moyen âge* (Paris, 1893; repr. New York, n.d., and Hildesheim, 1976), 37–41; M. B. Parkes, 'The Scriptorium of Wearmouth–Jarrow', Jarrow Lecture 1982 (Jarrow, 1983), 3 *et passim*; D. H. Wright, 'Some Notes on English Uncial', *Traditio* 17 (1961), 441–56; R. L. S. Bruce-Mitford, 'The Art of the Codex Amiatinus', Jarrow Lecture 1967 (Jarrow, 1968) and *Journal of the British Archaeological Association* 3rd series, 32 (1969), 1–25; Fischer, *Lateinische Bibelhandschriften*, 9–34 and 67–9.

[13] See Bede's *Historia abbatum*, ch. 15, and the anonymous *Vita Ceolfridi*, ch. 20, in *Venerabilis Baedae Opera Historica*, ed. C. Plummer, 2 vols. (Oxford, 1896), I, 379 and 395, respectively; and Parkes, 'Scriptorium of Wearmouth–Jarrow', 3.

[14] The first post-Conquest English Vulgate Bibles, all dating from the close of the eleventh century, include Cambridge, Trinity College, B. 5. 2 (148), Gneuss, no. 169, from Lincoln; Durham, Cathedral Library, A. II. 4, Gneuss, no. 217, from Durham; Lincoln, Cathedral Library, 1 (A. 1. 2), Gneuss, no. 270, from Lincoln; and San Marino, California, Henry E. Huntington Library, HM 62, Gneuss, no. 934, from Rochester (the Gundulf Bible).

[15] Brown, 'A New Fragment', at 41–3. Brown gives the dimensions of the manuscripts dating from the seventh century to the beginning of the ninth century.

[16] These leaves are all now in the British Library, as Add. 37777, Add. 45025 and Loan MS 81.

and Add. 34652 (with a text area probably of about 345 × 260 mm), are the remains of large-format, complete Bibles. We cannot tell whether these were two-volume Bibles, like the third late witness, Royal 1. E. vii–viii, or pandects.[17] Looking at the full list of eleven Anglo-Saxon biblical manuscripts containing the Old Testament, we may conclude that we have witnesses to five complete Bibles, including each of the three late ones, and to six part-Bibles.[18]

This Anglo-Saxon evidence for two main formats, a larger one for pandects (or multi-volume Bibles) and a smaller one for volumes containing a limited number of biblical books, is paralleled on the Continent, where far more manuscripts from the whole early medieval period survive.[19] There remain about forty part-Bibles and almost fifty complete Bibles (most of them pandects) written up to the beginning of the eleventh century.[20] Thus part-Bibles, as in England, are outnumbered by complete Bibles, but undoubtedly these figures give a distorted view of Bible production and Bible use during this period. Economic pressures and purely practical demands must have caused the smaller books to be made in greater numbers. We may assume that pandects survived better because they were valued more highly, often as prized possessions, and were less likely to be in daily use either for reading or for copying.[21] Some fourteen of the part-Bibles consist of, or include, collections of the wisdom books, like our Egerton codex; Job is frequently included. Almost equally popular are codices containing the major or minor prophets (or a combination of both) and others containing the deuterocanonical books, Judith, Esther, Ezra, I–II Maccabees and Tobit, or a selection of three or four of these, and again Job is often added. St Gall is particularly notable as a thriving centre for the production of such part-Bibles during the second half of the ninth century.[22] There is comparatively little Continental evidence for the circulation of the Pentateuch, Heptateuch or Octateuch independently, though obvious exceptions are the illustrated Pentateuch from Saint-Gatien and an Octateuch from Saint-Martin, Tours, both more or less contemporary with *Amiatinus*.[23] There are at least three cases, however, where a Pentateuch, a

---

[17] The question of whether Royal 1. E. vii–viii was in fact always a two-volume book is discussed below.

[18] Royal 1. E. vii–viii, with a text area averaging 440 × 240 mm on pages of 550 × 345 mm, differs from our Anglo-Saxon witnesses in its vertical dimensions. The other complete Bibles fall within the range 350–70 × 255–65 mm (text) and 480–505 × 335–40 mm (page). The page format of Royal 1. E. vi (see n. 8 above) is somewhat squarer, at *c.* 470 × 345 mm. On this see Brown, 'A New Fragment', 42.

[19] Although the Continental Bibles, as we might expect in view of their greater number, show a larger range of page size, the same division into two format groups is generally applicable, although there are of course notable cases of small-format pandects, such as those produced under Theodulf at Fleury. For example, the pages of London, British Library Add. 24142 (the Saint Hubert Bible) measure 325 × 245 mm.

[20] The most useful source of information is still the annotated list in Berger, *Histoire*, 374–422, although some of Berger's dates must be treated with caution. Further Bibles or part-Bibles are listed in library catalogues. My estimates are based on the contents of Berger's list and the catalogues of the Stifts-bibliothek at St Gall and the Bibliothèque Nationale in Paris, the two largest repositories of early medieval Latin Bibles.

[21] Fischer, *Lateinische Bibelhandschriften*, 33.

[22] Berger, *Histoire*, 413–18; Fischer, *Lateinische Bibelhandschriften*, 180–5.

[23] Paris, Bibliothèque Nationale, n.a. lat. 2334, and Tours, Bibliothèque Municipale, 10, respectively.

Heptateuch or an Octateuch have been included in a volume with other Old or New Testament books.[24]

The picture of Bible circulation in late Anglo-Saxon England suggested by our three surviving late tenth- or early eleventh-century manuscripts, which all represent complete Bibles, is certainly the result of the same aberration which we see in the Continental record. In England, too, economic factors and the practicalities of production, transmission and use must have meant that the smaller part-Bibles were more numerous, though none has survived. Two Anglo-Saxon booklists offer some confirmation of this, although both date from very late in our period. One of them, made between 1069 and 1072, probably lists the books procured for the church of Exeter by Bishop Leofric after his arrival there in 1050 and includes a volume of the four major prophets, separate volumes of Isaiah, Ezekiel and Maccabees, and a fifth volume containing the Song of Songs.[25] The other list, made in about 1070 and perhaps representing the personal library of Sæwold, abbot of Bath, at the time of the Conquest, includes a Heptateuch among its volumes.[26] Neither of these lists, nor others that survive, includes complete Bibles. This may be an indication of the relative rarity of these, but complete Bibles, where they existed, would have been permanent fixtures of the monastic churches and we would not expect them to share the mobility of part-Bibles or to feature in the personal booklists of abbots.

So far I have discussed purely biblical manuscripts, but we know that the Old Testament circulated in other ways also, either as complete individual books collected with miscellaneous non-scriptural texts, or in the form of substantial extracts of relevance to the theme of a particular exegetical or devotional work. For the purposes of textual history such witnesses are hardly less important than the Bibles or part-Bibles themselves. Two manuscripts containing the texts of complete Old Testament books survive from the Anglo-Saxon period. One is a copy of Proverbs, included in a volume of patristic and devotional texts which is now British Library, Cotton Vespasian D. vi., fols. 2–77, made at St Augustine's, Canterbury, in the mid-tenth century.[27] The second is a copy of Tobit, probably made likewise in the tenth century and included among patristic and devotional texts in Oxford, Bodleian Library,

24 St Gall, Stiftsbibliothek, 2 (s. viii, the Pentateuch, plus Acts and Revelation) and 80 (s. x, the Heptateuch, plus the Pauline epistles and Acts), and Vatican City, Biblioteca Apostolica Vaticana, Pal. lat. 2 (s. ix 1, the Octateuch, plus Kings and Chronicles).

25 M. Lapidge, 'Surviving Booklists from Anglo-Saxon England', in *Learning and Literature*, ed. Lapidge and Gneuss, 33–89, at 64–9.

26 *Ibid.*, 59. The Heptateuch, or in some manuscripts the Hexateuch, circulated also in an Old English translation, made at about the turn of the millenium. It is edited in S. J. Crawford, *The Old English Version of the Heptateuch, Ælfric's Treatise on the Old and New Testament and his Preface to Genesis*, EETS 160 (London, 1922; repr. 1969, with the text of two additional manuscripts transcribed by N. R. Ker); see also C. R. Dodwell and P. A. M. Clemoes, eds., *The Old English Illustrated Hexateuch: British Museum Cotton Claudius B*, iv, Early English Manuscripts in Facsimile 18 (Copenhage, 1974).

27 Gneuss, no. 389; N. R. Ker, *Catalogue of Manuscripts Containing Anglo-Saxon* (Oxford, 1957; reissued with suppl., 1990), no. 207. The text of Proverbs is on fols. 2–37 and is glossed extensively in Old English. The manuscript includes also a Latin work by Alcuin and an Old English paraphrase of Psalm 50.

Bodley 572, a manuscript of Cornish and Welsh origin.[28] Among the late Anglo-
Saxon manuscripts containing substantial extracts from the Vulgate Old Testament,
the following are noteworthy.[29] A continuous extract from Sirach 25–6 is included in
a series of texts concerning sin which follows Defensor's *Liber Scintillarum* in London,
British Library, Royal 7. C. iv, dated to the first half of the eleventh century. The
manuscript is believed to have originated at Christ Church, Canterbury, and is glossed
in Old English.[30] A version of the *Liber ex lege Moysis*, a work of Irish origin and
including substantial extracts from Exodus, Leviticus, Numbers and Deuteronomy,[31]
survives in London, British Library, Cotton Otho E. xiii, a tenth-century manuscript
from St Augustine's, Canterbury.[32] Another version of the *Liber*, known to have
reached Worcester but written in France in the second half of the ninth century, is in
Cambridge, Corpus Christi College, 279, fols. 55v–80r.[33] Finally, a fragment of a
liturgical version of portions of Lamentations is preserved in Columbia, Missouri,
University of Missouri Library, Fragmenta Manuscripta 1. The manuscript dates from
the mid-tenth century and, to judge from its format and annotations, may come from a
volume containing biblical readings needed for Nocturns. A Glastonbury provenance
has been suggested.[34]

    Tracing the origin of the late Anglo-Saxon Old Testament texts is problematical.
Ought we to follow the model of Hans Glunz's account of gospel book transmission
and think purely in terms of a Continental origin for all the tenth-century Vulgate
texts?[35] This view would envisage a flow of biblical texts from the Continent to
accompany and complement the influx of monastic ideals and practices which inspired
and underpinned the English reforms.[36] Such Continental texts would inevitably have

[28] Gneuss, no. 583; Ker, *Catalogue*, no. 313; F. Madan *et al.*, *A Summary Catalogue of Western Manuscripts in the
Bodleian Library at Oxford*, 7 vols. (Oxford 1895–1953; repr. Munich, 1980), ii, 170–4; W. M. Lindsay, *Early
Welsh Script* (Oxford, 1912), 26–32. The dating of the various parts of this interesting manuscript remains
uncertain.

[29] I take no account here of the numerous short scriptural citations which occur in the works of Anglo-Latin
authors and in liturgical material.

[30] Gneuss, no. 470; Ker, *Catalogue*, no. 256. See also T. A. M. Bishop, 'Notes on Cambridge Manuscripts, Part
vii: the Early Minuscule of Christ Church Canterbury', *Transactions of the Cambridge Bibliographical Society* 3
(1959–63), 413–23, at 420–3.

[31] On the use and transmission of the *Liber*, see R. Kottje, 'Der *Liber ex lege Moysis*', in *Irland und die Christenheit:
Bibelstudien und Mission*, ed. P. Ní Chatháin and M. Richter (Stuttgart, 1987), 59–69.

[32] Thomas Smith, *Catalogus Librorum Manuscriptorum Bibliothecae Cottonianae* (Oxford, 1696), 79; Ker, *Medieval
Libraries*, 43; Kottje, '*Liber ex lege Moysis*', 62. The manuscript was severely damaged in the Cotton fire but a
substantial proportion of the text remains legible.

[33] M. R. James, *Descriptive Catalogue of the Manuscripts in the Library of Corpus Christi College Cambridge*, 2 vols.
(Cambridge, 1912), ii, 42–4; Ker, *Medieval Libraries*, 206; Kottje, '*Liber ex lege Moysis*', 62.

[34] See L. E. Voigts, 'An Anglo-Saxon Liturgical Manuscript at the University of Missouri', *Anglo-Saxon England*
17 (1988), 83–92, at 86–9. The manuscript contains Lam. 2.22–3.14, 3.19–35, 40–56 and 60–6. See also n. 46
below.

[35] Glunz, *History*, esp. 61–5 and 133–6. As we shall see, Glunz's views must be treated with extreme caution.
The question of the influence of the Carolingian Vulgate textual traditions is discussed further below. On
some of the problems involved in assessing the extent of Continental influence on English monasticism
during the tenth century, see E. John, 'The Sources of the English Monastic Reformation: a Comment', *Revue
Bénédictine* 70 (1960), 197–203; but cf. T. Symons, 'Some Notes on English Monastic Origins', *Downside Review*
80 (1962), 55–69.

[36] D. Knowles, *The Monastic Order in England*, 2nd edn (Cambridge, 1963), 515, apparently following Glunz, saw
a single Vulgate text as part of 'all that was best' that had been brought from the Continent during Dunstan's
time.

shown evidence of the great Carolingian Vulgate textual reforms of the ninth century, associated primarily with Theodulf and Alcuin.[37] Specifically, according again to Glunz's account of the Gospels, they will have transmitted Alcuin's text, as developed at Tours. On the other hand, did any of what we might call the 'native' Bible texts, written mainly in Northumbria in the later seventh and the eighth centuries (and prominently represented among our early manuscripts), survive the apparent monastic decline of the ninth century and continue to be used and copied during the monastic revival of the later tenth century, perhaps alongside new arrivals from the Continent? Such questions can only be answered adequately by an exhaustive study, not only of the surviving Anglo-Saxon Bible manuscripts but also of derived material, such as scriptural citations in Anglo-Latin writers and the vernacular translations made in the late tenth century.[38]

The evidence of the manuscripts must be viewed in the context of our knowledge of manuscript transmission between the Continent and England during the tenth century. Following the apparent decline in Latin learning and virtual standstill in manuscript production in England during the middle years of the ninth century,[39] Alfred used scholars from the Continent in his efforts to revive learning and this may be seen as the first potential opportunity for the transmission of the new Carolingian Vulgate texts to England, but there is no evidence of this.[40] The renewed contacts between the Wessex royal family and continental religious houses were consolidated during the reigns of Alfred's successors,[41] and Athelstan (who succeeded in 924) provides us with the first firm evidence of the importing of scriptural books. He was a collector of books and presented many as gifts, including gospel books to both Christ Church and St Augustine's at Canterbury and to the community of St Cuthbert at Chester-le-Street. Almost all Athelstan's books, including the gospel books, were written on the Continent, although some may well have been imported before his reign.[42] The continental connections of the progenitors and engineers of the monastic

---

[37] Fischer, *Lateinische Bibelhandschriften*, 135–47 and 127–34, respectively. The Alcuinian Bibles are surveyed in detail on 203–403. See also the essays by David Ganz and Rosamond McKitterick, chs. 3 and 4 above.

[38] For Old Testament translations, see above, n. 26.

[39] On the decline in learning, see Alfred's well-known remarks in the letter which prefaces his translation of Gregory's *Regula Pastoralis*, printed in *King Alfred's West-Saxon Version of Gregory's Pastoral Care*, ed. H. Sweet, 2 vols., EETS OS 45 and 50 (Oxford and London, 1871), I, 2–6, and the appraisals by H. Gneuss, 'King Alfred and the Anglo-Saxon Libraries, in *Modes of Interpretation in Old English Literature: Essays in Honour of Stanley B. Greenfield*, ed. P. R. Brown, G. R. Crampton and F. C. Robinson (Toronto, 1986), 29–49, and N. P. Brooks, *The Early History of the Church of Canterbury* (Leicester, 1984), 164–74. Cf., however, the arguments of Jennifer Morrish in 'Dated and Datable Manuscripts copied in England during the Ninth Century: A Preliminary List', *Medieval Studies* 50 (1988), 512–38, and in 'King Alfred's Letter as a Source on Learning in England in the Ninth Century', *Studies in Earlier Old English Prose*, ed. P. E. Szarmach (Albany, NY, 1986), 87–107.

[40] Glunz, *History*, 61, accepted as a fact the introduction at this time of gospel books in the new Carolingian textual traditions, especially the Alcuinian, but he gave no evidence and his account here is confused.

[41] See D. A. Bullough, 'The Educational Tradition in England from Alfred to Ælfric: Teaching *Utriusque Linguae*', *Settimane* 19 (1972), 453–94.

[42] S. Keynes, 'King Athelstan's Books', in *Learning and Literature*, ed. Lapidge and Gneuss, 143–201, at 198–201. The donated gospel books have been identified with London, British Library, Cotton Tiberius A. II (Christ Church), Royal 1. A. xviii (St Augustine's), and Cotton Otho B. IX (St Cuthbert's). See F. A. Rella, 'Continental Manuscripts acquired for English Centres in the Tenth and Early Eleventh Centuries: A

revival during the following decades are well known, although their relative significance as influences on the monastic reforms is still debated.[43] In the 950s, Dunstan spent a period of exile at the reformed monastery of St Peter's, Ghent. Æthelwold, abbot of Abingdon and bishop of Winchester (963–84), and arguably the most influential of the reformers, was prevented from visiting the Continent himself but sent his pupil Osgar to Fleury. Later, he is credited with summoning monks from Corbie to instil into those of Abingdon proper standards in the practice of chant. Oswald, future bishop of Worcester and archbishop of York, was sent to Fleury (*c.* 950–8) by his uncle Oda, archbishop of Canterbury, and he was followed by his colleague Germanus of Winchester, who stayed for two years at Fleury before moving back to England and soon to Ramsey. In turn, Lantfred of Fleury was at Winchester in the 970s, while Abbo came from Fleury to teach at Ramsey in 985.

The evidence that scriptural works were among the books brought to England during this extended period is restricted, as we have seen, to gospel books, and certainly these had a prime place in monastic liturgical practice, along with the Psalter.[44] Yet Old Testament materials must have been in demand also and their existence is confirmed by the booklists noted above. Helmut Gneuss has observed that scriptural readings for the Night Office were mainly from the Old Testament and that, to provide them, there was needed either a special book containing all the biblical lessons or a complete Bible.[45] While no Bible or part-Bible showing signs of having been used for this purpose is known, the recently-described fragment of a liturgical version of Lamentations preserved in Missouri may well have belonged to a special book of the sort Gneuss posits.[46]

To return once more to Glunz's account of gospel book transmission, undoubtedly it was an overstatement and an oversimplification. Glunz identified what he called a 'Winchester text', represented by several surviving manuscripts, which he believed had a Continental prototype, probably brought from Fleury to Winchester during the time of Æthelwold, and copied there several times.[47] In fact, although the group of

---

Preliminary Checklist', *Anglia* 98 (1980), 107–16, nos. 7, 18 and 13. A Psalter, London, British Library, Cotton Galba A. xviii, was probably donated by Athelstan to the Old Minster, Winchester (Rella's no. 12). Rella lists a total of thirty-four books known to have reached England from the Continent in the tenth and early eleventh centuries.

[43] See Knowles, *Monastic Order*, 39–40; E. John, 'The King and the Monks in the Tenth-century Reformation', in his *Orbis Britanniae and Other Studies* (Leicester, 1966), 154–80; Bullough, 'Educational Tradition', 482–3; P. Wormald, 'Æthelwold and his Continental Counterparts', in *Bishop Æthelwold: His Career and Influence*, ed. B. Yorke (Woodbridge, 1988), 13–42, at 22–5.

[44] Brooks, *Church of Canterbury*, 275. There are six gospel books, a gospel lectionary and five Psalters in Brooks' list of Canterbury books, 267–70. He also includes Royal 1. E. vii–viii, which would thus be the only witness in his list to the Old Testament, but there is no evidence that this Bible was at Canterbury before the Conquest; see below.

[45] Gneuss, 'Liturgical Books', 122.

[46] It could be the remains of a biblical lectionary or even a 'proto-breviary'. See the interesting discussion by Voigts in 'Liturgical Manuscript', 87–9, and the note on breviaries by Gneuss in 'Liturgical Books', 110–12.

[47] Glunz, *History*, 133–6.

'Winchester' gospel texts does have a degree of textual coherence and an obvious Continental origin,[48] none of the surviving gospel books can be assigned to that centre with certainty on palaeographical grounds. Glunz's theory may yet have substance; grounds for at least the suspicion of a 'Fleury' connection in some Old Testament books will be presented below. In general, however, in the absence of clear and specific evidence it is quite unsafe to posit simple lines of transmission for any part of the Anglo-Saxon Bible during this period. New biblical manuscripts arriving in England from the Continent are likely to have supplemented those already there, however few they were, and not simply replaced them, and both old and new texts may then have been copied.[49] With monasteries being founded or re-founded at an unprecedented rate, above all during the 960s and 970s,[50] Bible texts of all kinds (as well as liturgical and other books) must have been at a premium and transmission may have been largely haphazard. Linda Brownrigg has highlighted some evidence for Æthelwold's supplying of new libraries from the resources of established centres, as well as the more unpredictable role played in the movement of books by peripatetic abbots such as the above-mentioned Sæwold of Bath.[51] In general, however, we can only speculate on patterns of demand for biblical manuscripts and the logistics of their supply. I am aware of no contemporary reference to such matters.

LONDON, BRITISH LIBRARY, ROYAL 1. E. VII–VIII

The two-volume Bible comprised in London, British Library, Royal 1. E. vii–viii is our most important source of information about the form and text of the Old Testament in late Anglo-Saxon England. The volumes have 208 and 203 folios, respectively, and were rebound in the early part of this century. According to inscriptions on fol. 2r of the first volume and fol. 1r of the second, they belonged successively to Henry Fitz-Alan, Earl of Arundel, and John, Lord Lumley. A slip of paper inserted between fols. 34 and 35 of volume I bears writing in a sixteenth-century hand and the signature of Robert Lenton. The Bible has long been associated with Christ Church, Canterbury on the basis of an inscription in the right-hand margin of the recto of fol. 193 in volume II. This is in a hand of the second half of the thirteenth or early fourteenth century and reads *bibilioteca*

---

[48] McGurk, 'Text', 51–5.

[49] For an interesting general view of the complexities of manuscript transmission during this period, see C. E. Hohler, 'Some Service Books of the Later Saxon Church', in *Tenth-Century Studies: Essays in Commemoration of the Millennium of the Council of Winchester and 'Regularis Concordia'*, ed. D. Parsons (London and Chichester, 1975), 60–83.

[50] Most new foundations, more than twenty, were made during Edgar's reign (959–75); P. A. Stafford, 'Church and Society in the Age of Ælfric', in *The Old English Homily and its Backgrounds*, ed. P. E. Szarmach and B. F. Huppé (Albany, NY, 1978), 11–42, and Knowles, *Monastic Order*, 48–52.

[51] L. L. Brownrigg, 'Manuscripts Containing English Decoration 871–1066, Catalogued and Illustrated: A Review', *Anglo-Saxon England* 7 (1978), 239–66, at 261–2. See also her comments on late Anglo-Saxon book production at 239–40.

(sic) *ecc[lesi]e chr[isti]*.[52] Warner and Gilson seem to have been first to make a connection between the inscription and an entry in Henry of Eastry's book catalogue for Christ Church, Canterbury, from the period 1284–1331, which records a 'Biblia bipartita in infirmaria in duobus uoluminibus'.[53] Although such a description would fit a large number of medieval Bibles, there is now, as we shall see, good reason to accept that our Bible was indeed at Christ Church at the latest immediately after the Conquest, but not that it was written there.

Structure and contents

As already indicated, Royal 1. E. vii–viii does not survive completely in its original form. Leaves at the beginning and end of both volumes, and at another point within volume II, have been replaced during what appear to be two different phases of reconstruction, in the late fourteenth or early fifteenth century and in the sixteenth century. It is not clear whether the Bible was always in two volumes, and the present tight bindings prevent a close investigation of just how they were originally made. The need for the reconstruction of the opening and closing pages of the present volumes, which had either been lost or perhaps were discarded because of their damaged state,[54] indicates only that these were separated some time before Eastry's Christ Church list was made. The impressive bulk of even the present single volumes might seem to be an argument against an original pandect form.[55] The Bible was well used, at least after the Conquest, to judge from the many textual corrections and annotations (which are discussed below), and by the reading marks which occur throughout the text and which draw attention above all to word division at the end of lines. The original quire signatures, all but two of which survive, are continuous throughout the two volumes.

Only one original leaf remains from the first quire in volume I. It is the present fol. 1 but must formerly have been fol. 2, for it carries on its recto the end only of Jerome's prologue to Genesis, followed by the list of Genesis capitula headings as far as LXXVI. On the verso is the end of the capitula list, LXXVII–LXXXIII, followed by a large illustration of the Creation and, at the very bottom, the heading for Genesis proper. The present fols. 2–9, containing Genesis as far as 29.35, have been supplied in a hand of the late-fourteenth century or fifteenth century. In its use of space, this hand differs little from the original hand which wrote the rest of Genesis, so that the original first quire must have consisted similarly of eight leaves, plus both the present fol. 1 and the lost leaf before it – that is, a total of ten leaves. The present folio numbering, which

---

[52] At the bottom of the same page, adjacent to the quire signature of the last quire (49), the same scribe has written *xii liber*, for which no explanation is apparent, unless it be a pen test.

[53] Warner and Gilson, I, 21. For the catalogue entry, see M. R. James, *The Ancient Libraries of Canterbury and Dover* (Cambridge, 1903), 51, no. 321.

[54] The replaced folios may have been in the same poor state as the present fol. 1 of the first volume, the only folio now surviving from the first gathering, which was probably retained on account of the illustration on its verso. The capitula on its recto are hardly legible.

[55] The *Codex Amiatinus* is, of course, a single volume, as were its two sister pandects. Its format is somewhat smaller than that of Royal 1. E. vii–viii but it has 1,030 leaves.

may have been added at the time of a previous binding in the sixteenth or seventeenth centuries, ignores a double transposition of leaves in the supplied section of Genesis, where the present fols. 4–7 would have to be re-ordered in the sequence 5, 4, 7, 6 to restore a coherent text. The second quire is marked as beginning at the present fol. 10, which is in the original hand; it continues the text of Genesis from 29.35. It is complete and has eight folios, as do all the quires which survive complete in either volume. Quires 3–21 are complete, but quire 22 wants a leaf between fols. 171 and 172, where the text of Ezekiel 44.5–46.20 is consequently missing. Quire 23 is complete and ends with fol. 184. The continuing quire numeration in volume ii shows that quire 24 must have been the last quire in volume i, but it has been totally lost. It has been replaced not by eight but by twenty-four leaves (fols. 185–208), written in a sixteenth-century hand and supplying the text of the minor prophets from Obadiah 1.19 to the end of Malachi (fols. 185r–192v), and of Baruch and III–IV Esdras (fols. 193r–208v). It seems likely that, as in the sixteenth-century version, the text of the minor prophets originally occupied eight folios, thus completing a 'standard' quire. Baruch and III–IV Esdras were therefore very probably a sixteenth-century addition, not a replacement, so that, in the original sequence of books, the minor prophets were followed directly by Job. Other evidence, discussed below, reinforces this probability.

In the second volume, Royal 1. E. viii, the first leaf of the first quire, with the signature 25, has been supplied, like Genesis 1–29.35, in a fourteenth- or fifteenth-century hand.[56] It carries the opening chapters of Job. The next six leaves are original, and they complete the quire. Thus the supplied first leaf (fol. 1 of volume ii) appears to replace two lost leaves. Written in the original hand, the text of Job 1.1–6.21 would certainly not have required more than a single folio, as in the supplied version,[57] but it is very likely that prefatory material occupied the first leaf of the quire. A majority of surviving Vulgate Bibles of the early medieval period include Jerome's prologue to Job, beginning 'Cogor per singulos Scripturae diuinae'.[58] This would have needed about one and a half columns. A second and far shorter prologue, 'iuxta emendationem grecam', is found in some Bibles and could well have been in Royal 1. E. viii also, although it is much rarer.[59] Together, however, the two prologues would still have filled little more than a single page. It is possible that the rest of the space on our conjectured first folio was taken up by a capitula list, although such lists for Job are again rare, occurring in no Bibles of the Alcuinian

---

[56] The hands in the leaves supplying the first twenty-nine chapters of Genesis, the opening of Job and the end of Revelation (see below) are clearly contemporary, but at least two scribes were involved. Similarly, at least two scribes helped to supply the fourteenth- or fifteenth-century leaves of the minor prophets, Baruch and III–IV Esdras, and of parts of Psalms (see below).

[57] The replacement leaf supplies rather more text than necessary, continuing to 6.27, so that there is an overlap of six verses.

[58] See *Biblia Sacra iuxta Latinam Vulgatam Versionem ad codicum fidem*, ed. H. Quentin *et al.*, 18 vols. (Rome, 1926–), ix, *Liber Hester et Iob* (1951), 68–74 (hereafter *Biblia Sacra*). (Only vol. xviii, *Liber Macchabeorum*, of this critical edition remains to be published). The prologue occurs in all Bibles in the Theodulfian tradition and at least four of those in the Alcuinian tradition.

[59] *Biblia Sacra* ix, 74–6. This prologue is absent from all surviving Alcuinian Bibles but is in three of the Theodulfian and in a small number of others.

tradition.[60] It is more likely that it was left blank, a common practice at the start of a volume, although the possibility of another illustration might be considered also; both these explanations would of course require that there were two volumes from the start.[61]

As already indicated, fol. 8 carries the quire signature 26. The quires then continue regularly and completely until quire 48, with the single exception of quire 28. Here the middle four leaves have been lost and they have been replaced with five leaves, written in a sixteenth-century hand. The supplied text is Psalms 110.1–143.2 and the extra leaf seems to have been required as a result of rather extravagant use of space by the later scribe, whose writing varies greatly from page to page and whose ruling ranges between fifty-four and sixty-two lines per column. The final signed quire in volume II is number 49, which begins at fol. 193 and ends at fol. 198; its original structure is uncertain. Five leaves have been needed (fols. 199–203), to supply, in a fourteenth- or fifteenth-century hand, the final part of Revelation.[62] Thus quire 49 may have had eight folios, with a bifolium added, or it may originally have been a gathering of ten leaves, like the first quire of volume I.

To summarise, it is likely that Royal 1. E. vii–viii originally possessed a total of 396 leaves, contained in forty-nine quires, of which the first and last may have had ten leaves and the rest eight. It is possible that there were two further leaves, either in quire 24 or in quire 25. It is not clear whether the arrangement in two volumes was original.

Our Royal Bible lacks decoration in the text and in the Gospels there are no canon tables, so often used as an opportunity for lavish illustrative work in medieval Bibles. Colour is much used, however. Each book starts with a large capital letter in red, and red or purple is used for a few of the small capitals which punctuate some parts of the text. A notable display of coloured (and in this case extremely large) capital letters occurs in the book of Psalms. The uncial incipits and explicits are mostly in red, along with the numerals in some of the capitula lists.

The painted illustration on the verso of fol. 1 of the Royal Bible has long interested art historians.[63] It depicts in diagrammatic form the Creation, as described in Genesis

---

[60] Two Theodulfian Bibles, however, have a list, and others include the Maurdramnus and Biasca Bibles; see *Biblia Sacra* IX, 78. If our Bible was indeed always in two volumes, another possibility is that the (conjectured) unfilled space on the opening folio was taken up with another illustration.

[61] Another explanation, that some material continued from volume I onto the first leaf of the present volume II, cannot be ruled out. If our Royal Bible had after all been supplied originally with a copy of Baruch (which is certainly more likely than III–IV Esdras), an extra bifolium in quire 24 (such as that supplied to the first quire) plus the first page of the first leaf of quire 25 would have been sufficient to accommodate its fairly short text. Alternatively, the extra bifolium could have been supplied to the beginning of quire 25.

[62] They were thus supplied at the same time as the Genesis and Job replacement leaves. Warner and Gilson, *Catalogue* I, 21 wrongly attributed them to the sixteenth-century reconstruction.

[63] See esp. F. Wormald, *English Drawings of the Tenth and Eleventh Centuries* (London, 1952), no. 37, with nos. 15, 32 and 56, and pls. 20, 30 and 31; A. Heimann, 'Three Illustrations from the Bury St Edmunds Psalter and their Prototypes. Notes on the Iconography of some A–S Drawings', *Journal of the Warburg and Courtauld Institutes* 29 (1966), 39–59, at 53–4; E. Temple, *Anglo-Saxon Manuscripts 900–1066*, A Survey of Manuscripts Illuminated in the British Isles 2 (London, 1976), no. 102, pp. 119–20, 100, 115 and ill. 319.

1.6–10.[64] Within the circular cosmos are clearly represented both the separation of the waters above the firmament from the waters below it and the gathering together of the lower waters in one place so that dry land may appear. God's hirsute and nimbed head appears above the circle of the cosmos, over which he presides. Within the circle, at the top, one of the deity's hands holds rather awkwardly a pair of dividers or compasses and a pair of scales. The most intriguing feature of this illustration is the inclusion of two long horns, which protrude from either corner of God's mouth and extend on each side down into that area where the waters have been, or are being, divided. Adelheid Heimann has noted that this combination of the horn theme (whose origin is unknown) with the dividers and scales is uniquely English, but no version clearly predating that in our Royal Bible has survived.[65] The most accomplished version of the motif, following a prototype different from that of Royal, is in the Tiberius Psalter, which was produced in Winchester in the mid-eleventh century.[66] Two other Anglo-Saxon witnesses to the design, the Eadwig Gospels and the Bury Psalter, are both eleventh-century books. The former is certainly from Christ Church, the latter possibly so.[67] It seems, then, that a prototype of our illustration was known at both Winchester and Canterbury during the first half of the eleventh century, though perhaps earlier at Canterbury. Francis Wormald has assigned the style of drawing in the Royal version to the mid-eleventh century and linked it with such books as the British Library, Cotton Tiberius A. iii, the *Regularis Concordia*, which probably originated at Christ Church.[68]

On the evidence of the marginalia described above, the origin of our Royal Bible at Christ Church, Canterbury, has persistently been promoted. Yet its script offers nothing to confirm this. A good round Anglo-Caroline minuscule of Bishop's 'style I',[69] clear and firm but never monumental, and almost without Insular features (though an occasional uncial **d** is an exception), it probably dates from the end of the tenth century. We should perhaps look for its origin not at Canterbury but, as David Dumville has suggested, in one of the houses connected with Æthelwold and Winchester.[70] Wormald's dating of the creation picture to the mid-eleventh century merely provides a *terminus ante quem* for the text. It is likely that the picture was added some time after the writing of the manuscript, along with the elaborate heading to

---

[64] 'et fecit Deus firmamentum diuisitque aquas quae erant sub firmamento ab his quae erant super firmamentum ... dixit uero Deus congregentur aquae quae sub caelo sunt in locum unum et appareat arida' (Gen. 1.7, 9).

[65] A. Heimann, 'Three Illustrations', 53.

[66] London, British Library, Cotton Tiberius C. vi (Gneuss, no. 378).

[67] Hannover, Kestner-Museum, W. M. xxia, 36 (Gneuss, no. 831) and Vatican City, Biblioteca Apostolica Vaticana, Reg. lat. 12 (Gneuss, no. 912).

[68] Wormald, *English Drawings*, no. 37.

[69] T. A. M. Bishop, *English Caroline Minuscule* (Oxford, 1971), xxi–xxiv. The work seems to have been done by three scribes.

[70] D. N. Dumville, 'On the Dating of Some Late Anglo-Saxon Liturgical Manuscripts', *Transactions of the Cambridge Bibliographical Society* 10 (1991), 40–57, at 47–8. Dumville accepts a probable late-tenth-century date; see also Warner and Gilson, Catalogue I, 21 and Ker, *Medieval Libraries*, 36. On the monasteries associated with Æthelwold see the editor's introduction to *Bishop Æthelwold*, ed. Yorke, 2–4.

Genesis which the artist provided at the bottom of the same page. They could have been done after the manuscript's arrival at Canterbury.[71]

There is indeed firm evidence that it was there, at the latest, immediately after the Conquest. The text has been corrected or emended assiduously through the two volumes, mostly in a single post-Conquest hand, and this has now been identified by Tessa Webber as belonging to a Christ Church scribe who was working in the early years of the eleventh century. Among the manuscripts which the same scribe wrote and corrected are Cambridge, Trinity College, B. 1. 17 and B. 3. 9.[72] Corrections in the Royal Bible are in fact few, for copying errors are rare. Emendations are more numerous and, in general, they introduce the sort of variant readings which were to become widely current in Vulgate texts of the twelfth and thirteenth centuries. The Christ Church corrector was also much preoccupied with imposing his own orthographical conventions. For example, original *adp-* has been emended persistently to *app-*, *adf-* to *aff-*, *opp-* to *obp-* and *inm-* to *imm-*, and every occurrence of *idcirco* seems to have been altered to *iccirco*. Remarkable also is the corrector's habit of altering word-breaks at the ends of lines, sometimes with very odd results. For example, on fol. 14r of volume I, *ip/se* has been emended, by erasure of *p* at the end of one line and its addition to the start of the next, to *i/pse*, and on fol. 15r the division of *uic/timis* has been changed to *ui/ctimis*. Throughout both volumes there are occasional alterations or annotations in later hands.

Canon and capitula

In the selection and arrangement of the books of the Old Testament, Royal 1. E. vii–viii reflects the pattern established in the Alcuinian Bibles produced at Tours.[73] The sequence of books is as follows: the Pentateuch, Joshua, Judges, Ruth, I–IV Kings, Isaiah, Jeremiah, Ezekiel, Daniel, twelve minor prophets, Job, Psalms, Proverbs, Ecclesiastes, Song of Songs, Wisdom, Sirach, Chronicles, Ezra, Esther, Tobit, Judith, I–II Maccabees. This sequence occurs in no recension before the Alcuinian; notable is the placing of Job after the minor prophets and before Psalms. I believe, for the reason noted above, that Baruch and III–IV Esdras were not included in the original Bible but were first inserted between the minor prophets and Job (on fols. 193–208 of Royal 1. E. vii) as part of the sixteenth-century reconstruction. Their

---

[71] For the precise design of the heading, the artist made use of the pre-existing scored lines which cover the whole page. Temple, *Anglo-Saxon Manuscripts*, 119–20, judges the illustration, which she attributes on stylistic grounds to Canterbury, to be a late addition of the period *c.* 1050–70.

[72] T. Webber, 'Script and Manuscript Production at Christ Church, Canterbury after the Norman Conquest', in *Canterbury and the Norman Conquest: Churches, Saints and Scholars, 1066–1109*, ed. R. Eales and R. Sharpe (London, forthcoming). Dumville, 'Anglo-Saxon Liturgical Manuscripts', 47, notes similarities also with the corrector's hand in London, British Library, Arundel 155.

[73] Thus Zürich, Zentralbibliothek, C. 1, written during the abbacy of Fridugisus, 807–34, and Paris, Bibliothèque Nationale, lat. 3 (the Rorigo Bible) and London, British Library, Add. 10546 (the Moutier Grandval Bible), both from the abbacy of Adalhard, 834–43. However, two later Alcuinian Bibles, Rome, Biblioteca Vallicelliana, B. 6 and Rome, Abbazia di San Paolo fuori le Mura, s.n., associated with Rheims, differ in some details. The Theodulfian Bibles differ from the Alcuinian mainly in the separation of Daniel from the other prophetical books and in the order of the wisdom books.

absence originally is not surprising, for they are in none of the Tours Bibles or their immediate successors. Baruch appears characteristically in Bibles from Fleury, but III–IV Esdras are confined mainly to a few Spanish Bibles.[74]

In their provision of prologues or prefaces to the Old Testament books, early medieval Bibles varied considerably. In the books of law, the histories and the prophets, Royal 1. E. vii–viii reflects again in general the tradition of the Alcuinian Bibles, even down to the wording of headings; but there are exceptions and anomalies, especially in the wisdom and deuterocanonical books. Wisdom has a prologue, originally from Isidore, which occurs in the Theodulfian Bibles and in a Bible from Corbie.[75] Proverbs is supplied with a set of three prologues, although no Alcuinian Bible has more than one. The three are found together also in a few other Bibles, including one Theodulfian, but the order in our Royal Bible is unique. Judith has the expected Hieronymian prologue but in addition, preceding it, a prologue from Isidore, which is recorded in four other Bibles, including one Theodulfian.[76] Tobit has also been supplied with an extra prologue from Isidore, which occurs in only three Bibles, each of them among those just noted as having the extra prologue to Judith.[77]

The considerable influence of the Alcuinian tradition on the ancillary features of Royal 1. E. vii–viii is again apparently in the supplying of lists of capitula headings for the Old Testament books. There are fourteen such lists, including one each for the two parts of I–IV Kings (Samuel and Malachi). These books do not include Ruth, and in this respect our Bible differs from the usual Alcuinian tradition.[78] However, in the number of divisions which they indicate and in their texts, the capitula headings, while continuing to adhere basically to the Alcuinian tradition, show frequent anomalies, many of which have no known parallels in other Bibles. In the Pentateuch, for example, while the first three books have headings which are textually extremely close to the consistent Alcuinian tradition, those in Numbers are expanded in a unique way. Deuteronomy, however, again follows the Alcuinian tradition very closely, and so also do Joshua and Judges. The two lists in Kings, on the other hand, have features which seem to be unique to our Royal Bible. They are firmly based on a capitula series which is found only in two Alcuinian Bibles and five other early medieval

[74] Baruch is today recognised among the prophets in the Vulgate canon, but III–IV Esdras were rejected by the Council of Trent (1546) as apocryphal. Both Baruch and the Esdras books are relegated to the aprocrypha in the English protestant Bible; I–II Esdras are known as Ezra, which is canonical.

[75] Paris, Bibliothèque Nationale, lat. 11532–3, the so-called 'Corbie Bible' (830–50). See Berger, *Histoire*, 104–8, and Fischer, *Lateinische Bibelhandschriften*, 154–5. It occurs also in two thirteenth-century Paris Bibles and one later printed edition. For the text of the prologue, see *Biblia Sacra* XII, *Sapientia Salomonis, Liber Hiesu Filii Sirach* (1964), 3.

[76] Paris, Bibliothèque Nationale, lat. 9380 (the Mesmes Bible, CLA v, no. 576), along with Milan, Biblioteca Ambrosiana, E. 53. inf. (the Biasca Bible); Paris, Bibliothèque Nationale, lat. 6 (the Rosas Bible); and Stuttgart, Württembergische Landesbibliothek, HB. II. 35 (CLA IX, 1358). See D. De Bruyne, *Les Préfaces de la Bible Latine* (Namur, 1920), 36, no. 6; and C. C. Gómez, *Isidoro de Seuilla: De Ortu et Obitu Patrum* (Paris, 1985), 189, no. 63.

[77] That is, the Mesme, Rosas and Biasca Bibles. See De Bruyne, *Préfaces*, 36, no. 5, and Gómez, *De Ortu*, 183–5. no. 58. The text in Royal most closely matches the version in the Mesme Bible.

[78] The entry in the Warner and Gilson, *Catalogue*, I, 21, incorrectly omits Ruth from its list of books without capitula lists. Two Alcuinian Bibles (along with all the Theodulfian Bibles) also lack the list, however: *Biblia Sacra* IV, *Libri Iosue, Iudicum et Deuteronomi* (1936), 363.

Bibles, including the *Codex Amiatinus*,[79] but there has been much alteration. Two other examples may be given. In Wisdom, whose non-Alcuinian prologue was noted above, the capitula headings follow the Alcuinian tradition closely (except for a few errors), whereas in Sirach, which in its prologue and epilogue is conventionally Alcuinian, the headings begin in a form very close to the Alcuinian tradition but then show many omissions and alterations, some of them quite radical and, apparently, unique.

Text

In theory, the idiosyncrasies and variant readings of Vulgate texts offer a key to their transmissional history and their origins. In practice, the complexities of transmission in the early medieval period and the uneven survival of the manuscripts create almost insuperable difficulties.[80] Nevertheless, sufficient comparative material is now available, in the form of collations of several dozen manuscripts, for textual analysis of Bibles such as Royal 1. E. vii–viii to be worthwhile.[81] The preliminary results of such an analysis, which so far has included complete collations of a few books and partial collations of others, allow some tentative conclusions to be made about the relationship of our late Anglo-Saxon text to Continental texts of the ninth and tenth centuries, above all to the dominant Theodulfian and Alcuinian recensions.[82]

Several related points may be made at once about the text of the Old Testament in Royal 1. E. vii–viii. First, there is no consistency of textual tradition followed by the Old Testament books as a whole, and even in an ostensibly coherent group like the Pentateuch there is variation. Such textual eclecticism, however, is a characteristic feature of Vulgate Bibles at all periods, including our earliest Anglo-Saxon Bible, the *Codex Amiatinus*.[83] Secondly, there is no necessary correlation between the traditions apparently followed in the capitula lists and prologues and the traditions which appear to have influenced their texts; the ancillary features seem to have been transmitted independently and, as we have seen, with limited consistency. Thirdly, whatever its complexities, the text of Royal 1. E. vii–viii is firmly based on an

---

[79] *Biblia Sacra* v, *Liber Samuhelis* (1944), 15; *Biblia Sacra* vi, *Liber Malachim* (1945), 3. The two Alcuinian Bibles – one of which in fact lacks the second (Malachi) list – are the same and are without a capitula list for Ruth.

[80] The most detailed account of medieval Vulgate textual history (especially for the Old Testament) will be found in the essays of Bonifatius Fischer collected in *Lateinische Bibelhandschriften*. The more general approach of Jean Gribomont usefully complements Fischer's work; see, for instance, 'Les Editions Critiques de la Vulgate', *Studi Medievali*, 3rd series, 2 (1961), 363–77 and 'L'Eglise et les Versions Bibliques' *La Maison-Dieu* 62 (1960), 41–68. Berger, *Histoire* remains invaluable. The only substantial account of medieval Vulgate history in English is R. Loewe, 'The Medieval History of the Latin Vulgate', *The Cambridge History of the Bible II: The West from the Fathers to the Reformation*, ed. G. W. H. Lampe (Cambridge, 1969), 102–54. Loewe's essay is sometimes misleading, especially where it relies on the work of Glunz.

[81] The collations are in the multi-volume edition of the *Biblia Sacra* issued by the Benedictines in Rome. See n. 58 above.

[82] In these paragraphs I summarise the results of my own collations of seven books, including those of the Pentateuch, and partial collations of a further eight books. For a detailed textual analysis of the Royal Bible's Pentateuch, see my 'The Text of the Pentateuch in Late Anglo-Saxon England: The Latin and Old English Evidence' (unpublished Ph.D. thesis, University of Cambridge, 1991), from which all the statistics relating to the Pentateuch in the following footnotes are taken.

[83] Fischer, *Lateinische Bibelhandschriften*, 18–34, 67–9 and 438–52.

exemplar or exemplars whose texts originated in, or were at least strongly influenced by, the Carolingian textual traditions associated largely with Fleury and Tours in the first half of the ninth century.[84] Fourthly, in connection with these traditions, the text of Royal 1. E. vii–viii confirms as fallacious the theory, still widely propagated until recently,[85] that it was one of these – the Alcuinian – which dominated Vulgate transmission from the end of the ninth century. Neither our Royal Bible nor its exemplar was an 'Alcuinian' Bible. Elsewhere in this volume Rosamond McKitterick uses the Continental manuscript evidence of the ninth and tenth centuries to show that the 'Alcuinian' orthodoxy was always based on false assumptions.[86] We have of course already noted considerable Alcuinian influence on the non-textual features of Royal 1. E. vii–viii, and certainly such influence was widespread and lasting, yet it was rarely consistent and never complete. A fifth and final point complements the 'negative' Alcuinian finding and may prove to be the most interesting of all. The indications from a preliminary analysis of the text of Royal 1. E. vii–viii are that, in the significant number of books where one textual tradition dominates, it is the Theodulfian.[87]

A summary of the textual features of the Pentateuch and a few other books must suffice to illustrate the above points. In Genesis, although variant readings associated with the Alcuinian Bibles are somewhat more numerous than those which may be categorised as Theodulfian, the difference is not sufficiently great, and the independent element (consisting of variants which are characteristic of neither of the two main traditions) is too obtrusive, for any clear account of the book's textual history to be possible.[88] In Exodus, there are firm indications that two different textual traditions were joined at some point during transmission to Royal 1. E. vii, with the result that the book should probably be divided approximately into two halves as far as its textual history is concerned. While forty per cent of the variant readings identified appear to

---

[84] The textual history of the Vulgate is written around the small proportion of readings in which significant variation occurs among the surviving mansucripts. A majority of the variants in the Royal Bible can be traced to one or other of the Carolingian traditions. On some of the problems of Vulgate textual analysis, see the comments of D. C. Chapman, 'The Families of Vulgate Manuscripts in the Pentateuch', *Revue Bénédictine* 37 (1925), 5–46, 365–403, at 7–8; 12–13; 21, n. 1; and 402–3.

[85] See, for instance, Glunz, *History*, 3; F. L. Ganshof, 'La Révision de la Bible par Alcuin', *Bibliothèque d'Humanisme et Renaissance* 9 (1947), 7–20, at 11; Loewe, 'Medieval History', 139 and 146. Fischer, in his *Die Alkuin-Bibel*, Vetus Latina 1 (Freiburg, 1957), 19, stated that Alcuin's text became, at least in France, the 'Normaltext', but his later views decisively contradict this; see *Lateinische Bibelhandschriften*, 155, 392–3 and 402.

[86] See ch. 4 above.

[87] The question of whether we can safely identify an 'Alcuinian' or a 'Theodulfian' reading is an important but complex one. Many readings characteristic of the Tours or the Fleury Bibles were already widely current before the end of the eighth century and may therefore have been transmitted to later Bibles via other, 'independent' pre-Carolingian traditions which have not otherwise survived. One complication is that, at an early stage of their production, Theodulf's Bibles were taking over some of Alcuin's readings, either in the main text or in marginal notes, long before the major period of Tours production. See the discussion in ch. 2 of Marsden, 'The Text of the Pentateuch'.

[88] 39 per cent of significant variant readings are independent of the two main traditions, while 35 per cent are apparently Alcuinian and 26 per cent Theodulfian. Some independent readings (such as *octoginta* for *septuaginta* in Gen. 1.3) are probably simple errors (at whatever stage of transmission they were made); others (such as *benedixitque Iacob filios Ioseph* for *benedixitque Ioseph filio suo* in Gen. 48.15, a reading shared by only one other surviving Vulgate manuscript) are unlikely to be accidental.

be Theodulfian overall, most are concentrated in Exodus 20–40, while the twenty-seven per cent of Alcuinian readings are fairly evenly distributed through the book. Thus, while the first half of Exodus (like the whole of Genesis) can be ascribed no definite textual character, even if Alcuinian readings do slightly outnumber Theodulfian, there can be little doubt that the second half of Exodus originated in, or was very strongly influenced by, a Theodulfian text. In Leviticus, the pattern seen in the second half of Exodus is more or less repeated, with well over half the variants being Theodulfian and fewer than a quarter Alcuinian.[89] In Numbers, the statistics reveal a similar picture, but in this case we must be cautious, for a large number of the Theodulfian readings are of a sort that might have arisen coincidentally through scribal carelessness, while the most positive readings (those least likely to have arisen accidentally) are among those few which are characteristic of the Alcuinian recension.[90] Most of the latter involve the use of extra words or phrases, and it could be that here we have an example of a text which was deliberately emended from an Alcuinian exemplar, but only to the extent of selecting the most obvious variants. Deuteronomy offers the most convincing evidence of a text which we can hardly doubt originated in one of Theodulf's Fleury Bibles. In the earlier chapters it is hard to find any positive evidence of Alcuinian influence at all and, overall, sixty per cent of the variant readings are characteristically Theodulfian. A mere seventeen per cent are unequivocally Alcuinian, and several of the most significant of these are readings which were also entered in one or more Theodulfian manuscripts as emendations or alternative readings, so that Fleury could then have been responsible for their further transmission. Yet in Deuteronomy there is also a comparatively high proportion of readings which are independent of the two main traditions and are not paralleled in other collated manuscripts.

Even within an apparently coherent group of books like the Pentateuch, then, we are dealing with a complex text or set of texts. We might rationalise by assuming that, at some point during transmission to our Royal Bible (perhaps even at the moment of its copying), one exemplar was used for Genesis and the first half of Exodus, and a second, with an unequivocal Theodulfian character, for the rest of Exodus, Leviticus, Numbers and Deuteronomy. But the history of the two conjectured exemplars cannot in turn have been simple. In the case of Numbers, for instance, it seems that emendations, few but highly noticeable, were made deliberately at some point from a Tours text.

Collations of other books in the Old Testament of Royal 1. E. vii–viii have revealed a similar alternation of textual uncertainty with apparent Theodulfian dominance in the variant readings. Especially notable is Judith, where the 'Theodulfian' case is even

---

[89] Examples of exclusively-Theodulfian readings occurring in Leviticus in Royal 1. E. vii are *et ad filios* for *et filiis* (6.25), *purgator* for *purificator* (14.4) and *et quod mutat et quod mutatum est* for *et quod mutatum est et pro quo mutatum est* (27.33).

[90] The Theodulfian readings tend to involve simple variations in grammatical termination (such as *uesperam* for *uesperum* in 9.11) or the substitution of one conjunction or preposition for another (such as *ac* for *et* in 11.32 or *super* for *per* in 6.5). Among the Alcuinian readings are *cunctis* + *uidentibus* (14.10), *arietes* + *per singulas aras* (23.29), and a long eighteen-word interpolation in 8.2.

stronger than in Deuteronomy and there can be little doubt of an ancestry leading more or less directly back to Fleury. Interestingly, Judith shows a strong affinity with the text in two other surviving manuscripts, the Biasca and Corbie Bibles.[91] It will be recalled that Judith also has a prologue found only in the Biasca and a few other Bibles. This suggests, of course, parallel Theodulfian influence on both Biasca and Royal 1. E. vii, not a direct connection between the two. In the Royal Bible's Tobit there is again clear and consistent evidence of Theodulfian influence, and in this instance a high proportion of the readings is to be found again in the Corbie Bible. Proverbs seems to present us with another divided text; an unequivocal Theodulfian character is reversed after chapter six with the appearance of a succession of highly positive and highly characteristic Alcuinian readings. The textual bias of Song of Songs is more equivocal throughout; overall, there is little to choose between the two main traditions. This seems to be the case also in the three prophetical books which have so far been examined, Isaiah, Lamentations and Ezekiel.

OTHER OLD TESTAMENT EVIDENCE

Although Royal 1. E. vii–viii is our only late Anglo-Saxon witness for many books of the Old Testament, the two Bible fragments and three of the non-biblical witnesses offer invaluable supplementary textual evidence. They will be dealt with as a single group. The complete book of Proverbs which opens London, British Library, Cotton Vespasian D. vi (fols. 2–77), has been dated to the mid-tenth century and may have been written at St Augustine's, Canterbury. Scholarly interest has mainly centred on the Old English glosses which accompany the text of Proverbs and several other items in the manuscript.[92] A comparative analysis of selected portions of the Vespasian and Royal 1. E. viii texts has revealed no consistent correspondence between the two. The older version, that of Vespasian, adheres in general more closely to the Alcuinian tradition, and lacks a number of characteristic Theodulfian readings which occur in the Royal version. The picture in the latter is not clear-cut, however, for it too has some good Alcuinian readings (where the few correspondences between the Royal and Vespasian versions occur). One of the most interesting aspects of the Vespasian text is the use of some idiosyncratic readings which seem to be unparalleled until their re-appearance in an early thirteenth-century Paris Bible.[93]

Little can be said about the biblical fragment of the minor prophets now in the University of Missouri Library. Accurately and well written in a formal but not mannered Caroline minuscule which has many Insular features, the surviving leaf

---

[91] Milan, Biblioteca Ambrosiana, E. 53. inf. (s. ix/x), and Paris, Bibliothèque Nationale, lat. 11532–3 (830–50), respectively.

[92] On the manuscript, see Ker, *Catalogue*, no. 207; James, *Ancient Libraries*, 204, no. 131; *The Anglo-Saxon Poetic Records*, ed. G. P. Krapp and E. V. K. Dobbie, 6 vols. (London and New York, 1931–42), vi: *The Anglo-Saxon Minor Poems*, lxxviii–lxxix. For the glosses, see J. Zupitza, 'Kentische Glossen des neunten Jahrhunderts', *Zeitschrift für deutsche Alterthum* 21 (1877), 1–59 and H. Sweet, *A Second Anglo-Saxon Reader: Archaic and Dialectal*, 2nd edn, rev. by T. F. Hoad (Oxford, 1978).

[93] Paris, Bibliothèque Nationale, lat. 7.

probably belonged, as already indicated, to a complete Bible. The small amount of surviving text, Micah 7.15–20 and Nahum 1.1–6 (recto) and Habakkuk 2.5–17 (verso), permits no definite conclusions to be drawn about its origins, although some Alcuinian influence is apparent. Unfortunately, no useful textual comparisons can be made with Royal 1. E. vii, since the books concerned are part of the sixteenth-century reconstruction.

The text of the book of Tobit preserved in Oxford, Bodleian Library, Bodley 572 is one of our most interesting Insular biblical witnesses.[94] Fols. 2–50 of Bodley 572 are a book of Cornish and Welsh origin, written in a variety of Continental and Insular scripts and containing, apart from Tobit, some prayers, a treatise on the mass, two epistles of St Augustine and a Latin conversation lesson. Evidence in a paschal table indicates that all the items were written in or before 981. The book was at one time at St Augustine's, Canterbury, as shown by the addition of material there in the eleventh or twelfth century, and may previously have been at Glastonbury.[95] The Vulgate text of Tobit on fols. 14–25 is complete and includes the Hieronymian prologue beginning *Chromatio et Heliodoro*. It is an idiosyncratic text, with many readings without parallel in other known Vulgate versions, but most remarkable is an unequivocal textual connection with Ceolfrith's recension of Tobit contained in the *Codex Amiatinus*. There is persuasive evidence that one of the two sister pandects of *Amiatinus* was at Worcester from perhaps the end of the eighth century until, possibly, the sixteenth. Thus it seems likely that we should look here for the origin of the Cornish Tobit, which seems to be the witness to an otherwise unknown Insular Vulgate tradition quite untouched by the Carolingian textual reforms.[96]

In the extract from Sirach in London, British Library, Royal 7. C. iv, written in the first half of the eleventh century, we have a text whose writing is more or less contemporary with that of 1. E. viii and which also belonged to, and may possibly have been written at, Christ Church, Canterbury. Like the version of Proverbs discussed above, the Sirach text has attracted interest primarily because of its Old English glosses.[97] The extract concerns women and sin. It constitutes the first two items in a section headed 'Hic pauca incipiunt de uitiis et peccatis', which follows a copy of Defensor's *Liber Scintillarum*. The subheading 'Apostrapha de Muliere nequam' proceeds the first item (Sir. 25.17–36) and 'Item de Muliere Bona et Mala' preceeds the second (Sir. 26.1–28).[98] In both Royal 1. E. viii and 7 C. iv the character of the text is particularly difficult to pin down. In terms of the main Carolingian textual

[94] For bibliography, see above, n. 28. The text is analysed in my 'The Survival of Ceolfrith's Tobit in a Tenth-century Insular Manuscript', *Journal of Theological Studies* (forthcoming). The manuscript's non-biblical contents are discussed in M. Lapidge, 'Latin Learning in Dark Age Wales: Some Prolegomena', *Proceedings of the Seventh International Congress of Celtic Studies*, ed. D. E. Evans, J. G. Griffith and E. M. Jope (Oxford, 1986), 91–107.

[95] Part of the contents is listed in a late medieval catalogue from St Augustine's: see James, *Ancient Libraries*, 204, no. 129.

[96] Marsden, 'The Survival of Ceolfrith's Tobit'.   [97] Ker, *Catalogue*, no. 256.

[98] The Latin and Old English texts are edited by E. W. Rhodes, *Defensor's Liber Scintillarum*, EETS 93 (1889), 223–6.

traditions, both texts lack a clear identity, suggesting either that they were never substantially influenced by Tours or Fleury, or that such influence has largely dissipated after successive copying in different textual environments. Analysis shows that the two versions are independent, for both have several notable readings peculiar to themselves. Two readings in the extracted version are of great interest, for they appear to link it with a specific but much earlier textual tradition, that of Amiens, Bibliothèque Municipale, 12. This manuscript forms part of the multi-volume Bible written at Corbie under Abbot Maurdramnus between 772 and 781, and has been shown, at least for the Octateuch, to be an important textual precursor of Alcuin's Bibles.[99] The Sirach text of Royal 7. C iv shows also a significant number of readings which have no recorded parallels in other manuscripts.

Finally, the fragment bound as fol. 6 in London, British Library, Add. 34652, whose dimensions indicate that it is from a complete Bible, probably has textual connections with our Royal Bible. The fragment includes the last half of Song of Songs (4.7–8.14) and about two-thirds of a capitula list for the following book, Wisdom. It has been dated to the first half of the eleventh century and was thus almost certainly copied sometime after Royal 1. E. vii–viii. Several notable readings in the Song chapters correspond with those in the Royal version but this in itself is not significant, for the readings are Alcuinian and need indicate no more than that both texts evolved at least partly under the influence of that tradition. In the list of Wisdom capitula headings, however, Add. 34652 has six omissions or idiosyncratic readings which are also in Royal 1. E. viii but in no other Vulgate manuscript that has so far been examined.[100] For example, in both Royal and Add. 34652 the whole text of the cap. XXII heading and the final clause in cap. XVIII are omitted. In both manuscripts, too, the last three words of cap. VII are incorporated in the text of cap. VI, so it seems that in some common antecedent exemplar they were written above the line because of a lack of space and then carelessly copied as though belonging to the preceding heading.

SOME DESIDERATA

According to the evidence of our single substantial witness, Royal 1. E. vii–viii, and our two Bible fragments, the dominant influence on the text of the Old Testament during the late Anglo-Saxon period was known Continental Carolingian traditions. This is not unexpected, in view of the huge debt owed to the Continent by the English monastic reform movement. Yet we should remember that even the Royal Bible has a small but persistent stratum of readings which seem to be independent of the main

---

[99] CLA vi, 707; Fischer, *Lateinische Bibelhandschriften*, 90 and 350; Berger, *Histoire*, 102–3. One of the readings in question, *uita uecordis* for *uidebit cordis* in Sir. 25.18, is so eccentric (and erroneous) that coincidence is hardly in question.

[100] *Biblia Sacra* xii, 7–12.

Continental traditions and for which, in many cases, no parallels in other manuscripts have been found. Significantly, this same pattern has been found in an analysis of the Old English version of the Heptateuch, which was made by two or more translators around the end of the tenth century. There are anomalies in the Old English text which seem to reflect independent readings in the translators' Latin exemplars.[101] A comprehensive study of all Old Testament citations in the vernacular literature of Anglo-Saxon England may well produce more such evidence.

Do such readings show that pre-Carolingian textual traditions survived in England itself long enough to exert their influence in the monastic scriptoria of the second half of the tenth century? The text of Sirach in Royal 7. C. iv, with its apparent affinities with a Corbie text, might seem to bear witness to an early textual import, a generation or so before the scriptoria of Fleury or Tours began to flourish. Yet the manuscript is comparatively late, and we cannot be sure, without the evidence of more specific parallel cases, that the anomalous reading had not survived on the Continent and been imported late to England. More work on other manuscripts may produce such evidence. The survival of at least one old Insular textual tradition is of course confirmed in the copy of Tobit in Bodley 572; it was probably associated with houses untouched by the monastic reforms.

In as far as the late Anglo-Saxon Bibles owed most to the late Carolingian traditions in their texts, however, have we enough evidence to be more specific about the likely origin of their exemplars? In Royal 1. E. vii–viii we have seen that, although the Alcuinian tradition profoundly (but not exclusively) influenced the ancillary features, the same could not be said of the text. There are, to be sure, many Alcuinian readings, and in a few books the tradition may be stronger than any other, but often its influence seems to be little more than vestigial or tangential. In none of the books is it overwhelming. The historian of the Vulgate text in the tenth and eleventh centuries must often concede that the mixing of textual traditions has precluded any productive analysis of particular texts, and some parts of our Royal Bible, such as Genesis (at least that part of it which survives in its original form) and the beginning of Exodus come into this category.[102] Yet there are books or parts of books which may justly be described as Theodulfian in their texts; they are not the result of random mixing or selective emendation but must have originated at Fleury. The best examples are Deuteronomy, Judith and the second half of Exodus. At this stage, the explanation of this can only be guessed at, for we do not know whether the Old Testament text of Royal 1 E. vii–viii arrived in England already in the form preserved there, or whether it was an English product, copied from a variety of available exemplars, some perhaps more recently imported than others. Whatever the case, we must note the many direct contacts between English monasteries and Fleury and its associated houses during the middle of the tenth century, and we may recall, with due reserve, Glunz's theory of gospel book transmission. If the Royal Bible was indeed written

---

[101] See Marsden, 'The Text of the Pentateuch', ch. 4. It should be noted that the anomalies are not the same as those found in the Heptateuch of Royal 1. E. vii.

[102] The assessment of Berger, *Histoire*, 329, is pertinent.

at one of the houses associated with Æthelwold and Winchester, this is precisely where the influence of Fleury was at its greatest. We know that a liturgical sequence from Fleury was used at Winchester and that hymns were sung according to the Fleury tradition; there may also be a textual connection between the Latin exemplar of the *Regula Benedicti* used by Æthelwold for his Old English translation and one written at Fleury.[103]

Yet we must be cautious. Even if volumes of the Old Testament had been brought from Fleury to England in the tenth century, would their texts still have been recognisably 'Theodulfian' – direct heirs of the Bibles written under Theodulf's direction at the turn of the eighth century? There is in fact some evidence that they might be, but in general we know as yet too little about Fleury books.[104] Our knowledge of many of the surviving Continental Bibles relevant to our period is merely superficial; in the Bibliothèque Nationale alone, some twenty manuscripts await detailed study. The greatest desideratum is the collation of these Continental texts, or at least a representative selection of them.[105]

APPENDIX: SURVIVING MANUSCRIPTS

Bibles and part-Bibles

Durham, Cathedral Library, B. IV. 6 (s. vi, written in Italy; I Maccabees; fragment of part-Bible)

London, British Library, Add. 37777 + 45025 + Loan MS 81 (*c.* 700; III–IV Kings, Sirach; twelve leaves, and fragments of another, from pandect)

Florence, Biblioteca Medicea Laurenziana, Amiatino 1 (s. viii in; complete pandect)

Durham, Cathedral Library, C. IV. 7 (s. viii; Leviticus; fragment of part-Bible)

London, British Library, Egerton 1046 (s. viii; Proverbs, Ecclesiastes, Song of Songs, Wisdom, Sirach; almost complete part-Bible)

Cambridge, Gonville and Caius College, 820(h) (s. viii ex; minor prophets; fragment of part-Bible)

Cambridge, Magdalene College, Pepysian 2981(4) (s. ix in?; Daniel; fragment of part-Bible)

Oxford, Bodleian Library, Lat. bib. c. 8 (P) + Salisbury, Cathedral Library, 117, fols. 163–4 + Tokyo, T. Takamiya, private collection (s. ix; Numbers, Deuteronomy; four leaves of part-Bible)

Columbia, Missouri, University of Missouri Library, Fragmenta Manuscripta 4, (s. x 2; minor prophets; fragments of Bible)

London, British Library, Sloane 1086, fol. 109 (s. x 2; Numbers; fragment of Bible, as yet unanalysed)

London, British Library, Royal 1 E. vii–viii (s. x ex; almost complete 2-vol. Bible)

London, British Library, Add. 34652, fol. 6 (s. xi 1; Song of Songs (text), Wisdom (capitula); leaf of Bible)

---

[103] See M. Gretsch, 'Æthelwold's Translation of the *Regula Sancti Benedicti* and its Latin Exemplar', *Anglo-Saxon England* 3 (1974), 125–51, at 136.

[104] See Berger, *Histoire*, 177–8, on Orléans, Bibliothèque Municipale, 14 (11) and 16 (13) and M. Mostert, *The Library of Fleury: a Preliminary List of Manuscripts* (Hilversum, 1989).

[105] I am grateful to Michael Lapidge and Richard Gameson for valuable criticism of earlier drafts of this paper.

The Old Testament in non-biblical volumes

London, British Library, Cotton Vespasian D. vi. fols. 2–37 (s.x med; complete Proverbs)
Oxford, Bodleian Library, Bodley 572, fols. 14–25 (s. x 2; complete Tobit)
London, British Library, Royal 7 C. iv, fols. 100v–106 (s. xi 1; extract from Sirach)
Cambridge, Corpus Christi College 279, fols. 55v–80r (s. ix 2, written in France; extracts from
    Exodus, Leviticus, Numbers, Deuteronomy)

7

The Italian Giant Bibles: aspects of their Touronian ancestry and early history

LARRY M. AYRES

The second half of the eleventh and the twelfth century saw an unprecedented production of illuminated Bibles throughout Romanesque Europe. The new vitality in Bible production can be related to the broad geographical scope of the religious renewal of the period, and this is reflected in the fact that illuminated manuscripts of the Vulgate survive from scriptoria as far afield as Rome, Limoges, Stavelot, Salzburg, Canterbury and Durham, among other centres.[1] The pictorial and ornamental embellishment of Romanesque Bibles rank among the most glorious expressions of medieval manuscript illumination; and in terms of variety and inventiveness, the decorative programmes of these volumes place them in the mainstream of medieval scribal art and painting. In this paper the artistic heritage of ornamental initial styles in a group of Romanesque Bibles produced in Italy will be explored, establishing the role of transalpine Carolingian models in a particular eleventh-century renewal of manuscript illumination. Art historical considerations will then assist in tracing the early life of a particular Italian scriptorium which employed a distinctive decorative vocabulary. The ornamental outfitting of pages of this group of Italian Romanesque pandects furthermore contributed to produce a standardised effect or institutional character for these volumes, which are here related to the patronage of the reform circle.

Rome emerged early as one of the leading centres in the cultivation of the Romanesque Bible.[2] The impressive folio dimensions of the pandect Bibles which were created in the papal city have promoted their designation as the Italian Giant Bibles (hereafter: Giant Bibles).[3] The rise of Rome as a centre of Romanesque

---

[1] C. Nordenfalk, 'Romanesque Book Illumination', in A. Grabar and C. Nordenfalk, *Romanesque Painting from the Eleventh to the Thirteenth Century* (Geneva, 1958), 133–206, at 133–44; W. Cahn, *Romanesque Bible Illumination* (Ithaca, 1982), 251–93, cats. 1–150.

[2] Nordenfalk, 'Romanesque Book Illumination', 135–7; K. Berg, *Studies in Tuscan Twelfth-Century Illumination* (Oslo/Bergen/Tromsö, 1968), 18–23; F. Avril, 'Les arts de la couleur', in X. Barral i Altet, F. Avril and D. Gaborit-Chopin, *Le temps des croisades: Le monde roman, 1060–1200* (Paris, 1982), 131–226, at 159–60.

[3] The term 'Riesenbibel' was employed by G. Swarzenski, *Die Salzburger Malerei von den ersten Anfängen bis zur Blütezeit des romanischen Stils* (Stuttgart, 1913), 64–5 and G. Ladner, 'Die italienische Malerei im 11. Jahrhundert', *Jahrbuch der Kunsthistorischen Sammlungen in Wien*, n.f. 5 (1931), 38–160, at 51–61. 'Giant Bible' was established as standard nomenclature in the publications of E. B. Garrison, *Studies in the History of Medieval Italian Painting*, 4 vols. (Florence, 1953–62). For the term 'bibbia atlantica', see P. Toesca, 'Miniature romane dei secoli XI e XII', *Rivista del Reale Instituto d'archeologia e storia dell'arte* 1 (1929), 69–96, at 73–80.

manuscript production and illumination may be connected to the spirit of religious renewal and the institutional reform of the Church which characterised the era of the Gregorian Reform. Reform movements had already touched the monastic life of Latin Christendom during the tenth and eleventh centuries, as expressed in the foundation of the Order of Cluny in Burgundy and in the Lotharingian monastic revivals, but the Gregorian Reform movement showed the spirit of renewal taking strong hold in Italy. It was promoted by papal authority and initiatives in Rome as the Church moved to secure its freedom from secular powers and lay intervention. The ongoing struggles between Papacy and Empire over the issue of the freedom of the Church were dramatised historically by the Investiture Controversy, being personified in the conflict between Pope Gregory VII and the German king (1056–1106) and emperor (1084–1106) Henry IV, whom Gregory VII excommunicated twice, once in 1076 and again in 1080. Essential objectives of the reform in Gregorian terms were the restoration of the spiritual life of the clergy and the canonical affirmation of the hierarchy of Church governance which set forth the role of the Church in a Christian society.[4] Books were fundamental instruments in restoring the religious observances of the clergy, and the most celebrated class of illuminated volume which emanated from Rome in the period was the folio Bible, a large lectern or display manuscript which contained both Old and New Testaments in one or several volumes. Such volumes were used in the choir and in the refectory for prescribing public readings. That Cluniac communities adopted a practice of readings from the Bible throughout the year is confirmed, for example, by Ulrich of Zell's report of Cluniac customs to Abbot William of Hirsau.[5] These large volumes of Scripture not only defined the biblical canon but also mirrored the new emphasis on collective devotion for the clergy, who were exhorted to live a common religious life according to a monastic observance or following a rule such as that of the Augustinian canons.[6]

Before turning to the art historical dimensions of our subject, the state of research on the origins and early history of the Giant Bibles needs to be reviewed, because these volumes stand apart from other Romanesque Bibles in several important ways. The relatively large number of surviving Giant Bibles and other related manuscripts from the same centre of production – what might be termed 'a heavy industry'[7] – and their

---

[4] A review of the political and religious dimensions of the era of reform is supplied by F. Kempf, *The Church in the Age of Feudalism, History of the Church* III, ed. H. Jedin and J. Dolan (New York, 1980), 320–472. Further studies on the religious life include G. Constable's 'Renewal and Reform in Religious Life: Concepts and Realities', *Renaissance and Renewal in the Twelfth Century*, ed. R. L. Benson and G. Constable (Cambridge, Mass., 1982), 37–67, and the contributions by G. Picasso, 'Gregorio VII e la disciplina canonica: clero e vita monastica', and W. Goez, 'Riforma ecclesiastica – Riforma gregoriana', to Relazioni del Congresso Internazionale di Salerno, 'La riforma gregoriana e l'Europa' (20–5 May 1985), in *Studi Gregoriani* 13 (1989), 151–66 and 167–78.

[5] P. H. Brieger, 'Bible Illustration and Gregorian Reform', *Studies in Church History* 2 (1965), 154–64, at 161; H. E. J. Cowdrey, *The Cluniacs and the Gregorian Reform* (Oxford, 1970), 204; Cahn, *Romanesque Bible*, 95–6.

[6] G. Olsen, 'The Idea of the *Ecclesia Primitiva* in the Writings of the Twelfth-Century Canonists', *Traditio* 25 (1969), 61–86, at 65–6.

[7] Nordenfalk, 'Romanesque Book Illumination', 135–6 and 163–6.

appearance at an early date not only within Italy but also in transalpine regions[8] suggest that the scriptorium which spawned these manuscripts functioned as an 'export' scriptorium to provide widespread distribution of books on a considerable scale.[9] To no other Romanesque scriptorium can be assigned so great a productivity in multiple copies of illuminated texts. Indeed the scriptorium of the Giant Bibles might be viewed as a Romanesque 'Tours', or an eleventh-century Romanesque counterpart to what Paris became for Gothic illuminated Bible production in the thirteenth century.

The scriptorium of the Giant Bibles has also gained significance in another way because recent studies have placed its activity as early as the third quarter of the eleventh century. Seen in this light the Giant Bibles as a group stand in the vanguard of Romanesque Bible production and antedate by many decades the great flowering of Romanesque Bible illustration in the monastic scriptoria of Northern Europe. It seems likely that the Giant Bible which Henry IV gave to Hirsau (Munich, Bayerische Staatsbibliothek, Clm 13001) and that which Archbishop Gebhard of Salzburg presumably presented to his foundation at Admont (Admont, Stiftsbibliothek, MSS C–D) arrived at their Northern destinations in the 1070s.[10] Furthermore, a date in the third quarter of the eleventh century has now been proposed for one of the most celebrated early products of the scriptorium, the Giant Bible which belonged to the church of Santa Cecilia in Trastevere in Rome (Vatican City, Biblioteca Apostolica Vaticana, Barb. lat. 587).[11] The shift to such earlier dates represents a significant revision, since E. B. Garrison, a pioneer in the study of the Giant Bibles, favoured dates which were considerably later. Garrison, for example, argued that the Santa Cecilia Bible postdated 1097 and could have originated as late as 1117/1118.[12] The decoration of the Hirsau, Admont and Santa Cecilia Bibles represents advanced stages in the artistic embellishment of such manuscripts and, consequently, the earliest Giant Bibles may have originated in the 1060s if not before.

Whereas Rome has often been claimed as the site of the scriptorium of the Giant Bibles, scholars have been reluctant to localise the scriptorium to a specific Roman

---

[8] L. M. Ayres, 'A Fragment of a Romanesque Bible in Vienna (Österreichische Nationalbibliothek, Cod. ser. nov. 4236) and Its Salzburg Affiliations', *Zeitschrift für Kunstgeschichte* 45 (1982), 130–44; 'An Italianate Episode in Romanesque Bible Illumination at Weingarten Abbey', *Gesta* 24 (1985), 121–8; and 'Gregorian Reform and Artistic Renewal in Manuscript Illumination: The *Bibbia Atlantica* as an International Artistic Denomination', to Atti del Congresso Internazionale di Salerno, 'La riforma gregoriana e l'Europa' II, *Comunicazione* (20–5 May 1985), in *Studi Gregoriani*, 14 (1991), 145–52.

[9] A. Boeckler, *Abendländische Miniaturen bis zum Ausgang der romanischen Zeit* (Berlin/Leipzig, 1930), 71, was among the first to consider the possibility of a great 'export' scriptorium: 'Wie bei dieser mag der Stil Schöpfung eines oder zweier Klöster sein und sich von dort schnell und unter vielfachen Abwandlungen und Durchkreuzungen in weitem Umkreis verbreitet haben. Oder handelt es sich um einige grosse Export-Ateliers?'

[10] K. Berg, 'Notes on the Dates of Some Early Giant Bibles', *Acta ad Archaeologiam et Artium Historiam Pertinentia, Institutum Romanum Norvegiae* 2 (1965), 167–76, at 174–6; L. M. Ayres, 'The Bible of Henry IV and an Italian Romanesque Pandect in Florence', *Studien zur mittelalterlichen Kunst, 800–1250: Festschrift für Florentine Mütherich* ed. K. Bierbrauer *et al.* (Munich, 1985), 157–66, at 157–9.

[11] P. Supino-Martini, *Roma e l'area grafica romanesca (secoli X–XII)*, Biblioteca di Scrittura e Civiltà 1 (Alessandria, 1987), 108–17.

[12] Garrison, *Studies* III, 23, '*c.* 1117–18'; his review of Berg, *Studies*, in *The Art Bulletin* 52 (1970), 310–15, at 312; Cahn, *Romanesque Bible*, 287, cat. 132, 'First quarter of the twelfth century'.

monastery or basilica. The problem of isolating a precise location is bound up with the type of script employed in the Giant Bibles, a script which is clearly distinguished from the *romanesca* favoured by the hands of the Roman region in the eleventh century. In its consistent use of *carolina* at the expense of *romanesca* the 'export' scriptorium of the Giant Bibles stands apart and promotes a 'uniformità grafica'.[13] Berger, in his study of the history of the Vulgate recognized that the Giant Bibles represented a 'veritable edition'.[14] Quentin, in his investigations of Octateuch texts of the Vulgate suggested that only Rome could have provided for the creation of such an 'edition'.[15] If we are to accept the existence of a scriptorium in Rome, utilising *carolina* almost exclusively and devoted to the production of sacred texts for distribution throughout Latin Christendom, then, as Supino-Martini has observed, this new book culture must have developed with the spiritual authorisation and direct intervention of the Church of Rome.[16]

An exception to this practice of excluding the *romanesca* in the Giant Bibles is found in the San Pietro Bible (Vatican City, Biblioteca Apostolica Vaticana, Archivio di San Pietro, Codex A. 1) where a hand which is typically *romanesca* wrote portions of the Octateuch.[17] It is also of interest that this same *romanesca* scribe of the San Pietro Bible incorporated three *tituli* of the famed Carolingian Bible of the basilica of San Paolo fuori le Mura into the San Pietro Bible as prologues at Deuteronomy and Joshua.[18] Another link to the Carolingian San Paolo Bible in the tradition of the Giant Bibles has been observed in the Barberini Bible (Biblioteca Apostolica Vaticana, Barb. lat. 588),[19] which contains a copy of the dedication prologue by the scribe of the San Paolo Bible, a certain Ingobertus. The San Paolo Bible itself was probably brought to Rome at the time of Charles the Bald's imperial coronation in 875. This Carolingian manuscript was evidently in Rome or its vicinity in the eleventh century since an oath of fealty taken by Robert Guiscard to Pope Gregory VII in 1080 is found recorded in the San Paolo Bible.[20] But in evaluating the Carolingian components of the Giant Bibles, references to the illuminated Bibles of Tours overshadow by far the preceding references to the San Paolo Bible which had originated at Rheims.

[13] Supino-Martini, *Roma*, 21–33. See her further comments at the 1987 Madrid conference of the Comité International de Paleographie, 'La scrittura delle Scritture (secoli XI–XII)', *Actas del VIII Coloquio del Comité Internacional de Paleografía Latina* (Madrid, 1990), 225–7; a more ample version of this paper was published as 'La scrittura delle Scritture (sec. XI–XII)', *Scrittura e Civiltà* 12 (1988), 101–18, at 102. For the question of Bible typology as it pertains to miniatures, see G. Dalli-Regoli, 'Per una storia del libro illustrato. Note sulla tipologia di alcune Bibbie miniate in Italia fra l'XI e il XII secolo', *Quaderni della ricerca scientifica* 106 (1980), 515–28; Supino-Martini, *Roma*, 31, note 20.

[14] S. Berger, *Histoire de la Vulgate pendant les premiers siècles du moyen âge* (Paris, 1893), 142.

[15] H. Quentin, *Mémoire sur l'établissement du texte de la Vulgate*, Collectanea Biblica Latina 6 (Rome and Paris, 1922), 384.

[16] Supino-Martini, *Roma*, 30; she further suggests (*Scrittura e Civiltà*, 107–8) a possible localisation of the Lateran for the production of the Giant Bibles.

[17] Supino-Martini, *Roma*, 28, note 14.

[18] L. Ayres, 'An Italian Romanesque Manuscript of Hrabanus Maurus' *De Laudibus Sanctae Crucis* and the Gregorian Reform', *Dumbarton Oaks Papers (Studies on Art and Archaeology in Honor of Ernst Kitzinger)* 41 (1987), 15–27, at 25–6.

[19] Garrison, *Studies* III, 284–5, figs. 350–2, 'possibly Roman, fourth quarter, eleventh century ... script is a Caroline'; Berg, *Studies*, 26, figs. 21–3, 'Tuscan, fourth quarter, eleventh century'.

[20] P. Schramm and F. Mütherich, *Denkmale der deutschen Könige und Kaiser* (Munich, 1962), I, 136–7, cat. 56; F. Mütherich and J. E. Gaehde, *Carolingian Painting* (New York, 1976), 27–8.

In creating its new illuminated Romanesque Vulgate 'edition', the scriptorium of the Giant Bibles turned time and time again for inspiration to the Carolingian Bibles of Tours. In his study of the text of the Octateuch of the Giant Bibles, Quentin saw the influence of the ninth-century Touronian pandects.[21] The use of the *Gallicanum* rather than the *Romanum* as the favoured version for Psalms in the Giant Bibles also finds its roots in the Touronian heritage.[22] The Canon Tables of the Giant Bibles are distributed on four pages following a practice which originated in the Touronian Bibles.[23] Furthermore the decorative initials of the Giant Bibles feature styles of ornamental lettering which are indebted to Touronian designs.[24] Indeed, in the use of large ornamental and historiated initials to punctuate artistically the text divisions of the Vulgate, the scriptorium of the Giant Bibles was allied in its approach to decorative embellishment to the solutions of early medieval illumination which had flourished in Northern Europe rather than to the schemes of manuscript decoration found in the Christian culture of late Antiquity. Tours had defined a type of Vulgate Bible which endowed text pages with masterful graphic dimensions.[25] By capitalising on Touronian traditions, the designers of the Giant Bibles of the reform epoch associated themselves with a Carolingian cultural heritage of book typology which had already been spread throughout Europe by the manuscripts of Tours and which had been one of the great achievements in the art of the book in Latin Christendom. Like the Bibles of Tours, the Giant Bibles display a distinct character as books. They have, however, survived in greater number than their Touronian predecessors, and their page dimensions are in general somewhat larger than those of the Tours pandects. Whereas some changes or latitude in development may be seen in their production over decades, the Giant Bibles share a striking family resemblance. They constitute a distinctive Vulgate family in format, text and decoration, and they were designed as a manifestation of the new ecclesiastical unity promoted by the Church of Rome in the era of the Gregorian Reform.

In their investigations of Italian Romanesque illumination, E. B. Garrison and Knut Berg have noted the influence of Carolingian models on the most prevalent initial style which was invented to decorate pages of the Giant Bibles, the 'geometrical' initial.[26] 'Geometrical' initials are normally placed at the beginning of each book of the Bible and introduce artistic punctuation to the text page. The 'geometrical' form of the ornamental letter displays an especial respect for the script character and stresses its alphabetic shape. The skeletal structures of such initials are invariably painted yellow,

---

[21] Quentin, *Mémoire*, 374.

[22] B. Fischer, 'Zur Überlieferung altlateinischer Bibeltexte im Mittelalter', *Lateinische Bibelhandschriften im frühen Mittelalter*, Vetus Latina 11 (Freiburg, 1985), 404–21, at 413.

[23] C. Nordenfalk, 'Beiträge zur Geschichte der turonischen Buchmalerei', *Acta Archaeologica* 6 (1936), 281–304, at 298–304; Ayres, 'Bible of Henry IV', 158.

[24] Nordenfalk, 'Romanesque Book Illumination', 181; Berg, *Studies*, 18; Cahn, *Romanesque Bible*, 103; Ayres, 'Bible of Henry IV', 158.

[25] F. Mütherich, 'Die Buchmalerei', in Atti del XXIV Congresso Internazionale di Storia dell' Arte 1, *Riforma religiosa e arti nell' epoca carolingia*, (Bologna, 1983), 77–88, at 82–3. See also the discussion by David Ganz, ch. 3 above.

[26] Garrison, *Studies* 1, 43–6; Berg, *Studies*, 18.

perhaps to imitate the golden lettering found in the most ambitious Carolingian Bibles. The letter armatures therefore appear constructed from individual rectangular or triangular panels bordered in yellow and filled with either floral, foliate, interlace, scrollwork or rosette ornament executed in red, green, blue, grey, brown or purple. As a result, the 'geometrical' initial assembly exhibits an additive component in its design. The ornamental elements are strictly confined to the panels within the initial structure and seldom trespass on the borders of the script framework. This calculated elaboration of decorative components or insets in reference to the skeleton of the initial is one of the reasons that the 'geometrical' initials have been compared to the ornamental letters which Wilhelm Koehler designated 'Rahmentypus' in his study of Carolingian illumination at Tours.[27]

Whereas many initials in the early phases of the decorative outfitting of the Giant Bibles are executed in a rudimentary fashion which often obscures their artistic ancestry, several manuscripts contain more elaborate 'geometrical' letters which more clearly reveal their Touronian heritage. The translation of Carolingian traditions into an Italian Romanesque idiom, signifying the convictions of a different era, took place rapidly, suggesting strict supervision or the early use of pattern- or model-books within the scriptorium.[28] Nevertheless certain examples of Italian 'geometrical' lettering reveal particulars of their Touronian ancestry which can be associated more precisely within the span of ninth-century production at Tours. A case in point is the initial for Ruth in the fragment of a Giant Bible which dates from early in the development of the group (ill. 7.1; Rome, Biblioteca Angelica, MS 1272).[29] The **I** initial at Ruth in the Angelica Bible may be compared to the ornamental lettering in a gospel book made at Tours in the 860s (ill. 7.2; Paris, Bibliothèque Nationale, MS lat. 261).[30] The Italian 'geometrical' initial in the Angelica Bible still has a long way to go to match the calligraphic harmony found in the Carolingian past; nevertheless in its use of foliate panels in alternation with interlace bands it clearly shares fundamental aspects of the Touronian artistic vocabulary.

The organisation of the **I** at Ruth in the Angelica Bible points to artistic habits which were common in late Touronian illumination. As Koehler noted, in the period after the Norman devastation of 853 the bulk and solidity of Touronian initial designs were often dismantled by an interest in sharp contrasts between fields of interlace and panels of foliate infilling within the stalk of the letter.[31] This rivalry between elements led to important changes in the construction of the stem, for individual elements now vie for attention within the overall scheme and diminish the unified effect of the design. This formal rivalry among elements is shared in the Angelica 'Ruth' which is

[27] C. Nordenfalk, 'Italian Romanesque Illumination', *Burlington Magazine* 112 (1970), 401–3, at 401.

[28] For a twelfth-century series of such patterns, see J. J. G. Alexander, *The Decorated Letter* (New York, 1978), 24–5, pl. XXV; E. Sebald, in *Ornamenta Ecclesiae*, 3 vols. (Cologne exh. cat., 1985), I, 304, 316, cat. B 88.

[29] Garrison, *Studies* III, 122, figs. 133–5; Berg, *Studies*, 26–8, 300–1, figs. 18–20.

[30] W. Koehler, *Die karolingischen Miniaturen I: Die Schule von Tours*, 2 vols., (Berlin, 1930–3), 291–309, cat. 54 (pp. 416–18), Taf. 118 c, d; B. Fischer, 'Die Alkuin-Bibeln', *Die Bibel von Moutier-Grandval, British Museum Add. MS 10546*, ed. J. Duft *et al.* (Bern, 1971), 49–98, at 64. This gospel book, which belonged to Le Mans Cathedral in the eleventh century, is usually dated after 860.

[31] Koehler, *Die karolingischen Miniaturen* I, 305.

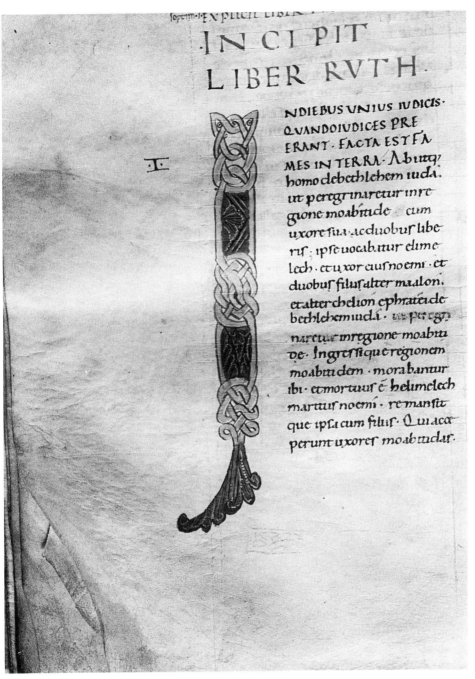

foptum. if X plicit libe

INCIPIT
LIBER RVTH·

NDIEBUS VNIUS IUDICIS·
QVANDOIUDICES PRE
ERANT· FACTA EST FA
MES IN TERRA· Abiitq;
homo debethlehem iuda.
ut peregrinaretur inre
gione moabitide cum
uxore sua. acduobus libe
rif· ipse uocabatur elime
lech. etuxor eiusnoemi· et
duobus filiusalter maalon.
etalterchelion ephrateide
bethlehem iuda· ut peregri
naretur inregione moabiti
de· Ingressique regionem
moabiti dem· morabantur
ibi· etmortuur é helimelech
martiur noemi· remansit
que ipsa cum filiis· Quiacce
perunt uxores moabitidas.

7.2 *Tours gospel book (Paris, Bibliothèque Nationale, MS lat. 261, fol. 53r: initial at St Mark)*

7.3   Barberini Bible (Vatican City, Biblioteca Apostolica Vaticana, MS Barb. lat. 588, fol. 312v: initial at St Mark).

thus clearly reiterating late Touronian conventions. On the other hand, the **I** initial which opens the Gospel of St Mark in the Barberini Bible (ill. 7.3; Vatican City, Biblioteca Apostolica Vaticana, Barb. lat. 588) shows a different approach to modulating the shaft of the initial. In this case the interlace panel which articulates the shaft is fitted to continuous bars which define the basic shape of the letters and hence it does not dissolve the fundamental contours of the letter-form. Prototypes for this type of design may also be found in Touronian illumination.[32]

The construction of the Angelica initial also includes the use of broad, flat leaves as a foliate or floral infilling. Garrison observed that illuminators of the early Giant Bibles were often partial to such ornament which was shaped into fan-like patterns.[33] Here, too, a late Touronian antecedent seems likely, because the use of coloured,

[32] As, for example, in the Lothar Gospels of *c.* 849–51 (Paris, Bibliothèque Nationale, MS lat. 266), Koehler, *Die karolingischen Miniaturen* I, 241–3, 260–9, Taf. 103b, cat. 41 (pp. 403–05); Fischer, 'Die Alkuin-Bibeln', 64. It is not without interest that Koehler (p. 307) observed that models of the type used for the initials in the Lothar Gospels were still influencing the illuminators who decorated the Le Mans Gospels (for which see n. 30 above).

[33] Garrison, *Studies*, I, 43; III, 121.

modelled leaf-work as an infilling for initial stems became more pronounced in Touronian production in the time of Abbot Vivian (843–51) and was especially prevalent in several volumes which postdate the Norman incursion of 853.[34] Fan-leaf or palmette patterns were taken up as a characteristic ornamental device in the 'geometrical' lettering of the earliest Giant Bibles and some variation can be observed. The Italian interpretation of the fan-leaf decor lacks the clarity of definition given to individual leaf forms at Tours, but the bright edging of the leaves in the Italian pandect enhances the vitality of their contours. Like their Touronian predecessors the leaf forms exhibit a sense of confinement and recede into the interstices of the initials, but the 'geometrical' leaf patterns appear more locked into position and create less intricate carpets of leaf ornament than the Carolingian prototypes mentioned above. Such fan patterns were not restricted to the Carolingian ateliers of Tours and they can be found, for example, on the ornamental pages of the Codex Aureus from the Court School of Charles the Bald (Munich, Bayerische Staatsbibliothek, Clm 14000),[35] and later in Ottonian illumination at Regensburg, especially as border ornament in the gospel book which Henry II gave to Monte Cassino (Vatican City, Biblioteca Apostolica Vaticana, Ottobon. lat. 74).[36] Although fan-leaf decor was widespread in other centres of early medieval illumination, it seems likely that the taste for this decor in the Giant Bibles was inspired by the Touronian models that were available in the scriptorium which first formulated the artistic dimensions of the Italian Romanesque pandects.

The initial to St Mark in a fragment of a Giant Bible at Monte Cassino (ill. 7.4; Archivio della Badia, MS 515 AA)[37] exhibits an adaptation of such leaf ornament, characteristic of the early 'geometrical' repertoire of the Giant Bibles, whereby the shaft of the letter is filled with a continuous pattern of foliate ornament or another type of decor. By comparing the St Mark initial from the Giant Bible at Monte Cassino with the initial at Ezra in the Barberini Bible 588 (ill. 7.5), it is evident that fan-leaf ornament was accommodated to initial designs of basic alphabetic shape as well as to more complex designs featuring interlaced rhythms or terminals. Also indicative of their early position in the definition of the decorative embellishment of the Giant Bibles, the Barberini and Monte Cassino codices display the embryonic form of a characteristic ornamental design for the letter **A** (ills. 7.6–7.7). The initial **A** is crested with a foliate comb and this basic design was often repeated in other manuscripts from the family of the Giant Bibles. Whereas decorative vocabulary, as outlined in the above comparisons, links such manuscripts as the Angelica, Barberini and Monte Cassino volumes, it is noteworthy that the text of the Octateuch of the Barberini Bible contains none of the six variant readings considered by Quentin as particularly

---

[34] Koehler, *Die karolingischen Miniaturen* I, 297, 308–9; F. Mütherich, 'Die Initialen der touronischen Bibel von St. Maximin', *Schatzkunst Trier: Forschungen und Ergebnisse*, ed. F. J. Ronig (Trier exh. cat., 1991), 137–46, at 137.

[35] W. Koehler and F. Mütherich, *Die karolingischen Miniaturen V: Die Hofschule Karls des Kahlen* (Berlin, 1982), 26–7, Taf. 50, 53b, 55a and 68.

[36] F. Mütherich and U. Kuder, 'Die ottonische Zeit', *Regensburger Buchmalerei* (Munich exh. cat., 1987), 23–38, at 34, Taf. 13, cat. 18.

[37] Garrison *Studies* I, 26, note 42, 55, 68.

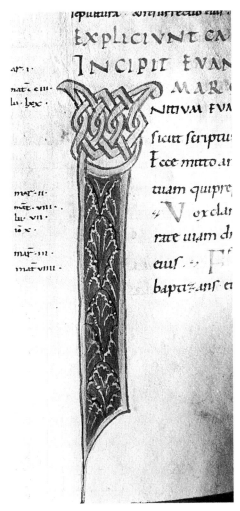

7.4 *Monte Cassino Bible (Monte Cassino, Archivio della Badia, MS 515 AA, p. 752: initial at St Mark)*

7.5 *Barberini Bible (Vatican City, Biblioteca Apostolica Vaticana, MS Barb. lat. 588, fol. 268v: initial at Ezra)*

characteristic of this Italian group of Vulgate manuscripts.[38] On the other hand, our knowledge of Touronian Bible production suggests that there existed even in Alcuin's time significant differences among Tours manuscripts, and recent work has underlined the heterogeneity of subsequent textual traditions.[39] Accordingly such textual variations among these three Giant Bibles should not surprise us, and it might also reflect the fact that they stand near to the earliest phases of composition in the tradition of the Giant Bibles.

[38] Quentin, *Mémoire*, 381.

[39] Fischer, 'Die Alkuin-Bibeln', 68. See also the discussions by Rosamond McKitterick and Richard Marsden, chs. 4 and 6 above.

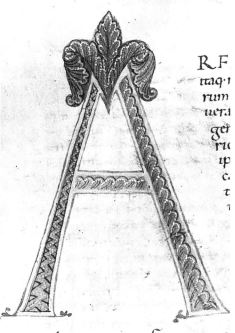

7.6 Barberini Bible (Vatican City, Biblioteca Apostolica Vaticana, MS Barb. lat. 588, fol. 180r: initial at Daniel)

7.7 Monte Cassino Bible (Monte Cassino, Archivio della Badia, MS 515 AA, p. 670: initial at Judith)

As has already been noted in previous studies, one of the artistic hallmarks of the Vulgate 'edition' is the major ornamental accent given to the Prologue **F** (*Frater Ambrosius* ...) and the **I** of Genesis (*In principio* ...) at the beginning of each Giant Bible.[40] The Giant Bible which Bishop Frederick of Geneva gave to his cathedral displays the form which these monumental letters had taken by the 1070s (ills. 7.8–7.9; Geneva, Bibliothèque Publique et Universitaire, MS 1).[41] Each letter is as tall as its adjacent column of text and each is supplied with an interlace terminal. Foliate ornament is the main decorative filling employed for the shafts of the letters and for the arms of the prologue initial. The body of the Genesis initial is veined with scrollwork, an ornamental element employed also in Touronian illumination. The use of a central veined panel within the shaft was already anticipated in the Genesis initial of the Angelica Bible, where the veined effect was achieved through painted contrasts

[40] Quentin, *Mémoire*, 381; Garrison, *Studies* I, 47–68; for the Tours practice, Fischer, 'Die Alkuin-Bibeln', 66–7.

[41] Garrison, *Studies* I, 14–15; Berg, *Studies*, 13–14; M. de Tribolet, 'La bibliothèque de Frédéric, évêque de Genève, fin du XIe siècle', *Bulletin de la Société d'Histoire et d'Archéologie de Genève* 14 (1970), 265–75; B. Gagnebin, *L'enluminure de Charlemagne à François Ier* (Geneva exh. cat., 1976), 36–8, cat. 8; Cahn, *Romanesque Bible*, 284, cat. 122; P. Monnier, in *Saint-Pierre, Cathédrale de Genève* (Geneva exh. cat., 1982), 78–9, cat. 109.

in colour within the foliate field of the shaft of the initial (ill. 7.10).[42] In the Angelica Bible, the Genesis initial is still nested within a text column and does not stand free as in the Geneva Bible.

Frederick of Geneva's episcopate can be documented between the years 1032 and 1073, but it is unclear how far his office continued into the time of Pope Gregory VII (1073–85). Frederick was last mentioned in 1073 and the next reference to a bishop of Geneva, in 1083, concerns Bishop Guy.[43] As Garrison and Berg have noted, the possibility that Frederick's tenure in office may have continued for some years after 1073 cannot be ruled out, but art historical considerations based on the initials in another early Giant Bible, which belongs to the same artistic phase as the Geneva Bible in the development of the 'geometrical' style, add support to a date in the 1070s for the Geneva Bible. The related Giant Bible is now in the possession of the Biblioteca Guarneriana (MSS 1–2) at San Daniele del Friuli (ills. 7.11–7.12) and its creation antedates 1078 since it contains the later addition of an obit for an Abbess Gerlenda and documents the dedication of three altars in the crypt of San Poziano near Spoleto in that year.[44]

Garrison was the first to associate the Geneva and San Daniele Bibles with one another, and he demonstrated their chronological proximity on the basis of the close resemblances in the execution of the 'geometrical' letters in these volumes. For Garrison the decorative programmes of these two books epitomised the earliest stages in the growth of the 'geometrical' style, and he noted characteristics in the Caroline derived script of the San Daniele Bible which he saw as 'typical of Urban Rome and its immediate vicinity'.[45] Whereas Garrison was apparently willing to localise these Vulgate manuscripts to the Umbro-Roman region, he was reluctant to see them as products of the same scriptorium. To the nucleus of the group centred around the Geneva (ill. 7.13) and San Daniele volumes may be added such other Giant Bible manuscripts as those now in Sion (Bibliothèque du Chapitre, MS 15),[46] and Mantua (ill. 7.14; Biblioteca Comunale, MS 131 [A.V.1]).[47] The Sion Bible displays initials which are based on a model of the same ancestry and age as that which guided the illuminator of the Genesis initial of the Geneva Bible. The Mantua volume once belonged to the monastery of San Benedetto di Polirone. If this Giant Bible from San Benedetto di Polirone was originally destined for that house, one could consider two occasions in the 1070s as likely contexts for its arrival. On the one hand there was the time when Pope Alexander II (1061–73) renewed the sanction for the consecration of

---

[42] Garrison, *Studies* III, fig. 133.   [43] Berg, *Studies*, 14.

[44] Garrison, *Studies* I, 16–17; Berg, 'Notes on the Dates', 175–6; M. D'Angelo, 'Inventari Quattrocenteschi della Chiesa di San Michele a San Daniele del Friuli', *Quaderni Guarneriani* 7 (1983), 8, 51 and 62, with Tav. VI; C. Scalon, in *La Guarneriana: I tesori di un'antica biblioteca*, ed. L. Casarsa *et al.* (San Daniele del Friuli, 1988), 88–90.

[45] Garrison, *Studies* I, 47; III, 121–22.

[46] J. Leisibach and A. Jörger, *Livres sédunois du Moyen Âge* (Sion, 1985), 44–8.

[47] Garrison, *Studies* III, 286, 299; P. Piva, 'Contributo al recupero di un grande centro scrittorio: La miniatura romanica nel monastero di Polirone', *Codici miniati e artigianato rurale* (San Benedetto Po [Mantova] exh. cat., 1978), 13–65, at 16, 32, cat. 6 (p. 32); G. Z. Zanichelli, 'Lo *scriptorium* di San Benedetto al Polirone nei secoli XI e XII', *Wiligelmo e Matilde*, ed. A. C. Quintavalle (Milan, 1991), 507–660, at 632–3.

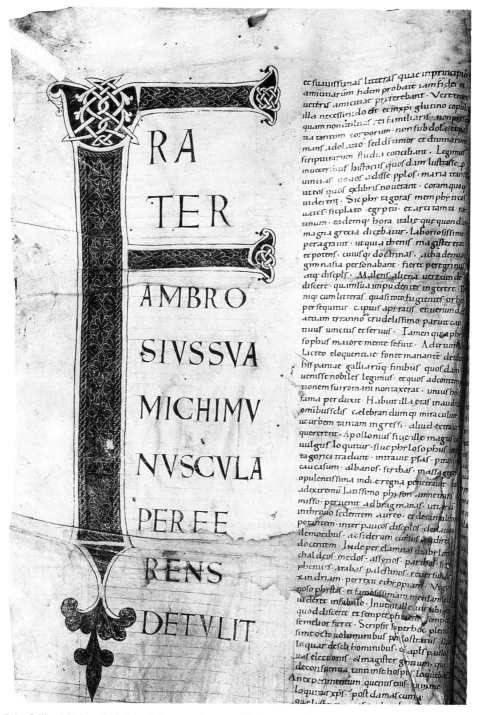

7.9 *Bible of Bishop Frederick of Geneva (Geneva,
Bibliothèque Publique et Universitaire, MS 1, fol. 5r:
Genesis initial)*

7.10 *Angelica Bible (Rome, Biblioteca Angelica,
MS 1272, fol. 4v: Genesis initial)*

its church, which is thought to have taken place between 1074 and 1076.[48] On the
other hand, the Bible may have arrived at Polirone in the wake of Pope Gregory VII's
grant of papal protection and its transfer to the family of Cluny in 1077.[49] In either

[48] H. Schwarzmaier, 'The Monastery of St. Benedict, Polirone, and its Cluniac Associations', *Cluniac Monasticism
in the Central Middle Ages*, ed. N. Hunt (London, 1971), 123–42, at 126–7; P. Piva, *Da Cluny a Polirone*,
Biblioteca Polironiana di Fonti e Studi IV (San Benedetto Po, 1980), 42–3.
[49] For the chronology of historical events, see P. Piva, in *I secoli di Polirone* (San Benedetto Po [Mantova] exh. cat.,
1981), 19, 25.

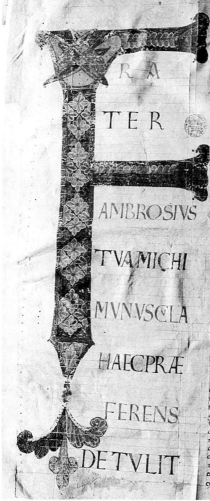

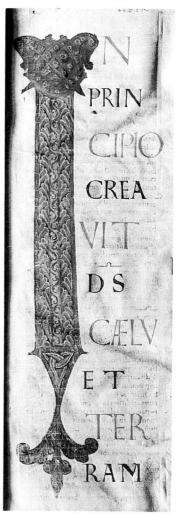

*7.11 San Daniele Bible (Friuli, San Daniele, Biblioteca Guarneriana, MS 1, fol. 1v: Prologue **F** initial)*

7.12 San Daniele Bible (Friuli, San Daniele, Biblioteca Guarneriana, MS 1, fol, fol. 5: Genesis initial)

event, Matilda of Canossa, who ceded the abbey to the protection of the Holy See, comes to mind as a likely benefactor.[50]

Let us return to consider further the monumental 'geometrical' lettering which inaugurates the texts of the Prologue and Genesis initials in the Geneva Bible, and the character of the monumental letters at the same places in the Bibles of Tours. It is noteworthy that of the surviving Tours pandects which have ornamental Genesis

---

[50] H. Fichtenau, ' "Riesenbibeln" in Österreich und Mathilde von Tuszien', *Beiträge zur Mediävistik* 1 (Stuttgart, 1975), 163–82, at 179–82. Fichtenau's proposal that a scriptorium functioned at Polirone for the production of Giant Bibles has, however, not found many adherents.

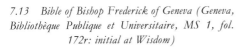

7.13   *Bible of Bishop Frederick of Geneva (Geneva,*
Bibliothèque Publique et Universitaire, MS 1, fol.
172r: initial at Wisdom)

7.14   *Polirone Bible (Mantua, Biblioteca Comunale,*
MS 131 (A.V.1), fol. 13r: initial at Wisdom)

initials only two contain Genesis initials with interlace terminals which are not bound to the stem within rectangular grids or connected with both the stalk of the letter and an ornamental framing device for the page. These are the Munich Bible (Bayerische Staatsbibliothek, Clm 12741) from the late years of Fidugisus' abbacy (807–34),[51] and the Hermann Bible in Cologne which postdates the Norman incursion of 853 (ills. 7.15–7.16; Cologne, Dombibliothek, Dom MS 1).[52] Furthermore of the Tours Bibles only the Hermann Bible has an interlace terminal or capital for the Genesis initial which steps free of the stalk (ill. 7.16), as well as an **F** initial at *Frater Ambrosius* (ill. 7.15) which has an interlace terminal which steps free from the stalk and which also functions as the connection for the upper arm of the **F** to the stalk of the letter.[53] The artistic pattern for the use of interlace at these junctures in the design of the monumental letters in the Giant Bibles may therefore descend from late Touronian models.

   Although closely comparable in some respects, as we have seen, there remain perceptible differences between the Romanesque initials and their Touronian ante-

[51] For the Munich Bible, Fischer, 'Die Alkuin-Bibeln', 63 (*c.* 830–4); E. J. Beer, 'Die Initialen', *Die Bibel von Moutier-Grandval*, ed. Duft *et al.*, 121–48, Abb. 59, at 141.

[52] Koehler, *Die karolingischen Miniaturen* I, 291, 296–303, Taf. 115g, h, i, 116, cat. 49 (pp. 410–12); Fischer, 'Die Alkuin-Bibeln', 63–4; A. von Euw, 'Das Buch der vier Evangelien: Kölns karolingische Evangelienbücher', *Kölner Museums-Bulletin*, Sonderheft 1 (1989), 24, 34, 46–7, Abb. 3–6, 18, 23, cat. 4 (pp. 46–7). This Tours Bible is usually dated between 857 and 862, and was given to Cologne Cathedral by Archbishop Hermann (890–925).

[53] Examples of the artistic connection of such initials to ornamental frames of the text pages may be seen in the Vivian Bible: Koehler, *Die karolingischen Miniaturen* I, Taf. 87a, c.

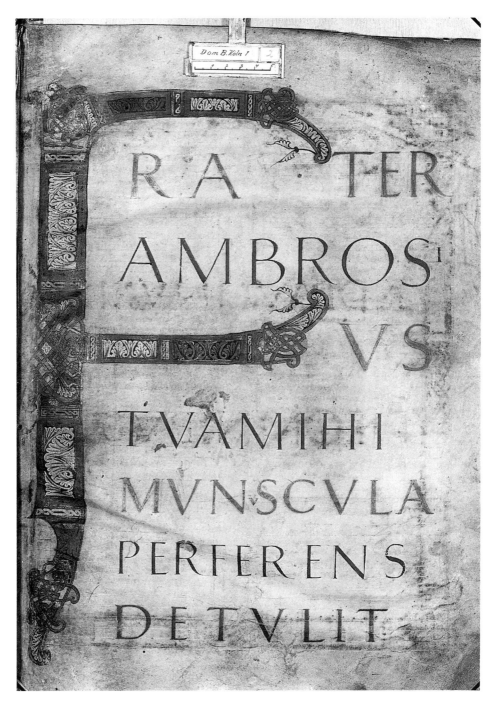

7.15 *Tours Bible of Archbishop Hermann of Cologne (Cologne, Dombibliothek, Dom MS 1, fol. 2r: Prologue* **F** *initial)*

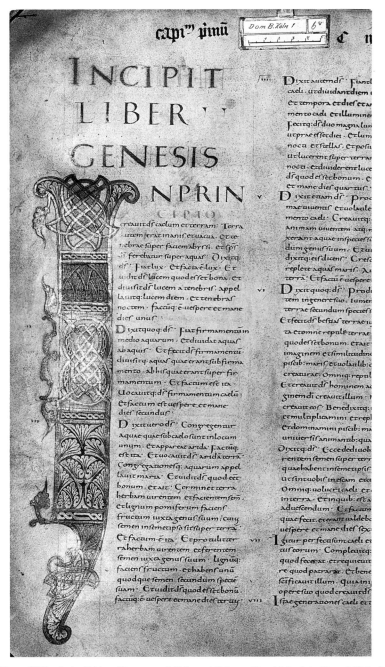

7.16   *Tours Bible of Archbishop Hermann of Cologne (Cologne, Dombibliothek, Dom MS 1, fol. 6v: Genesis initial)*

cedents. A comparison between the Genesis initials of the Geneva and Hermann Bibles (cf. ills. 7.9 and 7.16) reveals that Italian illuminators of the Early Romanesque period decided against subdividing or breaking the vertical axis of the stem of the Genesis initial into framed sections or panels. On the contrary, the Italian artists created a strong rectangular, compacted format, a more architectonic beam whose roots were executed as a trefoil of floral or leaf forms and whose upper terminal or capital blossomed into a field of interlace. By adopting this type of construction the ornament was strictly confined within the body of the initial along a continuous vertical axis. The components of the early 'geometrical' Genesis initials do not, therefore, come together or blend into dynamically unified formations of the types found in Touronian illumination.[54] Similarly, whereas the modulation of the stem of the Touronian Genesis initials often articulates the foliate roots or tails of the letters in a lateral direction, in the Italian 'geometricals' such artistic dynamic is subordinated to a partiality for symmetry, and the tail of the initial gives the impression of a stabilising weight or anchor. The Italian 'geometricals' of the early period do not, therefore, express the unifying 'inner dynamic' which informed so much of Touronian illumination, but return to a compact stateliness which fortifies the basic shape of the script character.[55]

Two distinct groups have been perceived among the early Giant Bibles: a Roman group centred on the Geneva, San Daniele, Admont and Palatine Bibles (ill. 7.17; Vatican City, Biblioteca Apostolica Vaticana, MSS Pal. lat. 3–5), and a Tuscan one exemplified by the Angelica, Barberini, Mugellano (Florence, Biblioteca Medicea Laurenziana, MS Mugel. 1) and Fiesole Bibles (Florence, Biblioteca Medicea Lauren-ziana, MS Fesul. 4).[56] The study of the initials of the Mugellano and Fiesole Bibles in relation to those of the Roman group may throw some additional light on the character or existence of a Tuscan branch for the production of such manuscripts.[57] The Genesis initial of the Mugellano Bible (ill. 7.18), like that of the Angelica Bible (ill. 7.10), has not yet declared its independence from the script column, but the Genesis initial of these same manuscripts share a number of design elements with manuscripts of the Roman group. Their interlace terminals feature sabre-like branches which spring from the belled terminals or capitals of the letters, and such interlace patterns seem to grow from leaf profiles tucked neatly into the sides of the drum of the capital. Fan-leaf decoration is employed as the main ornamental filling for the body of the letter. The fan-leaf belt was eventually modified and provided with another ornamental motif, the continuous scroll, which functions as a central vein for the

[54] For the Touronian approach, see Koehler, *Die karolingischen Miniaturen* i, 202–4.

[55] Nordenfalk, 'Italian Romanesque', 401, suggests that the stress placed on the basic alphabetical shape of the 'geometricals' may be influenced by such late Antique initial designs as those in the *Vergilius Augusteus*. See his analysis of such decoration, C. Nordenfalk, *Vergilius Augusteus: Codex Vaticanus Latinus 3256 der Biblioteca Apostolica Vaticana und Codex Latinus Fol. 416 der Staatsbibliothek Preussischer Kulturbesitz, Codices Selecti: LVI,* (Graz, 1976), 27–30.

[56] Berg, *Studies,* 24–7. For the Palatine Bible, see also the contributions by W. Berschin, in *Bibliotheca Palatina* i (Textband) (Heidelberg exh. cat., 1986), 133–4, cat. C 8.2.

[57] For these volumes, Garrison, *Studies* iii, 121–2, 270, figs. 130–2; Berg, *Studies,* 26–7, 270–1, figs. 24–6; Garrison, *Studies* i, 54, 68, figs. 75–6; iii, 121–2, figs. 130–2; Berg, *Studies,* 27–8, 269, fig. 30.

7.17 Palatine Bible (Vatican City, Biblioteca Apostolica Vaticana, MS Pal. lat. 3, fol. 5v: Genesis initial)

7.18 Mugellano Bible (Florence, Biblioteca Medicea Laurenziana, MS Mugel. 1, fol. 5r: Genesis initial)

initials at Genesis in the Geneva, San Daniele and Palatine Bibles. An early stage in this process can be observed in the Genesis initial of the Mugellano Bible. The central panel of fan leaves is separated into two zones of different colour in the Mugellano example; it is divided into three in the Angelica example; and the process is taken even further in the Geneva, San Daniele and Palatine Bibles by the conversion of the central zone into a pattern of running scrollwork. What was inaugurated as a play of colour to divide the leaves into sections is transformed in the Geneva group to create a central vein of another type of ornament altogether. This feature of scrollwork veining is also found in a Genesis initial in another manuscript claimed for the Tuscan group, the Fiesole Bible (ill. 7.19), a Vulgate fragment which belonged to the monastery of Santa Maria de Fregionaia near Lucca and later to the house of San Bartolomeo at Fiesole. The Genesis initial of the Fiesole Bible displays a design which is nearly identical to that in the Geneva, San Daniele and Palatine Bibles of the Roman group.

Garrison noted that the 'geometrical' repertoire of the Fiesole Bible depended heavily on that found in the Geneva and San Daniele Bibles, but he also perceived anomalies which prompted him to remove this important volume from the Umbro-Roman sphere and to situate its origin in Tuscany.[58] Berg has also observed variant features in the initials of the Fiesole Bible which suggested to him that the book be removed from the immediate context of the Geneva and San Daniele Bibles. He noted a greater degree of standardisation in the rendering of the ornamental decor and the tendency to replace foliate designs with panels of beaded interlace in the execution of the 'geometrical' alphabets. Berg, like Garrison, assigned the Fiesole Bible to a Tuscan scriptorium. He dated the volume to the late eleventh century and saw it as a member of a Tuscan branch of the early 'geometrical' style, tracing, 'a rather parallel course to that which can be observed in the standard version of this style'.[59]

Garrison noted an unusual feature in the distinctive borders which frame the text pages of the *Frater Ambrosius* and Genesis initials in the Fiesole Bible (ill. 7.19), and this 'un-Roman' feature figured among his reasons for disassociating the Fiesole Bible from the workshop which created the Geneva Bible.[60] On the other hand, these frames might equally well be explained by the fact that the Fiesole Bible dates from early in the fashioning of the Giant Bibles: they could represent an experimental imitation of the Touronian ornamental text pages which carried such display borders.[61] The illuminators of the Giant Bibles quickly abandoned the framing of such monumental letters in favour of framing the Preface frontispiece to the Vulgate of St Jerome. In early Giant Bibles such as the Geneva Bible the Preface frontispiece remained unframed and without artistic embellishment; however it was framed at this time, presumably under the influence of Touronian practices, in the Giant Bible which Archbishop Gebhard of Salzburg may have given to his foundation at Admont, perhaps as early as 1074. Moreover it is worth drawing attention to the fact that the contents of the Fiesole Bible link it to the Roman group. Although the Fiesole Bible does not survive in its entirety, it is nevertheless noteworthy that the selection of prologues and capitula for supplements in the surviving portions is identical to that found in the Geneva Bible.

Although the 'geometrical' style of ornamental lettering was first employed on pages of the Giant Bibles, it was soon applied to the embellishment of other texts. Furthermore, it became, in decorative terms, something of an international artistic

[58] Garrison, *Studies* III, 121–2.   [59] Berg, *Studies*, 28.   [60] Garrison, *Studies* I, 54.

[61] For example, Koehler, *Die karolingischen Miniaturen* I, Taf. 42 (Preface frontispiece, *Die Bibel von Moutier-Grandval*, ed. J. Duft *et al.*) Taf. 87a, c (*Frater Ambrosius* and Genesis initials, Vivian Bible).

7.19   *Fiesole Bible (Florence, Biblioteca Medicea Laurenziana, MS Fesul. 4, fol. 5v: Genesis initial)*

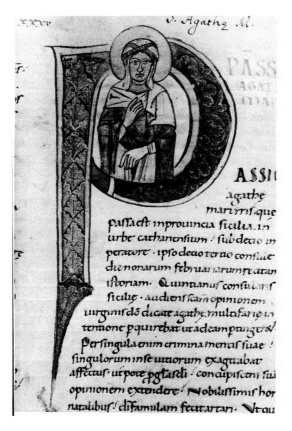

*7.20 Passional (Florence, Biblioteca Nazionale Centrale, MS F.N. II. I. 412, fol. 44r: **P** initial, Lection for St Agatha)*

currency and influenced initial designs not only in other Italian scriptoria but also in transalpine centres of manuscript illumination such as Salzburg, Hirsau/Zwiefalten, Weingarten and Cluny.[62] Among its more successful applications in Italian manuscripts other than the Vulgate is the illustrated Passional now in Florence (Biblioteca Nazionale Centrale, MS Fondo Nazionale II. 1. 412).[63] The Passional was owned by the house of SS. Flora and Lucilla in Arezzo before it entered the collection of Santa Maria Assunta in Florence (Badia Fiorentina). Garrison's and Berg's studies of the hagiographical programme of the volume point to an original destination for the Passional in the 'Tusco-Umbrian-Sabine region'. Although smaller in its dimensions than the Giant Bibles, the Passional is nevertheless abundantly adorned with 'geometrical' initials. Fan-leaf patterns are a standard foliate motif in the ornamental repertoire, as can be seen in the **P** initial for the lection of St Agatha (ill. 7.20). The leaf decor in the curved lobe of the **P** describes a foliate pattern in a centrifugal splay which

[62] See note 8 above.

[63] Garrison, *Studies* III, 281–3, figs. 347–9; IV, 194–6, figs. 145–50; Berg, *Studies*, 23–37, 71–81, 283–7, figs. 1–17, cat. 103 (pp. 283–7); M. B. C. Dupré dal Poggetto, 'Introduzione', in R. Passalacqua, *I codici liturgici miniati dugenteschi nell' Archivio Capitolare del Duomo di Arezzo* (Florence, 1980), 4–5, figs. 1–4; A. D. Domenico, in *Biblioteca Nazionale Centrale* (Florence, 1989), 30–1.

is arranged in step with the curvature of the contour of the letter. Such foliate ornament recalls similar designs in the bows of initials in the Geneva and Mantua Bibles (cf. ills. 7.13 and 7.14).

While drawing close parallels between the decoration of the Passional and several early Giant Bibles, Garrison and Berg do not affiliate this liturgical volume with the scriptorium responsible for the latter. For Berg the Passional is the cornerstone in the definition of a Tuscan dialect of the early 'geometrical' style. Among his reasons for disassociating the Passional initials from the 'leading center in the development of the geometrical style, which, as stated, must have been Rome',[64] are the absence of interlace patterns in the Passional's ornamental repertoire and the more restrained palette employed in the painted execution of its letters.

The Passional, however, contains not only 'geometrical' lettering but is also decorated with an initial based on an Ottonian-derived rinceau style. The **S** on fol. 12 is the case in point. The alphabetic shape of the **S** initial is rendered with two shafts of a different colour, while a bulbed or spurred tendril springs from this structure (ill. 7.21). This Italian Romanesque rinceau style has its antecedents in the Ottonian schools of illumination which flourished at such centres as Reichenau, Cologne and Echternach in the late tenth and first half of the eleventh centuries. Ottonian rinceau initials were often animated by dynamic tendril rhythms and are celebrated as particularly fine expressions of medieval calligraphic art. The rinceaux of such designs not only overlap one another, they also pierce and thread through and around the shaft elements which define the basic letter form to produce a knitted pattern which combines vegetal movement with the abstract form of the letter. And this is precisely what we see in our **S**. The influence of Ottonian initial styles was widespread in Italian illumination of the eleventh century, and it does not, therefore, seem particularly surprising to find Ottonian-derived designs in the decoration of the Giant Bibles and their relatives.[65] They were nevertheless used quite sparingly in the early Giant Bibles, and they stand out as foreign bodies amidst the 'geometrical' repertoire. The rinceau type of initial eventually discarded much of its Ottonian ancestry, and in due course blossomed into one of the great decorative accomplishments of Italian illumination, the *bianchi girari* or white vine-scroll initials.[66]

The Ottonian pedigree of the **S** initial at III John in the Palatine Bible (ill. 7.22) has been explored elsewhere,[67] and it is clear that the Ottonian-derived **S** in the Passional (ill. 7.21) belongs to the same family tree. Moreover the rinceau style of the Palatine Bible is also evident in the Mugellano Bible (ill. 7.24). In terms of the elaboration of the rinceau component of the initial, the tendril patterns of the Passional appear more

[64] Berg, *Studies*, 23–32.

[65] *Ibid.*, 20, note 40, and more recently, J. J. G. Alexander, 'A Manuscript of the Gospels from Santa Maria in Trastevere, Rome', *Studien zur mittelalterlichen Kunst, 800–1250*, ed. Bierbrauer *et al.*, 193–206, at 201; L. Ayres, 'An Italian Romanesque Manuscript of Gregory the Great's *Moralia in Job*', *Florilegium in Honorem Carl Nordenfalk Octogenarii Contextum* (Stockholm, 1987), 33–46, at 40; and F. Mütherich, 'Die Brüsseler Handschrift MS 9219 aus dem Aachener Münster', *Litterae Medii Aevi: Festschrift für Johanne Autenrieth*, ed. M. Borgolte and H. Spilling (Sigmaringen, 1988), 109–16, at 109–10, 115.

[66] Ayres, 'Italian Romanesque Manuscript of Hrabanus Maurus', 25.

[67] Ayres, 'Fragment of a Romanesque Bible', 140.

7.21 Passional (Florence, Biblioteca Nazionale Centrale, MS F.N. II. I. 412, fol. 12r: **S** initial, Lection for the Invention of SS. Diodorus and Marianus)

7.22 Palatine Bible. (Vatican City, Biblioteca Apostolica Vaticana, MS Pal. lat. 5, fol. 17r: initial at Third Epistle of St John)

7.23 San Daniele Bible (Friuli, San Daniele, Biblioteca Guarneriana, MS 2, fol. 164v: initial at Third Epistle of St John)

7.24 Mugellano Bible (Florence, Biblioteca Medicea Laurenziana, MS Mugel. 1, fol. 75v: initial at Joshua) abundant and animated than those of the **S** in the San Daniele Bible (ill. 7.23) yet less dynamic than those of the **S** in the Palatine Bible. The key point, however, is that this consonance of two types of ornamental lettering in the Passional and Mugellano Bible with that in two Bibles of the Roman group not only confirms the derivative character of the Tuscan branch of the Giant Bibles but questions its early existence. In the light of the above comparisons it might be argued that the Passional and the Mugellano Bible, monuments claimed as central to the early Tuscan school, could be attributed to the immediate orbit of a group of Giant Bibles which has been localised to Rome. The closely shared artistic pedigrees in both initial styles which are common to these books, the geometrical and the rinceau type, argue against the separation of these manuscripts into different workshops. The 'geometrical' initials of the Passional may lack some of the crisp definition and brightness of those of the Geneva group, but such distinctions hardly require a difference in origin: they might also readily be explained in terms of the inevitable variations in the work of a large scriptorium.

There is an alternative to the hypothesis of an early Tuscan school: the early history of these Giant Bibles can be understood in terms of the growth of a major scriptorium in Rome. This scriptorium created a new Vulgate 'edition' for widespread distribution, a Bible which expressed an authorised manuscript typology in format, text, script and decorative vocabulary, and, as such, cultivated a distinctive institutional appearance which affirmed the ecclesiastical unity pursued by the reforming Papacy. A manuscript trade evidently emerged in Rome at this time to provide the source books for religious guidance and renewal. The Giant Bible was but one of many illuminated texts which issued from Rome, and in terms of labour and material the production of these volumes must have been a costly undertaking. Much needs to be learned about who underwrote this enterprise. Were such volumes ordered by such monarchs as Henry IV or prelates like Frederick of Geneva or Gebhard of Salzburg or even Abbot Desiderius of Monte Cassino? Or should we think rather in terms of a commercial trade with its attendant financial risks? With the expansion of the tradition of the Giant Bibles in the twelfth century arises the question of the role of lay professionals employed as scribes, rubricators and illuminators.[68]

In view of the recently revised dating of the Santa Cecilia Bible, Desiderius of Monte Cassino may be considered as a possible donor of Giant Bibles. No direct evidence links the Giant Bible from Monte Cassino (MS 515 AA) with Desiderius' term of office as abbot of this great Benedictine foundation (1058–87), but a connection is likely given that the volume belongs to the early group of Giant Bibles which probably antedate the 1070s. Similarly, the Santa Cecilia Bible may have affiliations with Desiderius by way of his activities in Rome. This handsomely decorated manuscript, which was written in *carolina* and belonged to the church of Santa Cecilia in Trastevere (Biblioteca Apostolica Vaticana, Barb. lat. 587), strikes a sharp contrast with manuscripts written in Santa Cecilia's own scriptorium in the 1060s and 1070s.[69]

---

[68] Berg, *Studies*, 218–20; Berg, 'La miniatura romanica in Toscana', *Atti del I convegno sulle arti minori in Toscana* (Florence, 1973), 41–52, at 50–2; Dalli-Regoli, 'Tipologia', 520.

[69] Berg, 'Notes on the Dates', 167–73.

After the arrival of the Santa Cecilia Bible at the church, supplementary leaves were inserted into the manuscript and the scripts of the supplement are based on the characteristic *romanesca* employed in its own scriptorium.[70] It is now thought that a scribe of the supplement to the Bible was one and the same as a *romanesca* hand found in the Gradual of Santa Cecilia, a manuscript written at Santa Cecilia and dated 1071.[71] If the supplementary leaves were indeed made for this Giant Bible, then the date of the Santa Cecilia Bible is considerably earlier than previously thought.[72]

The church of Santa Cecilia already had in its possession another Bible, a composite volume with one portion dating from the ninth century and another from later in the eleventh century. This product of the scriptorium of Santa Cecilia, until recently owned by the Brooklyn Museum in New York, was auctioned in London in 1987.[73] The eleventh-century portion, perhaps a replacement for a worn or damaged Carolingian original, has also been related to the phase of scribal activity at Santa Cecilia which produced the Gradual of 1071 and other volumes. Therefore with the arrival of the Santa Cecilia Bible the church would have found itself in possession of two copies of the Vulgate. Could it have been that the need to produce a new or replacement copy of the Vulgate for the church, as represented by the eleventh-century campaign in the Brooklyn volume, was brought to the attention of the great patron, Desiderius, who held not only the abbacy of Monte Cassino but also served as cardinal–priest of Santa Cecilia in Trastevere?[74] Desiderius, who succeeded Gregory VII as Pope Victor III (1086–7), was a prelate known for his many gifts to Monte Cassino. The miniature which opens the Lectionary of Monte Cassino (Vatican City, Biblioteca Apostolica Vaticana, lat. 1202), a volume which is thought to have been made for the consecration of the new abbey church at Monte Cassino in 1071, depicts Desiderius offering books and buildings to St Benedict.[75] Perhaps Desiderius' benefactions also extended to his titular church in Rome, and accordingly he may be considered a possible donor of the Santa Cecilia Bible to that foundation. If Desiderius were the donor of the manuscript, the Santa Cecilia Bible would have to date before 1087, so his role as donor would accord well with recent paleographical investigations favouring a date for the manuscript in the 1070s or 1080s.

Returning to the problems associated with the localisation of the early Giant Bibles, the question of the 'Tuscan' group might be approached from another direction by

[70] Supino-Martini, *Roma*, 27–8, 108–13.

[71] M. Lütolf, *Das Graduale von Santa Cecilia in Trastevere (1071), I: Kommentar und Register* (Cologny/Geneva, 1987), 44.

[72] Supino-Martini, *Roma*, 109–10.

[73] C. de Hamel, *Western Manuscripts and Miniatures*, Sotheby's Auction Catalogue, 23 June 1987, (London, 1987), 74–83, lot 72.

[74] R. Hüls, *Kardinäle, Klerus und Kirchen Roms, 1049–1130*, Bibliothek des Deutschen Historischen Instituts in Rom xlviii (Tübingen, 1977), 154–6; H. E. J. Cowdrey, *The Age of Abbot Desiderius* (Oxford, 1983), 52, note 17; Lütolf, *Graduale*, 45–6.

[75] For the dedication picture, P. Mayo and P. Meyvaert, 'The Illustrations, Captions and Full-page Initials of the *Codex Benedictus*', *The Codex Benedictus: An Eleventh-Century Lectionary from Monte Cassino*, ed. P. Meyvaert (New York, 1981/2), 59–91, at 59–60; B. Brenk, *Das Lektionar des Desiderius von Montecassino* (Zürich, 1987), 27, Abb. 2A; V. Pace, 'Studi sulla decorazione libraria in area grafica beneventana', *L'età dell'abate Desiderio, II: La decorazione libraria*, Miscellanea Cassinese LI (Montecassino, 1989), 65–93, at 69–71.

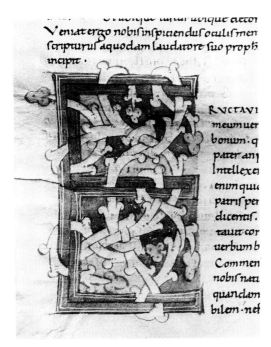

7.25   St Augustine, Enarrationes in Psalmos (Lucca, Biblioteca Capitolare, MS 24, fol. 103r: initial at Psalm 44)

identifying patrons who would have had connections with both Rome and Tuscany or ecclesiastical initiatives which would have bridged the two areas. In the brief pontificate of Nicholas II (1059–61), Florence for a time functioned as the head-quarters of the reform party.[76] Nicholas II, a Cluniac monk, had served as bishop of Florence since 1045; while the elevation of its bishop, Anselm of Baggio (1056–73) to the papal throne as Alexander II (1061–73) placed Lucca at the heart of the reform papacy. The dissemination of the Giant Bibles in Tuscany might also be viewed against the expansion of the Roman reform in Alexander's time. Alexander's predecessor as Bishop of Lucca, Johannes II (1023–56), had undertaken to improve the clerical discipline of the diocese and Alexander continued the policy. The latter's commitment to enhancing his church at Lucca was observed in his sponsorship of the rebuilding of St Martin's cathedral. In renewing the fabric of this church Alexander stands beside such other ecclesiastics of his era as Desiderius of Monte Cassino, Wido of Pisa, Peter of Anagni, Benedict of Santa Pudenziana (Rome), Dominic of San Biago (Rome) and Odimund of San Cosimato in Trastevere (Rome).[77]

Although Alexander's pontificate was torn by schism, significant gains were nevertheless made in the consolidation of papal authority and in encouraging the

[76] W. Paatz, "Die Hauptströmungen in der Florentiner Baukunst des frühen und hohen Mittelalters und ihr geschichtlicher Hintergrund," *Mitteilungen des Kunsthistorischen Institutes in Florenz* 6 (1941), 33–72, at 67–9; E. Kitzinger, 'The Arts as Aspects of a Renaissance: Rome and Italy', *Renaissance and Renewal in the Twelfth Century*, ed. Benson and Constable, 637–70, at 651.

[77] T. Schmidt, *Alexander II. (1061–73) und die römische Reformgruppe seiner Zeit* (Stuttgart, 1977), 38.

renewal of the priestly life. Turning his attention to Rome, Alexander promoted the *communem vitam, exemplo primitivae ecclesiae*, for the canons of the Lateran.[78] Such renewal of the clerical life had already been championed by Hildebrand in the Lateran Synod of 1059. Now Alexander was simultaneously Pope and Bishop of Lucca. The pluralist dimensions of his career may then offer a partial explanation for the distribution of the Giant Bibles and the 'geometrical' style in both Rome and Tuscany.

An illuminated copy of St Augustine's *Enarrationes in Psalmos*, which belongs to the chapter library of Lucca Cathedral (ill. 7.25; Biblioteca Capitolare, MSS 24–5), also has the same style of rinceau initials as found in the Giant Bibles (ill. 7.24), and this manuscript may be included among the patristic works which issued from that same scriptorium.[79] According to Wilmart, the manuscript represents a tradition of Roman extraction, and Avril and Załuska have noted that another illuminated manuscript of this same work by St Augustine may be affiliated with the Lucca volume (Paris, Bibliothèque Nationale, MSS lat. 1980–1).[80] They have further observed that the Lucca and Paris volumes have at least one illuminator in common. When placed within the artistic context of the Giant Bibles, a date in the time of Alexander II might therefore be argued for these volumes of patristic commentary. Furthermore, the Lucca Augustine signals that the scriptorium responsible for the Giant Bibles provided multiple copies of works other than the Vulgate and affirms that its spiritual mission was allied to the teachings of the Church Fathers. Whether it sprang from a single urban scriptorium or from several centres, the 'edition' of the early Giant Bibles must have been sponsored by the reform party as an important instrument in promoting ecclesiastical unity in the era of spiritual renewal.

[78] T. Schmidt, 'Die Kanonikerreform in Rom und Papst Alexander II (1061–73)', *Studi Gregoriani* 9 (1972), 199–221, at 214–20.

[79] Garrison, *Studies* I, 54, 68, fig. 74; Berg, *Studies*, 29, note 50; G. Dalli-Regoli, 'La miniatura lucchese tra la fine dell' XI e gli inizi del XII secolo: forme di decorazione 'umbro-romano' e cultura grafica francese', *Romanico padano, Romanico europeo* (Parma, 1982) 273–88, at 275–7.

[80] A. Wilmart, 'La tradition des grands ouvrages de Saint Augustin', *Miscellanea Agostiniana* 2 (1931), 295–316, at 305–6. F. Avril and Y. Załuska, *Manuscrits enluminés d'origine italienne* I (Bibliothèque Nationale, Paris, 1980), 34–5, cat. 60.

8

French Bibles c. 1200–30: a new look at the origin of the Paris Bible

LAURA LIGHT

This paper will discuss a small group of Bibles copied in Northern France, most likely in Paris, during the first thirty years of the thirteenth century. In particular, it will examine the contents of these Bibles and explore their relationship with the Paris Bible. The discussion will focus on three aspects of the text, namely, the order of the biblical books, the prologues, the capitula lists and the chapters. The evidence provided by the existence of these Bibles alters the commonly accepted interpretation of the origin of the Paris Bible. The Paris Bible does not appear suddenly around 1230 as a completely new departure in the history of the Vulgate. Instead, each of its distinguishing elements is prefigured in this group of Bibles copied roughly between 1200 and 1230.

The term, 'Paris Bible' has been used since the late-nineteenth century to describe Bibles with certain characteristics.[1] First, these Bibles are arranged in an order closely resembling modern Bibles, beginning with the Octateuch, followed by I–IV Kings, I–II Chronicles, Ezra, Nehemiah, II Ezra (= III Ezra), Tobit, Judith, Esther, Job, Psalms, the Sapiential books (Proverbs, Ecclesiastes, the Song of Songs, Wisdom and Ecclesiasticus), the Prophets (Isaiah, Jeremiah, Lamentations, Baruch, Ezekiel, Daniel and the Minor Prophets) and then I–II Maccabees. In the New Testament the Gospels are followed by the Pauline Epistles, Acts, the Catholic Epistles and the Apocalypse.[2]

---

[1] The pioneering studies of the Paris Bible were: S. Berger, *Histoire de la Vulgate pendant les premiers siècles du moyen âge* (Paris, 1893; reprint Hildesheim, 1976), 27–30; his 'Des Essais qui ont été faits à Paris au XIIIe siècles pour corriger le texte de la Vulgate', *Revue de Théologie et de Philosophie* 16 (1883), 52–5; and his *La Bible française au Moyen Age* (Paris, 1884), 151–2; J.-P.-P. Martin, 'La Vulgate latine au XIIIe siècle d'après Roger Bacon', *Le Muséon* 7 (1888), 88–107, 169–96, 278–91, 381–93 and his 'Le texte parisien de la Vulgate latine', *Le Muséon* 8 (1889), 444–66; 9 (1890), 55–70, 301–16; H. Denifle, 'Die Handschriften der Bibel-Correctorien des 13. Jahrhunderts', *Archiv für Literatur- und Kirchengeschichte* 4 (1888), 263–311, 474–601.

H. Quentin, *Mémoire sur l'établissement du texte de la Vulgate*, Collectanea Biblica Latina 6 (Rome and Paris, 1922), 385–8, uses the term 'University Bible', a term I have avoided since it seems to imply that this particular type of Bible enjoyed a more official status at the University of Paris than is in fact likely; this point was stressed by R. Loewe, 'The Medieval History of the Latin Vulgate', *The Cambridge History of the Bible II: The West from the Fathers to the Reformation*, ed. G. W. H. Lampe (Cambridge, 1969), 145–52.

[2] The presence of the Prayer of Manasses [Stegmüller 93,2 – see note 4 below] following II Chronicles, II Ezra (= III Ezra), Baruch and the Epistle of Jeremiah (ch. 6 of Baruch) is characteristic of the Paris Bible; see P.-M. Bogaert, 'La Bible latine des origines au Moyen Age. Aperçu historique, état des questions', *Revue théologique de Louvain* 19 (1988), 298–9 and 291 (the Paris Bible did not, however, usually include IV Ezra). Baruch was lacking in most Bibles before the thirteenth century; see Bogaert, 'Le nom de Baruch dans la litterature

The biblical books are accompanied by a set of sixty-four prologues,[3] including a number of prologues new to the thirteenth century; scholars have traditionally pointed to the two prologues to Maccabees by Hrabanus Maurus and the prologue to the Apocalypse attributed to Gilbert de la Porrée, although as we shall see these are not the only new prologues in this set.[4] Chapter divisions closely related to the modern chapters still used today are found throughout the Bible.[5] The biblical text is followed by the version of the Interpretation of Hebrew Names beginning 'Aaz apprehendens'.[6] Accompanying these reforms there was a disappearance of features present in many earlier biblical manuscripts, notably the Eusebian canon tables and the summaries of the biblical books known as capitula lists.[7]

The history of the Paris Bible is still not written. Much work remains to be done to clarify its origins, and to trace the extent of its circulation in Paris and Northern France, as well as its influence on Bibles produced elsewhere in Europe.[8] However, the term is a useful one which describes a type of Bible that was produced in very large numbers beginning in around 1230. The earliest dated example known to me is Dôle, Bibliothèque Municipale, MS 15, which was copied in 1234 when it was signed and dated by its scribe, Thomas, *clericus* of Pontisara.[9] Nonetheless, it can be confusing when the term 'Paris Bible' is used too broadly, and a few words of caution may help to prevent misunderstandings. The term does not denote a Bible of a particular physical type, and it should not be confused with that other important thirteenth-century innovation, the pocket Bible.[10] Examples of the Paris Bible survive in many formats, ranging from very large monumental volumes to very small portable ones. Secondly, the text of the Paris Bible was never adopted as a standard text. Certain features of the Paris Bible, notably the order of the books, the modern chapters and the inclusion of the *Interpretation of Hebrew Names*, did quickly influence Bibles

pseudepigraphique: L'Apocalypse syriaque et la livre deuterocanonique', *La litterature juive entre Tenach et Mischna*, ed. W. C. van Unnik, Recherches bibliques 9 (Leiden, 1974), 56–72.

[3] Convenient lists of these prologues are found in N. R. Ker, *Medieval Manuscripts in British Libraries*, 4 vols. (Oxford, 1969–72), I: *London*, 96–8 and R. Branner, *Manuscript Painting in Paris during the Reign of Saint Louis. A Study of Styles*, California Studies in the History of Art 18, ed. W. Horn (Berkeley and Los Angeles, 1977), 154–5.

[4] Stegmüller 547, 553 and 839; prologues and other texts are identified by their numbers in F. Stegmüller, volumes IX–XI with the assistance of N. Reinhardt, *Repertorium Biblicum Medii Aevi*, 11 vols. (Madrid, 1950–80); S. Berger, *Les Préfaces jointes aux livres de la Bible dans les manuscrits de la Vulgate* (Paris, 1902), 28.

[5] The most recent study of these chapters is A. d'Esneval, 'La division de la Vulgate latine en chapitres dans l'édition parisienne du XIIIe siècle', *Revue des Sciences philosophiques et theologiques* 62 (1978), 559–68.

[6] Stegmüller 7709; A. d'Esneval, 'Le perfectionnement d'un instrument de travail au début du XIIIe siècle: les trois glossaires bibliques d'Etienne Langton', *Culture et travail intellectuel dans l'Occident médiéval. Bilan des Colloques d'humanisme médiévale (1960–1980)*, eds. G. Hasenohr and J. Longère (Paris, 1981), 163–75, citing earlier studies.

[7] Berger, *Préfaces*, 28.

[8] See note 1 above, and L. Light, 'Versions et révisions du texte biblique', *Le Moyen Age et la Bible*, eds. P. Riché et G. Lobrichon, Bible de tous les temps 4 (Paris, 1984), 75–93.

[9] 484 fols; 158 × 105 (110–08 × 70–69) mm; C. Samaran and R. Marichal, *Catalogue des Manuscrits en écriture latine portant des indications de date, de lieu ou de copiste* (Paris, 1959–), v, 41 and pl. XXIII.

[10] J. Case Schnurmann, 'Studies in the Medieval Book Trade from the late Twelfth to the Middle of the Fourteenth century with Special Reference to the Copying of Bibles', (unpublished B.Litt. thesis, St Hilda's College, Oxford, 1960); L. Light, 'The New Thirteenth-Century Bible and the Challenge of Heresy', *Viator* 18 (1987), 276–9.

made throughout Europe. Nonetheless, as studies of Bibles from England, Spain, Italy and even Paris have demonstrated, many thirteenth-century Bibles are not examples of the Paris Bible.[11] The corollary is also true. Copies of the Paris Bible were produced outside of Paris, and one cannot therefore argue with certainty that a Bible was copied in Paris just because in terms of its text it can be described as an example of the Paris Bible.[12]

It is a commonplace today to speak of the Paris Bible as a Bible created sometime around 1230 to serve as the Bible of the Paris classrooms. The circumstances surrounding the creation of this Bible have been much debated. Leaving aside the exact mechanism of how and by whom the Paris Bible was created, the group of early thirteenth-century Bibles we will examine in this paper does shed light on one aspect of this debate. These Bibles demonstrate that the Paris Bible, far from being the result of an extensive revision of the Vulgate, was the result of only minor modifications of a Bible already in existence which was created about thirty years before, sometime around the beginning of the thirteenth century.

The first thirty years of the thirteenth century were a tremendously exciting period in the history of the Vulgate. An acquaintance with the Bibles produced during these years leaves one with a feeling of experimentation and innovation – a richness that our concentration here on one group of textually related Bibles will mask.[13] It was during these years that a one-volume format was adopted as the usual format for the Vulgate.[14] In some senses all the other alterations in both the text and physical presentation of the Bible characteristic of this period can be seen as growing from this first change. This basic innovation raised the questions: what should a Bible contain, and how should these texts be presented?

This paper will focus on a group of fourteen one-volume Bibles.[15] I am indebted to

---

[11] Light, 'Versions', 91–2; English Bibles are discussed in A. L. Bennet, 'The Place of Garret 28 in Thirteenth-Century English Illumination' (unpublished Ph.D thesis, Columbia University, New York, 1973; University Microfilms, 1976), 36–63 and appendices 1A and 1B; lists of the prologues in a group of Spanish Bibles are found in F. Avril *et al.*, *Manuscrits enluminés de la peninsule ibérique*, Bibliothèque Nationale, Département des manuscrits, Centre de recherches sur les manuscrits enluminés (Paris, 1982), appendix II. The numerous exceptions in the prologues included in Parisian Bibles are apparent after examining the Bibles described in Robert Branner's catalogue of manuscripts (*Manuscript Painting*, appendix V); the variation exhibited should not be seen as surprising, since there is no evidence that the Paris Bible was an 'official' text of the University; for this reason Branner's use of the term 'canonic' to describe the common set of prologues is unfortunate.

[12] Light, 'Versions', 88.

[13] In comparison with the very large numbers of Bibles produced after *c.* 1230, the number of one-volume Bibles produced during the first thirty years of the century seems to have been fairly restricted; I have studied twenty-eight examples (fourteen of which belong to the textually related group examined here), preserved today in collections in Paris, London and Oxford. A complete census of Bibles produced during these years has never been attempted, but based on available sources I would guess that double the number that I have personally examined are still extant.

[14] This is not to say that earlier examples of pandects, or one-volume Bibles, did not exist; Cassiodorus' one-volume Bible, the *Codex Amiatinus*, and the great ninth-century Alcuinian and Theodulfian Bibles are among the more famous examples, on which see further the discussions by David Ganz, Rosamond McKitterick and Richard Marsden, chs. 3, 4 and 6 above. Christopher de Hamel has suggested that Thomas Becket and Robert of Adington probably owned one-volume Bibles in the late twelfth century; see C. F. R. de Hamel, *Glossed Books of the Bible and the Origins of the Paris Booktrade* (Woodbridge, 1984), 37, note 67. Nonetheless, the one-volume format was not adopted as the usual one for the Bible until the thirteenth century.

[15] For a list of these manuscripts, see the appendix.

the work of three art historians, Patricia Stirnemann, Robert Branner and François Avril, who have taught us much about manuscript painting in Paris during the early decades of the thirteenth century.[16] In particular, their studies have pointed out that many of the Bibles we shall examine here are products of Parisian ateliers.[17] This group of Bibles does not form a coherent family of manuscripts in the same sense as did earlier Bibles such as the ninth-century copies of Alcuin's Bible produced at Tours. Though produced in one geographical area, they were not the product of a single scriptorium. A quick survey of these Bibles would not immediately yield evidence of their relationship. Many of them are handsomely illuminated, even luxurious manuscripts, but others are quite modest. They differ significantly in their physical characteristics, such as size, format, presentation of the text and script. However, their close textual relationship – even if there is some variation from Bible to Bible – allows us to study them as a coherent group, and sets them apart from both earlier Bibles and other contemporary Bibles.

Before turning to an examination of the text of these books, it is appropriate to say a few words about their physical characteristics. They all include the complete Bible in one volume. The majority are large books, ranging in size from about 48 × 30 cm to 26 × 19 cm; the measurements of their written spaces, however, range from about 27 × 16 to 18 × 12 cm.[18] One Bible in the group is exceptionally small, measuring only 231 × 164 mm, with a written space of 143–2 × 88–7 mm.[19] Despite the large size of most of these Bibles, they exhibit a new organisation of the text on the page. The twelfth-century monastic Bible was usually written in a large, uncramped script, suitable for public reading.[20] In many of these Bibles, by contrast, there is a new reduction in the size of the script and a new tendency to reduce the space between each line of script, resulting in a smaller written space and large margins. The number of lines per column – in most of these books between 62 and 58 – is another measure of the new compression of their text.[21]

Overall, they can be seen as a new type of Bible. Most are certainly too large to be packed in one's baggage and carried effortlessly. They would, however, have been

---

[16] I owe special thanks to Patricia Danz Stirnemann, who introduced me to several examples of this group, and encouraged me to study their text; her help was especially valuable in establishing the dates of various manuscripts; some of these manuscripts are mentioned in her article, 'Nouvelles pratiques en matière d'enluminure au temps de Philippe Auguste', *La France de Philippe Auguste. Le Temps des mutations*, ed. R.-H. Bautier, Colloques internationaux du Centre National de la Recherche Scientifique 602 (Paris, 1982), 955–80. Branner, *Manuscript Painting*, 22–31, and appendix v A, 'Early manuscripts'; F. Avril, 'A quand remontent les premiers ateliers d'enlumineurs laïcs à Paris?', *Les Dossiers de l'Archéologie. Enluminure gothique* 16 (1975), 36–44, and 'Un Manuscrit d'auteurs classiques et ses illustrations', *The Year 1200. A Symposium* (New York, 1975), 267–8, note 3.

[17] Of the fourteen manuscripts in this group, only Paris, Bibliothèque Mazarine, MSS 7 and 70, Paris, Bibliothèque Nationale, MSS lat. 11933, 15470 and 15471 have not been assigned to such ateliers; see my appendix for the remaining manuscripts and references to relevant studies.

[18] Outer dimensions: London, British Library, Additional MS 15253, 479 × *c*. 300 mm; Oxford, Bodleian Library, MS Kennicot 15, 263 × 193 mm. Written space: Paris, BN, MS lat. 14233 276–3 × 163–60 mm; London, British Library, Additional MS 15253 272 × 165–4 mm; Troyes, Bibliothèque Municipale, MS 577 187–5 × 119–17 mm; Paris, BN, MS lat. 15475 180 × 110–05 mm.

[19] Paris, Bibliothèque Mazarine, MS 70.

[20] A good introduction to the monastic Bible is W. Cahn, *Romanesque Bible Illumination* (Ithaca, 1982).

[21] The number of lines in each Bible is listed in the appendix.

practical volumes for the scholar. They are large enough to be read without strain, yet compact enough to carry short distances. It is easy to imagine a master in Paris in the early thirteenth century transporting such a book from his lodgings to the home of another scholar for consultation. The new compactness and manageability of these Bibles, which contrasts so vividly with the monumentality of the multi-volume twelfth-century monastic Bibles, speaks eloquently of the fact that these Bibles were being used in new ways by a new community. The aspects of their text we will examine – the order of the books, choice of prologues, capitula lists and chapters – also underline the fact that the thirteenth-century Bible was being shaped by new needs and requirements.

ORDER OF THE BOOKS

The books of the Bible in this group of early thirteenth-century manuscripts are arranged in an order that is essentially that of the modern Bible, with the exception that Acts is found between the Pauline and Catholic Epistles instead of immediately following the Gospels.[22] This arrangement of the biblical books is also one of the distinguishing characteristics of the later Paris Bible; the widespread use of an uniform order has traditionally been seen as one of its achievements.[23] Less attention has been paid to the fact that this was a new order, used for the first time in the Middle Ages in the group of Bibles we are examining here.

Given the fact that the new thirteenth-century order is essentially that of the modern Bible, it is easy to take it for granted and to underestimate how significant a departure it was from the many orders current in earlier manuscripts of the Vulgate.[24] This new order of the biblical books was also a departure from the dominant trends in the tradition of medieval commentaries on the books included in the Canon and their relationship to one another. Jerome's discussion of the Canon in his prologue to the books of Kings was often the basis of medieval commentaries discussing the Canon; in the twelfth century it was the source most frequently cited in commentaries.[25]

The four books of Kings were the first books Jerome translated from the Hebrew and his prologue to these books was intended as a general introduction to his

---

[22] Listed in detail, p. 155, above.

[23] Berger, *Histoire*, 304; Martin, 'Le texte parisien' 8 (1889), 457; 9 (1890), 56, 304.

[24] The fundamental study is still Berger, *Histoire*, 301–6, and appendix I, 331–42. More recent discussions include: Bogaert, 'La Bible latine', 301–2 and 277–82; *Sapientia Salomonis*, ed. W. Thiele, Vetus Latina 11/1 (Freiburg, 1977–85), 222–32; and *Epistulae ad Philippenses et ad Colossenses*, ed. H. J. Frede, Vetus Latina 24/2 (Freiburg, 1966–71), 290–303. The literature on the related question of the biblical Canon is immense; see J.-D. Kaestli and O. Wermelinger, eds., *Le Canon de l'Ancien Testament. Sa formation et son histoire*, Le Monde de la Bible (Geneva, 1984), and B. M. Metzger, *The Canon of the New Testament. Its Origin, Development, and Significance* (Oxford, 1987), both with good bibliographies.

[25] Recent authors have warned that it is important not to overestimate the influence of Jerome's commentary on the actual order of the books in manuscripts of the Bible; cf. Bogaert, 'La Bible latine', 301 and Thiele, ed., *Sapientia Salomonis*, 231; nonetheless, it would seem to be an over-reaction to ignore the commentary tradition entirely.

translation.[26] Jerome defines the Old Testament as consisting of twenty-two books, which he divides into three orders based on the Hebrew Canon: first, the five books of Moses or the Law (Genesis, Exodus, Leviticus, Numbers and Deuteronomy); secondly, the order of the Prophets, including Joshua, Judges and Ruth considered together as one book, Samuel or I and II Kings, Malachi or III and IV Kings, Isaiah, Jeremiah, Ezekiel and the Minor Prophets; and thirdly, the Hagiographa or Sacred Writings, consisting of Job, the Psalter, Proverbs, Ecclesiastes, the Song of Songs, Daniel, I and II Chronicles, treated as one book, the book of Ezra, here including Nehemiah, and Esther.[27] In this prologue, Jerome states that the books not found in the Hebrew should be considered apocryphal, naming Wisdom, Ecclesiasticus, Judith and Tobit; he also did not include Maccabees among the canonical books, and adds that although he found the first book of Maccabees in Hebrew, the second book is Greek. Later, Jerome reluctantly translated Judith and Tobit. His translations of these two books and different versions of the remaining books he rejected as apocryphal were part of the biblical Canon throughout the Middle Ages, and were included in manuscripts of the Vulgate.[28] In Bibles arranged in an order patterned on Jerome's prologue these 'apocryphal' books are grouped together at the end of the Old Testament. A second distinguishing feature of Jerome's discussion is that the books of Chronicles and Daniel are grouped with the Hagiographa rather than with Kings and the Prophets respectively, although their contents would logically argue for the latter arrangement.

In contrast with the importance of Jerome's discussion in the commentary tradition, only a small number of Bibles were arranged exactly according to this order. Among the most important early examples of Bibles arranged in this order are the ninth-century Theodulfian Bibles.[29] In the twelfth century, Stephen Harding, abbot of Cîteaux, arranged the books of his Bible in this order.[30] His decision to use this order, based as it was on the Hebrew Bible, is of interest since he states that he corrected the text of his Bible against translations of the Hebrew text. These manuscripts all strictly follow the order described by Jerome, even grouping Wisdom and Ecclesiasticus with the other books Jerome considered apocryphal rather

[26] Stegmüller 323, inc. 'Viginti et duas litteras apud hebraeos . . .'; *Biblia Sacra iuxta Latinam Vulgatam Versionem ad codicum fidem*, ed. H. Quentin *et al.*, 18 vols. (Rome, 1926–), v, 1–11. Jerome's letter to Paulinus (Ep. 53[52]; Stegmüller 284), which circulated from the ninth century as a general prologue to the Old Testament, is also relevant to the question of the order of the books of the Bible; however, since it was much less influential than his prologue to Kings, it will not be discussed here.

[27] Berger, *Histoire*, 301, group I, no. 1; G. W. Anderson, 'Canonical and Non-canonical', *The Cambridge History of the Bible I: From the Beginnings to Jerome*, eds. P. R. Ackroyd and C. F. Evans, (Cambridge, 1970), 135–8.

[28] For a discussion of the biblical books not translated by Jerome but circulating with his translations in the Vulgate, see Bogaert, 'La Bible latine', 159 and 291; as Bogaert notes, Jerome's restricted interpretation of the Canon did not prevail, although Baruch did virtually disappear from the Latin Bible until the thirteenth century (see note 2 above). On Jerome's attitude towards the deutero-canonical books, cf. O. Wermelinger, 'Le Canon des latins', in Kaestli and Wermelinger, eds., *Le canon de l'Ancien Testament*, 184–93 and E. F. Sutcliffe, 'Jerome', *The Cambridge History of the Bible II*, ed. Lampe, 92–3.

[29] Berger, *Histoire*, 331, group I, no. 3; Quentin, *Mémoire*, 260–2; and cf. *Biblia Sacra* I, 38–41.

[30] Dijon, Bibliothèque Municipale, MSS 12–15; Berger, *Histoire*, 331, group I, no. 2, listed as Dijon 9 bis; Cahn, *Romanesque Bible*, 270–1, with bibliography.

than with the three books of Solomon. Other pre-thirteenth-century Bibles follow Jerome's order but group the five Sapiential books together.[31]

Although the numbers of Bibles arranged exactly according to Jerome's order is relatively small, the order found in Alcuin's Bible influenced numerous later Bibles. The books in the ninth-century Alcuinian Bibles are arranged according to the order described by Jerome, except that Daniel is grouped with the three Major Prophets rather than with the Hagiographa, and Wisdom and Ecclesiasticus follow the books of Solomon.[32] This practical adjustment of Jerome's sequence to the realities of the Church's traditions and teachings helps to account for the popularity of Alcuin's order. Many of the great monastic Bibles of eleventh- and twelfth-century Italy, England and France are arranged in this order, or in closely related ones.[33]

In contrast with Jerome, Augustine's view of the Canon found in his *De doctrina christiana* was based on the Septuagint.[34] Curiously, it was cited very rarely by medieval commentators, and seems to have little influence on the order of the biblical books in manuscripts of the Vulgate. Augustine begins with 'the books of history which contain a connected narrative of the times and have an orderly arrangement', that is, the Octateuch, Kings and Chronicles. These books are followed by 'histories of a different order which are not united to the aforementioned order or to one another', Job, Tobit, Esther, Judith, I and II Maccabees and the two books of Ezra. The Prophets, defined very broadly to include the Psalter and the five Sapiential books followed by the twelve Minor Prophets and the Major Prophets complete the Old Testament.

In this discussion of the Canon and the divisions of the Bible, Augustine's arrangement is very close to the new thirteenth-century order. The small differences between Augustine's sequence and the new order should not be allowed to mask the fact that the principles underlying both are identical. Both make no distinction between the canonical and deutero-canonical books, and arrange the Old Testament purely on the basis of the contents of the books. Moreover, Augustine's second group of historical books, Job, Tobit, Esther, Maccabees and the two books of Ezra, are, with the exception of Maccabees, placed after the Octateuch, Kings and Chronicles in both Augustine's discussion and in the new thirteenth-century order. Augustine's

---

[31] Berger, *Histoire*, 331, group I, nos. 6–9.

[32] B. Fischer, 'Die Alkuin-Bibeln', *Lateinische Bibelhandschriften im frühen Mittelalter*, Vetus Latina 11 (Freiburg, 1985), 275–87; Berger, *Histoire*, 332, group II, nos. 20 and 27; the order of the books in Alcuin's prefatory poem, 'In hoc quinque libri', does not follow this order, but rather that of Jerome's letter to Paulinus (Stegmüller 284); cf. Quentin, *Mémoire*, 286, but he is incorrect, however, in implying that manuscripts of Alcuin's Bible are arranged in this order.

[33] On Italy, see J. Gribomont, 'Les éditions critiques de la Vulgate', *Studi Medievali*, 3rd series, 2 (1961), 373–5 and Berger, *Histoire*, 332, group II, no. 41; France, see Berger, *Histoire*, 332, group II, nos. 21, 22 and 36, and Cahn, *Romanesque Bible*, cat. 76, 63, 81 and 104; England, see Berger, *Histoire*, 331, group II, no. 23 and C. M. Kauffmann, *Romanesque Manuscripts 1066–1190*, A Survey of Manuscripts Illuminated in the British Isles 3 (London, 1975), nos. 13, 69, 70, 83 and 98, arranged in an order very close to Alcuin's [Berger, *Histoire*, group II, no. 20].

[34] *De doctrina christiana*, ed. J. Martin, CCSL 32 (Turnhout, 1962) Book II, VIII, 13, pp. 39–40; English translation in J. Gavigan, *De doctrina christiana*, Writings of St Augustine 4 (New York, 1947); in general, see Wermelinger, 'Le Canon des latins' and A.-M. la Bonnardière, 'Le canon des divines Ecritures', *Saint Augustin et la Bible*, ed. A.-M. la Bonnardière, Bible de tous les temps 3 (Paris, 1986), 287–301.

discussion was available thoughout the Middle Ages, but, as we have noted, it had surprisingly little affect on the commentary tradition, especially when compared with the widespread influence of Jerome's discussions. Moreover, before the thirteenth century, I know of no Bibles in which all of the historical books are grouped together to form an unbroken series at the beginning of the Old Testament.[35] We are left, therefore, with the question of why in the thirteenth century for the first time in the Middle Ages there was a switch to an order similar to Augustine's.[36]

The answer to this question is found in the fact that the new thirteenth-century order, unlike those that circulated in earlier centuries, is based upon a grouping of the biblical books which corresponds to their literal meaning. The historical books are grouped together in an uninterrupted series. The books of Maccabees are the exception to this pattern. Since they retell events closest in time to the Gospel narratives, they were placed at the end of the Old Testament where they serve as a logical link between the Old and New Testaments. All of the books that can be classified as the doctrinal books, Job, the Psalms, the five Sapiential books and the Prophets, are similarly grouped together. The creation and acceptance of this order should be seen in the context of the increasing importance of the literal sense of the biblical text as the foundation of exegesis. Hugh of St Victor (c. 1097–1141) outlined this principle clearly in the *Didascalion*:

First you learn history and diligently commit to memory the truth of the deeds that have been performed, reviewing from beginning to end what has been done, when it has been done, and by whom it has been done.

This knowledge of biblical history is the necessary foundation for the exploration of the further meanings of the sacred text, as he expresses in a frequently quoted statement:

Nor do I think you will be able to become perfectly sensitive to allegory unless you have first been grounded in history. Do not look down on these things. The man who looks down on such small things slips little by little. If, in the beginning, you had looked down on learning the alphabet, now you would not even find your names listed with those of the grammar students.[37]

The principles outlined in the *Didascalion* were followed by other writers at St Victor, in the *Historia scholastica* of Peter Comestor, and in the commentaries of Peter the Chanter and Stephen Langton.[38] The fact that the commentators of the Paris schools of the late twelfth and early thirteenth centuries stress the importance of the

---

[35] Not surprisingly, Augustine's order can be compared with other orders based on the Old Latin (cf. Berger, *Histoire*, 333–4, group III and Bogaert, 'La Bible latine', 301), although they do not present an unbroken sequence of the historical books at the beginning of the Old Testament.

[36] Berger, *Histoire*, 304, pointed out that the new thirteenth-century order was the same as the order found in the Greek *Codex Vaticanus*; there is however, no reason to believe that this manuscript had any direct influence on the new order.

[37] J. Taylor, trans., *The Didascalion of Hugh of St. Victor. A Medieval Guide to the Arts*, Records of Civilization. Sources and Studies 64 (New York and London, 1961), VI, 3, pp. 135–6; B. Smalley, *The Study of the Bible in the Middle Ages*, 3rd edn, rev. (Oxford, 1983), 87.

[38] Smalley, *Study of the Bible*, 196–9 and 214–42.

literal sense of the scriptures, together with its allegorical and moral senses, meant that a Bible arranged in an order based upon the literal sense of the biblical books was well suited to their needs. The creation of a new order of the books of the Bible was a natural outcome of their teaching, whether it was arrived at independently or based on the order described by Augustine in the *De doctrina christiana*.

The creation and adoption of this new order of the biblical books may also be related to the actual sequence in which the later twelfth- and early thirteenth-century schoolmen commented upon the text. This is an area in which more research needs to be done. The order in which Stephen Langton composed his commentaries does, however, support the idea. As Beryl Smalley observed, the order in which Langton worked 'looks like a carefully thought-out programme, based on a study of the *Didascalion*'.[39] Langton glossed Peter Comestor's *Historia Scholastica* first, thus familiarising himself with biblical history. Next, following Hugh's advice on the order in which to study the allegorical sense, he commented on the Gospels. He then glossed the Sapiential books, the historical books, and the Epistles and the Prophets. The relationship between Langton's commentaries and the new order of the Bible is most apparent in his treatment of the historical books. He glossed the Octateuch first, and then continued with Kings, Chronicles and the remaining historical books. The surviving manuscripts of Langton's commentaries reflect the order in which he glossed these books. Chartres, Bibliothèque Municipale, MS 294, for example, includes his commentaries on the Octateuch, Kings, Chronicles, Tobit, Judith, Esther, Ezra, Nehemiah and Maccabees.[40] The study of the commentaries of Langton's teachers and contemporaries would very probably shed additional light on the question of the new order of the books of the Bible.

PROLOGUES

The prologues that are found in our group of early thirteenth-century Bibles are closely related to the set of sixty-four prologues associated with the Paris Bible.[41] I would like to examine a handful of prologues of particular interest, and to define the differences between the prologues in our early thirteenth-century Bibles and those in the later Paris Bible.[42] The new order of the books of the Bible was well suited to the needs of the classroom. As we shall see, it is much more difficult to show that the prologues in this set were chosen for such well-defined reasons.

---

[39] *Ibid.*, 198–9.

[40] G. Lacombe and B. Smalley, 'Studies on the Commentaries of Cardinal Stephen Langton', *Archives d'histoire doctrinale et litteraire du Moyen Age* 5 (1931), 65, 69–73 and 163.

[41] See note 3 above.

[42] Essential studies of the biblical prologues include D. de Bruyne, *Les Préfaces de la Bible Latine* (Namur, 1920); Berger, *Préfaces*; Stegmüller, *Repertorium Biblicum* I, 253–306 and VIII, 220–9; and M. E. Schild, *Abendländische Bibelvorreden bis zur Lutherbibel*, Quellen und Forschungen zum Reformationsgeschichte 39 (Gütersloh, 1970); many of the prologues are edited in *Biblia Sacra*, and *Novum Testamentum Domini Nostri Iesu Christi Latine secundum editionem S. Hieronymi ad codicum manuscriptorum fidem*, ed. J. Wordsworth and H. J. White, 3 vols. (Oxford, 1889–1954).

Six prologues deserve special consideration; namely, the prologues introducing
Ecclesiastes (Stegmüller 462), Amos (Stegmüller 513), Matthew (Stegmüller 589) and
the Apocalypse (Stegmüller 839), and two of the three prologues used before
Maccabees (Stegmüller 547 and 553). Each of these prologues appears in the Vulgate
for the first time in our group of early thirteenth-century Bibles, and are also found
later in manuscripts of the Paris Bible. Since these prologues are new to the Vulgate,
they raise the questions: where do they come from, and why were they included in
these Bibles? I have tried to determine whether the source of these new prologues can
be tentatively traced to the Paris classroom, asking whether they circulated with the
Glossa ordinaria, and whether late twelfth- and early thirteenth-century masters,
particularly Peter the Chanter and Stephen Langton, whose commentaries are glosses
on the Gloss, comment on them.[43] The answers in most cases have proven to be sadly
inconclusive.

It seems likely that three of these prologues were included in manuscripts of the
Vulgate because they circulated with the Gloss and were customarily commented on
in the classroom. The prologue to Ecclesiastes (Stegmüller 462), which begins,
'Memini me ante hoc ferme', is Jerome's preface to his commentary on the book.[44]
Although new to manuscripts of the unglossed Bible, it did appear as a prologue to
Ecclesiastes in the Gloss, and both Peter the Chanter and Stephen Langton discuss it
in their commentaries.[45] Similarly, the prologue to Amos (Stegmüller 513), beginning
'Hic est Amos', is of special interest, since it is new to manuscripts of the Vulgate.[46]
The source of this anonymous prologue is unknown, but like the prologue to
Ecclesiastes, it circulated in manuscripts of the *Glossa Ordinaria*.[47]

The new prologue to Matthew is particularly interesting. Matthew is introduced by
two prologues in our group of early thirteenth-century Bibles and in the Paris Bible.
The first (Stegmüller 590), beginning 'Matheus ex iudeis', was a standard accompaniment to the Gospel in the medieval Vulgate. The second prologue (Stegmüller 589),
however, beginning 'Matheus cum primo', does not appear in manuscripts of the
unglossed Bible before the thirteenth century.[48] It is a revision by an unknown author
of Jerome's prologue to his commentary of the four Gospels beginning 'Plures fuisse',

[43] There has been little research into the question of which prologues circulated with the *Glossa Ordinaria*, and to
what extent and when these prologues became standard; the prologues listed in Stegmüller's summary of the
Gloss (*Repertorium Biblicum* IX, nos. 11781–853) provide only a rough guide; I have tried to supplement this
information with evidence of a few randomly selected manuscripts of the Gloss; all my results should be
regarded as preliminary. On the practice of commenting on prologues in the Paris classroom, see Smalley,
Study of the Bible, 216 and her 'Peter Comestor on the Gospels', *Recherches de théologie ancienne et médiévale* 46
(1979), 84–129, at 110–11.

[44] De Bruyne, *Préfaces*, 120 and Berger, *Préfaces*, no. 138; Hieronymus, *Commentarius in ecclesiasten*, ed. M. Adriaen,
CCSL 72 (Turnhout, 1959); this prologue is not edited in *Biblia Sacra* XI.

[45] Paris, BN, MS lat. 15504, glossed Wisdom, *c.* 1230, includes this prologue; Stegmüller 6481 (Peter the Chanter)
lists this prologue, although it is not included in BN, MS lat. 15565, *c.* 1230; Stegmüller 7806 (Langton), also
lists this prologue and it is included in BN, MS lat. 384, s. xiii 2/4–med.

[46] See *Biblia Sacra* XVII; De Bruyne, *Préfaces*, 150; Berger, *Préfaces*, no. 187.

[47] In Paris, BN, MS lat. 131, s. xii 4/4, the Gloss on Amos is introduced by three prologues including 'Hic est
Amos'. Peter the Chanter seems not to have commented on it (cf. Stegmüller 6492); it is not included in his
Commentary in BN, lat. 16793, s. xii 4/4.

[48] De Bruyne, *Préfaces*, 183; Berger, *Préfaces*, no. 200.

a prologue that did circulate widely in earlier Bibles.[49] Jerome's long discussion of which Gospels were canonical, still an important question in Jerome's day, is reduced in the new version to an explanation of the spiritual and mystical reasons of why there are four Gospels. In place of Jerome's discussion of each of the four evangelists, is an account of how the Gospel of Matthew was written. Jerome's discussion of the four symbols of the evangelists is also shortened, and the emphasis is placed on the correspondence between these four symbols and the life of Christ. Throughout, the focus is on the importance of the message of the Gospels, rather than on the historical circumstances of their composition.[50] Nothing is known about the author of this prologue, but modern scholars have usually associated it with the *Glossa Ordinaria*.[51] This hypothesis is supported by a passage in Peter Comestor's commentary on Matthew in which he explains that commenting on the usual prologue to Matthew, 'Matheus ex iudea', would not fill an entire lecture; therefore a second prologue to the book was added.[52] The content of this prologue seems an adequate explanation of why it was included in these Bibles from the *Glossa Ordinaria*.

The prologues to Maccabees (Stegmüller 553 and 547), which begin 'Memini me' and 'Cum sim promptus', are from the commentary on these books by Hrabanus Maurus.[53] The Gloss on Maccabees was probably assembled from Hrabanus Maurus' commentary and other sources very late in the twelfth century.[54] Peter the Chanter did not comment on these prologues, although in the next generation, Stephen Langton did. It is likely, therefore, that these prologues also made their way into the Vulgate from the classroom.[55]

The first prologue to Maccabees (Stegmüller 551) in our Bibles begins 'Maccabeorum libri duo prenotant'. This prologue and the prologue to the Apocalypse (Stegmüller 839), beginning 'Omnes qui pie', are of interest because they are used in manuscripts of the Vulgate before they circulate in Glossed Bibles. The anonymous prologue to Maccabees circulated in a minority of manuscripts of the Vulgate beginning in the ninth century.[56] It was usually attributed to Jerome, which may explain its use in our Bibles. It does not, however, routinely appear in manuscripts of Maccabees with the Gloss until around the middle of the thirteenth century, and it is

---

[49] Stegmüller 596; Wordsworth and White, eds., *Novum Testamentum* I, 11–14.

[50] Schild, *Abendländische Bibelvorreden*, 55–6.

[51] Two early thirteenth-century copies of Matthew with the Gloss include this prologue: Paris, BN, MS lat. 621 and 11558; Wordsworth and White, eds., *Novum Testamentum* I, 15, notes that it occurs in a number of editions and ascribes it to Walfridus Strabo (PL cxiv, 63); they do not list any manuscripts, nor do they print the prologue.

[52] Smalley, *Study of the Bible*, 217 and her 'La Glossa Ordinaria', *Recherches de théologie ancienne et médiévale* 9 (1937), 369.

[53] De Bruyne, *Préfaces*, 152; Berger, *Préfaces*, nos. 192 and 199.

[54] G. Lobrichon, 'Une nouveauté: les gloses de la Bible', *Le Moyen Age*, ed. Riché and Lobrichon, 111 and note 40. Paris, BN, MS lat. 2438, an early thirteenth-century copy of glossed Maccabees includes both these prologues.

[55] Cf. Stegmüller 6502–3 (Peter the Chanter), no prologues specified; Stegmüller 7764 (Langton), with both prologues; his commentary in Paris, BN, MS lat. 393, s. xiii 1, includes these prologues.

[56] De Bruyne, *Préfaces*, 151; Berger, *Préfaces*, no. 189.

therefore possible that its use in our group of Bibles led to its inclusion in the Gloss, rather than the other way around.[57]

The prologue to the Apocalypse (Stegmüller 839) circulated under the name of Gilbert de la Porrée; its real author and origin are unknown.[58] Although it was not routinely used in twelfth-century manuscripts of the Gloss, Stephen Langton did comment on it in his commentary on the Apocalypse.[59] It circulated in our group of Bibles at the beginning of the thirteenth century, but apparently was not commonly used in manuscripts of the Gloss until *c.* 1220.[60]

The presence of these six prologues which are new to the Vulgate in both this group of early thirteenth-century Bibles and in the later Paris Bible underlines the close connection between the two. The set of prologues in our group of Bibles is not, however, identical to the prologues found in the Paris Bible of after *c.* 1230. Three major differences distinguish the two sets. First, although no prologue is used before II Chronicles in our early thirteenth-century Bibles, in the Paris Bible this book is introduced by the prologue beginning 'Quomodo grecorum' from Jerome's earlier translation of the Septuagint (Stegmüller 327). Jerome's prologue to his translation from the Hebrew, 'Si septuaginta interpretum pura' (Stegmüller 328), is found before I Chronicles in both groups of Bibles. Job is introduced in our group of early thirteenth-century Bibles and in the Paris Bible by both Jerome's Vulgate prologue 'Cogor per singulos' (Stegmüller 344), and the prologue from his translation of the Greek (Stegmüller 357), which begins 'Si aut fiscellam'. The hexaplaric prologues to both Job and II Chronicles were uncommon in earlier manuscripts of the Vulgate.[61] Why they circulated in our group of early thirteenth-century Bibles, and in this pattern is difficult to explain. There is nothing about their content that obviously recommends them, since both are simply a discussion of the difficulties of translation. Their use in the commentaries of Peter the Chanter and Stephen Langton, moreover, is exactly the opposite of the pattern found in manuscripts of the Bible. Although the hexaplaric prologue to Chronicles is lacking in our group of early thirteenth-century Bibles, both of Jerome's prologues to Chronicles were routinely commented upon.[62]

---

[57] Lobrichon, 'Une nouveauté', 113 and note 47; in Paris, BN, MS lat. 2438, glossed Maccabees, early thirteenth century, this prologue is added.

[58] De Bruyne, *Préfaces*, 262–3; Berger, *Préfaces*, 320; no commentary by de la Porrée on the Apocalypse survives, although there is one manuscript claiming to include extracts from it (Stegmüller 2529, with this prologue); later in the Middle Ages the prologue was attributed to Gilbert (cf. Stegmüller 5926 and 2872).

[59] Peter the Chanter apparently did not comment on it (cf. Stegmüller 6531, and it is lacking in Paris, BN, MS lat. 15565, *c.* 1230), although Langton did (Stegmüller 7935); this prologue is included in Paris, Bibliothèque de l'Arsenal, MS 64, s. xiii 1, although it is lacking in BN, MS. 393, s. xiii 1.

[60] Lobrichon, 'Une nouveauté', 113 and note 46; Paris, BN, MS lat. 621 includes a copy of the glossed Apocalypse with this prologue, and dates from the first quarter of the thirteenth century.

[61] Edited in *Biblia Sacra* VII, 7–10 and IX, 74–5; see also De Bruyne, *Préfaces*, 31 and 39 and Berger, *Préfaces*, nos. 37 and 56; on Jerome's translation of the Septuagint and the surviving prologues, see Loewe, 'Medieval History of the Latin Vulgate', 121; and Bogaert, 'La Bible latine', 157–8.

[62] Peter the Chanter commented on both (Stegmüller 6438, 1 and Paris, Bibliothèque de l'Arsenal, MS 44, 1220s), as did Langton (Stegmüller 7756, and Paris, BN, MS lat. 14414, s. xiii 2/4); BN, lat. 384, s. xiii 2/4–med, however, includes neither prologue.

Our group of Bibles do include both prologues to Job; nonetheless, in commentaries on Job, it is common to find only the Vulgate prologue, 'Cogor per singulos'.[63]

Secondly, the book of Wisdom is introduced in the Paris Bible by the prologue from Isidore's *Etymologiae* vi, 2, 30 which begins 'Liber sapientiae' (Stegmüller 468). The use of this prologue was not a thirteenth-century innovation. It is first found in manuscripts of the Vulgate in the ninth century. Before the thirteenth century, however, it circulated in only a comparatively small number of manuscripts.[64] Like Jerome's hexaplaric prologue to Chronicles, it appears regularly only after *c.* 1230. I know of no reason to account for its sporadic use in the early thirteenth-century Bibles we are studying. It may be noted that although Peter the Chanter does not comment on it, Stephen Langton not only commented on it but attributed it to Jerome, a practice also followed in later thirteenth-century commentaries.[65]

Finally, in the Paris Bible, the Pauline Epistles are introduced by a series of very brief prologues. Most modern scholars agree in attributing these prologues to Marcion. In the Middle Ages, however, Marcion's prologues, together with a very similar short prologue to Hebrews, were accepted as completely orthodox, and indeed were a very common, almost standard, accompaniment to the Pauline Epistles.[66] It is noteworthy, therefore, that the prologues used before the Pauline Epistles in our early thirteenth-century Bibles are far from standardised, and generally include only part of the series. The particular prologues used vary from Bible to Bible, with the prologues to Romans and Galatians being the two most frequently omitted.[67] I can offer no completely satisfactory explanation. However, it is interesting to note that late twelfth- and early thirteenth-century manuscripts of commentaries on the Pauline Epistles also seem to follow this curious pattern of including only some of the Marcionite prologues. The original version of Peter Lombard's commentary on the Pauline Epistles included none of the Marcionite prologues. In thirteenth-century manuscripts of this commentary, the prologues are often included, with the exception of the prologue to Romans, which is instead preceded by Peter Lombard's general prologue.[68] It is possible that the frequent omission of this prologue in our group of early thirteenth-century Bibles reflects the influence of this commentary.

---

[63] Peter the Chanter seems only to have commented on the Vulgate prologue (Stegmüller 6474 and Paris, BN, MS lat. 15565, *c.* 1230); the same is true of Stephen Langton (Stegmüller 7798, and BN, MS lat. 384, s. xiii 2/4–med).

[64] Edited in *Biblia Sacra* xii, 3; De Bruyne, *Préfaces*, 121; Berger, *Préfaces*, no. 142.

[65] It is not included in Peter the Chanter's commentary (Stegmüller 6483 and Paris, BN, MS lat. 15565, *c.* 1230). Langton does comment on it (Stegmüller 7811 and Paris, Bibliothèque de l'Arsenal, MS 64, s. xiii 1).

[66] Edited in Wordsworth and White, *Novum Testamentum* ii; Stegmüller 677, 684/5, 699/700, 715, 728, 736, 747, 752, 765, 772, 780 and 793. Most recently, see K. T. Schäfer, 'Marius Victorinus und die marcionistischen Prologe zu den Paulus Briefen', *Révue Bénédictine* 80 (1970), 7–16. See also D. de Bruyne, 'Prologues bibliques d'origine Marcionite', *Révue Bénédictine* 14 (1907), 1–16 and A. von Harnack, 'Der marcionitische Ursprung der ältesten Vulgata-Prologe zu der Paulus Briefen', *Zeitschrift für die neutestamentliche Wissenschaft* 24 (1925), 204–18.

[67] Listed in the appendix.

[68] Paris, BN, MS lat. 648, a late twelfth-century copy of the Lombard's commentary, includes none of these prologues; Paris, BN, MS lat. 660, in contrast, dating from *c.* 1205–10, includes all the Marcionite prologues except for Romans and Galatians (those for I and II Corinthians may be added). Stegmüller 6654–68 lists all of the Marcionite prologues except for the prologue to Romans, with the Lombard's commentary.

To summarise, the formation of the set of prologues that circulated with the Paris Bible involved three changes in the set of prologues circulating in our group of early thirteenth-century Bibles: Jerome's prologue from his earlier translation of the Septuagint was added as a prologue to II Chronicles, and the prologue to Wisdom from Isidore's *Etymologiae* and all of Marcionite prologues to the Pauline Epistles were routinely used before these books. These changes are evidence that the Paris Bible was the product of a second revision of the Vulgate. Apart from these minor differences, however, the prologues used in the Paris Bible are those found in our group of early thirteenth-century Bibles.

CAPITULA LISTS

Most of the Bibles in our group of manuscripts, like the majority of Bibles dating before the thirteenth century, include capitula lists, that is lists at the beginning of each book of the Bible which summarise its contents, chapter by chapter.[69] The mere presence of capitula lists in Bibles of this date is not surprising. The series of capitula lists in these Bibles, however, are unique to Bibles from Northern France dating after *c.* 1200, and were a product of the reform of the Vulgate that also included the creation of a new order of the biblical books and the choice of a new set of prologues. They have never been discussed by scholars of the thirteenth-century Bible, although their existence was first recorded in the late nineteenth century by Berger, and De Bruyne, a member of the Benedictine commission to revise the Vulgate, recognised that they were thirteenth-century texts.[70]

This new set of capitula lists included entirely new texts, revised versions of texts found in earlier manuscripts of the Vulgate, and unrevised, earlier texts. A look at a few of these texts will illustrate their character, and the type of revisions that produced them. The capitula list for Genesis, which begins 'De die primo in quo lux facta est', is almost identical to a very ancient capitula list composed for the Old Latin Bible that circulated in numerous manuscripts, including Bibles of the Alcuinian recension. The Benedictine critical edition of the Vulgate prints these two texts in parallel columns to stress their close relationship.[71] The similarities between these texts are certainly striking. The first capitula in both is identical. The older version generally has eighty-one or eighty-two capitula; in the critical edition the new version has eighty-one. In our group of Bibles the number of capitula range from seventy-six to eighty-two. Such

---

[69] The fundamental work on capitula lists is [D. De Bruyne], *Sommaires, divisions et rubriques de la Bible latine* (Namur, 1914); some of the lists printed by de Bruyne are re-edited in *Biblia Sacra* and Wordsworth and White, eds., *Novum Testamentum*. See also Berger, *Histoire*, 307–15, and O. Schmid, *Über verschiedene Eintheilungen der Heiligen Schrift insbesondere über die Capitel-Eintheilung Stephan Langtons im XIII. Jahrhunderte (Graz, 1892), 25–55.

[70] Berger, *Histoire*, appendix II, 343–62; de Bruyne, *Sommaires*; cf. A. d'Esneval, 'La division de la Vulgate latine', 565, hinting at an attempt to revise the capitula lists early in the thirteenth century, but citing only Paris, BN, MS lat. 26, a later Bible, dating from the second quarter of the thirteenth century, which includes the capitula lists found in our group of early thirteenth-century Bibles. These lists are found in another later Bible, BN, MS lat. 31.

[71] *Biblia Sacra* I, series Λa (older list) and Λb (revised list); cf. De Bruyne, *Sommaires*, series A (older list) and Fr (revised list).

variations in the number of capitula included in any given list is a common characteristic of these texts.

A close examination of the text of the old and the new version of this capitula list indicates that we are dealing with two separate versions, and, moreover, that the newer version was the result of a deliberate revision of the old one. In general, the new list is lengthier than the old. The fifty-eighth capitula in both lists, for example, summarises Genesis 32.1–33.17 of the modern Vulgate, in which Jacob sets up camp at the 'fortress of God', wrestles with the Angel and sends messengers to his brother Esau. The older lists states simply:

58. Vidit Iacob castra Dei et misit nuntios ad fratrem suum et occurit ei.

Jacob saw the fortress of God and sent messengers to his brother and runs to meet him.

The new version is slightly longer:

[58.] Ubi vidit Iacob castra Dei et luctatus est cum angelo et misit nuntios ad fratrem suum et occurit ei

Where Jacob saw the fortress of God and wrestled with the angel and sent messengers to his brother and hastened to meet him.[72]

To cite another example, we may note that in the older version, the sixty-third capitula consists of the very brief statement: 'De generationibus Esau.' The new version adds, '. . . et hic dicit, qui invenit aquas calidas'.[73] Other examples of such additions could be cited. In each case, it seems sensible to believe that these additions represent a conscious attempt by the reviser of the capitula list to emphasise portions of the text ignored in the older version. In the *Historia scholastica*, Peter Comestor's treatment of Genesis 36.24, like the sixty-third capitula in the new version, emphasises the importance of the finding of the hot springs.[74] It is possible that a thorough search through contemporary commentaries would enable us to reconstruct the logic behind many such additions.

Two further examples may complete our examination of the changes made in this new version of the capitula list. The older list divides what is now the thirty-sixth chapter of Genesis into three sections:

63. De generationibus Esau [36.1];
64. De principibus Esau [36.15];
65. Qui regnaverunt in Edom priusquam esse rex in Israhel [36.31].

The new version divides this same portion of the text into two:

[63.] De generationibus Esau et hic dicit: qui invenit aquas calidas [36.1–24];
[64.] De primogenitis eius qui regnaverunt in Edom priusquam rex esset in Israhel [36.31].[75]

---

[72] *Biblia Sacra* I, 98.   [73] *Ibid.*   [74] PL CXCVIII, 1124.   [75] *Biblia Sacra* I, 98.

Finally, one capitula may have been changed because the text of the older version included a reading from the Old Latin not found in the Vulgate. Capitula seventy-five of the old version reads: 'Cum septuaginta quinque animabus intravit Iacob in Aegyptum.' This passage in the Vulgate, however, records that Jacob entered Egypt with seventy, not seventy-five, souls. The new version states simply: 'Nomina filiorum Israhel qui ingressi sunt in Aegyptum.'[76] Overall, the text of the new version of this capitula list does not depart from the old significantly. When the two do diverge, however, it was the result of a deliberate revision of the older text.

The capitula lists for Exodus, Joshua, Judges and I and II Chronicles were also the result of minor revisions of older texts.[77] The capitula lists for the remaining books of the Octateuch – Leviticus, Numbers, Deuteronomy and Ruth – and the four books of Kings, by contrast, were all products of revisions of older capitula lists that were so thorough that the resulting lists can be thought of as completely new texts.[78] A more detailed study than I have attempted would be necessary to characterise the nature of the revisions which created these texts. In general, they seem to be an attempt to eliminate many of the small divisions in the old lists by grouping a number of the capitula together. At the same time, their language is usually clearer and more direct. The capitula lists for the remaining books of the Bible are all older capitula lists, which were included in this series without revisions of any kind.[79] These older capitula were, however, an integral part of the new series of capitula lists. Each of the Bibles which include the new capitula lists for Genesis through Chronicles, contain the same capitula for the remaining biblical books.[80]

In Bibles with capitula lists it is usual for the biblical text to be divided into chapters that correspond to the lists, although it is certainly easy to find Bibles that do not follow this pattern. Indeed, an examination of the chapter divisions in our group of Bibles shows that they are an exception to this rule. In books such as Genesis, where the revision of the capitula lists entailed only a slight change in the number of capitula, the number of chapters usually agree with the number of capitula. However, in the case of books prefaced by new capitula lists, there was no corresponding new division of the biblical texts. In these books, the number of chapters differs markedly from the

---

[76] *Ibid.*, I, 100 [Genesis 46.27].

[77] The capitula lists for Exodus, Joshua and Judges are edited in *Biblia Sacra*, where they are assigned the *sigla* Λb, and printed in parallel columns with the older series Λa. The capitula lists for I and II Chronicles are edited as 'unica b'. De Bruyne, *Sommaires* prints the revised series of capitula lists as 'Fr'.

[78] The capitula lists for Leviticus, Numbers, Deuteronomy and Ruth are edited in *Biblia Sacra* as 'K'; the series circulating with I–IV Kings are edited as 'E'. De Bruyne, *Sommaires*, prints these lists with the *sigla* 'Fr'.

[79] Some of the shorter Old Testament Books lack capitula lists (namely Nehemiah, II (III) Ezra, Canticles, Baruch and the Minor Prophets); the capitula lists for the remaining Old Testament books are edited in de Bruyne, *Sommaires*, as 'Bed' (Ezra) and 'A'; the series for the Sapiential Books and the Prophets are printed in *Biblia Sacra* as 'Aa'. My examination of the New Testament capitula lists in these Bibles was cursory, although sufficient to conclude that they all include the same series of older capitula lists.

[80] The discussion of the capitula lists in this group of Bibles provided here is only the briefest of summaries. One of the points not discussed is the variation in the capitula lists included; in particular, it may be noted that Paris, Bibliothèque Mazarine, MS 70, and Paris, BN, MS lat. 15471 do not include capitula lists; the series found at the beginning of BN, MS lat. 15475 is unique to this manuscript, although the capitula lists in the 'Paris' series are retained before Exodus and Leviticus, and finally, although BN, MS lat. 15470 includes some of the 'Paris' capitula lists, it also includes some not from this series.

number of capitula.[81] When one understands the function of capitula lists, this anomaly is not as odd as it might seem at first. The traditional function of capitula lists was to provide a summary of the biblical text. If these summaries aided in the location of information within the text, it was only because it is easier to find a specific passage by skimming through the capitula lists than by reading through the entire biblical book. The accompanying chapters were intended as aids to comprehension that divided the text into sections reflecting its sense. These functions are reflected in the manuscripts. In the majority of the Bibles studied here, the capitula in these lists are unnumbered. Chapter divisions within the text, moreover, are usually indicated by unnumbered coloured initials, placed immediately following the preceding chapter. This layout was a functional way to indicate textual divisions intended to aid readers of the text. Modern chapters, in contrast, are primarily important as systems of reference, and are therefore always numbered.

The creation of a new series of capitula lists at the beginning of the thirteenth century demonstrates that these traditional texts were still useful at that time.[82] Around 1230, however, when the Paris Bible was created, the capitula lists were omitted, and the text of the Bible was divided into numbered chapters.[83] These chapters, which are essentially those used today, were probably created by Stephen Langton at the end of the twelfth century or the beginning of the thirteenth – certainly before he left Paris in 1206.[84] The chapters found in Bibles copied during the first thirty years of the thirteenth century underline the fact that this was a transitional period in the history of the Vulgate. Although the text of most Bibles from this period is divided according to older systems of chapters, indications of modern chapters are found in the margin.

It is admittedly often difficult to determine whether these marginal indications of modern chapters are original or subsequent additions. Of our group of Bibles, I would argue that five were definitely copied with original indications of modern chapters, and that an additional five very probably were. In the case of the remaining four Bibles, the modern chapters may have been additions.[85] The early appearance of modern chapters in manuscripts of the Vulgate has largely been ignored. It is, however, simply what the history of the practice of citing biblical passages by means of a numbered chapter leads one to expect. Chapter references were almost never used

---

[81] For example, in Paris, BN, MS lat. 14233, the number of the capitula in the lists for Genesis, Joshua, Judges and I and II Chronicles corresponds fairly closely to the textual divisions (listed second): Gen. 82 (81), Jos. 36 (34), Jud. 27 (26), I Chron. 23 (23) and II Chron. 20 (21); this is not the case for the following books: Lev. 44 (89), Num. 37 (74), Deut. 37 (156) and Ruth 7 (5). Exodus, with 92 capitula in the capitula lists and a double series of chapter divisions numbered 1–16 and 1–139, is an exception to this rule.

[82] The function of biblical capitula lists, however, was probably different from that of the chapter lists appended to other works with growing frequency from the mid-twelfth century on; cf. R. H. and M. A. Rouse, 'Statim invenire: Schools, Preachers, and New Attitudes to the Page', *Renaissance and Renewal in the Twelfth Century*, ed. R. L. Benson and G. Constable (Cambridge, Mass., 1982), 205–6.

[83] For a discussion of the context in which the modern use of chapters developed, see R. H. and M. A. Rouse, 'Statim invenire', 221–4.

[84] Langton's chapters are discussed in A. d'Esneval, 'La division de la Vulgate latine', 559–68; Schmid, *Über verschiedene Eintheilungen*, 56–117; and Martin, 'Le texte parisien', 8 (1889) 457–65; 9 (1890) 55–9.

[85] See the appendix for the chapters used in each manuscript.

in this way before the middle of the twelfth century. The commentaries of Peter Comestor (d. 1169), Peter the Chanter (d. 1197) and Stephen Langton, who, it will be recalled, left Paris in 1206, illustrate the growing frequency of the practice during the course of the second half of the twelfth century. In the works of Peter Comestor, biblical citations are not identified by chapter numbers.[86] Peter the Chanter, by contrast, frequently includes chapter references. All his references, however, are to older systems of chapters.[87] Not surprisingly, the earliest use of the new chapters is found in manuscripts of Langton's commentaries. However, in most of his works these are not the only chapters used, and references to old chapters exist side by side with references to the new chapters. In the classroom, Langton seems to have used older chapters to identify his citations.[88] This pattern continues through the first thirty years of the thirteenth century, and it is only from about 1230 that the new chapters are consistently used by the Paris theologians. It is a pattern that corresponds perfectly with the pattern in the Bibles of the period.

The group of early thirteenth-century Bibles which we have studied here is evidence that there was a revision of the Vulgate in Paris around 1200. The Bible produced by this revision was characterised by a certain order of the biblical books, a set of prologues which included six which were new to manuscripts of the unglossed Bible and a new series of capitula lists. Many of these Bibles also included indications of modern chapter divisions copied in the margins. Overall, these reforms of the text of the Vulgate are best understood in the context of the new needs of the Paris classroom. On the one hand, the commentary tradition and teaching practices influenced the new order of the biblical books and the new set of prologues. This is especially true for the new order, which can be seen as a response to the emphasis on the literal sense of the biblical text. The long tradition of the *Glossa Ordinaria* seems to have influenced the new set of prologues. Alongside the use of the Bible in lectures and commentaries, the growing emphasis on preaching also changed how the Bible was used. The new one-volume Bible may have been a convenient tool in the classroom, but it was certainly an essential reference tool for the working scholar, who was not only taught, but also composed sermons. The modern chapter divisions as well reflect the use of the Bible as a repository of texts that was searchable. In this paper we have been able only to skirt the edges of these topics; they certainly deserve to be explored more fully.

Interesting for themselves, these Bibles are equally important because of their close relationship to the Paris Bible. The Paris Bible of *c.* 1230 is the product of only minor revisions of this earlier group. Paris Bibles are arranged in an identical order, and include a closely related set of prologues. Perhaps the most visible difference between these two types of Bibles is the fact that in the Paris Bible modern chapters are used exclusively. The disappearance of capitula lists and older chapter divisions is a

---

[86] A. Landgraf, 'Die Schriftzitate in der Scholastik um die Wende des 12. zum 13. Jahrhundert', *Biblica* 18 (1937), 77–8; Smalley, *Study of the Bible*, 222.

[87] Landgraf, 'Die Schriftzitate', 78–84; Smalley, *Study of the Bible*, 222.

[88] Landgraf, 'Die Schriftzitate', 84–7; Smalley, *Study of the Bible*, 222–4.

reflection of the fact that the practice of citing passages by means of numbered chapter references had been firmly adopted by around 1230.

In conclusion, I would like to emphasise that this brief survey has neglected a number of important topics. In particular, we have not discussed the actual text circulating in this group of early thirteenth-century Bibles and in the Paris Bible, despite the obvious importance of the topic. The *Interpretation of Hebrew Names* that circulated independently of the Vulgate between 1200 and 1230, and became a feature of the Paris Bible in *c.* 1230, is another part of this story that has been omitted. Nonetheless, I hope that even a partial discussion such as this may serve as an introduction to a neglected group of Bibles. Their evidence must be part of any reconstruction of the origin of the Paris Bible.

EARLY THIRTEENTH-CENTURY BIBLES RELATED TO THE PARIS BIBLE

Note: Order of the biblical books, prologues and capitula lists are identified as 'Paris' according to the criteria discussed in the text of the paper; text is classified as 'Paris' according to a test of selected readings from the Octateuch and the Gospels. Bibliography is selective, concentrating on recent literature.

1. Paris, Bibliothèque Mazarine, MS 7, Bible (Paris?, *c.* 1200–10)
   302 fols., 335 × 243 (211–08 × 130–26) mm, 2 columns, 58 lines
   order: Paris
   prologues: Paris except lacks Stegmüller 327 (II Chron.), Stegmüller 468 (Wis.) and Stegmüller 677 (Rom.); + Stegmüller 463 (Cant.)
   capitula lists: Paris
   text: Paris
   chapters: older chapters and original modern chapters

2. Paris, Bibliothèque Nationale, MS lat. 14233, Bible (Paris, *c.* 1200–10)
   324 fols., 425 × 290 (276–3 × 163–60) mm, 2 columns, 60 lines
   order: Gen.–Esth.; I–II Macc.; Prophets; Job; Ps., Prov., Ecces., Cant., Wis., Eccus.; Gosp.; Acts; Ca. Ep.; Pa. Ep.; Apoc.; II (III) Ezra
   prologues: Paris except lacks Stegmüller 327 (II Chron.), Stegmüller 468 (Wis.), Stegmüller 677 (Rom.) and Stegmüller 707 (Gal.)
   text: Paris
   capitula lists: Paris
   chapters: old, marked with two line initials, and modern (both systems original and carefully numbered)
   Bibliography: P. Danz Stirnemann, 'Nouvelles pratiques en matière d'enluminure au temps de Philippe Auguste', *La France de Philippe Auguste. Le Temps des mutations*, ed. R.-H. Bautier, Colloques internationaux du Centre National de la Recherche Scientifique 602 (Paris, 1982), 967, note 20 and 970, no. 10: s. xii–xiii

3. Paris, BN, MS lat. 16747, Bible (Paris, *c.* 1200–10)
   337 fols., 380 × 255 (228–4 × 137) mm, 2 columns, 61–2 lines
   order: Paris
       prologues: Paris except lacks Stegmüller 327 (II Chron.), Stegmüller 468 (Wis.),
       Stegmüller 677 (Rom.) and Stegmüller 707 (Gal.)
   text: Paris
   capitula lists: Paris
   chapters: older chapters and modern chapters, possibly original
   Bibliography: F. Avril. 'Un Manuscrit d'auteurs classiques et ses illustrations', *The Year
       1200. A Symposium* (New York, 1975), 267–8, note 3 and 'A quand remontent les
       premiers ateliers d'enlumineurs laïcs à Paris?', *Les Dossiers de l'Archéologie. Enluminure
       gothique* 16 (1975), 37–8; Stirnemann, 'Nouvelles', appendix, 971, no. 19: 1200–10

4. Paris, BN, MS lat. 14232, Bible (Paris, *c.* 1200–10)
   336 fols., 427 × 304 (247–5 × 155–8) mm, 2 columns, 60 lines
   order: Paris
   prologues: Paris except lacks Stegmüller 327 (II Chron.), Stegmüller 468 (Wis.), Stegmüller
       677 (Rom.), Stegmüller 707 (Gal.)
   text: Paris
   capitula lists: Paris
   chapters: older chapters and added modern chapters, possibly contemporary
   Bibliography: Avril, 'Un Manuscrit', 267–8, note 3 and 'A quand remontent', 37–8

5. Oxford, Bodleian Library, MS Kennicot 15, Bible (Paris, *c.* 1200–10)
   816 pp., 263 × 193 (223–5 × 124–5) mm, 2 columns, 58–9 lines
   order: Paris (includes double Psalter and Canon Tables)
   prologues: Paris except lacks Stegmüller 327 (II Chron.), Stegmüller 357 (Job) and
       'Quoniam quidem' (Luke); + Stegmüller 430 and 'Liber iste quem hebrei nablum' (cf.
       Stegmüller 8448; Psalter), Stegmüller 596 (Gosp.), Stegmüller 651, 670, 674, 677, 690,
       697, 709, 724, 733, 741, 743, 759, 761, 771 and 775 (Pa. Ep.)
   text: Paris
   capitula lists: Paris
   chapters: old divisions marked by one line initials; modern chapters added but possibly
       contemporary
   Bibliography: Avril, 'Un manuscrit', 267–8, note 3 and 'A quand remontent', 37–8;
       O. Pächt and J. J. G. Alexander, *Illuminated Manuscripts in the Bodleian Library*, 3 vols.
       (Oxford, 1966–73), III, 37, no. 385, pl. XXXIV; *Manuscripts at Oxford: An Exhibition in
       Memory of Richard William Hunt (1906–1979)*, eds. A. C. de la Mare and B. C. Barker-
       Benfield (Oxford, 1980), 69 and plate, back cover

6. London, British Library, Additional MS 15253, Bible (Paris, *c.* 1210–20)
   329 fols., 479 × *c.* 300 (272 × 165–4) mm, 2 columns, 58 lines
   order: Paris
   prologues: Paris except lacks Stegmüller 327 (II Chron.), Stegmüller 468 (Wis.), Stegmüller
       677 (Rom.) and Stegmüller 707 (Gal.)
   text: Paris
   capitula lists: Paris

chapters: original old and modern chapters

Bibliography: R. Branner, *Manuscript Painting in Paris during the Reign of Saint Louis. A Study of Styles* (Berkeley and Los Angeles, 1977), appendix v A, Early manuscripts, Almagest Atelier, 202, pl. I; Avril, 'A quand remontent', 38–40; G. Haseloff, *Die Psalterillustration im 13. Jahrhundert* (n.p., 1938), 110, tab. 8: N. France, around 1230–40

7. Troyes, Bibliothèque Municipale, MS 577, Bible (Paris, *c.* 1210–20)

326 fols., 322 × 218 (187–5 × 119–17) mm, 2 columns, 57 lines

order: Paris

prologues: Paris except lacks Stegmüller 327 (II Chron.), Stegmüller 468 (Wis.), Stegmüller 707 (Gal.); beginning of Romans missing

text: Paris

capitula lists: Paris

chapters: older chapters and modern, possibly original

Provenance: Given by Garnier de Rochefort, Bishop of Langres to Clairvaux, after *c.* 1220, before *c.* 1226 (fol. 326v)

Bibliography: Branner, *Manuscript Painting*, appendix v A, Early manuscripts, Almagest Atelier, 202; Avril, 'A quand remontent', 38–40

8. Paris, Bibliothèque Mazarine, MS 12, Bible (Paris, *c.* 1210–20)

273 fols., 305 × 210 (179–8 × 122–6) mm, 2 columns, 67 lines

order: Paris

prologues: Paris except lacks Stegmüller 327 (II Chron.) and Stegmüller 468 (Wis.); + 'Liber iste quem hebrei nablum' (cf. Stegmüller 8448; Psalms), Stegmüller 670, 659, 672, 651, 674 (Rom.), 799 (Heb.)

text: Paris

capitula lists: Paris

chapters: older chapters and modern, possibly original

Bibliography: Branner, *Manuscript Painting*, appendix v A, Early manuscripts, Almagest Atelier, 202; Avril, 'A quand remontent', 38–40; Haseloff, *Psalterillustration*, 110, Tab. 8: N. France, around 1230–50

9. Paris, Bibliothèque Mazarine, MS 70, Bible (Paris?, *c.* 1210–20)

528 fols., 231 × 164 (143–2 × 88–7) mm, 41 long lines

order: Paris, except Job follows Ps. and Cant. follows Eccus.

prologues: Paris except lacks Stegmüller 327 (II Chron.), Stegmüller 677 (Rom.), Stegmüller 707 (Gal.)

text: Paris

capitula lists: none

chapters: older chapters and original modern chapters

Bibliography: G. Lobrichon, 'Une nouveauté: les gloses de la Bible', in *Le Moyen Age et la Bible*, eds. P. Riché and G. Lobrichon, Bible de tous les temps 4 (Paris, 1984), 101, note 17, s. xiii med

10. Paris, BN, MS lat. 15470, Bible (Paris?, *c.* 1210–20)

381 fols., 335 × *c.* 240 (235–20 × 145–40) mm, 2 columns, 49–52 lines

order: Paris except: I Ezra, Neh., Tob., II (III) Ezra, Jud., Esth.

   prologues: Paris except lacks Stegmüller 327 (II Chron.), Stegmüller 468 (Wis.) and
      Stegmüller 487 (Jer.); + Stegmüller 5190 (Tob.) and Stegmüller 5191 (Jud.)
   text: OT: Paris, NT: non-Paris
   capitula lists: mixed
   chapters: older chapters; modern chapters added, possibly contemporary

11. Paris, BN, MS lat. 15471, Bible (Paris?, *c.* 1210–20)
    308 fols., 310 × 225 (210–200 × 140–20) mm, 2 columns, 62–59 lines
    order: Paris except: Esth., Tob., Jud.; Acts and Ca. Ep. follow Apoc.
    prologues: Paris except lacks Stegmüller 468 (Wis.) and Stegmüller 589 (Mat.);
       + Stegmüller 307 (Jos.), Stegmüller 350 (Job), and Stegmüller 834 (?) and 829 (Apoc.)
    text: non-Paris
    capitula lists: none
    chapters: older chapters, and added modern chapters, possibly contemporary

12. Paris, BN, MS lat. 11933, Bible (Paris?, *c.* 1210–20)
    292 fols., 294 × 220 (200–198 × 123–5) mm, 2 columns, 60 lines
    order: Paris
    prologues: Paris except lacks Stegmüller 327 (II Chron.), and Stegmüller 677 (Rom.);
       + 'Iohannes de testimonio Iheusu' (Apoc.)
    text: OT: Paris, with some non-Paris readings; NT: non-Paris
    capitula lists: Paris
    chapters: older chapters and modern, possibly original

13. Paris, BN, MS lat. 15475, Bible (Paris, *c.* 1210–30)
    365 fols., 268 × 180 (180 × 110–05) mm, 2 columns, 62 lines
    order: Paris except Col. follows II Thess.
    prologues: Paris except lacks Stegmüller 327 (II Chron.)
    text: Paris
    capitula lists: included at the beginning of the manuscript (set unique to this manuscript),
       and before Ex. and Lev. (Paris)
    chapters: older chapters and original modern chapters
    Bibliography: Branner, *Manuscript Painting*, appendix V A, Early manuscripts, Alexander
       Atelier, 203 (incorrectly listed as MS 15457); Avril, 'A quand remontent', 40–4

14. Paris, BN, MS lat. 11536, Bible (Paris, *c.* 1210–30)
    353 fols., 390 × 270 (228–6 × 159) mm, 2 columns, 59–8 lines
    order: Paris
    prologues: Paris except lacks Stegmüller 327 (II Chron.), Stegmüller 468 (Wis.); prologues
       to Rom., Gal.–I Thess. added in margin in another hand
    text: Paris
    capitula lists: Paris
    chapters: older chapters and modern, possibly original
    Bibliography: Branner, *Manuscript Painting*, appendix V A, Early manuscripts, Alexander
       Atelier, 203 and fig. 21; Avril, 'A quand remontent', 40–4; Stirnemann, 'Nouvelles',
       appendix, 973, no. 28: 1210–20

9

The textual basis for visual errors in French Gothic Psalter illustration

ELIZABETH A. PETERSON

The Psalter is universally recognised as a favourite medieval devotional text precisely because its use was ubiquitous in public and private sectors.* As a copied text, it demonstrates a longevity similar to Bible manuscripts, and the oldest preserved Psalm codex, the sixth- or seventh-century Verona Psalter, even includes decoration.[1] The Book of Psalms, the core of the Psalter, also appealed to patristic and medieval exegetes: the text served as a focal point of the Divine Office but provided contemplative and homiletic literary formulas as well. The numerous surviving examples of Psalm commentaries attest to this popularity, underscored by the high proportion of Psalm manuscripts which received artistic attention. Researchers in this arena have directed their scholarly efforts towards cataloguing, comparing and interpreting pictorial repertories. Studies address fundamental questions about illustrative programmes embedded in Psalm books: their formation in the workshop, their transmission to other contexts and their utilitarian function in private devotions.

As a series of unrelated poems, typically considered to be hymns of praise or plaints of supplication, the Psalms inspire non-sequential illustration that bears an as yet undefined relationship to the text. Nevertheless, assessing schemes of decoration has yielded insights into medieval visual responses to textual stimuli, and has shed light on mechanisms by which a canon of images is incorporated into historical sequences. Since their first appearance in Anglo-Saxon Psalters, full-page miniatures depicting the Life of Christ exemplify the rich corpus of narrative schemes available to medieval artists, and sharpen our understanding of the use of typological iconography. In examining the various loci of illustration within Psalm books, Victor Leroquais summarised four systems of decoration that partition the Psalm text with historiated initials into three, five, eight or ten sections, based on traditional biblical or theological

---

* Apart from shortening the title and adding footnotes, I have left the body of the paper, as presented at the conference, substantially unchanged. Dr Gameson, the editor, has kindly permitted me to update the bibliography and to add a few comments that clarify some of the arguments and that address the issue of minor Psalm illustration in a broader context.

[1] Verona, Biblioteca Capitolare, cod. 1. See A. Goldschmidt, 'Die ältesten Psalterillustrationen', *Repertorium für Kunstwissenschaft* 23 (1900), 265–73.

divisions or liturgical requirements.[2] Systematic tabulations of subjects in Psalters grouped by temporal and geographical relationships have commanded further analysis as repositories of conventional scenes, and narrative patterns which evolved for the 'major' Psalms have been well-documented. Leroquais also distinguished a special family of luxury Psalters in which it was intended that each Psalm should be illustrated. Although more than fifty of these books or fragments of books have survived, they constitute a relatively small proportion of the output of medieval Psalters.[3] The situation is further complicated: these fully-illustrated books are linked by the quantity of figural representation, yet isolated by the apparent lack of overall affinity among narrative sequences in the Psalters.

Too often there is no direct path to locating the sources used for historical iconography in these manuscripts, and we are confronted with miniatures whose models are not readily identifiable. This is particularly so when looking at text that is only sporadically illuminated. However, if a study of this kind of illustration in books, containing also conventional pictorial sequences, is pursued in tandem with an examination of the texts, the result can sometimes inform us about the selection process. A group of French Gothic manuscripts constitute part of a rich phenomenon of fully-illustrated Psalm books, illustrating text rarely selected for pictorial treatment. The following list places them in approximate chronological order, with both their popular name and their current location and shelfmark.

H: *La Charité Psalter* (London, British Library, Harley MS 2895), *c.* 1190

G: *Geneviève Lombard Commentary* (Paris, Bibliothèque Ste-Geneviève, MS 56), *c.* 1200

R: *Jeanne de Navarre Psalter* (Manchester, John Rylands University Library, Latin MS 22), *c.* 1225–30

L: *'Leningrad' Psalter* (St Petersburg, Saltykov-Scedrin State Public Library, MS Q. v. I. 67), *c.* 1225–30

Ph: *Lewis Psalter* (Philadelphia, Free Library, Lewis Collection, European MS 185), *c.* 1235

B: *Bute Psalter* (Malibu, J. Paul Getty Museum, 92.MK.92 (MS 46), formerly of the collection of the Marquis of Bute), *c.* 1285

C: *Cambridge Psalter* (Cambridge, University Library, MS Ee. iv. 24), *c.* 1280

P: *Amiens Psalter* (Paris, Bibliothèque Nationale, MS lat. 10435), *c.* 1295

The group comprises seven Psalters and one manuscript containing the mid-

---

[2] Abbé Leroquais quantifies 'major Psalm' illumination in *Les psautiers manuscrits latins des bibliothèques publiques de France*, 3 vols. (Mâcon, 1940–1), I, xc–xcviii, based on A. Goldschmidt, *Der Albanipsalter in Hildesheim und seine Beziehung zur symbolischen Kirchenskulptur des XII. Jahrhunderts* (Berlin, 1895), 1–23 and A. H. Springer, *Die Psalterillustration im frühen Mittelalter mit besonderer Rücksicht auf den Utrechtpsalter*, Abhandlungen der philologisch-historischen Classe der königlich Sächsischen Gesellschaft der Wissenschaften no. II, Bd. 8 (Leipzig, 1880). See also particular groups described by H. Schneider, 'Die Psaltererteilung in Fünfziger- und Zehnergruppen', in *Universitas. Dienst an Wahrheit und Leben. Festschrift für Bischof Dr. Albert Stohr*, ed. L. Lenhart, 2 vols. (Mainz, 1960), I, 36–47 and by L. Gjerløw, *Liturgica Islandica I: Text; II: Facsimiles*, Bibliotheca Arnamagnaeana xxv, ed. J. Louis-Jensen *et al.* (Copenhagen, 1980), esp. I, 98–101.

[3] The oldest manuscripts preserved, the Utrecht, Stuttgart, Chludoff and Pantocrator Psalters (see notes 8, 9 and 11 below), have been used to buttress arguments for the Early Christian origin of fully-illustrated picture Bibles. Consequently, extensive narrative programmes, by virtue of the quantity of illustration, could signal a different historical meaning, quite apart from liturgical considerations.

twelfth-century Commentary on the Psalms composed by Peter Lombard. Each book is decorated with, among other things, historiated initials for most of the 150 Psalms, which provide a rich, if somewhat unwieldy, corpus from which to pose questions of identification of subject, source of iconography or pinpointing of visual models, not to mention the formation, as well as transmission, of the 'programme' as a whole.[4] The eight manuscripts range in date from the late twelfth to the late thirteenth century, and seven workshops were responsible for their execution;[5] yet the subjects in the initials to a particular Psalm manifest a high degree of iconographic correspondence among the books. How the transference of subject was effected within the group, and the iconographic alterations undergone by some of the subjects during the process, is the focus of this paper.

I refer to these manuscripts, for purposes of convenience, as the French Psalter Group. The last six books (R, L, Ph, B, C, P) in the list contain approximately 171 historiated initials apiece, one for each of the Psalms and one for each of the twenty-two standard divisions of Psalm 118, *lacunæ* due to non-execution or subsequent loss notwithstanding.[6] The first two books (H, G) in the list are less densely-illustrated,[7] although they have a significantly greater number of narrative depictions than the 'classic' eight or ten historiated initials placed before those Psalms which mark the liturgical divisions. No source – that is, no previously-executed fully-illustrated Psalter – has yet come to light that might have served as the exact single model for the illumination in the French Psalter Group; yet, a review of the subjects of the Psalms reveals that the painters did not make random selections. Each manuscript represents a conscious effort to expand the standard decoration of the Psalter, and while the pictorial sequences are not identical to each other throughout the family, many of the scenes in one manuscript echo those for the same Psalms in one or more of the other manuscripts.

In the period from the ninth to the mid-fifteenth centuries, densely-illustrated, even fully-illustrated, Psalters are not by any means an exceptional phenomenon. The earliest surviving Western examples, the well-known Stuttgart[8] and Utrecht

---

[4] Samuel Berger wrote an introductory essay on a portion of the group (R, C, P): 'Les manuels pour l'illustration du psautier au XIIIe siècle', *Mémoires de la Société nationale des Antiquaires de France*, 6e série, 7, 57 (1898), 95–134. A more recent essay begins to reassess the evidence for the iconogrpahy and texts that link together the eight manuscripts: see my 'Accidents in Transmission Among Fully-Illustrated Thirteenth-Century French Psalters', *Zeitschrift für Kunstgeschichte* 50 (1987), 375–84, with selected bibliography on the group. For a fuller study of the iconography of the minor Psalm illustration in these French Psalters, see my thesis, 'Iconography of the Historiated Psalm Initials in the Thirteenth-Century French Fully-illustrated Psalter Group' (University of Pittsburgh, 1991).

[5] For evidence that R and L were created in the same workshop, R. Haussherr, 'Ein Pariser martyrologischer Kalender aus der ersten Hälfte des 13. Jahrhunderts', in *Festschrift Matthias Zender: Studien zur Volkskultur, Sprache und Landesgeschichte*, ed. E. Ennen and G. Wiegelmann, 2 vols. (Bonn, 1972), ii, 1076–103; and R. Branner, *Manuscript Painting in Paris during the Reign of Saint Louis. A Study of Styles*, California Studies in the History of Art 18, ed. W. Horn (Berkeley and Los Angeles, 1977), cat. pp. 206–7.

[6] R is missing initials for Psalms 1 and 32; L has two initials each for Psalms 68 and 70; and Ph lacks an initial for Psalm 99.

[7] H has been badly mutilated: of the remaining Psalm initials, fifty-five are historiated and nineteen are foliate. G has thirty-two figural and one unexecuted initial; the rest are foliate.

[8] Stuttgart, Württembergische Landesbibliothek, Bibl. fol. 23, hereafter referred to as the Stuttgart Psalter: *Der Stuttgarter Bilderpsalter. Bibl. Fol. 23 der Württembergischen Landesbibliothek. I: Faksimile; II: Untersuchungen*, ed. B. Bischoff *et al.*, 2 vols. (Stuttgart, 1965–8).

Psalters,[9] date from the ninth century, and several ninth-century Byzantine counter-parts also manifest narrative scenes for most of the Psalms.[10] In addition to sixteen Eastern Psalters with extensive illustration,[11] thirty-nine Western Psalm manuscripts from England and the Continent incorporate figural illumination for a great number of minor Psalms.[12] Investigations to date suggest that, in general, these varying Psalter 'programmes' were assembled from diverse sources, impeding perhaps attempts to trace any direct contribution to the formation of the iconographic 'programme' in the French Psalter Group. Indeed, one must use the term 'pro-gramme' cautiously since analysis has so far indicated no underlying concept to guide the artist in the selection of his subjects. A majority of the scenes show Old and New Testament events, while others stem from a variety of sources, including bestiaries, patristic exegesis and ecclesiastic activities. While the themes in this family of French Psalter manuscripts are often inspired by one of the Psalm verses or by the *titulus*, illustrating literally the Sacred Word,[13] the subjects of the initials in this group of books, which include historical events, frequently derive from exegetical writings. More than forty of these commentary essays on some or all of the Psalms have been published in modern critical editions.[14]

In focusing my remarks on the means of transmission for some of the historiation

---

[9] Utrecht, Universiteitsbibliotheek, MS 32 (Script. Eccl. 484), hereafter referred to as the Utrecht Psalter: *Utrecht-Psalter: vollständige Faksimile-Ausgabe im Originalformat des Hs. 32, Utrecht-Psalter, aus dem Besitz der Bibliothek des Rijksuniversiteit te Utrecht*, Codices selecti 75, comm. K. van der Horst, trans. J. Rathofer, 2 vols. (Graz, 1982–4). The images in three Psalter manuscripts are based on this book: London, British Library, Harley MS 603; Cambridge, Trinity College, R. 17. 1; and Paris, Bibliothèque Nationale, lat. MS 8846. Diagrams of a proposed inter-relationship between these four manuscripts appear in *English Illuminated Manuscripts 700–1500. Brussels, Bibliothèque Royale Albert 1er, 29 September–10 November 1973*, ed. J. J. G. Alexander and C. M. Kauffmann (Brussels, 1973), 36, and nos. 14, 15, 17, 18, pp. 35–9, 41–3; and A. Heimann, 'The Last Copy of the Utrecht Psalter', *The Year 1200. A Symposium* (New York, 1975), 313–38. Patricia Stirnemann discredits these earlier attempts to establish direct link between Trinity R. 17. 1 and BN, lat. 8846 in F. Avril and P. D. Stirnemann, *Manuscrits enluminés d'origine insulaire VIIe–XXe siècle* (Paris, 1987), no. 76, 45–8, with pls. E, XXII–XXIV.

[10] Until the manuscript is properly evaluated in this context, I do not include Verona, Biblioteca Capitolare, cod. 1, whose illuminated initials sometimes contain animals or busts of figures, see note 1.

[11] Suzy Dufrenne compiled comparative tables of iconography of Byzantine Psalters and the Utrecht and Stuttgart Psalters: *Tableaux synoptiques de 15 psautiers médiévaux à illustrations intégrales issues du texte* (Paris, 1978). Other Byzantine examples are discussed in A. Baumstark, 'Frühchristliche-syrische Psalterillustration in einer byzantinischen Abkürzung', *Oriens Christianus* 5 (1905), 295–320; A. Cutler and A. Weyl Carr, 'The Psalter Benaki 34.3: An Unpublished Illuminated Manuscript From the Family 2400', *Revue des études byzantines* 34 (1976), 281–323.

[12] Of the Western Psalters still extant from six and a half centuries, more than twenty percent, represented by the French Psalter Group, date to a single hundred-year period.

[13] While scholars have briefly addressed the issue of Eastern and Western attitudes to Psalter illustration, definitions of and function of the *ad verbum* technique versus the historical approach remain unclear. See, for example, S. Dufrenne, *Les Illustrations du psautier d'Utrecht: sources et apport carolingien*, Association des publications près les universités de Strasbourg, fasc. 161 (Paris, 1978), 29–33; also F. Mütherich, in *Der Stuttgarter Bilderpsalter*, II, 151–202. A recent study discusses examples of word illustration in a thirteenth-century Provençal chansonnier: A. Rieger, ' "Ins e.l cor port, dona, vostra faisso": Image et imaginaire de la femme à travers l'enluminure dans les chansoniers de troubadours', *Cahiers de civilisation médiévale* 28e année, no. 4 (Octobre–Décembre 1985), 385–415. I thank Dr Patricia Stirnemann for bringing this article to my attention.

[14] *Patrologia latina*, ed. J.-P. Migne, 221 vols. (Paris, 1844–64). Re-attributions of author and date for some of the Psalm commentaries appear in, among others, P. Glorieux, *Pour révaloriser Migne: tables rectificatives*, Mélanges de science religieuse, IXème année, Cahier supplémentaire (Lille, 1952); in E. Dekkers, ed., 'Clavis Patrum latinorum', *Sacris erudiri* 3 (1961), incl; in W. Affeldt, *Die weltliche Gewalt in der Paulus-Exegese. Rom. 13, 1–7 in den*

among the eight family members, I will demonstrate how certain iconographic particulars depended not on visual models but on textual ones. Altogether, four of the eight manuscripts (the Jeanne de Navarre, the Lewis, the Cambridge and the Amiens Psalters) include the rare feature of descriptive legends or inscriptions in the form of short titles accompanying the historiated initials. Those in the Jeanne de Navarre (R) and the Lewis (Ph) manuscripts are written in Latin, while legends in Old French appear in the Cambridge (C) and Amiens (P) Psalters. The inscriptions are not written in the text column, and they do not correspond to any of the edited series of *tituli*. The latter serve as standard literary formulas to introduce each Psalm and to ground the hymn in Christian interpretation, either by identifying the author of the Psalm, by recounting the occasion on which the author, often King David, wrote the Psalm, by describing the contents of the Psalm or by explaining its purpose.[15] The inscriptions are written in the margin near the initials in R, Ph and P; in C, however, they are collected together in a single list on one bifolium, which has been inserted between the gatherings containing the calendar and the first Psalm. The display script, the careful lettering of the legend, does not preclude it from being workshop (and therefore impermanent) instructions to the illuminator, but the red and blue ink in the Jeanne de Navarre and Lewis Psalters and the red ink in the Amiens Psalter suggest rather that they are meant for the reader. They seem to function as picture captions to the historiated initials. Apart from the French Psalter Group, I know of three fully-illustrated Psalters, dating to the late twelfth, the mid-thirteenth and the mid-fifteenth centuries, which also have such titles, each series different from the other and all of them unpublished.[16] The equally unpublished marginal legends written in the Lewis Psalter are generally verbatim quotes from, or paraphrases of, Peter Lombard's Commentary on the Psalms. Not so the inscriptions in the other three Psalters (R, C, P), which have been published previously in comparative tables. These three, like the subjects of the historiated initials, exhibit considerable similarity, but not repetition. The phrasing in Old French in both the Cambridge and Amiens manuscripts frequently resembles the Latin wording in the Jeanne de Navarre book. It is these texts which will prove to be a significant factor in determining how some of the iconographic details were selected by the painters.

As might be expected among books linked temporally and geographically, the sequences of subjects for the historiated initials in these manuscripts sometimes follow

---

Römerbriefkommentaren der lateinischen Kirche bis zum Ende des 13. Jahrhunderts (Göttingen, 1969), 256–85; and in R. Sprandel, *Altersschicksal und Altarsmoral: Die Geschichte der Einstellungen zum Altern nach der Pariser Bibelexegese des 12.–16. Jahrhunderts*, Monographien zur Geschichte des Mittelalters, Band 22, ed. Karl Bosl (Stuttgart, 1981), 5–8. Newer critical editions appear in two series: CCSL and CSEL.

[15] Pierre Salmon edited six series in manuscripts from the eighth to the twelfth centuries in *Les 'Tituli Psalmorum' des manuscrits latins*, Collectanea Biblica Latina 12; Études liturgiques 3 (Paris, 1959), esp. 9–39. Further series appear in his *Analecta liturgica: extraits des manuscrits liturgiques de la Bibliothèque Vaticane. Contribution à l'histoire de la prière chrétienne*, Studi e Testi 273 (Vatican City, 1974), 12–46.

[16] Respectively, Berlin, Kupferstichkabinett, MS 78 A 5; Oxford, Bodleian Library, Ashmole MS 1525; London, British Library, Additional MS 16999. None of the three sets of inscriptions corresponds to any of the sets published by Salmon and remains an unknown factor in the selection process for illustration. For bibliography on the first two manuscripts, see notes 25 and 30. The third manuscript is unpublished. Indeed, this feature is not always recorded: a 1982 catalogue entry of a fully-illustrated Psalter failed to mention their presence.

the same pattern. The point is reinforced by comparing initials where painters have faithfully rendered one particular subject for the same Psalm in each of the manuscripts, and the rubricators have done the same with the descriptive legends. Before discussing the iconographic shifts in several of the Psalm initials, I will present, for Psalm 8, the degree to which similarities can occur.[17]

The Psalm, *Domine Dominus noster* ('O Lord our Lord, how admirable is thy name in the whole earth!'), celebrates the glory of the Lord's creation. Yet, the *titulus* at the head of the Psalm inspires the theme for the initials in the French Psalter Group: *In finem pro torcularibus psalmus David* ('Unto the end, for the presses: a psalm for David').[18] The initial from the Lewis Psalter (fol. 36r), of *c.* 1235, defines the kind of press: David stands next to a winepress loaded with grapes and gestures to the head of God in a cloud.[19] The legend, referring to the *titulus*, says *Dauid loquitur domino pro torcularibus* ('David speaks to the Lord for the winepresses'). The inscription next to the initial in the Jeanne de Navarre Psalter (fol. 19r), of *c.* 1225–30, says, *Quidam erigit torcularia* ('A person constructs winepresses'). The title is rendered visually by a man in tunic and bonnet cap who stands behind the press and pushes down on the upper horizontal bar, but the presence of grapes inside implies that he is operating, rather than constructing, the winepress.[20] No legends have been inserted in the Leningrad Psalter (fol. 12), produced in the same workshop as R, but the activity in the initial correlates more precisely to the Rylands inscription. In this initial, a man, constructing a winepress, slides the top horizontal bar onto two vertical uprights of which the left one is threaded.[21] The subject is repeated in three of the later manuscripts of the French Psalter Group from the last quarter of the thirteenth century. Although inscriptions have also been omitted from the Bute Psalter (fol. 7v), of *c.* 1285, the initial shows a man fitting a vertical threaded post with base onto its platform. The two components of the scene, the man and the winepress, occur again in the initials in the Cambridge (fol. 7r), of *c.* 1280, and in the Amiens Psalter (fol. 6v), of *c.* 1295. In C, a man attaches a device onto a threaded post above two horizontal bars of the press, and the legend in Old French repeats the Latin one in R: *Uns homs dessce .i. pressoir* ('A man constructs a winepress'). In P, a man standing next to a press raises his hands over two horizontal bars fixed by two vertical threaded posts.[22] Dating from the late twelfth century, the La Charité Psalter (fol. 12r) does not depict the press's construction, but nevertheless features the object prominently in the image: a stream of blue liquid issues from the winepress and is collected by an angel while a devil

---

[17] I summarise here the salient points of the comparison in the French Psalter Group from Peterson, 'Accidents in Transmission', 378–9.

[18] For the Latin Bible, R. Weber, ed., *Biblia Sacra Iuxta Vulgatam versionem*, 2 vols., 3rd rev. edn (Stuttgart, 1983). English translations of Vulgate passages are quoted from *The Holy Bible Translated From the Latin Vulgate* . . . (Baltimore, 1899; repr. Rockford, n.d.). I cite only the Vulgate numbering of the Psalms.

[19] Peterson, 'Accidents in Transmission', fig. 2.   [20] *Ibid.*, fig. 1.

[21] I. P. Mokretsova and V. L. Romanova, eds., *Les manuscrits enluminés français du XIIIe siècle dans les collections soviétiques 1200–1270* (Moscow, 1983), p. 115, fig.

[22] The legend is only a problematic approximation of those in the Jeanne de Navarre and Cambridge Psalters: *Uns hons se dreche sur un pressoir* ('A man lifts himself up on a winepress'). More errors of transcription are treated below in detail.

9.1   *London, British Library, MS Harley 2895, fol. 12r: Psalm 8*

wields a blue hatchet on the grapes inside (ill. 9.1). The winepress, a central element in the compositions of the initials in the French Psalter Group, does not appear for Psalm 8 in earlier Psalm illustration,[23] thereby isolating the eight books under consideration here from traditional patterns of narrative.

In order to underline the close relationship among the scenes in our group of Psalters, it is worth reviewing the vastly different subjects used for the Psalm in other Psalters. While some densely-illustrated books omit figural illustration at Psalm 8, several Psalters include it. The ninth-century Utrecht manuscript (fol. 4v), has a composite miniature which includes Christ in glory, an angel with three demons and the moon, stars, cows, fish and birds mentioned in verses 3, 4, 8 and 9. Initials in the

[23] The subject appeared once for Psalm 83, *Quam dilecta*, in Engelberg, Stiftsbibliothek, cod. 12, fol. 101, a copy of Augustine's Commentary on the Psalms of 1180–1230, where it is recognised as a type for the Crucifixion of Christ. G. Staffelbach, 'Etwas über Keltertretermotive in Luzern und der Innerschweiz', in *Archäologische kirchen- und kunsthistorische Beiträge zur Vollendung des 70. Lebensjahres am 18. Januar 1966* [Festschrift Alois Thomas] (Trier, 1967), 405–10, esp. 409 fig. 94; cited in *Lexicon der christlichen Ikonographie*, ed. E. Kirschbaum *et al.*, 8 vols. (Rome, 1968), II, col. 500.

Stuttgart manuscript (fol. 8v) and many of the ninth- through eleventh-century Byzantine Psalters display a representation of the Entry of Christ into Jerusalem.[24] This particular Christological interpretation of verse 3 occurs again in a late twelfth-century North Italian Psalter (Berlin, Kupferstichkabinett, MS 78 A 5, fol. 13r) where inscriptions also accompany the illustrations.[25] In the margin at verse 3 the rubricator has written *Pueros hebreos obviam ihesu exire demonstrat* ('It shows Hebrew youths going forth to meet Jesus'), adjacent to a scene depicting the Entry into Jerusalem.[26] Further illustration occurs in this manuscript near verse 8 where David above points to the seated figures of the Father and the Son, flanked by men kneeling in prayer; the scene is rubricated by *David confitetur patrem dum subegisset dilecto filio suo* ('David acknowledges the Father when he had put down his [i.e. David's] own beloved son'). The early ninth-century Corbie Psalter (Amiens, Bibliothèque Municipale, MS 18, fol. 7r) includes a bust of the Lord blessing and holding a book.[27] The mid-eleventh-century Bury St Edmunds Psalter (Vatican City, Biblioteca Apostolica Vaticana, Reg. lat. 12, fol. 25r) shows the Lord crowning David, responding to verse 6, '. . . thou has crowned him with glory and honour'.[28] The St Albans Psalter (Hildesheim, St Godehard's, dating from the 1120s, p. 83) divides the interior of the initial into four quadrants in each of which is a seated mother and child.[29] Another English Psalter (Oxford, Bodleian Library, Ashmole MS 1525, fol. 10r), possibly for the use of the Cathedral Priory at Canterbury, is dated to the mid-thirteenth century;[30] its legend to Psalm 8, written in the text column, says, *Ecclesia decantat laudes domino in isto psalmo* ('Ecclesia sings praises to the Lord in this Psalm'); its historiated initial depicts the Massacre of the Innocents, perhaps a visual response to the liturgical reading of the Psalm during the feast of the Holy Innocents.[31]

[24] E.g. Vatican City, Biblioteca Apostolica Vaticana, Vaticanus graecus 1927, fol. 10v; London, British Library, Additional MS 19352, fol. 6; Vatican City, Biblioteca Apostolica Vaticana, Barb. graec. 372, fol. unpublished; London, British Library, Additional MS 40731, fol. 15v. The connection to the New Testament is found at Matthew 21.16; Christ quotes part of the Psalm 8.3 when the children acclaimed his solemn entry into Jerusalem: 'Out of the mouth of infants and of sucklings thou has perfected praise'.

[25] For description and provenance, P. R. Wescher, *Beschreibendes Verzeichnis der Miniaturen – Handschriften und Einzelblätter – des Kupferstichkabinetts der Staatlichen Museen, Berlin* (Leipzig, 1931), 21–4, fig. 24; W. Augustyn, 'Zu Herkunft und Stil des lateinischen Hamiltonpsalters in Berliner Kupferstichkabinett (78 A 5)', *Jahrbuch der Berliner Museen* 31 (1989), 107–26. For reproductions of all illustration in the manuscript, W. Augustyn, *Der lateinische Hamilton-Psalter im Berliner Kupferstichkabinett (78 A 5). Zur Ikonographie einer italienischen Handschrift des 12. Jahrhunderts*, forthcoming.

[26] I thank Dr Jeanne Krochalis, Penn State University, for her aid with translations from Latin.

[27] For bibliography, Leroquais, *Les psautiers manuscrits* 1, no. 4, pp. 6–9, pls. III–VI and U. Kuder, 'Die Initialen des Amienspsalter' (unpublished Ph.D. thesis, Munich, 1977).

[28] On the Bury Psalter, R. M. Harris, 'The Marginal Drawings of the Bury St Edmunds Psalter' (unpublished Ph.D. thesis, Princeton University, 1960); E. Temple, *Anglo-Saxon Manuscripts, 900–1066*, A Survey of Manuscripts Illuminated in the British Isles 2 (London, 1976), no. 84, pp. 100–2, ills. 262–4, fig. 26; T. Ohlgren, ed., *Insular and Anglo-Saxon Illuminated Manuscripts: An Iconographic Catalogue, c. A.D. 625 to 1100*, Garland Reference Library of the Humanities 631 (New York and London, 1986), no. 189, pp. 205–11.

[29] On this manuscript, O. Pächt *et al.*, *The St. Albans Psalter (Albani Psalter)*, Studies of the Warburg Institute 25 (London, 1960); and C. M. Kauffmann, *Romanesque Manuscripts 1066–1190*, A Survey of Manuscripts Illuminated in the British Isles 3 (London, 1975), no. 29, 68–70, ills. 72–4, 76, 78, fig. 22. See also R. M. Thompson, *Manuscripts From St. Albans Abbey, 1066–1235, I: Text no. 29, II: Plates*, 2 vols. (Woodbridge, 1982), I, 23. For folio references, I follow the pagination of the manuscript cited in Pächt *et al.*

[30] N. J. Morgan, *Early Gothic Manuscripts [1]: 1190–1250*, A Survey of Manuscripts Illuminated in the British Isles 4 (London and Oxford, 1982), no. 33, pp. 81–3, ills. 114–18.

[31] *The Jerusalem Bible*, ed. Alexander Jones (London, 1966), 791.

Yet, the winepress as object does occur in a contemporary manuscript, the so-called Oxford Moralized Bible, dated 1240–50.[32] It is one of the four copies of the Moralized Bible that depend principally upon sets of paired scenes to convey all the nuances of the excerpts of Bible text and the accompanying abbreviated moral instruction which are written alongside. The first medallion for this Psalm, juxtaposed to the text of the *titulus* and first verse (fol. 4r), shows a man working a winepress while King David observes him.[33] The commentary written next to the second medallion states, *Psalmus iste loquitur de institutione ecclesie ... Et invocatur ecclesia torcular quia sicut torcular segregat vinum ab amurca. Ita separantur boni a malis sententia excommunicationis* ('This Psalm speaks about the institution of the church ... And the winepress is called to mind by the church because just as the winepress separates the wine from the oil lees, in this manner the good are separated from the evil by a sentence of excommunication'). St Augustine focuses on the necessary presence of the good and the evil in the church in many sermons, where he draws a parallel between *torcularia* ('winepresses') and churches because we separate the grapes from the grapeskins in the press in the same fashion as we separate the good from the multitude of worldly people.[34]

[32] The Book of Psalms in the Oxford Moralized Bible is part of Paris, Bibliothèque Nationale, lat. MS 11560. A. Laborde, *La bible moralisée illustrée conservée à Oxford, Paris et Londres*, 5 vols. (Paris, 1911–27). For the recensional links among the various copies of the *Bibles moralisées*, see the diagram in R. Haussherr, 'Sensus litteralis und sensus spiritualis in der Bible moralisée', *Frühmittelalterliche Studien* 6 (1972), 356–80, at 367.

[33] Laborde, *La bible moralisée*, II, pl. 228.

[34] S. Hebgin and F. Corrigan, trans., *St Augustine on the Psalms*, Ancient Christian Writers: The Works of the Fathers in Translation, 2 vols. (Westminster, Md. and London, 1960), I, 96–7. Following Augustine, many of the Psalm commentaries edited in PL mention the function of the winepress, but I have not yet found an explanation for the act of building the winepress. None refers to that particular aspect but to the separation of grapes from the grapeskins associated with Christ treading grapes, an iconography that became popular in a variety of contexts. The object in the so-called 'Anagogical' window in the Abbey Church of St Denis mistakenly identified as a winepress by Anna Esmeijer in *Divina Quaternitas: A Preliminary Study in the Method and Application of Visual Exegesis* (Assen, 1978), 55, note 155 and 86, note 52, is reproduced in L. Grodecki, *Les Vitraux de Saint-Denis*, Étude sur le vitrail au XIIe siècle 1, Corpus Vitrearum Medii Aevi (Paris, 1976), 98, 101, 102, with fig. 122. Abbot Suger in his *De rebus in administratione sua gestis*, cap. XXXIV, mentions not the press but rather the Pauline mystic mill. For the Latin text and a translation, see E. Panofsky, *Abbot Suger On the Abbey Church of St.-Denis And Its Art Treasures*, 2nd edn by G. Panofsky-Soergel (Princeton, 1946; 1979), 74–5. Christ treading the grapes in the winepress is, however, one element of the image on fol. 241 in a reconstruction of the *Hortus Deliciarum* with the inscription: *Torcular calcavit solus pro omnibus ut omnes liberarentur; torcular calcavi solus; torcular est sancta crux* ('He has trodden the winepress alone for all so that all are liberated; alone I have trodden the winepress; the winepress is a holy cross'). See R. Green *et al.*, *Herrad of Hohenbourg, Hortus Deliciarum*, Studies of the Warburg Institute 36, ed. J. B. Trapp, 2 vols. (*Reconstruction* and *Commentary*) (London and Leiden, 1979), II, cat. no. 307, fig. 297 and I, pl. 133, on p. 405. This use of the winepress is found also in Munich, Bayerische Staatsbibliothek, Clm 14159, a twelfth-century *Dialogus de laudibus crucis*: fol. 4, *Torcular calcavi solus*, blessing Christ treads grapes in a winepress, and reproduced in Green *et al.*, *Herrad*, fig. 298. On this manuscript, E. Klemm, *Die romanischen Handschriften der Bayerischen Staatsbibliothek*, Katalog der illuminierten Handschriften der Bayerischen Staatsbibliothek in München, Band 3, Teil 1, 2 vols. (Wiesbaden, 1980), I: *Textband*, no. 35, pp. 34–7, colour pl. IV, figs. 66–70. A further use of the winepress appeared in the now lost twelfth-century fresco of the west transept of St Emmeram at Regensburg.

Another use of the winepress is found in Wiesbaden, Nassauische Landesbibliothek, cod. 1, the *Scivias* of Hildegard of Bingen. On fol. 22, the fifth miniature represents the creation of the soul and the struggle after sin, described in L. Baillet 'Les miniatures du "Scivias" de Sainte Hildegarde conservé à la Bibliothèque Wiesbaden', *Fondation Eugène Piot. L'Académie des Inscriptions et Belles Lettres. Monuments et Mémoires* 19 (1911), 49–149, esp. 65 and pl. VIII: *De la liberté, l'âme peut user pour le bien, ou abuser pour le mal. Mais l'âme pécheresse elle-même garde le pouvoir de se relever. Les diables ont beau l'enchaîner, la faire paître avec les pourceaux, l'écraser sous le pressoir.* See also M. Böckler, *Wisse die Wege: Scivias nach dem Originaltext des illuminierten Rupertsbergerkodex der Wiesbadener Landesbibliothek ins deutsche Übertragen* (Salzburg, 1954, repr. 1963), esp. 121 and colour pl. 5, p. 25 (Schau 1, 4): *Danach legten sie mich auf die Kelter und quälten mich mit vielen Qualen.*

Such Psalm analysis serves to confirm the iconographic inter-relationship of the members of the thirteenth-century French Psalter Group. The comparison with other fully-illustrated Psalters, demonstrating the versatility which shapes the compositions at Psalm 8, establishes the status of the eight books as a family. Simultaneously, comparing the initials within the French Psalter Group testifies to the independent treatment of the subject. That the compositions are not consonant in every detail suggests that the manuscripts themselves did not communicate the images to each other. Moreover, in a limited way, the analysis refines earlier scholarship on the family which generalised from the inscriptions to arrive at inadequate, sometimes incorrect, descriptions of the iconography in the historiated initial. Scholars failed to grasp the significance of the variants in the phrasing of some of the legends for the same Psalm among the Jeanne de Navarre, the Cambridge and the Amiens Psalters, and furthermore failed to query the occasional discrepancies between what the legend communicates and what the scene portrays in the same manuscript. Thus they misjudged the nature of the link between the manuscripts in the French Psalter Group and inadvertently implied that the manuscripts were the products of a model-copy relationship.[35] I shall examine how these iconographic deviations relate to the legends of the four manuscripts and how the wording in two or more legends corresponds to, or differs from, each other in order to prove that the earlier manuscripts themselves could not have functioned as a model for the later manuscripts. Moreover, I argue that the kind of model which might have transmitted the iconography from atelier to atelier was not even a visual one, but rather a textual exemplar.

Within the framework of similarity exhibited by Psalm 8, inspection of other initials in the French Psalter Group occasionally reveals astonishing variations among some of these closely-related narrative patterns. Of the different ways in which compositions have been altered, I have classified two types of modifications, both showing how distance in time and place of execution can be a factor affecting the transmission of iconography. Subjects selected by the painters of the Jeanne de Navarre and 'Leningrad' Psalters undergo modification for the same Psalm in the later manuscripts.

The first category of changes is represented by a complete break in the continuous transmission of theme for a specific Psalm whereby an alternative subject is chosen for the later Psalters. The difference is also reflected in the wording of the legend. Psalm 25 illustrates one of at least ten examples of this pattern of change in the French Psalter Group. David prays for deliverance in the Psalm so that he may worship the Lord in his tabernacle, and the text begins, *Iudica me Domine quoniam ego in innocentia mea ingressus sum* ('Judge me, O Lord, for I have walked in my innocence'). Two verses which mention the church perhaps prompted the ideas visualised in three of the books. Verse 8 says, 'I have loved, O Lord, the beauty of thy house; and the place where thy glory dwelleth'; and in verse 12: 'My foot hath stood in the direct way; in the churches I will

---

[35] This is the implied premise of Samuel Berger in 'Les manuels', 95–134. He transcribed the rubrics in R, C and P; the texts are, in turn, largely repeated by G. Haseloff, who also gave brief descriptions of the intials in H and G, two manuscripts of the French Psalter Group without legends: *Die Psalterillustration im 13. Jahrhundert: Studien zur Geschichte der Buchmalerei in England, Frankreich und den Niederlanden* (Kiel, 1938), 33–9. A transcription of some legends in Ph is found in Peterson, 'Iconography of the Historiated Psalm Initials'.

9.2   Manchester, John Rylands University
Library, Latin MS 22, fol. 35v: Psalm 25

9.3   Paris, Bibliothèque Ste-Geneviève, MS
56, fol. 43v: Psalm 25

bless thee, O Lord'. Either of these may have inspired the subject of the initial in the late twelfth-century La Charité Psalter (fol. 20r); the Psalmist stands in the doorway of the church, raising his arms orant to a blessing Christ who rises above the roof. The first distinct iconographic change occurs in the Jeanne de Navarre Psalter (fol. 35v); the legend, *Ecclesia tenet calicem* ('Ecclesia holds a chalice'), is written next to Ecclesia, standing on green water, holding a chalice in her right hand (ill. 9.2). The subject, indeed even the composition as a whole, is nearly duplicated in the 'Leningrad' Psalter (fol. 28v) from the same workshop: crowned, veiled Ecclesia stands holding a chalice in her veiled left hand.[36] St Augustine mentions Ecclesia in his comments on the *titulus Psalmus David* ('A Psalm of David') and writes, 'David himself may here signify, not the Mediator Christ Jesus in His humanity, but the whole Church now perfectly established in Christ'.[37] Pseudo-Jerome, in a Psalm commentary once thought to be of seventh- or eighth-century Irish provenance, characterises the Psalm as the voice of Ecclesia addressing itself to Christ,[38] and later on, Peter Lombard includes Ecclesia in his Commentary: *Domus dei ecclesia est* ('The house of God is Ecclesia').[39] Another member of the French Psalter Group, G, an early thirteenth-century copy of Peter Lombard's Commentary on the Psalms, may also represent Ecclesia: in the initial (fol. 43v), a woman (perhaps Ecclesia?) stands on a pedestal, holding a chalice in her right hand and a palm branch in her left (ill. 9.3). The rarity of the theme is underscored by its absence in other Psalters with an illustration for Psalm 25. Only one seems to reflect a similar impulse, or perhaps it is only by coincidence that a mid-thirteenth-century Psalter (Melk, Stiftsbibliothek, MS 1833, fol. 32r) from the diocese of Bamberg-Eichstatt includes a standing female figure within the initial **I** for the same Psalm.[40]

    None of the subjects in the earlier fully-illustrated Psalters can account, however, for a second iconographic shift in two of the later Psalters of the French Psalter Group. In the initial from the Cambridge Psalter (fol. 10r), an angel flies up from a well-head; from the top of the mound issues water (ill. 9.4). The initial from the Amiens Psalter (fol. 26r), shows a high degree of fidelity: an angel flies up with wings spread from the top of a well-head in a mound. Water, the common element in R, C and P, is not found in L, and Ecclesia of the Jeanne de Navarre and Leningrad Psalters has been replaced in the Cambridge and Amiens Psalters by an angel performing an action explained neither by Psalm verse nor by commentary. Pushing C and P further away from R and L, the inscriptions in both the Cambridge and Amiens Psalters are identical to each other but quite different from R: 'An angel exits from a

---

[36] Mokretsova and Romanova, eds., *Les manuscrits enluminés français*, 116 fig.
[37] Hebgin and Corrigan, *St. Augustine on the Psalms*, 238.
[38] PL XXVI (1884), 948. For suggested date and provenance, B. Fischer, *Verzeichnis der Sigel für Kirchenschriftsteller*, Vetus Latina, Die Reste der altlateinischen Bibel 1/1 (Freiburg, 1963), 307.
[39] PL CXCI (1880), 464.
[40] H. Swarzenski, *Die lateinischen illuminierten Handschriften des 13. Jahrhunderts in den Ländern an Rhein, Main und Donau*, Die deutsche Buchmalerei des XIII Jahrhunderts, Denkmaler Deutscher Kunst I, 2 vols. (Berlin, 1936), I, 163, II, pl. 194/1051. The woman in the initial may relate to the source for the legend in the North Italian Psalter (Kupferstichkabinett 78 A 5, fol. 26), whose rubric says, *Mulierem querentes lapidare iudei. Illa dominum ipsum orat* ('The Jews are seeking the woman to stone. She prays to the Lord himself'). It is written next to a scene of an adultress flanked on one side by blessing Christ and on the other side by five Jews raising square-shaped rocks.

9.4   Cambridge, University Library, MS Ee. IV. 24, fol. 10r: Psalm 25

fountain, renewed'. (The inscription in C declares *Li angle ist de fontaine renouelez*; that in P: *Uns angles ist dune fontaine renouueles*.) M. R. James, in his description of the Cambridge manuscript, felt that the scribe had mistakenly written 'angel' (OF *angle*) in place of 'eagle' (OF *aigle*), who, by diving into a certain fountain, renewed its youth.[41] Nevertheless the accounts of angels and eagles and water offer only partly suitable solutions to finding an explanation for the choice of a new subject in the C and P initials.

Concerning the angel and water, John 5.2–3 says,

Now there is at Jerusalem a pond, called Probatica, which in Hebrew is named Bethsaida, having five porches. In these lay a great multitude of sick, of blind, of lame, of withered; waiting for the moving of the water. And an angel of the Lord descended at certain times into the pond; and the water was moved. And he that went down first into the pond after the motion of the water, was made whole, of whatsoever infirmity he lay under.

In this instance, however, the renewal affects the invalid, not the angel. Regarding the eagle and water, a legend, deriving from medieval bestiaries and usually mentioned in connection with Psalm 101, describes the eagle that has become infirm with age, his wings growing heavy and his eyes growing dim. 'It seeks a fountain, then flies above it into the region of the sun where its wings are burned and the mist consumed. Descending, the eagle plunges three times into the fountain and is wholly renewed.'[42] McCulloch, whose key work on bestiaries records the story of the eagle, mentions a manuscript tradition that calls for multiple images representing different stages of the renewal process.[43] How might the conjunction of these two events, the scene of renewal and an angel emerging from fountain be reconciled? Could the scene in the Cambridge and Amiens Psalters result, then, from a rubricator mistakenly writing *angle* for *aigle*, and the painter, using one of the bestiary compositions, substituting an angel for an eagle to accord with the legend? Despite any speculations generated that this thematic switch represents a mere transcriptional error, I do not exclude other logical links, as yet unclear, existing between two different scenes for the same Psalm in the French Psalter manuscripts.

More interesting than the Psalms displaying eccentric subject changes in the course of the thirteenth-century, such as for Psalm 25, are those which reveal how some

---

[41] M. R. James, 'On a MS Psalter in the University Library', *Communiations of the Cambridge Antiquarian Society*, 8 [ns 2 (1891–4)] (1895), 151. I thank Dr Barbara Sargent-Baur, University of Pittsburgh, not only for her aid with translations from French, but also for discussing how scribes might have made changes in the text.

[42] The seminal study of medieval bestiaries is F. McCulloch, *Medieval Latin and French Bestiaries*, University of North Carolina Studies in the Romance Languages and Literatures 33 (Chapel Hill, 1960), esp. 113–14. A translation of Physiologus is given in M. J. Curley, trans, *Physiologus* (Austin and London, 1979), esp. 12–13. The most complete list of sources in antique and medieval writings for this aspect of the eagle's behaviour is in N. Henkel, *Studien zum Physiologus im Mittelalter*, Hermaea, Germanistische Forschungen, Neue Folge, Band 38, ed. H. De Boor and H. Kunisch (Tübingen, 1976), 192–3.

[43] McCulloch, *Bestiaries*, 115. For an example of multiple illustration, Brussels, Bibliothèque Royale, MS 10074, fol. 144v, a Mosan Physiologus from the last years of the tenth century, now preserved as part of a collection of manuscripts, MSS 10066–77, texts of 'natural science' of different dates. C. Gaspar and F. Lyna, *Les principaux manuscrits à peintures de la Bibliothèque Royale de Belgique*, 2 parts (Brussels, 1937; repr. 1984), I, no. 7, esp. p. 24. For separate images of burning and diving, C. Cahier and A. Martin, *Mélanges d'archéologie d'histoire et de littérature*, 2 vols. (Paris, 1847–9), II, pl. XXIII.

factor of 'contamination' contributed to a modification in iconography. Occurrences of iconographic changes which did not depend on visual prototypes represent the second of the two patterns of change mentioned above and confirm the influence of a textual source. In these cases, the transformations in the illustration are not owed to a selection of a different Psalm verse or even a different section of a Psalm commentary as a textual foundation. They are based rather on the source which governed the formation of the original 'programme'. This, I suggest, was a written one. While trying to preserve the same subject, a misreading of one or more words of the legends in our postulated textual exemplar led to incongruities in iconography for at least sixteen Psalms. On occasion, the deviation is no more than the product of a reinterpretation on the part of the painter.

In Psalm 75, the Psalmist sings a hymn of thanksgiving for deliverance already achieved, and he begins *Notus in Iudaea Deus* ('In Judea God is known'), and verse 5 inspires the images of the French Psalter Group: 'Thou enlightenest wonderfully from the everlasting hills'. The initial in the 'Leningrad' Psalter (fol. 78r) depicts God holding a book in one hand and raising his other hand to remove the blindfold from Synagoga, who holds a single Table of the Law.[44] In the corresponding initial in the Jeanne de Navarre Psalter (fol. 83r), God pushes a scarf back from the forehead of Synagoga standing in prayer. The lifting of the veil from Synagoga is described by the legend in the margin which says, *Deus aufertur velum ab oculi sinagoge* ('God pulls the covering from the eyes of Synagoga'). The subject is faithfully transferred to the Bute Psalter (fol. 104v): God raises both hands to remove the blindfold from the eyes of Synagoga who drops a single Table of the Law. The enlightenment of Synagoga does not, so far as I know, occur for this Psalm in manuscripts with minor Psalm illustration outside the French Psalter Group,[45] although examples of the subject can be found elsewhere.[46] Peter Lombard's Commentary on the *titulus* may provide the impetus, however indirect, for the choice of theme; he observes, *Judaeos confutat, et devotos ad reddenda vota monet. Primo frangit gloriam Judaeorum. Secundo, dicit quod Christus illuminat, quod salvat, et judicat, ibi illuminans . . .* ('He [i.e. the Psalmist] refutes the Jews and he warns those already pious that they ought to fulfill their vows. First he breaks the Jews' source of pride. Second he tells how Christ enlightens, how he saves, and judges, therein shedding light . . .').[47]

---

[44] Mokretsova and Romanova, eds., *Les manuscrits enluminés français*, 118 fig.

[45] It is not to be confused with the rejection of Synagoga appearing in the initials for Psalm 73 in the French Psalter Group.

[46] For example, a twelfth-century Sacramentary for St-Martin at Tours (Tours, Bibliothèque Municipale, MS 193, fol. 71) shows an historiated initial for *Vere dignum et iustum est . . .*, the remainder of the Preface prayer before the opening of the Canon: Christ, half-length in a mandorla, is flanked by Ecclesia, holding a chalice and a sphere and Synagoga, whose blindfold is being raised by a Hand above her head: reproduced in B. Blumenkranz, *Juden und Judentum in der mittelalterlichen Kunst. Franz Delitzsch-Vorlesungen 1963*, ed. K. H. Rengstorf (Stuttgart, 1965), fig. 72. See also V. Leroquais, *Les sacramentaires et les missels manuscrits des bibliothèques publiques de France*, 4 vols. (Paris, 1924), I, no. 158, pp. 313–17. In the 'Anagogical' window in the Abbey Church of St Denis, one of the roundels that is not mentioned by Suger in his writings but is dated as original by Grodecki portrays the lifting of the veil of Synagogue: Christ with the seven doves of the Gifts of the Holy Spirit crowns Ecclesia standing on his right and lifts a white veil from the head of Synagoga standing on his left. L. Grodecki, *Les Vitraux*, esp. 100–1, colour pl. XI on 101.

[47] PL CXCI, 704–5.

9.5   *Cambridge, University Library, MS Ee. iv.*   9.6   *Paris, Bibliothèque Nationale, MS lat. 10435,*
         24, fol. 20v: Psalm 75   *fol. 88v: Psalm 75*

The covering to which the legend of the Jeanne de Navarre Psalter refers has been
interpreted as the blindfold of Synagoga. In both the Cambridge and Amiens Psalters,
the legends furnish more or less the same statement as in the Jeanne de Navarre
Psalter: 'God pulls the covering from off the synagogue'. The legend in C says, *Diex
oste la couverture de sus de la synagoge*; that in P: *Dix oste la couuerture de sus le sinagogue*. Yet
both initials betray an artistic malapropism. In the very damaged initial in the
Cambridge Psalter (fol. 20v) a blessing God, half-length in a sphere, lifts a blanket off a
king, his eyes closed (ill. 9.5). Has the covering been re-interpreted as a blanket, and
has Synagoga been reconceived as a crowned figure in bed? Even more extraordinary
is the initial in the Amiens Psalter (fol. 88v): God lifts a domed roof off a stone
structure (ill. 9.6). Here, Synagoga is rendered as the temple, and the covering has
become the building's roof.

Psalm 67, similarly, demonstrates that two painters could visualise a different
meaning for the same word that the rubricators faithfully recorded. The Psalm, which
begins *Exsurgat Deus et dissipentur inimici eius* ('Let God arise and let his enemies be
scattered'), speaks about the establishment of the church of the New Testament,
prefigured by the benefits bestowed on the people of Israel. Verse 8, 'O God, when
thou didst go forth in the sight of thy people, when thou didst pass through the
desert', perhaps suggests the figure of Moses who led them through the desert as
reported in Exodus 13, 14 and 19. Peter Lombard certainly mentions him in
connection with the Ark of the Covenant in his commentary for this Psalm, *Elevata
quippe arca Domini, hostes suos superabant atque in elevatione arcae verbis his similibus Moses
usus fuisse dicitur: Exsurgat, etc . . . Arca vero Christum significat in quo omnes sunt thesauri
sapientie et scientie dei absconditi . . .* ('For when the ark of the Lord was lifted up, they
overcame their enemies and in the raising of the ark, Moses is said to have used these
same words: "Let [God] arise", etc. . . The ark, indeed, signifies Christ in whom all the

9.7   *Manchester, John Rylands University Library, Latin MS 22, fol. 72v: Psalm 67*

9.8   *Cambridge, University Library, MS Ee. IV. 24, fol. 18r: Psalm 67*

9.9   *Paris, Bibliothèque Nationale, MS lat. 10435, fol. 75r: Psalm 67*

treasures of God's wisdom and knowledge are hidden').[48] Part of the Lombard's Psalm Commentary about the ark is quoted in the Oxford Moralized Bible for this Psalm (fol. 19v), and the first medallion, illustrating the Biblical text, depicts two men raising the Ark of the Covenant, in which a crown and lamp(?) hang behind opened

[48] *Ibid.*, 601.

doors; the composition is partly framed by a group of men turning to flee.[49] Like the commentary, it seems to refer to the battle before the walls at Jericho in Joshua 6.6: 'Then Josue the son of Nun called the priests, and said to them: "Take the ark of the covenant: and let seven other priests take the seven trumpets of the jubilee, and march before the ark of the Lord" '. A survey of earlier manuscripts reveals that in no Psalter is this particular event selected to illustrate Psalm 67.[50] Indeed even the painters of the French Psalter Group chose a different moment involving the Ark of the Covenant: that of its construction, recorded in Exodus 37–9. The initial in the Jeanne de Navarre Psalter (fol. 72v), where horned Moses and Aaron hold up the Ark between them, is described by the legend, *Moises et aaron erigunt archam* ('Moses and Aaron build the ark') (ill. 9.7). The subject is roughly preserved in the initials to the Psalm in L (fol. 67v)[51] and in Ph (fol. 89). In the first Psalter, Moses and Aaron flank a table, placing their hands on the top surface; and in the second manuscript, a man in a hooded mantel raises both hands before a table on whose other side stands a youth. The scene is less clearly identifiable in the Bute Psalter (fol. 88v), and the painter has perhaps modified the composition to incorporate a number of events involving the Ark of the Covenant: two kings (David? and Joshua?) struggle to stand up under the weight of the Ark on their shoulders.

Dated towards the end of the thirteenth century, the French legends in the Cambridge and Amiens Psalters read as literal translations of the Latin one in the earlier Jeanne de Navarre Psalter; they both state, 'Moses and Aaron build the ark'. (The inscription in C says, *Moyses et aaron drescent larche*; and in P it says, *Moises et aaron drechent larche*.) Yet the initials disclose how the artists interpreted that one element somewhat differently. The word *arca* has conveyed to the painters of these two manuscripts the ark of Noah rather than the Ark of the Covenant. The initial of the Cambridge Psalter (fol. 18r) portrays Moses and Aaron directing the activities of two workers with axe and auger in the body of the ship (ill. 9.8). In the Amiens Psalter (fol. 75r), Moses and Aaron undeniably hold up a boat between them (ill. 9.9).

These two examples of the enlightenment of Synagoga and the construction of the ark by Moses and Aaron argue that transmitted text unaccompanied by picture can result in misunderstandings by the painter. The next group of initials show how textual models assume such importance that textual errors demanded artistic invention in order to retain some degree of affinity between the legend and the initial.

The words of Psalm 13, beginning *Dixit insipiens in corde suo non est Deus* ('The fool

---

[49] Laborde, *La bible moralisée* II, pl. 243.

[50] The initial of the mid-thirteenth century Wilton Psalter depicts two tonsured priests carrying an ark-type reliquary shrine on a pallet while two men below recline (London, Royal College of Physicians, MS 409, fol. 81v); on this manuscript, N. Morgan, *Early Gothic Manuscripts [2]: 1250–1285* (London, 1988), no. 99, pp. 55–7, ills. 18–19. The fourth copy of the Utrecht Psalter shows Aaron and Hur supporting the arms of Moses during battle (Paris, BN, lat. 8846, fol. 114), referring to the battle with Amalec in Exodus 17.11–12, 'And when Moses lifted up his hands, Israel overcame: but if he let them down a little, Amalec overcame. And Moses' hands were heavy: so they took a stone, and put under him, and he sat on it: and Aaron and Hur stayed up his hands on both sides'. On this manuscript, Morgan, *Early Gothic Manuscripts [1]*, no. 1, pp. 47–9, ills. 1–7.

[51] Mokretsova and Romanova, eds., *Les manuscrits enluminés français*, 118 fig.

9.10 Manchester, John Rylands University Library, Latin MS 22, fol. 23v: Psalm 13

9.11 Paris, Bibliothèque Nationale, MS lat. 10435, fol. 11v: Psalm 13

9.12 Cambridge, University Library, MS Ee. IV. 24, fol. 7v: Psalm 13

hath said in his heart: "There is no God" '), expresses the corruption of man before his salvation by Christ, and the Psalm commentary of Pseudo-Jerome likens the *insipiens* ('fool') of the first verse to the Jewish people.[52] In the initial from the Jeanne de Navarre Psalter (fol. 23v) a seated man in a pointed hat puts his hand to his cheek in a gesture of despair (ill. 9.10), and a similar scene appears in the 'Leningrad' Psalter (fol. 16r).[53] The legend in R properly describes the attitude of the figure in the initials:

52 PL XXVI (1884), 900. Peter Lombard echoes this thought: see note 54 below.
53 Mokretsova and Romanova, eds., *Les manuscrits enluminés français*, 115 fig.

Quidam iudeus respiciens terram flet ('A certain Jew, looking at the ground, weeps'). The lamenting Jew is not so designated either in the words of the Psalm or in the Psalm commentaries, however, and no Psalm illustration from the earlier manuscripts that we have been using as comparative material relates to the subject in the historiated initials of the French Psalter Group. Yet, commenting on the first verse, Peter Lombard writes, . . . *Propheta in suam vel Christi persona loquens, increpat hic insipientiam et duritiam Judaeorum, qui Christo praesenti quem optaverunt, non credunt . . . Intentio. Prophetae est confutare Judaeos, Christi contemptores* ('. . . The Prophet, speaking on his own or in the person of Christ, reproaches here the folly and insensibility of the Jews who, with Christ in their very presence, had desired him, but did not believe him . . . The intention of the prophet is to refute the Jews, the despisers of Christ').[54]

In the initial from the Amiens Psalter (fol. 11v), a man in a pointed hat bends to look at grey rocks topped by brown pointed projections (ill. 9.11). This last peculiar iconographic detail may be identified, if we compare the Latin legend in the Jeanne de Navarre manuscript with the one in Old French in the Amiens Psalter. The legend in P is not so very different from R, *Uns iuis regarde le tere qui pleure* ('A Jew looks at the ground which weeps'), but the addition of a relative pronoun has changed the scene in a curious fashion to make the ground cry, not the Jew. The same inscription is written in the Cambridge manuscript, *Uns iuis regarde la terre qi pleure*, although the pictorial treatment (fol. 7v) does not relate as well: a man in a pointed hat looks at a tree growing from a mound that does not seem to be weeping (ill. 9.12). Finally, the error is also found in the Bute Psalter (fol. 14r): a man in a pointed hat points to the weeping ground.

The initials for Psalm 98 superficially demonstrate a similar form of misunderstanding, but the analysis is more problematic because the iconographic differences based on textual changes in R, C and P may have resulted from inadvertent errors or possibly intentional ones. The Psalm, beginning *Dominus regnavit irascantur populi* ('The Lord hath reigned, let the people be angry'), praises the power and justice of the Lord and speaks about the Old Testament priests – Moses and Aaron – and Samuel, who kept his commandments. Verse 6 of Psalm 98, 'Moses and Aaron among his priests: and Samuel among them that call upon his name. They called upon the Lord, and he heard them', suggests the inspiration for the subjects in the initials of the French Psalter Group. In the Jeanne de Navarre Psalter (fol. 108r), Moses gestures to the bust of God at the top of a tree (ill. 9.13), and the legend in the manuscript says, *Dominus in rubo apparet moisi* ('The Lord in the bush appears to Moses'), referring to the event in Exodus 3.2–4 when Moses spoke to the Lord in the burning bush. Verse 7 of the Psalm states, however, 'he spoke to them in the pillar of the cloud', another occasion reported in Exodus 34.4–5. The column of the cloud is accordingly included in the

---

[54] PL CXCI, 161, 162. Cf the Oxford Moralized Bible, Paris, BN, lat. MS 11560, fol. 5v, *In psalmo isto d(aui)d in p(er)sona sua v(el) in p(er)sona ih(es)u (christ)i loq(ue)ns incriperat insipientiam 7 duritiam iudeor(um) qui negabant cotidie (christe)m 7 desiderabant eum 7 n(on) credebant et ip(s)e minat(ur) eis s(ed) concedit reliquias iudeorum salvas fore in fine . . .* ('In this Psalm David, speaking in his own person or the person of Jesus Christ, here reprimanded the foolisness and harshness of the Jews who daily denied Christ, and expected him, and did not believe; and he himself threatens them, but concedes the rest of the Jews to be about to be saved at the end . . .').

North Italian Psalter (Kupferstichkabinett, 78 A 5, fol. 85r) and the Bury Psalter (Biblioteca Apostolica Vaticana, Reg. lat. 12, fol. 103r).[55] That detail is also depicted in another member of the French Psalter Group, the Bute Psalter (fol. 139v), although Moses has been inexplicably replaced by King David who addresses Christ, the two figures separated by a vertical undulating cloud column. The episode is transmitted to the Cambridge and Amiens Psalters, and both C and P mention the cloud in their legends. Nevertheless, comparing the inscriptions of R, C and P displays a breakdown in the transmission of text.

R: *Dominus in rubo apparet moisi*	C: *Dex parole a moysen en la columbe de la riue* (sic).	P: *Dix parole ad moisem en la columbe.*
The Lord in the bush appears to Moses	God speaks to Moses in the column of the cloud.	God speaks to Moses in the column.

Might one invent several scenarios to account for the variant phrasing in the legends? The Jeanne de Navarre Psalter does not include the cloud of verse 7, but speaks rather of the burning bush. Is it attributable to scribal error? Did the scribe of the Jeanne de Navarre Psalter, ignoring the Psalm text and following a written list of legends as a model in the preparation of his own legends, simply add the phrase 'in the bush' to a textual model which stated only 'The Lord appears to Moses'? Or did the rubricator read the Latin word *rubo* (bush) instead of *nube* (cloud)?[56] Can the wording in R be construed as an 'error' in a comparison with the initial in the 'Leningrad' Psalter (fol. 102r) where horned Moses gestures to the head of God at the top of a cloud column (as stated in verse 7)?[57] Is it further possible that the scribe of the Cambridge Psalter, also working from a textual model which stated, 'God speaks to Moses in the cloud', added the words 'column of the'? Did the scribe in the later Amiens Psalter read the model used directly by the creator of the Cambridge manuscript and drop the phrase 'of the cloud', leaving its legend to say, 'God speaks to Moses in the column'? Again the initial in C does not correspond very well to its own legend: horned Moses, seated with the Tables of the Law, raises his right hand to blessing God above, half-length in a sphere. On the other hand, the curious legend in the Amiens Psalter (fol. 117v) more than adequately conforms to iconographic particulars in the initial, where

---

[55] The scene is part of Suger's glass programme at St Denis. 'In the same window, where the Lord appeared to Moses in the burning bush:
"Just as this bush is seen to burn yet is not burned,
So he who is full of this fire Divine burns with it yet is not burned".'
Panofsky, *Abbot Suger*, 74–5

[56] Peter Lombard, whose Commentary on the Psalms seems to be a source for many of the subjects in the initials of the French Psalter Group, also writes about the cloud to the exclusion of the bush: *Et nota quod non ait in nube sed in columna nubis. Columna enim fortitudo est, et decor domus. In hac specie, loquebatur eis, quae annuntiabat Ecclesiam, vel carnem christi; s(ed) tunc in nube loquebatur, qui modo per Filium aperte loquitur* ('And note that it does not say in the cloud but in the column of the cloud; for the column is strength and an ornament of the house. In this shape he spoke to them, when he declared the Church or flesh of Christ, but then he spoke in the cloud which now speaks openly through the Son'). PL *CXCI*, 896A–B.

[57] Mokretsova and Romanova, eds., *Les manuscrits enluminés français*, colour pl. on p. 139.

9.13   Manchester, John Rylands University Library,
        Latin MS 22, fol. 108r: Psalm 98

9.14   Paris, Bibliothèque National, MS lat. 10435
        fol. 117v: Psalm 98

9.15   Manchester, John Rylands University Library,
        Latin MS 22, fol. 34v: Psalm 24

9.16   Cambridge, University Library, MS Ee. IV.
        24, fol. 10r: Psalm 24

the head of God appears at the top of a column without any trace of cloud whatsoever
(ill. 9.14). Further research may elucidate workshop methods contributing to ways in
which 'errors' occur at the moment of copying text. Linguistic analysis may, in fact,
verify whether the legends in R served as the Latin exemplar from which the French
legends were composed, or whether C itself provided an exemplar of the legends
written in P.

9.17 Paris, Bibliothèque Nationale, MS lat.   9.18 Malibu, J. Paul Getty Museum, 92. MK. 92
         10435, fol. 24v: Psalm 24   (MS 46), fol. 30r: Psalm 24

So far, I have posited textual errors of this kind inspiring sometimes ludicrous images in the Jeanne de Navarre, the Cambridge and the Amiens Psalters, all of which contain legends for the initials. They are not alone. On a single occasion for Psalm 24 the painter of the Bute Psalter, which contains no inscriptions, has apparently been misled by text.[58]

Psalm 24, *Ad te domine levavi animam meam* ('To thee, O Lord, have I lifted up my soul'), describes the need for protection from enemies, and artists of fully-illustrated Psalters have selected several verses for illustration.[59] The exegetical tradition is partly summed up in the Oxford Moralized Bible (fol. 8r) which says, *Ecclesia loquitur in psalmo isto qui graviter penitens de verbere permisso in exemplum aliorum ne murmurent in adversis et expertum est quod in psalmo isto est misericordia et iusticia dei quia mulcet per misericordiam et terret per contriciam* ('Ecclesia speaks in this Psalm as a serious penitent about enduring beatings as an example to others not to grumble in adversities; and

[58] I thank Dr M. Alison Stones for bringing the Bute Psalter to my attention and for lending me her colour slides of this manuscript.

[59] Verse 10 says, 'All the ways of the Lord are mercy and truth, to them that seek after his covenant and his testimonies.' At this point in the text a ninth-century and two eleventh-century Byzantine Psalters include a marginal image of a martyr. Chludov Psalter (Moscow, Gosudarstvennij Istoriceskij Muzej, grec. 129D, fol. 22v), Theodore Psalter (London, British Library, Add. MS. 19352, fol. 26v), and Barberini Psalter (Vatican City, Biblioteca Apostolica Vaticana, Barb. graec. 372, fol. unpublished). See comparative table in Dufrenne, *Tableaux synoptiques*, unpaginated. The first copy of the Utrecht Psalter (Harley 603, fol. 14) shows a group of armed enemies for verses 8–9, 'The Lord is sweet and righteous: therefore he will give a law to sinners in the way. He will guide the mild in judgment: he will teach the meek his ways'. The third copy of the Utrecht Psalter (BN, lat. 8846, fol. 41v) shows the enemies of David loosing arrows at him. For verse 15 which says, 'My eyes are ever towards the Lord: for he shall pluck my feet out of the snare', the legend in the North Italian Psalter (Kupferstichkabinett, 78 A 5, fol. 25v) says *Petrus vinculis catenarum ligatus orat ut liberentur et angelus confestim venit* ('Peter, bound in chain fetters, prays that they would be freed, and the angel comes immediately'), illustrated by an angel, who pokes a long red pole at the feet of a reclining man while a nimbed man reclines in a building.

what is found in this Psalm is God's mercy and justice because he soothes through mercy and frightens through humility'). In the medallion which accompanies this text, Christ raises a branch to strike a man, bowing in prayer, while a tonsured priest speaks to a group of standing men gesturing in despair.[60] The historiated initial to this Psalm in the Jeanne de Navarre Psalter manifests the same theme, although not the same composition. The legend says, *Quidam respiciens in celum verberatur* ('One looking into the sky is beaten'), and the initial (fol. 34v) shows a stereotypical thirteenth-century scene of martyrdom; a man raises a club to strike another man kneeling in prayer; true to the description, the praying man looks up (ill. 9.15). The artists of the later Cambridge and Amiens Psalters have made only a small, and on this occasion very straightforward, modification to the iconography. The initial in C (fol. 10r) shows a man beaten by *two* men; and the initial in P (fol. 24v), repeats approximately the same composition (ills. 9.16 and 9.17). They do not duplicate the phrasing in the Jeanne de Navarre legend, however, but have separated into two clauses the information given in the legend of R. In C the legend says, *Deus homes batent le tierche et il regarde vers le cel*; and in P the legend says, *Doi houme batent le tierch et il regarde le chiel*. 'One looking into the sky is beaten' becomes 'Two men strike the third, and he looks towards the sky'. This separation may have occurred during the translation of the legends from Latin to French; the two-phrase statement, then, seems to explain the variant iconography that appears in the initial to this Psalm in the Bute Psalter (fol. 30r), where an error has changed the meaning of the first clause. A misreading of the word 'third' (OF *tierch*) has led to an understanding of the word 'earth' (OF *terre*), and we see the mistake rendered as a tonsured cleric and a man flexing their knees to beat the earth with hammers while one of them looks towards the sky (ill. 9.18).

Two other sets of initials from the lengthy Psalm 118 signal the importance of the wording of the inscriptions as a source or inspiration for the image. The Psalm is divided into twenty-two sections, each one beginning with a letter of the Hebrew alphabet and, in the French Psalter Group, each one historiated. The eighth section begins with the letter Heth, *Portio mea Dominus dixi custodire legem tuam* ('O Lord, my portion, I have said, I would keep thy law'), and it is likely that verse 61 provides the basis for the illustration: 'The cords of the wicked have encompassed me: but I have not forgotten thy law'. In the initial from the Jeanne de Navarre Psalter (fol. 132r), whose legend states, *Quidam post tergum ligatis manibus studet* ('One studies with his hands tied behind his back'), a tonsured man with bound hands held at his side is seated before a desk with an open book[61] (ill. 9.19). In a similar composition in the Cambridge Psalter (fol. 30v) a tonsured man with hands behind his back, presumably also bound, is seated at a lectern with an open book; the inscription paraphrases the legend in the Jeanne de Navarre Psalter: *Uns sestudie* (sic) *ses mains lies deriere le dos*

---

[60] Laborde, *La bible moralisée* II, pl. 232.

[61] While there are no exact parallels among the compositions for the Psalm in books created before the French Psalter Group, two manuscripts illustrate the same verse. The Stuttgart Psalter (fol. 136) shows David, wrists and legs bound together, led away by a soldier; and the Albani Psalter (p. 318) shows two furry demons holding a red rope; one grasping the wrist of the nimbed Psalmist who points with one hand to the verse in the textblock and with the other to Christ, half-length above in a sphere.

('One endeavours, his hands bound behind his back') (ill. 9.20). Surely the legend and concomitant picture in C is owed to scribal error so that the letter **s** precedes the word *estudie* ('studies'). Perhaps he meant to write *homs*, or perhaps he inadvertently repeated the letter from the end of *uns*.[62] In what way has this error contributed to the very different picture appearing in the Amiens Psalter? The enigmatic initial (fol. 147r) depicts a man standing, his hands behind his back (bound, we wonder?) with a sword through his abdomen (ill. 9.21). A comparison of the title in P demonstrates an equally radical change in phrasing: *Uns hons se tue dun coutel les mains loies deriere le dos* ('A man kills himself with a knife, his hands bound behind his back'). Has the rubricator mentally separated the syllables of *sestudie* and created three words, *se tue de*, which then compelled the painter to devise the abdominal wound shown in the initial?

One last comparison serves to reinforce forcefully the links between image and inscriptional text in the French Psalter Group. The last section of Psalm 118, headed by the letter Thav, begins, *Adpropinquet deprecatio mea in conspectu tuo domine* ('Let my supplication, O Lord, come near in thy sight'). The Jeanne de Navarre Psalter depicts the recovery of the lost sheep in its initial (fol. 136v, ill. 9.22) in accordance with verse 176, 'I have gone astray like a sheep that is lost: seek thy servant, because I have not forgotten thy commandments'; the legend in the manuscript says simply, *Quidam fert ovem* ('A person carries a sheep').[63] The iconography is largely repeated in the initials to the same Psalm in L (fol. 132v),[64] and in Ph (fol. 154v), where a man carries a sheep on his shoulders. The iconographic pattern established is sustained in the initial in the Cambridge Psalter (fol. 31v), described correctly by the legend which says, *Uns home porte une oeille sus ses espaules* ('A man carries a sheep on his shoulders') (ill. 9.23). The title in P is not so different: *Uns hons porte une orille sur ses espaules*, but reveals how the rubricator of the Amiens Psalter has made another orthographic change. He has misread the letter **e** in the word *oeille* and copied instead an **r**, changing radically the meaning of the word. A sheep (OF *oeille*) has been transformed into an ear (OF *orille*), and as I have already demonstrated, the painter of P has been compelled to invent a new composition that harmonises with the legend (fol. 154r): a man carries an ear on his shoulder (ill. 9.24).

In a preliminary effort to address the complex iconographic relationships among seven densely-illustrated Psalters and a copy of Peter Lombard's Commentary on the Psalms, I have juxtaposed pictorial compositions and attendant text. The French Psalter Group seems to have benefitted in part from one iconographic 'programme' that circulated among the various workshops responsible for them since a relatively high percentage of related themes appears for the same Psalm in two or more of the manuscripts. On the one hand, certain iconography transferred from manuscript to manuscript with some fidelity; on the other hand, treatment of the same subject can vary substantially within the family, denying that the earliest manuscripts in the

[62] I thank Dr Sargent-Baur for suggesting various possibilities to me.

[63] Only the Albani Psalter (p. 331) includes sheep in the illustration for the Psalm but not in a fashion that corresponds to our group; King David stands at left and looks at the bust of Christ above, points with his right hand to verse 176 and points with his left hand to a lion crouching below eating sheep.

[64] Mokretsova and Romanova, eds., *Les manuscrits enluminés français*, 122 fig.

9.19   Manchester, John Rylands University Library, Latin MS 22, fol. 132r: Psalm 118 Heth.

9.20   Cambridge, University Library, MS Ee. IV. 24, fol. 30v: Psalm 118 Heth.

9.21   Paris, Bibliothèque Nationale, MS lat. 10435, fol. 147r: Psalm 118 Heth.

9.22   Manchester, John Rylands University Library, Latin MS 22, fol. 136v: Psalm 118 Thav.

group acted as the visual model for any of the later manuscripts. Selected comparisons have illustrated examples of discrepancies between the legend and the accompanying iconography of the historiated initial, and examples of one manuscript visualising another manuscript's legend better than its own. Yet more significantly, the analysis of the iconography in the initial in conjunction with the legend that accompanies it has demonstrated the unquestionable inter-relationship of picture and legend. Peculiar, even bizarre, images resulted from inscriptions which do not always link with ideas communicated by the Psalm text or by Psalm exegesis. On the basis of this evidence, I would suggest that the illuminator(s) exercised some care in their selection of images and argue for a separate written list of subjects

9.23   Cambridge, University Library, MS Ee. IV. 24, fol. 31v: Psalm 118 Thav.

9.24   Paris, Bibliothèque Nationale, MS lat. 10435, fol. 154r: Psalm 118 Thav.

serving as the immediate vehicle to disseminate iconography within the French Psalter Group.

The restricted temporal and geographic boundaries of a group of books with textual contents programmed by liturgical concerns and with analogous narrative sequences suggests broader implications and invites a consideration of the wider context of illustration.

The thirteenth-century French Psalter Group finds echoes of its own iconographic schemes elsewhere, and it may offer a suitable *accessus* to discovering the means of and motive for transmission. For example, nearly the whole of the 'programme' has been preserved in a small format fifteenth-century French Psalter (British Library, Additional MS 16999).[65] While similar narrative patterns can be detected between the French Psalter Group and this manuscript, the latter's three-line historiated initials, also described by legends in Old French, reduce the populous compositions in the thirteenth-century books to abridged sequences. The descriptive titles, however, most often repeat in full or paraphrase the wording found in the Cambridge and Amiens Psalters.[66] A second set of unusual iconography, drawn from the major initials in the Cambridge Psalter, appears in a late thirteenth-century French Psalter (New York, Pierpont Morgan Library, M 730) and in two fourteenth-century English Psalters (Oxford, Exeter College, MS 46 and Vienna, Österreichische Nationalbibliothek, s.n.

[65] I have found no recent mention of this manuscript; G. F. Warner, *Illuminated Manuscripts in the British Museum. Miniatures, Borders, and Initials Reproduced in Gold and Colours. Series I–IV: Sixty Plates* (London, 1899–1903), series II, pl. 26. I reserve a discussion of the relationship of the illustration in this manuscript to the books of the French Psalter Group for more detailed treatment elsewhere.

[66] It is interesting to note that of the eight books in the French Psalter Group, H, R and C made their way to England; Ph arrived in the US via an English owner. The routes of travel cannot be tracked, excepting possibly for R. The signature of *Royne Jahanne* on fol. 2v, identified by Léopold Delisle as Jeanne de Navarre, the wife of Henry IV, King of England, provides a fifteenth-century date for the rebinding of the Psalter in brown leather with English-style stamped ornament. L. V. Delisle, 'Notice sur un Psautier de XIIIe siècle appartenant au Comte de Crawford', *Bibliothèque de l'École des Chartes* 58 (1897), 381–93.

2611).[67] Further research may explore the link between the historiated initial and its immediate textual context or define the visual or textual inspiration for the motifs in these books. Linguistic analysis of the legends by specialists may provide better descriptions about workshop practices that use oral or written exemplars in the copying of texts.[68]

Yet, the wider view of Psalters with a wealth of illustration mandates a fresh assessment of their significance. The selection of subject for the 'minor Psalms' from a literary and visual inheritance forms part of a context of which the patron is one component, and analysis of illustration of Psalm text disconnected from specific liturgical needs may reveal the intellectual concerns of the artistic director or reader. Changes in medieval attitudes towards the relationship of image to text might be carefully chronicled, and further research may discover whether iconographic or compositional alterations form part of a visual shorthand intended to recall several incidents of a single story. The long life of the 'cycle' in the French Psalter Group and the episodic appearance of fully-illustrated Psalters may inform us about medieval perceptions concerning not only the Psalms but the role of Psalm illustration as mnemonic devices in private devotions. Future discussions would also be shaped by a closer evaluation of the recurring legends, both their physical connection to the image on the page and their function in the course of ritual devotions.[69] Indeed, the concurrent move from Latin to vernacular texts, paralleling the change from a more oral to a more literate society, and the resultant effect on the *mise-en-page* arrangement of image and text provokes careful consideration of the interest in and use of prayer manuscripts. The manuscripts of the French Psalter Group represent an advanced stage of development in an evolution of private devotional books that led to the Book of Hours. The continued production of Psalters in a period in which Books of Hours enjoyed considerable popularity adumbrates a fluid conception of the book's role in a private world of daily devotion and, simultaneously, in the public world as a luxury object.

[67] On PML, M 730, W. Voelkle, ed., *Medieval and Renaissance Manuscripts: Major Acquisitions of the Pierpont Morgan Library, 1924–1974* (New York, 1974), no. 19 and pl. On Exeter 46, L. F. Sandler, *Gothic Manuscripts: 1285–1385*, A Survey of Manuscripts Illuminated in the British Isles 5, 2 vols. (London and Oxford, 1986), I, no. 102, pp. 112–13, ills. 259–61. On ÖNB, s.n. 2611, M. Krieger, *Gotische Bilderbibel. Faksimile der Handschrift cod. ser. n. 2611, fol. 1–22, der Österreichischen Nationalbibliothek, Wien*, 2 vols. (Stuttgart, 1988).

[68] I thank Dr Barbara Sargent-Baur and Dr Jeanne Krochalis for discussing the possible scenarios in which visual 'errors' corresponding to 'errors' in transcription were the result of one reading aloud the list of legends to the scribe. Whether or not these peculiar scenes represent intentional visual puns inserted at the request of the reader remains a problematic issue.

[69] Michael Camille has detected different modes of illustration consistently governed by the language of the text in 'Visualising in the Vernacular: A New Cycle of Early Fourteenth-Century Bible Illustrations', *Burlington Magazine* 130, no. 1019 (February, 1988), 97–106. See also the cogent arguments of Paul Saenger about the impact of the changes in reading practices; 'Silent Reading: Its Impact on Late Medieval Script and Society', *Viator* 13 (1982), 367–414. I thank Dr M. Alison Stones for bringing these references to my attention and for discussing some of their implications with me.

10

The Bible as subject and object of illustration: the making of a medieval manuscript, Hamburg 1255

ERIK PETERSEN

Copenhagen, Kongelige Bibliotek, MS G. K. S. [= Old Royal Collection] 4 2°, is a monumental work in three volumes, a Vulgate, well documented with respect to its origin and history.[1] An inscription in each of the volumes, addressed to the blessed Virgin and written as fourteen Latin hexameters, tells that the scribe was *Karolus*, and that the work was made on the initiative of the dean *Bertoldus*; and it also gives us the date of the work: 1255.[2]

In the year 1284 Hamburg was almost entirely consumed by fire, a catastrophe that is recorded in a notice at the end of the second volume: 'Anno domini millesimo ducentesimo octogesimo quarto in die sancti ciriaci que est ante uigiliam Sancti Laurencii proxima . exusta est tota ciuitas hamburgensis . eciam homines innumerabiles viri mulieres et pueri . ita quod infra muros una domus non remansit'. Our Bible, however, was saved from the fire, and remained in Hamburg for exactly 500 years more, until it was sold at the auction of the Chapter Library, and acquired by the Royal Library in Copenhagen together with some twenty-five other manuscripts.[3] Copenhagen itself had suffered a severe fire in 1728, totally devastating the University Library, which at that time housed the most important collection of medieval manuscripts, not least manuscripts of Danish provenance. But the grave losses of Danish manuscripts in the eighteenth century were remedied by astute private and public collecting of manuscripts, bought where they could be obtained on the European market.

The Hamburg Bible (as it is sometimes called) has received attention from scholars almost exclusively because of a series of illuminations contained in it showing the production of a medieval book. They have been used primarily for illustrative

---

[1] Cf. E. Jørgensen, *Catalogus codicum Latinorum medii ævi Bibliothecæ Regiæ Hafniensis* (Copenhagen, 1926), 1f.; for a survey of the literature on the manuscript, cf. E. Petersen, 'Bertoldus' Bibel. Bøger, billeder og bogstaver i et håndskrift fra 1255', *Fund og Forskning* 32 (1993).

[2] The dedication is found on fol. 1r in II, on fol. 230v in II and on fol. 218v in III. The text is printed on p. 219 below.

[3] *Bibliotheca capitularis sive apparatus librorum ex omni parte eruditionis in reverendo capitulo Hamburgensi huc usque asservatorum: jam vero inde a Die XVIII. Octob. A. O. R. MDCCLXXXIV. in Templi Cathedralis loco vulgo* Reventher *dicto publica auctione distrahendorum* (Hamburg, 1784), p. 2, no. 18–20.

purposes, with no attention paid to their context. In the following essay, by contrast, I would like to examine them as parts of a whole, and to offer an explanation for their occurrence in our Bible. The Hamburg Bible is, in my opinion, a well composed, coherent entity. In my attempt to prove this, I shall proceed as follows. First I shall give a summary description of the three individual parts of the manuscript. Next I shall discuss certain aspects of the 'freedom' that could be involved in the production of a medieval book of this period. Then I shall examine some of the pictures in the Hamburg Bible and consider their arrangement. After that I will offer a few words on the dean Bertoldus, the scribe Karolus and the anonymous painter. And finally I shall attempt to outline what may be considered as the main steps and intentions in the genesis and process of production of the Hamburg Bible.

1. Description

The first volume of G.K.S. 4 2°, consists of 241 folios, measuring 51.1×35.8 cm, with 41 lines per column. As in all three volumes, the text is written in two columns (a: 10.7; b: 10.5 cm). It contains approximately 4,170 metres of written text, which is close to 36 per cent of the total written text in the three volumes.

Volume II has fewer folios – 230 – but in terms of its dimensions is the largest of the three. It measures 55.2×39.1 cm, with 43 lines in two slightly broader columns (a: 11.1; b: 11.3 cm), thus containing approximately 4,430 metres of writing, or close to 38 per cent of the entire text.

Volume III is the smallest. According to its present foliation it consists of 218 folios, but one leaf was omitted in this foliation, and one leaf – that with the opening of the Gospel of St Luke – was cut out at an unknown date, probably after 1784. Thus the original number of folios was 220. It measures 44.5×31.7 cm, and the columns of writing (a: 8.8; b: 8.8 cm) are more than 2 cm narrower than those in volume II. It contains approximately 26 per cent of the entire text, equalling a distance of 2,940 metres.

The bindings seem to be contemporary with the contents. The three volumes differ in weight and dimensions, so they do not conform to the ideal of uniformity in a modern edition of, for example, a Vulgate in more than one volume – a fact which will have made them more easily identifiable on the shelf or table. Everybody who came into contact with the books in the chapter at Hamburg will rapidly have learned that the Gospels were to be found in the smallest volume and the prophets in the biggest – and he will have appreciated this knowledge, since there is a difference in weight of more than five kilos between the two! The three volumes have a total weight of close to 40 kilos, and their collective written text amounts to a line of more than eleven and a half kilometres in length.

The Bible is made in three parts, thus forming a physical tri-unity of the holy scripture, and naturally leading from the Law in volume I, via the Prophets in volume II, to the Gospels in volume III.

2. 'Licentia pictoria'

In various respects the production of books offered little freedom for those who made them. The texts and basic structure of a book, in this instance the Latin Bible, naturally imposed restrictions, as did various elements in what might broadly be termed tradition and convention. Yet the talented painter also had a certain amount of freedom to make choices concerning the form and motif of his illuminations. The degree of his talent and education had a direct bearing on this. The better he was able to perform his craft, the greater his freedom, because his ability made it possible for him to realise things and ideas that a lesser artist could not do. But the object itself, the Latin Bible, also offered room for manoeuvre. There was, to some degree, a choice to be made concerning the letters selected for illumination. Clearly tradition dictated that the *initial letters* of each individual section of the Bible should be painted. 'Each individual section', however, is an ambiguous term in the context of the medieval Vulgate, a complex and heterogenous book – or rather set of texts. The individual biblical books have different forms and contents which have different implications for the decoration; and apart from the biblical texts proper, manuscripts of the Vulgate often contain several other texts which added to the number of initials and offered additional possibilities for decoration – texts such as *argumenta*, prologues and other prefatory matter of Jerome and others. Even the number of biblical books contained in different manuscripts of the Vulgate may vary. Thus the Book of Psalms is not copied in G. K. S. 4 2°, probably because the text was already present in the cathedral in another manuscript. Moreover certain sections that are often separate could be amalgamated. Thus in the second volume of our Bible, the *liber secundus Ezrae* (also called Nehemias) is divided from the *liber primus* only by an insignificant rubric ('liber neemie' on fol. 6r), so that these two individual sections have coalesced to become what is called the 'liber hesdre primus'. It is followed (on fol. 13v) by what is called the 'liber hesdre secundus' – which is, in fact, the apocryphal *liber tertius Ezrae*. The *liber quartus Ezrae* is also present in our Bible, although in a slightly complicated manner: it has been placed at the end of the volume, and divided into three individual books, 'liber primus prophete hesdre' on fol. 218v (beginning with the words: 'Liber hesdre prophete secundus. filij sarei. filij azarie . . .'), 'liber secundus' on fol. 219v and 'liber tertius' on fol. 228v, ending with the words '. . . et mittitur ad devoracionem ignis' (= IV Ezrae 16.78) on fol. 230v.

    We shall return to the books of Ezra later. In the context of the issue of 'individual sections' it suffices to point out that the canonical and apocryphal books of Ezra as they are represented in our Bible offered five or six opportunities – depending on how we assess the division represented by the rubric *liber nehemie* on fol. 6r – for the painter to illuminate an initial. Yet he only painted three, *viz*. at the beginning of each of the first two books as they appear in our manuscript (that is at the beginning of the canonical I and II Ezra and at the beginning of the apocryphal III Ezra), and at the beginning of what is conceived as *liber secundus* of the apocryphal IV Ezra. The Books of Ezra may be atypical, since all biblical books proper are as a rule headed by painted initials. Nevertheless it is clear that the painter had a degree of freedom to choose the letters to be illuminated also in relation to the non-canonical texts of the Latin Bible.

The decision about how much a given initial letter was going to be decorated provided a further element of freedom. Broadly speaking the initials in our manuscript belong to one of three degrees of elaboration. The most elementary merely received a simple colouring in red or blue or both. They were probably drawn as part of the writing process, and reflect ornamental rather than artistic intentions. I have not taken these into account in this paper. The remaining two categories, the illuminated letters proper, are ornamental and historiated initials. Altogether in the three volumes there are 89 illuminations, 81 of which are historiated, whereas only 8 are merely ornamental. The distribution of these illuminations in the three volumes is as follows:

I – 18 illuminated letters = 15 historiated + 3 ornamental
II – 38 illuminated letters = 36 historiated + 2 ornamental
III – 33 illuminated letters = 30 historiated + 3 ornamental

It is tempting to interpret the total numbers of illuminations as a result of a deliberate planning; the number 3 – the figure of the Holy Trinity – can be discerned in them in several ways, e.g. when the total number is interpreted as $(3 \times 3) \times (3 \times 3)$ plus $2 \times 2 \times 2$. Lacking evidence from more explicit sources, I shall not offer further interpretations of them here. I will, however, point out that 89 far exceeds the number of books in the Vulgate, but that it is less than the total number of individual sections (that is biblical books plus prologues and prefaces, *argumenta*, etc.). In other words, the freedom to chose among illuminable initial letters was actually used.

Altogether seventeen different letters of the alphabet have been illuminated in our Bible. The number of occurrences of the individual letters are as follows:

P	18	F	4	D	2
U	13	H	4	L	2
I	9+3	S	3+1	Q	2
E	5+2	C	3	B	1
A	5	N	3	M	1
O	5	T	1+2		

P is by far the most frequently illuminated letter, a fact that is explained by St Paul's habit of introducing his letters by his own name: 13 occurrences of **P** are found consecutively in vol. III at the beginning of Paul's 13 letters (Romans to Philemon). In a similar way the high number of **U**s is due to the Prophets (major and minor) and their opening *Uisiones* (*Isaiae*, etc.) or *Uerbum domini*. No similar explanation seems possible for the frequency of the letter **I**. The illuminator (or his patron) seems to have chosen the letter **I** for illumination more often than other initial letters, and there are several possible explanations for his choice. The letter **I** has what may perhaps, using medieval terminology, be called an innate *anagogical* character. It leads from the Creature to the Creator, and raises the mind from the lower to the higher. It also has a unique significance in being the first letter of the name of the Lord, **I**esus; and, furthermore, it is the first letter of the Latin Bible.

We shall return to the question of the scope for individual expression involved in the designing of a medieval Bible. As we have seen, we find a measure of freedom in the process of selecting letters for illumination, and in deciding the degree to which an initial letter should be illuminated. Yet the selection of motifs for the individual letters might be even more appealing to the talented painter, since this could involve greater room for choice.

A prerequisite of a talented selection of motifs for the initials was familiarity with various models and a good knowledge of the Bible. Beyond this, the talented painter might give his personal touch to the picture – for example by not only depicting St Paul, but showing him actually in the act of writing his letter (he is, in fact, depicted as if he were writing books and not documents). This bestows a certain narrative quality on the picture, a quality which is generated by the mere process of writing and illuminating the book. With these remarks we are approaching the explicit witnesses of medieval book production – the Bible as object of illustration – as it is revealed in the pictures of Bertoldus' Bible.

3. The pictures and their arrangement

Some of the images of book production are, it should be said immediately, of a fairly common character – motifs that we encounter in almost every illuminated biblical manuscript. Books were often a source of fascination for those who produced them, and there was already a long tradition of representations of people writing books by the time our Bible was made in 1255. Yet our Bible does include some innovations – demonstrating that there was room for *licentia pictoria* at the interface of tradition and artistic talent.

All three volumes of Bertoldus' Bible contain historiated initials with motifs which relate to the production of books, but by far the greatest number are found in volume three. While there is but a single picture of this nature in vol. I, and only three in vol. II, there are no fewer than 15 in vol. III (if we include the initials of the Gospels). The pictures are part of initial letters to some of Jerome's prologues, to the Gospels, to the letters of St Paul (and of St Peter on fol. 199r in vol. III) and to the Apocalypse. Depictions of the evangelists as scribes almost invariably introduced the four Gospels of course, and they are correspondingly less interesting. Accordingly we shall concentrate on the other groups.

It is noticeable that with the exception of St Peter almost all the initials represent 'intellectuals' at work: the busy scholar and translator Jerome writing his prefaces, and the equally busy theologian St Paul writing his letters. These figures, who were known as 'men of letters', are here depicted as 'men of letters' in another more literal sense. Apart from Jerome who is represented in connection with prologues to Old Testament texts in volumes I and II of our Bible, all the depictions of people producing texts or books are found in the New Testament in the third volume. Thus the importance of the written word, the documentary nature of the New Testament, is subtly underlined in the design of the letters. Nevertheless one wonders why great intellectuals in the Old Testament such as Solomon who was credited with writing the Song of Songs and the Book of Proverbs were not depicted in the same way as those of the New Testament.

The contents of the pictures which relate to the production of a medieval Bible are summarised in the following synopsis. (The term 'writing' signifies general writing activity, including meditating, correcting, resting, etc.)

I, fol. 137v (Prologus Hieronymi in libros regum)
In a **U**: St Jerome marking the general layout and guidelines on a sheet of parchment (ill. 10.3)

II, fol. 38v (Prephatio in librum Iob)
In a **C**: St Jerome reading (proof-reading?) a written sheet on his desk

II, fol. 183r (Prologus in Danielem)
In a **D**: St Jerome and a parchment-maker (ill. 10.4)

II, fol. 195r (Prephatio in duodecim prophetas)
In an **N**: St Jerome cutting a piece of parchment into a sheet (ill. 10.5)

III, fol. 44r (Matthaeus)
In an **L**: St Matthew writing

III, fol. 65r (Marcus)
In an **I**: St Mark writing

III, fol. 80r (Lucas) – *excised folio*
[In a **Q**: St Luke writing?]

III, fol. 103v (Prologus in Johannem)
In an **H**: St Jerome at his desk, writing; at his side, books

III, fol. 104r (Johannes)
In an **I**: St John writing

III, fol. 125r (Ad Romanos)
In a **P**: St Paul at the desk with a ruled quire, writing

III, fol. 133v (Ad Corinthios I)
In a **P**: St Paul writing, with pen and knife, and horns for ink in the desk (ill. 10.6)

III, fol. 142v (Ad Corinthios II)
In a **P**: St Paul and Timothy: St Paul writing, Timothy preparing a sheet of parchment

III, fol. 148v (Ad Galatas)
In a **P**: St Paul writing

III, fol. 158v (1 Ad Thessalonicenses)
In a **P**: St Paul writing

III, fol. 161r (1 Ad Timotheum)
In a **P**: St Paul writing

III, fol. 165r (Ad Titum)

In a **P**: St Paul with lined sheet, ink, pen and knife, ready to write

III, fol. 166r (Ad Philemonem)

In a **P**: St Paul writing

III, fol. 199r (1 Petri)

In a **P**: Peter writing (cf. St Paul, e.g. fol. 165)

III, fol. 208r (Apocalypsis Johannis)

In a line connected to an **A**: Christ with the seven stars in his right hand (cf. Apocalypse 1, 13–18); underneath him, St John, and in a line connected to the initial **A**, the painter (ill. 10.7)

There are motifs relating to books in several other illuminations in the three volumes. Here we have gathered only those that illustrate the various aspects of the *production* of a book. It should be underlined that we have listed them in the order that they occur in the three volumes, and not according to how we conceive the stages in the production of a manuscript, which is the way in which they are often (not to say exclusively) reproduced, when used for didactic purposes.[4] This invites us to ask whether the pictures were designed to interrelate. Are they a 'series' of pictures, forming some kind of coherent sequence throughout the three volumes? And do they reflect the steps of production according to the practice in the medieval scriptorium? It would be natural, most scholars seem to think, to begin with the parchment-maker; to continue with the cutting of the 'raw' material into sheets; to look at the ruling and layout next; then to linger for a while on the actual process of writing, ending with the painter's craft, the last major step in the production of the book apart from the binding. This may well be an excellent procedure in theory or in the classroom, but it does conceal the intrinsic logic of the pictures as they are actually located. Indeed I think we may gain a valuable insight into medieval book production by simply following the series of pictures as they occur in the three volumes. They were clearly not made for abstract educational reasons; on the contrary they are, so it seems to me, structured from the point of view of a practising scribe. The very first image, it will be recalled, shows the working out of the general layout. This usefully reminds us that at the outset of any such project, decisions had to be taken about the type and format of the book that was to be produced, that is, someone had to decide what the dimensions and the layout of the sheets should be. Of course the scribe would need parchment in order to realise the decisions; but since we know that there was, at least in Bertoldus' time, a fairly regular production of books at the Hamburg chapter, it is reasonable to assume that there was always a certain amount of parchment in stock in the scriptorium. Consequently, the first thing a scribe did when he had to begin work on a new book was not necessarily to visit the parchment-maker; on the contrary he probably went to the storeroom, found some parchment of good quality, made his decisions about the general design of

---

[4] A selection of the pictures was first published, in a manipulated order, in A. A. Bjørnbo, 'Ein Beitrag zum Werdegang der Mittelalterlichen Pergamenthandschriften', *Zeitschrift für Bücherfreunde* 11 (1907), 329–35. For references to reproductions in more recent publications, cf. Petersen, 'Bertoldus' Bibel', note 15.

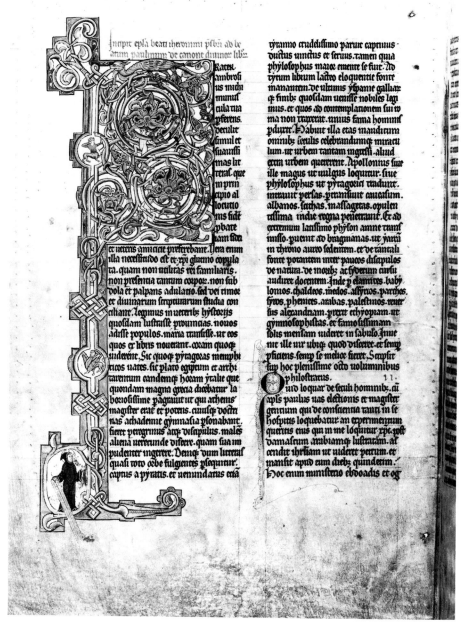

10.1   *Copenhagen, Kongelige Bibliotek, G. K. S. 4 2°, vol. 1, fol. 1v, Hieronymus ad Paulinum de canone divinorum librorum*

10.2 Copenhagen, Kongelige Bibliotek, G. K. S. 4 2°, vol. 1, fol. 5v, Genesis

10.3 Copenhagen, Kongelige Bibliotek, G. K. S. 4 2°, vol. I, fol. 137v, Prologus Hieronymi in libros regum

10.4 Copenhagen, Kongelige Bibliotek, G. K. S. 4 2°, vol. II, fol. 183r, Prologus in Danielem

10.5 Copenhagen, Kongelige Bibliotek, G. K. S. 4 2°, vol. II, fol. 195r, Prephatio in duodecim prophetas

10.6 Copenhagen, Kongelige Bibliotek, G. K. S. 4 2°, vol, III, fol. 133v, Ad Corinthios I

10.7   Copenhagen, Kongelige Bibliotek, G. K. S. 4 2°, *vol.* III, *fol.* 208r, *Apocalypsis Johannis*

the book and then drew the ruling and guide lines. At some time – and why not at fol. 195, when he was approaching the end of what had been planned as the content of the first volume? – all the suitable parchment 'in stock' would be used up, and it was then that he would visit the parchment-maker in order to get more material. When he had acquired this new stock he had of course to cut it into sheets of the right size for the project in hand, and the writing could begin again. The act of writing is shown in various ways – as we have seen St Paul provided plentiful opportunities for depicting such scenes. The final stage from the scribal point of view was the illuminating of the initial letters.

Thus I think we may say that the pictures displaying the production of the medieval book in the Hamburg Bible are not located randomly; rather they form a part of a planned series that connects the three volumes in their own fascinating way.

4. Bertoldus, Karolus, pictor

Bertoldus

I have stressed the element of coherence between the three volumes because it is important for an understanding of our Bible as an entity and a work of art in its own right. We shall now look at a text that may be considered as an external piece of evidence for our Bible.

The so-called *Necrologium Hamburgense* contains on 12 October a most interesting obituary notice concerning Bertoldus. The original manuscript is lost, but the text is known through two copies, both made in the last decades of the seventeenth century:

IV Id. Obiit Bertoldus, huius ecclesie decanus, qui suis laboribus priorem partem Biblie a Genesi usque ad librum Hester comparavit et huic ecclesie contulit; alios vero libros scripsit in expensis domini Jacobi de Mone. Contulit et huic ecclesie antiphonarium, graduale, collectarium, epistolarium, omeliarium, hyemale missale in duobus voluminibus, primas tres partes moralium, Job, gesta pontificum duplicia, librum Innocencii de miseria hominis, derivaciones maiores, Priscianum maiorem, exameron metricum magistri Andree archiepiscopi Lundensis, preterea casulam de rubeo exameto, duas cappas de exameto, unam rubeam, aliam croceam, duas pelves argenteas. Instituit eciam altare sancte Crucis, cuius vicario contulit villam Wulvoldestorpe cum omni iure, 5 modios siliginis in Barenvelde, 4 ortos iuxta Alstriam, 2 ortos sitos infra custodiam. Unum ortum qui fuit Ottonis Longi, 2 mansos in Suldorp, 2 mansos in Scenevelde, 7 iugera in Grieswerdere. Duos mansos in Nova villa, quos ad prebendam, que sita est in Thitmarsia ordinavit, et 1 campanam. Instituit eciam dari canonicis 1 sol. et vicariis 6 den., presentibus in vigiliis et in missa, quos dabit sue possessor vicarie, scilicet summi altaris.[5]

The notice may be divided into four parts according to what it tells. First, it mentions Bertoldus' efforts in providing *priorem partem Biblie* for the church – obviously this was something that was still thought of with respect when the Necrology was begun approximately a hundred years after his death. It then records

---

[5] Ed. K. Koppmann (based on copies by O. Sperling and G. Schroeder), *Zeitschrift des Vereins für hamburgische Geschichte*, Bd. 6, n.f. 3 (Hamburg, 1875), 129.

that Bertoldus himself wrote other books, financed by Jacobus de Mone. Jacobus de Mone is well known in Danish history: he was a member of one of the most influential families of his era, and his close ties to the chapter in Hamburg are attested, *inter alia*, by the obituary notices for Jacobus himself and two of his sons that occur in the Necrologium Hamburgense. Jacobus de Mone died in 1246.[6]

Next the Necrologium Hamburgense reveals that Bertoldus gave an impressive list of books *huic ecclesie*, and, finally, it mentions several other gifts for the Cathedral and its canons. The books may roughly be grouped into two categories, namely liturgical codices, and other books. The liturgical titles are relatively unambiguous; they are interesting not least because of their number. These volumes were central to the life of a cathedral, and they are so numerous that one wonders whether they were the result of liturgical reforms in the church of Hamburg; alternately they would seem to reflect a desire to replace older volumes with ones conceived according to the style of a new era. The list of non-liturgical books contains titles which were, or were to be, fairly common, such as *De miseria humane conditionis* by the later Pope Innocent III (1160/61–1216, elected pope 1198); a *Priscianus major* (*Institutiones grammaticae*); a work called *derivationes maiores* (possibly the *Liber derivationum* by Huguccio of Pisa, d. 1210); the *primas tres partes moralium Job* is likely to have been Gregory the Great's *Moralia in Iob*. The title *Gesta pontificum* with the word *duplicia* appended is open to interpretation; however since the list relates to Hamburg it seems reasonable to assume that the work in question is Adamus Bremensis' *Gesta Hammaburgensis ecclesiae pontificum*. Finally the list includes among the non-liturgical volumes the *Hexaemeron* in twelve books by the Archbishop of Lund, Andreas Sunesen (b. before 1170, d. 1228).[7] Bertoldus may have acquired a copy of this vast didactic poem for intellectual and educational reasons, and he had a personal motive as well: the author was the brother of the above-mentioned Jacobus de Mone. Since the Necrologium Hamburgense was first published in 1783,[8] it has been taken for granted that Bertoldus was actually the scribe of this lost *exemplar hamburgense* of the Hexaemeron, despite the fact that the text itself attests that this was not the case. In this context it is interesting to observe that Bertoldus himself commissioned this work, and that it was present in the chapter when our Bible was made.

Although the short text seems to be clear and concise it does contain some ambiguities. In particular, what exactly is meant by the passage which says that Bertoldus *suis laboribus priorem partem Biblie a Genesi usque ad librum Hester comparavit et huic ecclesie contulit*? In the first place this raises the fundamental question: is the obituary notice speaking about our Bible in three volumes? We can answer 'yes' with confidence, because our Bible is too monumental not to be mentioned in this connection, and we know that Bertoldus took part in its production, deliberately

---

[6] On Jacobus de Mone, cf. C. A. Christensen, 'Jacob Sunesen', *Dansk biografisk Lekiskom*, 3rd edn (Copenhagen, 1983), XIV, 212 and F. Bojsen, *Jakob Suneson of Møn* (Copenhagen, 1902).

[7] *Andreae Sunonis filii Hexaemeron*, post M. CL. Gertz ed. S. Ebbesen et L. B. Mortensen, Corpus Philosphorum Danicorum Medii Aevi xi.1 (Copenhagen, 1985); on the lost Hamburg manuscript, cf. 22.

[8] Eds. J. Langebek and P. F. Suhm, *Scriptores Rerum Danicarum Medii Ævi* v (Copenhagen, 1783); cf. note on the obituary notice on Bertoldus, 412f.

giving it such a monumentality that his name would remain connected with it for a long time. But why, then, does the notice speak only about *priorem partem Biblie a Genesi usque ad librum Hester* – and what does it mean?

The book of Esther is found on fols. 32v–38v of the second volume of our Bible, and it is thus located in a place that cannot have been a 'natural' division or partition. However, it will be recalled that the second volume also contains the first two canonical books of Ezra, on fols. 1r–13v, under the heading *liber hesdre primus*, and the apocryphal third book of Ezra, on fols. 13v–20v, under the heading *liber hesdre secundus*; while at the end of the volume on fols. 218v–230v we find the apocryphal fourth book of Ezra, under the headings *liber primus prophete hesdre*, *liber secundus* and *liber tertius*. Now if, as seems likely, we accept *liber Hester* as a misrendering of *liber hesdre*, there would seem to be two possible interpretations of the text in question, depending, amongst other things, on how we interpret *usque ad*. Either Bertoldus gave the first volume alone, or he gave both volumes I and II. *Huic ecclesie contulit* is less problematic: he gave it to the Church of Our Lady, that is, he paid for it.

For a just assessment of the Necrologium Hamburgense as a historical source it is important to remember that a primary aim of the obituary was to keep an account of gifts for the church and chapter. This, I believe, allows us to distinguish between Bertoldus' financial contribution on the one hand, and his intellectual one on the other. *Priorem partem Biblie a Genesi usque ad librum Hester* surely refers to what he paid for. However this does not mean that he did not take part in the planning of the overall design of the entire Bible – including the part that he did not pay for. *Suis laboribus* is probably a fairly precise expression of Bertoldus' personal involvement in the production of the Bible.

We should now enquire what the exact implications of the phrase *priorem partem Biblie* are likely to have been. I suggest that *partem* reflects the amount of money that Bertoldus was willing to or capable of paying. *Partem* again may be interpreted in relation to the process of making the Bible in terms of the various steps in the production, rather than as various completed subsections of the whole. Accordingly, it seems reasonable to assume that *priorem partem* means that Bertoldus paid for the inception of the entire Bible, but not for all the steps in its production; that is, he may have paid for the parchment and writing of it, but not, e.g., for the illuminating and the binding.

Assuming this is all correct, how then do I explain the text in the Necrologium? First, it should be remembered that the obituary notice was probably written approximately a hundred years after the period of Bertoldus and the production of the Bible. The three volumes were, of course, still in the cathedral, and it is likely that there was a strong tradition that Bertoldus was the man responsible for this marvellous treasure,[9] and also that he had paid for some but not all of it. He paid for part of it, and to people who knew the Bible and thought of it in terms of volumes, this could only mean that he paid either for volume I or for volumes I and II – that is *a genesi usque ad librum Hesdre* (if volume I alone) or *usque ad [prophetam] Esdre* (if

---

[9] This is attested by the fact that his role in connection with the Bible is mentioned first in the obituary notice.

volumes I and II). Now, the obituary also records that Bertoldus had worked as a scribe (*alios vero libros scripsit in expensis domini Jacobi de Mone*). In this case the person who commissioned the book was himself a (former) professional scribe, who had taken an active interest in the supply of books for his church and chapter. It was only natural therefore to suppose that he would have been deeply involved in the production of the special Bible that he wanted to bequeath to his own church.

I argued above that the series of pictures showing the production of a book were in various respects made from a *scribe's* point of view. Now if the overall structure and form of the book, the idea of showing the stages in the manufacturing of it, and the plan for its implementation were conceived and outlined by the scribe Bertoldus, we can understand why.

Karolus

We know who cooperated with Bertoldus on the Bible. His name was Karolus, as is attested by the dedicatory hexameters, written at the very beginning of the first volume, and at the very end of the two others. The close co-operation between Karolus and Bertoldus is mentioned:

> Virgo beata librum tibi scripsit karolus istum;
> In libro vite quod scribat eum pete christum.
> Currere fecit opus bertoldi cura decani,
> Nec labor amborum studio transivit inani.
> Venit ad effectum, jacet ordine scripta librorum,
> Biblia tota trium, pars hec est primus eorum.
> Ecclesieque tue cupiens augere decorem
> Contulit huic operi plenum chorus ipse favorem.
> Tu tibi prostratum pia mater respice clerum
> Quem iam multorum turbavit turbo dierum;
> Illi dignare maternum ferre iuvamen
> Vt tolerata diu cito passio transeat. amen.

> Mille ducentenis post partum virginis actis
> Vndecies quinis tibi liber hic est editus annis.[10]

> O blessed Virgin, Karolus wrote this book for you;
> Beseech Christ that He may inscribe him in the book of life.
> The attention of Dean Bertoldus made the work flow,
> And the labour of them both was not transformed into empty endeavour.
> It came to fulfilment: it reposes in a written row of books;
> A whole Bible in three parts, this part is the first of them.
> Desiring to enhance the beauty of your church
> The choir itself conferred full approval on this work.

---

[10] *primus eorum* in line 6 is changed to *alter eorum* in II, fol. 230v, and to *tercius horum* III, fol. 218v. The interpunctuation is mine.

You, O pious mother, regard the clergy prostrate before you
Whom already the round of many days has troubled;
Deign to bring maternal aid to it
So that the suffering which it has for a long time endured passes quickly. Amen.

When twelve hundred and fifty-five years had passed after the Virgin gave birth,
This book was produced for you.

This may, I think, corroborate the view that Bertoldus played an important role in the planning and design of his Bible. *Scripsit Karolus*, it says, whereas the odd expression *currere fecit opus bertoldi cura* excellently expresses Bertoldus' role in the general planning of the work. We may also perhaps point to the word *ordine* as an expression of his desire to underline the structural coherence of the three parts.

Again, the dedicatory verses express the process as seen from a scribal point of view. Why, one wonders, is the painter not mentioned at all? The painter may, of course, be identical with either Bertoldus or Karolus; however, I find this unlikely, and in any case it is the initiative, the planning and the craft of writing that is mentioned in the dedication. It is sometimes suggested that silence about the name and craft of painters is a symptom of their status; is this, perhaps, the case here?

We tend to see scribal remarks at the end of manuscripts as a sort of signature, as when an artist signs his work. Be that as it may, the dedication in our Bible is undoubtedly of quite a different nature from most scribal 'signatures'. It was probably neither written nor composed by Karolus. Accordingly I would like to offer a hypothesis concerning its meaning and implications: I suggest that Bertoldus is named in the dedication because he instituted the work on the Bible, because he had taken an active part in its execution, because he was an influential figure in the chapter and in particular because he had met most of the expenses of the production. Karolus was mentioned, because he had died shortly after the completion of the Bible. There is no external evidence for this hazardous statement, but there are, I think, a few indirect indications. In the first place, the dedication was not composed or written by Karolus, as we have noted. Secondly, the second line of the dedication (*In libro vite quod scribat eum pete christum*) may be interpreted as a prayer of the *clerus* for Karolus. Thirdly, the third volume of the Bible differs in one respect from the two others: none of the miniatures has text in the spaces that were reserved for it. This tells us that these little texts in the pictures were not added as an integral part of the painting process: they were (or were to be) written by the scribe, not by the painter who may not have known how to write.[11] I suggest, therefore, that the dedication should be read and understood as a commemoration of, and a prayer for, Karolus, and also as a celebration of the craft of the scribe. The silence about the painter says nothing about the status of *his* craft. He was allowed to add his signature to his work in his own way.

---

[11] Miniature writing in miniature paintings may often offer important information, and is a codicological phenomenon that deserves further research.

Pictor

For the scribe, the biblical text began with *In principio creavit deus* and ended, much later, with the final *Gratia Domini nostri Iesu Christi cum omnibus vobis AMEN*, occasionally being followed by personal expressions of relief and jubilation. For the painter of initial letters, assuming he followed the order of the text, the Bible began with the same **I** in the Old Testament, but ended with the initial **A** of Revelation in the New Testament. His first and last letter, then, would be an **I** (as in **I**esus) and an **A** (as in **A**dam). This could offer a possibility for the designer or artist of a Bible subtly to underline both the coherence between, and the corresponding natures of, the Old and the New Testament. For, in a way, the beginning points towards the end, while the end is contained in the beginning, underlining the fact that the whole Bible may be seen as the account about the Creation, the Sin and the Salvation of Mankind. The way from Creation, through Sin to Salvation is literally pointed out by the illumination of the initial **I** in the *In principio* of Genesis.[12] As it is designed, it leads in a vertical move from God to the Creature, and, with a scene showing Adam and Eve as turning-point, goes on horizontally to show the Expulsion from Paradise, the Ark of Noah, and *points* forward to what may already, on the first page of the holy scripture be conceived as the *historia salvationis humanae* (ill. 10.2). Iesus, the Saviour, is, by implication, present from the beginning, as is Adam at the end. By the illuminations of the initial **I** and the final **A**, Bertoldus and his *pictor* made visible a symmetry of fundamental theological importance in the design of Bible.

The **A** of the opening word of Revelation is to the painter what the *Amen* is to the scribe: the end of work. Accordingly it is in the vicinity of the **A** that we should look for the signature of the painter. And that is exactly where we find it: in a prolongation of the letter **A** at the bottom of the page, we find his portrait (ill. 10.7) – a fascinating equivalent to what scribes often did in prose or verse.[13]

The first and the last figures depicted in our Bible are non-biblical. The last, as we have just seen, is the artist himself; while on the fol. 1v of volume I, at the bottom of a page-long letter **F** (the initial of the first of Jerome's letters *ad beatum Paulinum de canone divinorum librorum*) the painter has depicted St Jerome – in point of fact he represents Jerome in a similar fashion to the way he depicts himself 650 folios later – he carries a scroll bearing a double line of text which states: 'me translatorem uoluit deus esse librorum/ne sit iudeus fallax interpres eorum' (ill. 10.1). Thus Jerome, the translator of languages is related by compositional means to the painter, himself a sort of a translator – of language into pictures.

---

[12] For the typology of the Genesis **I**, cf. J. Zahlten, *Creatio Mundi. Darstellungen der sechs Schöpfungstage und naturwissenschaftliches Weltbild im Mittelalter*, Stuttgarter Beiträge zur Geschichte und Politik, Band 13 (Stuttgart, 1979), 38, 59f., 105, 113, 116, 254 (no. 211); abb. 75.

[13] The motif of the initial **A** illustrates Apocalypse 1, 13–18.

5. Design and production of the Hamburg Bible

We are now in a position to offer a hypothetical reconstruction of the circumstances surrounding the production of the Hamburg Bible.

The Cathedral of Hamburg needed a monumental copy of the entire Bible (apart from the Book of Psalms). Bertoldus offered to pay as much for such a Bible as he could afford (he also needed money for the endowment of an altar dedicated to the Holy Cross, and for the *canonicis . . . et vicariis . . . presentibus in vigiliis et in missa* mentioned at the end of the notice in the Necrologium and elsewhere). Apart from the financing, the project was made possible by the presence in Hamburg of a dean who had worked as a scribe himself and who knew and respected the craft, a trained scribe, and an extremely gifted painter at the same time. Elaborating a traditional theme in miniature paintings, showing the Evangelists and other biblical authors at their writing desks, it was decided to include pictures of all the major stages in the production of the book.[14] Bertoldus planned the overall design of the Bible, probably discussing the project with Karolus the scribe and with the (anonymous) painter, and gave instructions concerning the way it was to be made. Eventually Bertoldus' money ran out; however alternative financing raised no problems, and the project continued as it had been planned. Shortly after completing his work, but before the Bible was finished and fully illuminated, Karolus died. All three volumes of the monumental Bible were finished in 1255. After its completion, Bertoldus wrote fourteen lines of hexameters on the first page of volume I, dedicating the work to the Virgin Mary, dating it and praying for the deceased Karolus.

The images of the production of the book in Bertoldus' Bible do not in themselves tell us much about the procedures involved that we cannot learn more clearly from other sources, e.g. from recipe books, and from the examination of the medieval manuscripts themselves. We are well aware that parchment was cut into sheets, that lines were ruled to receive text, that scribes sat at desks equipped with pen and inks and that initial letters were often subsequently illuminated by a separate painter – we can see most of this in the medieval books that we consult, refining our knowledge by means of written sources. Nevertheless, considered as a group in their original order and in context, they are uniquely informative. Bertoldus' Bible is of great interest to the historian of the medieval book. It is a valuable codicological document, not only because it shows the craft of manufacturing books in pictures, but also as a result and expression of that craft itself.

---

[14] Petersen, 'Bertoldus' Bibel', discusses the possibility that the pictures showing the production of the book were added after Karolus had died, as a tribute to him and his craft.

I I

The theology of the twelfth- and thirteenth-century Bible

LESLEY SMITH

In the beginning was the Word, and the Word was with God and the Word was God. He was in the beginning with God; all things were made through him and without him was not anything made that was made. In him was life, and the life was the light of men ... And the Word became flesh and dwelt among us ... full of grace and truth.[1]

The Word made flesh, the incarnation of God in Christ, is the central mystery of Christian belief. Interpretation of the place of the Word – its existence, powers and expression – are crucial doctrine; and misinterpretation of this mystical grammar is the stuff of the commonest heresies. In the beginning was the Word, and that Word became flesh and dwelt among us. In our medieval books this incarnation, this enfleshing, was real in the straightforward sense of the animal flesh which made up their folios. Turning the pages of a codex is a constant reminder of the intimate relation between word and flesh. See the similarities between the elevated host at the Eucharist – white, thin, smooth, flat, the very body of Christ, raised and offered in the hands of the priest – and the pages of the Gospel, carried in procession, kissed in veneration, surrounded by lights and incense – the emblems of reverence offered to Byzantine emperors.[2] As the bread of the Sacrament is *both* outward sign and inward truth, so too books take on, to the medieval reader – and I use that term in the widest possible sense – both the proclamation of the Word, and its character.

The Bible contains the record of the works of God; the Gospels proclaim the special history of salvation through the incarnate Word. Although they claim merely to set down the facts of the life, death and resurrection of Christ, as far as the reader is concerned the book is more real, more tangible, more credible, than its subject. The text *is* Christ as much as it is *about* Christ.

'In the beginning, God created the heavens and the earth ... God said, "Let there be light"; and there was light'.[3] God speaks the whole creation into existence. This Word of God makes everything that was made. This includes, of course, the text of

---

[1] John 1.1–4, 14.

[2] I am grateful to Professor Richard Schieder of York University, Toronto, for reminding me of the Little Entrance and Great Entrance in the Byzantine rite. In the first, the celebrant, deacon and acolytes carry the gospel book in procession at the beginning of the liturgy of the word; in the second, at the beginning of the liturgy of the sacrament, the procession is repeated carrying the paten and chalice.

[3] Gen. 1.1, 3.

the record of creation: the supremacy and primacy of the Word are reflected in the particular primacy of the Bible in creation. All creation may stand as *vestigia Dei*,[4] but the particular, creative power of the Word is mirrored in the primacy of the Bible. It is God's intention, all commentators agree, to be understood by all; and so it is the particular vocation of words to tell the truth.[5] Even God's Law, the ultimate Old Covenant statement of the relationship between Creator and created, is given by God as a simple Ten Words – the *Deca Logos* or Ten Commandments. Humanity is the *imago Dei* not least in its use of speech and language. The tragedy of the Fall finds expression in the Tower of Babel story,[6] where the simplicity of divine communication, a straightforward speaking of truth, is warped into the myriad misunderstandings of human language.[7] The Bible stands as particular revelation because, whilst creation may pass away, *verbum Dei manet in aeternum*.[8]

The correct use of a biblical text is no simple matter. The eighteenth-century hymn may claim: 'God is his own interpreter and he will make it plain'[9] but no medieval exegete takes quite such a sanguine view. Mediated through human hands, the words are, nevertheless, divinely inspired. Moreover, *all* the words in the text are divinely inspired. This is no red-letter edition with the *ipsissima verba* of Jesus rubricated to unhealthy prominence, nor the enterprise of modern New Testament critics who vote with coloured pebbles on the status of various sayings and parables. 'The entire text', Cassiodorus says, 'is full of excellence'[10] and must be accepted and wrestled with.[11] This taking the Bible as a whole is a corollary of its being *Verbum Dei*. The Word is One – single and complete – since it is the reflection and summation of the eternal Father. William of Auvergne in the early thirteenth century, considering the Trinity, holds a sophisticated view of the necessity and form of the first speech:

It will become clear from what follows that the first word by which the first speaker speaks himself and all else has to be one . . . [W]hat is one word but the expression of one truth, or the

---

[4] See E. Gilson, *Philosophie de Saint Bonaventure*, 2nd edn (Paris, 1978), 119ff. (divine exemplarism in creation); 165ff. (analogy and humanity as *imago Dei*); 304ff. (the creative Trinity, and hierarchy in the *Itinerarium*). See also Gilson, *Introduction à l'étude de St Augustin*, 3rd edn (Paris, 1949), 275–81 for Augustine on these ideas of similarity/participation.

[5] For this notion of words see, e.g., Augustine, *Enchiridion ad Laurentium*, ch. 22, CCSL 46, 62: 'Verba enim ideo sunt instituta: non sunt ut per ea homines invicem fallant, sed per ea in alterius notitiam suas cogitationes ferant.

[6] Gen. 11.

[7] Cf. Augustine, *De Doctrina Christiana* II, ch. iv, CSEL 80, 35–6. Trans. J. F. Shaw, in *The Works of A. Augustine of Hippo*, ed. M. Dods (Edinburgh, 1873), IX.

[8] Isa. 40.8; I Peter 1.25.

[9] William Cowper (1731–1800), 'God moves in a mysterious way':
      Blind unbelief is sure to err
      and scan His work in vain;
      God is His own interpreter
      and He will make it plain.

[10] Cassiodorus, *Institutiones*, ed. R. A. B. Mynors (Oxford, 1937), Bk. 1, ch. 16: *De virtute scripturae divinae*, 52: 'lectio cuncta virtutem est' (Trans. by L. W. Jones, *Divine and Human Readings* (Columbia, 1946), 'On the Excellence of the Divine Scriptures', 113).

[11] Hence, in part, the importance for all medieval biblical scholars of setting out clearly just which books are and are not to be included in the canon of scripture. Isidore, for example, in Book VI of the *Etymologiae: De Libris et Officiis Ecclesiasticis* (PL LXXXII, 229–60) begins by listing at some length the canonical books, their contents and their authors. Augustine has a similar exercise in *De Doctrina Christian* II, c. 8.

utterance or image of one intention? Therefore, since the first speaker has one truth and one intention in every way, there is necessarily one word, the expression of himself. For the first speaker intended to say only himself . . . Therefore, from the first one according to itself there comes neither a multitude nor a plurality.[12]

And:

Notice that it is natural for an intellect, as is obvious in us, to speak and generate words . . . Each thing speaks itself by its image as if by a kind of word and is in some sense generative of its image. Since all things speak, will the author of all speech be mute? And since all things manifest themselves through their images, will the author of all manifestations alone be hidden . . .? If it were not possible for him to speak himself and other things through a word which is his own clearest image and which ought to be called the first word, beyond which there is no word prior in act or thought, then he is necessarily mute and, therefore, blind. For his speaking *is* his seeing . . .[13]

God the first speaker has spoken Christ the first Word. The Word is a single One; and its singularity makes for comprehensibility, necessity and sufficiency. All things are contained in that Word, and the Word can be understood. It constitutes the permanent written record of God's intention in speaking. The expression of that Word, the Bible, is variously called *Scriptura*, *Pagina* or *textus*, (all stressing its nature as written or composed)[14] as well as *Auctoritas* – simply the authority – or, perhaps strongest of all, just *liber*.

At the beginning of each of the Gospels in a medieval Bible, we regularly find a scribal portrait of the Evangelist writing his book. The scene is so familiar that we may forget to question its presence; and yet it is not a moment ever to be found in an illustrated Bible of today. We have become thorough sceptics about the two kinds of authorship and authority that such a frontispiece declares, that is, the human authorship of the Evangelist, seated at a desk, writing the words, and the divine authorship of God, often shown as a dictating bird on the shoulder, or a hand or head in the air. Linking the two is the Evangelist's symbol, (the ox, eagle, lion or man: the four living creatures of Revelation 4.6–7). Deriving from the four living creatures full of eyes, gathered around the throne of God in the book of Revelation, the symbol stands as a reminder of the living nature of the text and of its all-encompassing vision. Taken together, the four symbols surround the Creator and summarise the creation. That the symbols stem from Revelation, that most opaque of books, brings into sharp relief the non-literal, allegorical or typological depths of the text. Indeed, the simple presence of a symbol beside each evangelist warns us that what is to follow will need interpretation: this is not merely John's book, it is the eagle's as well.

God as writer, it should be noted, has almost as old a history as God as speaker. As God speaks the creation in Genesis, so in Exodus God's finger writes the Ten Words

---

[12] William of Auvergne, *De Trinitate*, ch. 11, ed. B. Switalski (Toronto, 1976), 107–8. (Trans. R. J. Teske and F. C. Wade (Marquette, 1989), 140).
[13] *Ibid.*, chs. 18, 104; trans. 137.   [14] See p. 226 below and note 46.

of the Law. Traditional interpretation in the *Glossa Ordinaria*[15] (which for medieval schoolmen was almost as much the Bible as the canon of Scripture itself) equates the divine digit with the Holy Spirit. We can expound a Trinity of Father as Author, Son as Written and Spoken Authority and Spirit as Medium. God the Father is the intention behind divine communication, God the Son is its expression and God the Holy Spirit transports the word to the rest of creation through the Tradition. This notion of Father as Author of the Son finds its way into the commentary tradition via the *Sentences* where it is quoted from Hilary's *De Trinitate*.[16] Here is its appearance in Bonaventure's Sentence Commentary:

We might say, therefore, that the Son is born of the Father before time . . . for the Father is the author of the Son by procreation. So that, therefore, as the Father is eternal so is the Son eternal; but the Father is without author, whereas the Son is not; because the Father was not born, but the Son was born.[17]

God, then, speaks one word – Christ – and from Christ comes the One book. This equation of Christ with text reminds us of the tricks that Christian doctrine plays with time, conflating past, present and future. Just as the Eucharist calls the Eternal to enter the here-and-now through the body of the One who was, who is and who is to come, so the Word expressed in Scripture unites its readers through the ages. Cassiodorus again:[18]

Consider . . . how wonderful, how agreeable are the ordered words which flow through the Divine Scriptures, the object of ever-increasing desire, the endless sufficiency, the glorious object for which the blessed hunger . . . They describe the past without falsehood; they show the present as more than it seems; they report the future as if it had already been completed.

Scripture, like the Son of God, both describes and orders the past, present and future. We can see this, to begin with, in the Bible itself. The books of history tell the tale of the Jewish past. Old Testament Law and the precepts of the New Covenant both order life in the world and describe the running of the household of God. The books of the prophets use history as sermon, retelling the story to point out the errors of the past and to point to the inevitable consequences of present action. And this capacity to let age speak to age, a function of the eternity of the Word, is apparent in the medieval believer's confidence that this simple object, this confection of dead skin and pigment, should be venerated as a living emperor and could speak to them.

It is *not* the case that medieval interpreters had no historical sense, that they ignored

---

[15] *Glossa Interlinearis* on Ex. 31.18.
[16] Bonaventure, *Sentences* I, dist. 9, ch. 4, in *Bonaventurae Opera Omnia*, 10 vols. (Quaracchi, 1882–1902), III; Hilary, *De Trinitate*, 12, ch. 21, CCSL 62, 595.
[17] Bonaventure, *Sentences* I, dist. 9:
Dicamus ergo Filium natum de Patre ante tempora . . . Pater enim generatione auctor Filii est . . . Ut ergo Pater est aeternus, ita et Filius aeternus est; sed Pater sine auctore, Filius vero non; quia Pater innascibilis, Filius natus.
[18] Cassiodorus, *Institutiones*, ch. 16, 51; trans. 112.

etymology, philology, context, subtext or change over time;[19] but medieval interpreters proceeded by giving the Scripture a higher face-value than academic theologians might today, and they acted accordingly. I would argue that that face-value is
Christ.

This observation does not minimise the interpretation of Scripture, either in
medieval methods of exegesis or in their consciousness of its necessity. Rather, by
pointing out the identity of Christ with the text of scripture from the beginning, we
merely show what makes exegesis fundamentally both possible and worthwhile. All
books may be read, meditated upon and interpreted, but the Bible makes unique
claims – claims accepted by medieval interpreters – for the returns available for effort
expended: 'Everywhere in it truth holds sway; everywhere the divine excellence beams
forth; everywhere matters of use to mankind are related.'[20]

In allowing Scripture divine authorship, medieval interpreters gave it the sense of a
res by making it the supreme *signum*. When Augustine divides the world into *res* and
signa, 'things' which simply are, and 'signs' whose chief function, over and above
themselves, is to point to something beyond, he includes in that division words, which
'hold the chief place among signs.'[21] In one sense of this distinction, the Bible as a
collection of words is a collection of signs which point, through different methods of
interpretation, to various meanings, which separately and together point beyond
themselves to the Creator God.

In another focus, the Bible as a whole constitutes a different *signum*, a mirror which
reflects much more directly the Word made flesh and which shares his character. Since
God is the quintessential *res*, the thing beyond all things, the maker of language and
the maker of meaning, the Bible as mirror to God is the arbiter of meaning. This is the
final circularity behind all biblical interpretation: that the authority of the authority is
established by itself.

The single intent behind the Bible does not do away with a multiplicity of
meanings. Partly this is because the book is mediated through human writers, but it is
also part of the divine plan. Making the most of the paradox that God's message must
be accessible to all, whilst recognising that some parts of Scripture are so opaque as to
be largely incomprehensible, Augustine first chides the reader, then suggests what
God may have in mind:[22]

Hasty and careless readers are led astray by many and manifold obscurities and ambiguities,
substituting one meaning for another; and in some places they cannot hit upon even a fair
interpretation. Some of the expressions are so obscure as to shroud the meaning in the thickest

---

[19] William of Auvergne, discussing the problems relating to the 613 laws of the Old Covenant, notes differences
between Jews of the biblical period and the Jews of his day, and knows that 'his' modern Jews have just as
many questions of the text as he, a Christian, does (*De Legibus*, chs. 2, 15). See also B. Smalley 'William of
Auvergne, John of La Rochelle and St. Thomas Aquinas on the Old Law', in *Saint Thomas Aquinas.
Commemorative Studies. 1244–1274*, 2 vols. (Toronto, 1974), II, 37–8.
[20] Cassiodorus, *Institutiones*, ch. 16, 51; trans. 112.
[21] Augustine, *De Doctrina Christiana* II, ch. 3 CSEL 80, 35; trans. 36: 'For among men words have obtained far
and away the chief place as a means of indicating the thoughts of the mind.'
[22] *Ibid.*, II, ch. 6, CSEL 80, 36; trans. 37.

darkness. And I do not doubt that all this was divinely arranged for the purpose of subduing pride by toil, and of preventing a feeling of satiety in the intellect, which generally holds in small esteem what is discovered without difficulty.

Augustine is quoted, together with Jerome and Hilary, by Vincent of Beauvais[23] on the need for the reader to be open to the book. One must wait for the book to reveal its meaning, to expose itself, as William of Auvergne says,[24] and not impose oneself on it.

So the Bible embodies a series of paradoxes for the medieval reader, for it mirrors the paradoxical characteristics of Christ. It is already written and complete, and yet it exists in time and is continually subjected to exegesis. Derrida's distinction between 'writing' and the written book[25] describes not only the closed and finite nature of the canon of Scripture that was once composed but is now set and fixed, but also the theological person of the eternal Christ, begotten before all worlds, incarnate in a particular time and space and yet present to medieval believers. '[T]he idea of the book, which always refers to a natural totality, is profoundly alien to the sense of writing (*écriture*). It is the encyclopaedic protection of theology against the disruption of writing . . .'[26] So the figure of Christ, created before time, must be immutable and unchangeable, although incarnate once and present still. Like Christ, Scripture is undeletable: 'the moving finger' of God 'having writ, moves on'. *Quod scripsi scripsi*,[27] said Pilate to the chief priests, and the Gloss on this passage gives a medieval sense of the characteristics of Scripture: that it is done and unchangeable, that even the ignorant are used in the divine plan, that there is an order discernible beyond the letters and that it necessarily tells the truth.[28]

The Bible manifests that most difficult character of Christ in that both it and he are a revelation – literally an unveiling – by means of a veiling. In Christ, the divine nature is veiled in flesh; in Scripture, the divine wisdom is veiled in words. In both, without this veiling there could be no disclosure. For both there is a necessary exposition of the opaque and obscure. To both, most importantly, must come a reply – for it is the most Christ-like characteristic of the book that any real reading requires a reader response. For the medieval theologian, the response in both cases should be the direct building-up of love for God. Such is the necessity of response to the book that it matters, both in life and literature, whether it is open or closed. At the consecration of a bishop in the Roman rite, the open gospel book was laid on his head (the lappets still found on some mitres are survivals of the bookmarks) to signal the presence of Christ. In

---

[23] Vincent of Beauvais, *De Eruditione Filiorum Nobilium*, ed. A. Steiner (Cambridge, Mass., 1938), ch. 18, 67: *De Scribendi Exercicio Contra Aliena*. Hilary says: 'Optimus lector est, qui dictorum intelligenciam expectat ex dictis pocius quam imponit et refert magis, quam affert, nec id uideri dictis contineri cogit, quod ante lectionem intelligendum presumpserit' (*De Trinitate*, I, 18, PL x, 38).

[24] William of Auvergne, *De Fide et Legibus*, ch. 17: 'Quia vero nonnullos offendunt, et graviter scandalisant sacrae scripturae hujus expositiones, unde et abusive impositiones eis potius videntur, quam expositiones quaedam earum;' (*Opera Omnia* [repr. Frankfurt, 1963], 489).

[25] J. Derrida, *De la grammatologie* (Paris, 1967), 30–1. Trans. G. C. Spivak, *Of Grammatology* (Baltimore, 1976), 18.

[26] *Ibid.*   [27] John 19.22

[28] *Glossa Ordinaria* on John 19.22; Albertus Magnus on John 19.22 (*Opera Omnia* (Paris, 1899), XXIV, 657–8).

commenting on the book closed with seven seals, in Revelation, Peter of Celles notes that the book is closed for fear that even in the silence and secrecy of one's own room the heart might commit sin.[29] The open book of Revelation 10, which must be eaten, produces bitterness. The open books of Revelation 20 – the book of life and the books of the dead – are the most worrisome of all. Not only are these literally interpreted as lists of the saved and damned, written in eternity and unable to be changed, but medieval commentators lay on them (particularly the book of life) spiritual interpretations demanding a change in behaviour. In Albert the Great, for example, the open book of life is the saints who show us how we ought to behave. These books must be open to all, since all must be able to read their salvation in them.

It is suggestive that the act of reading is very often expressed by the nutritive metaphors of eating and drinking. Commentators bite, drink, chew, ruminate and digest. We all know Peter Comestor, whose diet was books. His name may come not so much from the quantity he had read as from the skill with which he had digested them. Scripture is sometimes drink, when it is easily understood and can be quaffed, and sometimes food, when it needs chewing and digestion before the meaning can be understood.[30] Much of the material on eating books comes from commentaries on Revelation 10.9–10, where an angel gives a book to John and tells him to eat it. The word used is not simply *comedite* (eat) but *devora* (devour). For Ambrose and the *Glossa Ordinaria*[31] this devouring should describe our longing for the words of salvation, and for the Sacrament. The similarity to the Eucharistic bread which, through the words of the priest becomes the flesh of the incarnate Word, is irresistible. The book is sweet in the mouth for it promises us eternal life, but bitter in the stomach since it causes us to recollect our sins. For later Mendicant commentators, Hugh of St Cher, Albert the Great and Bonaventure for example,[32] this eating of the book has developed a sense more specific to preachers: it signifies exposition or preaching; but this can be truly accomplished only if the book has been enfolded in the heart and retained in the memory.[33] In a late Gloss on Revelation the 'open book' signifies the power of the office of preacher.[34]

Books themselves are life-giving. In his exposition of the Ten Commandments, Stephen Langton[35] states that not lending your books to someone who asks for them is a form of homicide (and in fact is the only form of killing he discusses). This question of lending books is a repeated question in thirteenth-century commentary. It tends to become fixed in questions on scandal: whether, since someone may be scandalised (i.e. led into mortal sin), if I do not lend him my book, I am held to do

[29] P. de Celles, *De Disciplina Claustrali*, ed. G. de Martel, in *L'école du cloître* (Paris, 1977), 228.
[30] Haymo of Auxerre, *Glossa* on Rev. 10.9–10.   [31] Quoted in *Glossa* on Rev. 10.9–10.
[32] All commentaries on Rev. 10.9–10. On two types of books: Bonaventure on Psalm 103 (*Opera Omnia* (Paris, 1867), ed. A. C. Peltier, IX, 281).
[33] Hugh of St Cher on Rev. 10.9–10 (*Opera Omnia* (Venice, 1732), VII, fol. 397).
[34] *Glossa* on Rev. 10.9–10 (Nicolas of Lyra, *moraliter*).
[35] Commentary on Deut. 5.17 in Oxford, Trinity College, MS 65, fol. 258rb: 'Interlinearis: "Re vel voluntate vel subtrahendo alii quod potes prestare." Ergo de genere homicidii est quaternos non accommodare.' (A later hand has written *nota* in the margin at this point.)

so.[36] The basic answer is yes – on the grounds that one would be held to feed his corporeal body if he hungered, and so how much more must one feed the incomparably better spiritual body. And yet these academic commentators (Mendicants though many of them are) develop more and more elaborate occasions for circumventing the rules. William of Auxerre claims that it is just not to the common good to lend one's book to anyone who asks.[37] One is reminded of Peter the Chanter reporting the dictum that the brother who wishes to become librarian should not be allowed to take the job, since it will only bring out his most miserly qualities.[38]

The line between respect for the book as container of truth and bibliomania has always been fine. The Franciscan *Speculum Disciplinae* for novices has a section on looking after things, 'chiefly books',[39] where are expounded the dangers of dirty hands, stray food and violent handling. In the Rule of St Augustine books may be asked for, and given out only at certain hours of the day.[40] In the Eynsham Benedictine Customary, women who come to ask the abbey's protection were to kneel with a hand on 'the book' (called *textus* or *liber*) and kiss it. *Men* who came to the abbey kissed the monks![41]

To literate and illiterate alike, the practice of religion seemed ruled by books – Bibles, gospel books, missals, antiphonaries, penitentials, commentaries: at every turn there was a new leaf. Monastic life was cluttered with books, from the written rule onward. Many customaries and expositions dealt at length with the care, inspection, repair and provision of office books and books for spiritual reading. Lawyers, too, were ruled by books. Commenting on the open book in Revelation 10, Nicholas of Lyra claims that this book is the Code of Justinian.[42]

'Of the making of many books' says Ecclesiastes, 'there is no end, and much study [*meditatio*] is an affliction of the flesh.'[43] Comment on this verse suggests a weary mixture of resignation that more books will always be made, and a tone of disapproval that this is so. In the monastic Rule of Benedict, meditative reading, actively engaging the Scriptural text, was prescribed every day; but it was balanced with manual labour and the *Opus Dei*, or Divine Office. For some commentators, the *frequens meditatio* of Ecclesiastes 12.12 is going too far. People are not content with what they have – their

[36] E.g. Roland of Cremona, *Summa* [*Summae Magistri Rolandi Cremonensis, O.P.*, ed. A. Cortesi (Bergamo, 1962)], Liber III, ch. 440: 'Quid sit faciendum ne veniat scandalum. Utrum teneor dare Bibliam alicui ne scandalizetur'.

[37] William of Auxerre, *Summa Aurea* [*Magistri Guillelmi Altissiodorensis. Summa Aurea*, ed. J. Ribaillier, *cura et studio* (Paris, Grottaferrata, 1985)], Liber 3, tractatus 52, ch. 5: 'Quis faciendum est propter scandalum vitandum'.

[38] Peter the Chanter, *Verbum Abbreviatum*, PL CCV, 368.

[39] In Bonaventure, *Opera Omnia* XII, 492–3.

[40] See G. Lawless, *Augustine of Hippo and his Monastic Rule* (Oxford, 1987):
  Rule ch. 5: 'Codices certa hora singulis diebus petantur; extra horam qui petierit non accipiat' (p. 97) and also the *Regulations for a Monastery*:
  Operentur a mane usque ad sextam, et a sexta usque ad nonam vacent lectioni, et ad nonam reddant codices (p. 74).

[41] *The Customary of the Benedictine Abbey of Eynsham in Oxfordshire*, ed. A. Gransden, Corpus Consuetudinum Monasticarum 2 (Siegburg, 1963), 208–9.

[42] *Glossa Ordinaria* on Rev. 10.9–10.   [43] Ecces. 12.12.

curiosity is infinite, beyond reasonable bounds; everyone is looking for novelty; every book produces its own problems that must be explained by another book.[44]

The theological strength of the book is such that it is used as a metaphor for other revelations of God, particularly revelation through nature. A commentator mistakenly taken for Bonaventure, most mystical of academic theologians, puts it eloquently:

Note that the book in which we can read and understand and learn more about God is twofold. First, the book of the Scriptures, which was given by the Saviour to his disciples after the resurrection so that they might understand the mysteries of grace in the legal figures and prophetic signs which Christ worked; that is, so that, through what was done and said in the Old Testament they might understand those things fulfilled in the New. The other book is the book of creation, in which the discerning faithful person ought to seek God. Because there one can find the omnipotence of God in the greatness of creation, the wisdom of God in its beauty and order, the highest goodness of God in its unity and fruitfulness. Philosophers do not have this discernment, because they do not know how to rise from the greatness of creation to the greatness of God.[45]

Elsewhere he declares that there are two books: Scripture and clerics. 'We (he is addressing clerics) read Scripture, but the laity read us. Can they draw out of us what they should?'

Augustine uses the metaphor in reverse; the Bible is likened to the heavens:

For we are told that the sky shall be folded up like a scroll [Apoc. 6.14] and that, now, it is spread out like a canopy of skins above us [Psalm 104.2] . . . In the same way you have spread out the heavens like a canopy of skins, and these heavens are your Book, your words in which no note of discord jars . . . There in the heavens, in your Book, we read your unchallengeable decrees, which make the simple learned . . . [T]he heavens remain. Those who preach your word pass on from this life to the next, but your Scripture is outstretched over the peoples of this world, to the end of time . . .[46]

With immense arrogance, the Book describes the creation as like itself, a book: a description meant both to flatter and to explain.

In this short essay I have concentrated on the Bible (as opposed to other sorts of book) because it is *the* book in medieval terms, the *Liber librorum*. Brian Stock points out[47] that from the eleventh century onwards the word *textus* came to refer almost exclusively to the Gospels, both in their ceremonial, liturgical form, and in the direct notion of composed and woven meaning. This is supported, I would say, by an appreciation of the interlocking layers of the exegetical senses of Scripture. I have concentrated, too, on the twelfth and thirteenth centuries, where material from the commentaries of schoolmen abounds. But their attitudes were strongly influenced by

---

[44] Hugh of St Cher on Ecces. 12.12. Bonaventure on Ecces. 12.12.

[45] Probably not Bonaventure, *Diaetae Salutis*, tit. 6, ch. 3, 'On the seven gifts of the spirit: the gift of intellect' (*Opera Omnia* VIII, 310). For similar opinions in Bonaventure himself, see Bonaventure, *Sentences* III, dist. 24, articulus II, quaestio 3 (*Opera Omnia* III, 524); *Commentarius in Evangelium S. Luccae*, ch. 60: Luke 18, 37 (*Opera Omnia* VII, 470–1); *Quaestiones disputatae de scientia Christi, de mysterio SS. Trinitatis, de perfectione evangelica*, quaestio 1, articulus II, conclusion (*Opera Omnia* V, 54–8).

[46] Augustine, *Confessions* XIII, 15, CSEL 33, 357.

[47] Brian Stock, *Listening for the Text* (Baltimore, 1990), 41.

Augustine's writings on the authority of Scripture, and by Jerome and Isidore on the place of books and writers. The span of years is great, but the authority of the Fathers and the traditional nature of both Christianity and scholastic learning kept their voices fresh. For these twelfth- and thirteenth-century schoolmen, Scripture and its interpretation was the central core of their learning: only the most advanced students were allowed to lecture on Scripture in the University of Paris, *after* they had graduated from the 'theological' *Sentences* of Peter Lombard.

In the Christian world-view of the latin West the Sacred Page held the central place. For theologians, academics and many ordinary people 'the book' meant the Bible and its glosses. Christianity is amongst the most bookish of religions, intimately associated with the form of the codex. The medieval imagination is a biblical one. Their first response to any situation was likely to be a catena of Scripture. According to Augustine,[48] the third step to wisdom, after fear of God and piety, was knowledge[49] which meant knowledge of the Book. Scripture was undoubtedly superior to other books, as Haymo of Auxerre explains, commenting on Revelation 11. John is given a *calamus* (reed or rod) to hold:

By the *calamus* [Haymo says] we are to understand what is produced by the reed, namely, holy Scripture, because the ancients wrote with a reed. And the reed is said to be like a rod [*virga*]. For in this rod we understand the rectitude of sacred Scripture in which there is no lie and no error, as there is in the books of philosophers, Jews, and heretics, whose doctrine is full of lies. But sacred Scripture is right in every part.[50]

Right, complete, sufficient and necessary: Christ is the creation of the Book, which re-creates itself in His image, projecting its authority, and that of the written word, from the authority *it* accords *Him* as Word of God.

---

[48] Augustine, *De Doctrina Christiana* II, ch. 7, CSEL 80, 37–8.

[49] *Ibid.*, 'The most skillful interpreter of the sacred writings then, will be he who in the first place has read them all and retained them in his knowledge, if not yet with full understanding, still with such knowledge as reading gives ...' (II, ch. 8) 'For among the things that are plainly laid down in Scripture are to be found all matters that concern faith ... hope ... and love ...' (II, ch. 9), CSEL 80, 40.

[50] *Glossa Ordinaria* on Rev. 11.1

Index of people and places

Aaron 194; 196
Abbo of Fleury 108
Abingdon 108
Ada 22
Adalhard, abbot of Tours 57; 63; 71; 114, n.73
Adam of Bremen 217
Adelhard, abbot of St Germain-des-prés 96, n.52
Admont 127; 146
Æthelbert, archbishop of York 45, n.94
Æthelwold, bishop of Winchester 108; 109; 113; 123
Æthelwold of Lindisfarne 42
Africa 1
Albert the Great 229
Alcuin 44, n.89; 45, n.94; 55–6; 59; 60; 61; 63–77; 105, n.27; 107; 135; 158; 161
Aldred 42, n.80
Alexander II, pope (see also Anselm of Baggio) 137–9; 153–4
Alfred, king 46; 107
Amalarius 54
Amalric 57–8
Ambrose 229
Amiens 64
Anagni, Peter of: see Peter of Anagni
Andreas Sunesen, archbishop of Lund 217
Angelomus of Luxeuil 60
Angers 96
Angilbert, abbot of St Riquier 22
Aniane 57
Anselm of Baggio, bishop of Lucca (see also Alexander II) 153
Aquileia 19
Arezzo, SS. Flora and Lucilla 148
Argenteuil 69, n.33
Arn, bishop of Salzburg 99
Arundel, Earl of: see Fitz-Alan, H.
Athelstan, king 24; 28; 107; 108, n.42

Ato 21–2
Augustine of Canterbury 19; 45; 46, n.100
Augustine of Hippo 46; 54; 83; 96; 120; 154; 161–3; 185–8; 227–8; 231–2
Auvergne, William of: see William of Auvergne
Ava, *ancilla Dei* 56
Avril, F. 154; 158

Bamberg (-Eichstatt) 72; 188
Barking 45
Bath 45; 105
Bautrich, abbot of Regensburg 61
Beauvais, St Peter's 20; 67
Beauvais, Vincent of: see Vincent of Beauvais
Bede 46, n.100; 47; 50; 51; 76; 96
Benedict, St 152; 230
Benedict of S. Pudenziana 153
Berengar of Tours 96
Berengaria, duke of Friuli 20
Berg, K. 129; 137; 146; 148; 149
Berger, S. 128; 168
Bertoldus, dean of Hamburg 205; 206; 216–22
Bischoff, B. 58
Bobbio 1, n.2; 68
Boethius 46; 99
Boisil 48, n.108
Bonaventure 226; 229
Boniface, missionary 44, n.89; 45, n.91
Branner, R. 158
Breedon 45
Brown, J. 15
Brown, M. 103
Brownrigg, L. 109
Bruno, bishop of Würzburg 97

Caesarius of Arles 4
Canterbury 45; 49–50; 107; 113–14; 125
Canterbury, Christ Church 28, n.9; 102; 106; 109–10; 120; 184

233

Index of manuscripts